THE ENGLISH TOWN

A History of Urban Life

MARK GIROUARD

Yale University Press

New Haven and London 1990

For Blanche

Designed by Dorothy Girouard

Set in Linotron Times by Best-set Filmsetter Ltd., Hong Kong.
Printed in Italy by Amilcare Pizzi, Spa, Milan.
Library of Congress catalog number 90-70101
ISBN 0-300-04635-9

(Front and back endpapers) Details from *Panoramic View of Louth* by William Brown, *c*. 1844-55.
(half-title page) A view of Bagdale and St. Helen's Terrace, Whitby.
(previous page) Edward Burra, *Harbour, Falmouth*, 1975.
(right) Michael Andrews, detail from *Lights VI: The Spa,* 1974.

CONTENTS

ACKNOWLEDGEMENTS

My first debt in writing this book has been to libraries, public and private, museums, art galleries, and record offices all over England. The richness of their contents and the helpfulness of their staff makes using them a continual pleasure to all involved in research; the numbers are so great that I hope they will not mind sheltering under a general acknowledgement.

Among individuals I would especially like to thank the following: David Lloyd for help in Ludlow; Mrs Halford and Andrew Arrol for help in Shrewsbury; David Cheshire for information about theatres and music-halls; Laurence E. Klein for communicating his researches into politeness; Todd Longstaffe-Gowan for information about town gardens; Dr Eric Till for help and information in Stamford; Judge Lyall Wilkes for help in Newcastle; John Harris and John Cornforth for advice and information about illustrations, and other help; Alyson Cooper for information about Manchester warehouses; George Clark for hospitality and help in Dorchester; Peter Burton and Harland Walshaw, for their readiness to go anywhere at any time to take photographs; Peter Ferriday for hospitality and company in Lancashire and Yorkshire; and my sister Teresa James and her husband, and Laurence and Linda Kelly, for having me to stay when portions of the book were being written. Others who have helped me include Edward Piper, Neil Wright, Wilhelmine Harrod, Maureen Boddy, Lois Lamplugh, Barry Harling, J.G.A. Pocock, John Garland, Reresby Sitwell, Christopher Wakelin, Stefan Muthesius, and Wendy Baron.

Juliet Thorp has worked indefatigably on ordering illustrations, Jane Dorson has helped with the typing, and Elizabeth Manners has been a tower of strength in more ways than I can mention.

Finally I would like to thank the bed-and-breakfast landladies of England for providing a welcome and welcoming alternative to its ridiculously expensive hotels.

1. (right)   A view of Whitby through a window of St. Mary's parish church.

Introduction

I think the first occasion on which I became aware of an English town as something more than a place where one caught trains or went to the dentist was in 1944. I was at school in Sussex, aged thirteen. My interests had moved over from wild flowers to architecture about a year previously, but for me architecture still meant Norman, Early English, Decorated and Perpendicular. On free afternoons I bicycled to the little parish churches of West Sussex, and made dim little notes on them. Then, towards the end of the summer, my father came down to take me out, and we went to Chichester for the day.

Chichester knocked me over. It was not its medieval walls that excited me or its market cross, or even its cathedral, but its Georgian houses. Red brick, white sashes, fanlights and pediments, curling wrought iron, the dodos on the gate piers of Pallant House, the mellowness and harmony of the quiet streets (no cars on them in those days), what seemed an endless progression of houses, all related and all a little different — I licked it all up like treacle, and when I got back to school poured it out again in an essay for my English master, who encouraged my interest in architecture.

The holidays meant Ireland, Derbyshire and London. London, on the whole, I took for granted — when I was there, which was never for very long. My next school, in Yorkshire, brought moors, ruined abbeys, and Vanbrugh, but little in the way of towns — for York was too far to be easily accessible.

The next time a town really came alive for me was during my military service. When I was an officer cadet I drove to Yorkshire from Eaton Hall in Cheshire — the extravagant Gothic profile of which was my only consolation for the dreary business of being taught leadership in an English winter. The route was by way of Manchester. Manchester left no impression on me at all on this occasion, except for the speed and suddenness with which we drove up out of its suburbs into a landscape of moor and mountain, treeless and terrifying in the grey winter light. Then, with equal suddenness, we came down out of it into Huddersfield. What a city! For a mile or so we drove along a street of palaces — palaces which were admittedly as bleak and unadorned as the neighbouring Pennines, but still amazing in the height and power of their mighty stone façades, piled up storey after storey, and row after row of windows. I had never been to Florence, but this, it seemed to me, must be what Florence was like.

Up at Oxford in my final year, I lived in a crazy house on an island by Folly Bridge, with statues in alcoves on the front, and balconies from which one could feed the swans in the river. To one side were the High Street and the university, to the other the gas works, the railway station and the rows of little houses in St. Ebbes and St. Ald's which had been built for the gas and railway workers. The university was my everyday world, St. Ebbes and St. Ald's a private retreat, to which no one else from the university ever seemed to penetrate, so that walking there gave a sense of discovery unattainable in the colleges, where everything had been visited and written about. I grew attached to the long low terraces chequered in red-and-white brick, the mill stream that in places seemed about to flow up to their doorsteps, the dirty figures silhouetted against flame inside the gas works, and the dirty Thames alongside it, where the swans congregated far more thickly than in the picturesque reaches by the colleges.

For the next ten years my doctorate and my job took me to country houses rather than to towns. What few towns I wrote about were in Ireland or America. But I had memorable encounters from time to time, apart from my continuous experience of London, where I lived, and which, in the 1950s, was still full of extraordinary places, which have since disappeared or changed almost beyond recognition. Two of these encounters, at Bath and Bristol, remain in my memory with especial vividness.

My Bath memory is of Lansdown Crescent. I visited it for the first time on a summer evening. The long level road snaked along the hill, and below it a field dropped steeply down to a curving line of trees. In the field a herd of cows were chewing peacefully in the evening sun. Far below, beyond the trees, the lower half of Bath was spread out before me. Surveying the field, the cows, the trees and the view was a high curving line of exquisitely simple houses, each with an entrance arch of wrought iron silhouetted against its Bath stone façade. The cows munched, the houses hung still in the low sunlight; never had I seen such a sophisticated vision of how a town could be lived in. I had a sudden realization of a way of living in towns as enticing as it was sophisticated.

The visit to Bristol was an odd experience. It took place on a winter Sunday when bright sunshine alternated with blizzards. I spent the whole day walking round the city, and came through each blizzard with my long overcoat white on one side and dark blue on the other. Owing to the weather and its being Sunday, the streets were deserted. The town was extraordinarily dramatic. A terrace of Georgian houses perched high above a harbour. Warehouses and breweries as massive and exotic as Egyptian temples rose out of the streets. There was water everywhere; the town clung to hills as steep as those of Bath, but unlike Bath it exuded the flavour of ships, cargoes, merchants, manufacture and money.

In such ways I slowly gathered a sense of the variety of English towns — and have been increasing it ever since. The variety is as great as that of the English landscape, and just as enjoyable to experience or walk through. Townscapes, like landscapes, can be wild or tame, strange or serene, lonely or busy, sinister or homely, spacious or confined, sometimes all within the same town. There are towns which are harmonious and gentle, and others which are the result of violent collisions of buildings with nature or each other. It is often the collisions which make a town memorable, those with

3

nature in particular. For reasons of commerce or defence many towns were built in places where no sensible surveyor would ever have thought of putting one. England has no real water city (though guidebooks used to call High Wycombe 'the Venice of Buckinghamshire'), but it has hill towns of all types, dates and sizes, from Shaftesbury to Sheffield, Bath to Newcastle, and Lincoln to Hebden Bridge, in which buildings and streets can only make their way up the slopes by dramatic, and at times crazy, convolutions of gradient and level. Other collisions are man-made: collisions of use, as when houses and factories almost literally collide with railway viaducts or motorways; of scale, when churches, mills or castles tower above little terraces; of date, when Georgian red brick runs into magpie half-timbering or Victorian polychromy. Some towns have collisions of both kinds, none more dramatically than Newcastle along the Tyne, where streets and houses cling precariously to the steep slopes, and an enfilade of great bridges marches across the water and comes crashing over and into them.

Townscape is, after all, a form of landscape: both, except for the wildest landscapes, are the result of men putting their input into nature. The input is more intense in towns, but all towns are inevitably conditioned by the land on which they sit, or the materials which come out of it. In addition to the extreme cases already mentioned, hills and water mix with buildings to shape many English towns, or to loom in their near or middle distance: Beccles on its hilltop above the Waveney water-meadows; Rye, rising like a roof-covered island out of Romney Marsh; Todmorden beneath the long line and dip of the Yorkshire moors; the terraces of Weymouth following the giant curve of its bay; the flood of the Mersey, heaving and muttering like a living creature as it races past Liverpool; Whitby, rising like the sides of a crater round its harbour; the abbey mill-pond reflecting the towers of Lichfield Cathedral; the river loops round the hills of Shrewsbury and Durham. Above all trees and greenery are omnipresent in English towns, more so, perhaps, than in the towns of any other country: in the long gardens tangling together in the back lands of country towns; in the huge planes that make a Druids' grove of Berkeley Square; in the commons that come lapping into Harrogate and Tunbridge Wells; in the trees that line roads everywhere; in the forests, thickets and tangles of wild flowers that fill river banks, canal sides, embankments and waste places in industrial towns as the grip of pollution is loosened.

It is possible to walk through towns just as through country, and enjoy them in ignorance. But at some stage one is likely to start asking, Why? I enjoyed the back streets of Oxford without the slightest desire to know about the people who lived in them, or the origins or working of gas or the railways. I drove past the Huddersfield mills with only the most marginal interest in the past and present vicissitudes of the textile industry. I never thought of finding out how the people who first lived in Lansdown Crescent got through the day, or why they had come to live there in the first place.

Specifically architectural interests I did have, starting in the very earliest days and becoming stronger once architectural history and journalism became my livelihood. But it was only after my interest in country houses had widened to an interest in how they worked through the centuries that I began to ask similar questions about towns. It occurred to me that these could benefit from the same kind of approach, an attempt to widen understanding of architecture by trying to understand the way of life which produced it. A town, after all, supplied a community with shelter and services, just like a country house, even if the community was larger and more complicated. There were certain obvious resemblances. Towns had their rich and poor areas, just as country houses had their gentry and servant areas. Rich areas were served by mews and back streets, just as the gentry areas in country houses were serviced by basements and back stairs. Towns, like country houses, had to be warmed, lit and supplied with water and means of disposing of sewage, and succeeding generations found different and more sophisticated ways of doing this. One could trace hierarchies in both places, and changes of attitude which were common to both. At first, with innocent optimism, I tried to apply such a study to towns all round the world. The impossibility of doing this soon became apparent, and I split the project into two: a study of cities in the western world, which was published as *Cities and People* in 1985, and a study of towns of all sizes in England (but not Scotland or, except very marginally, Wales), of which this book is the result.

It soon became clear that the country-house analogy would only work to a limited extent. In a country house, even if its architecture is complex and confused, ownership by a single member of a single family imposes a continuous thread. Its history, at any given moment, is a drama, ostensibly, at least, controlled by a single director; where the control was complete and the director had genius, or knew where to find it, the result can have the perfection of a Hardwick or a Castle Howard. That kind of perfection is not to be expected in towns. In the Middle Ages many new towns were laid out by the owners of the land on a more-or-less regular plan, usually a grid, and a few planned towns followed in subsequent centuries – not very many, for the greater part of post-medieval urban growth took place piecemeal around a medieval core. But the buildings that were built on the basis of the plans seldom had any architectural unity, and if they did it was usually eroded by later rebuilding, just as the original plan was submerged by later extensions of the town around it. A few towns belonged over several centuries mainly or entirely to one ground landlord, who exerted a degree of control, which can still be felt if one walks round, for instance, Huddersfield or Eastbourne, most of which belonged to the Ramsdens and the Dukes of Devonshire, respectively. But control was always conditioned by a desire to make the property profitable, which produced a situation quite different from that involved in creating an appropriate setting for one family. Moreover, the more prosperous the town the more, and the more successfully, its inhabitants fought to reduce or escape from control.

The individuality and interest of towns comes from their being the result of thousands of decisions taken by thousands of people over, in most cases, several hundred years. Some led to collaboration, others to collision, between individuals and government, self-interest and idealism, man and nature. Enough decisions working in the same direction can produce a unity, of materials, function, or design. There are towns which were nearly all built of the same materials, usually because they were the easiest available. There are towns which were dominated by one particular building type, like the cotton mills of Lancashire or the kilns of the Potteries. Though there are no entire English towns of unified design there are, of course, many areas in towns, particularly those built in the eighteenth and early nineteenth centuries, which are completely and sometimes exquisitely of a piece.

Trying to find out about towns is as overpowering as it is absorbing. The sources of information are diverse and endless; a single person cannot hope to do more than sample them, to ask himself a limited number of questions and look for the answers. There is a huge literature of recent publications on towns, part written by local amateurs (who are often far from amateurish), part by professional urban or architectural historians. There is an equally huge literature of histories, guidebooks, directories and tours, published in increasing numbers since the seventeenth century. A mass of documentary records, of which only a fragment have been published, exist in county record offices and elsewhere, pertaining to corporations, private estates, and local and national bodies of all kinds. Local newspapers contain a reservoir of information so vast as to be overwhelming. Hardest to come by are the personal letters and diaries that, more than anything else, help one today to put oneself into the skin of someone in the past; the kind of material that has survived in the security of country-house archives tends to get scattered and lost in the changing and migratory life of the towns.

Contemporary visual records, in the form of paintings, drawings, plans and photographs, are rare before the eighteenth century, but survive in increasing numbers after 1700; local museums, libraries and town halls are full of riches which deserve to be better known. The Admiral Blake Museum in Bridgwater, for instance, holds on loan the water-colours of John Chubb, a local wine merchant and amateur artist who drew all the personalities of the town in the late eighteenth century. In the early 1800s a member of the Lord family made a record of St. James's Square, Bristol, in which she lived, of every detail of the long garden behind the house, and of herself looking out at it through the window. Between about 1840 and 1851, a local artist, William Brown, sat at the base of the church spire of Louth, drew everything he saw from its windows, and transferred the results onto two huge canvases. They hang today in the town hall and preserve an entire early Victorian town in aspic. The museum at Wisbech owns several hundred negatives of the town taken by Samuel Smith in the 1840s and 1850s. The museum at Whitby owns (but leases out to a shop in the town) the even larger collection of photographic negatives of Frank Meadow Sutcliffe, who walked round Whitby taking photograph after photograph for over sixty years, until his death in 1941. The list of riches could go on for ever; even sampling them has been a continual source of surprise and pleasure.

But writing this book has given me almost as much pain as pleasure. The pleasure came, initially, from research, from learning, bit by bit, the extraordinary complexity and richness of English towns, and building up, often out of nothing as far as I was concerned, a picture of individual town after town, learning how they developed, what their inhabitants bought, made and sold, who lived where, and why, who hated or loved what or whom, the different ways in which the different generations and classes amused themselves, and, finally, piecing together a picture of the slow accumulation of buildings which all this had produced over the centuries.

The pain came, all too often, when, armed with my bundle of index cards, my camera, and my carefully constructed mental picture, I visited the towns themselves, often for the first time, or for the first time for many years. I went back to Huddersfield, and found that its heroic street of mills had long since vanished under a ring road. I went back to Chichester and found too many of the Georgian houses which had excited me as a child pickled and preserved as little more than a screen to hide the car-parks. I saw how ruthlessly two-thirds of the centre of Worcester, and most of the centre of Gloucester, had been mangled; walked from the station to the Shire Hall through the corpse of what had once been Chelmsford; discovered how Taunton had destroyed in a year or two the town centre so carefully and creatively formed in the eighteenth century; wandered in Liverpool past gutted buildings and over the acres of desert which had once been covered by eighteenth-century squares and terraces; and wept in the screaming desolation of central Birmingham.

I came to know too well the boa-constrictor hug of the ring road; the cracked concrete, puddles and pornographic scribbles of the subways; the light standards rising out of tasteful landscaping on the roundabouts; the new telephone exchange pushing up its ugly head, with such inspired accuracy, exactly where it could do the most damage; the claustrophobic arcades, streaked surfaces and tattering glitziness of once-new shopping centres.

Yet often enough I fled in horror from the centre and recovered in the outskirts — or vice versa. And there are, of course, towns which remain a pure delight, because of the life in them as well as because of their buildings. There are unspoilt towns like Ludlow or

Richmond, which are much frequented by tourists, but are able to absorb them and go their own way; there are towns like Newark or Bury St. Edmunds which are comparatively little visited but are just attractive, busy places which have managed to remain prosperous and useful, while keeping their character. It is always a pleasure, for instance, to go into the modest town of Holt, in Norfolk, and see how it retains its centuries-old function as the place into which the surrounding countryside flocks to do its shopping; streets and shops are jammed, cars come in and out, everything is smart and up-to-date, friends and acquaintances call to each other across the street, yet it remains a bright and pretty town, which has not destroyed its old buildings.

But the richness or interest of English towns is not confined to small places, or the more obvious show spots. Its dominantly nineteenth-century towns, small and large, sea ports, mill towns, brewing towns, railway towns, spas and seaside resorts are all fascinating both to visit and to study, wickedly though many of them have suffered. If this book has heroes, they are the corporations of Victorian towns, especially of northern industrial towns. It has been a pleasure to find out about them, and savour their activities, in a climate so different from that of the present day. With unfailing energy and resourcefulness they took over services from inefficient private enterprise, and made them prosperous and fruitful, leaving behind them a rich harvest of town halls, court-houses, market halls, schools, viaducts, bridges, reservoirs, and pumping stations, all proudly flaunting the corporation coat-of-arms from ripely ebullient architecture.

As one learns, one finds oneself acquiring an increasing sense of companionship with the past inhabitants of the towns on which one is working. It is a companionship which can be acquired, of course, from documents on their own; but it gains an extra degree of reality when the buildings which those past inhabitants built, and the spaces through which they moved, are still recognizably there. It is this companionship with the past, combined with the beauty, character or interest of the buildings in themselves, and the variety which they give to their towns, which is an argument for keeping anything that can reasonably be kept, given the need of any town to change and grow. Keeping and understanding the past makes for tolerance; it also makes for creativity, in devising ways of altering and adding to towns, for nothing comes out of a vacuum. It is hard to believe that those who made the running in English towns in the 1950s and 1960s would have done what they did if they had known more about them.

2. (right)   The Tuesday market, King's Lynn, during the February Mart.

8

1

The
Market Place,
The Manor,
And The
Corporation

For five or six days a week most market squares in English towns are car-parks. The cars lap round a market cross, a war memorial, or the statue of some forgotten Victorian worthy, marooned on his island in a sea of metal. The shops around the cars are hardly ticking over. In the evening, when the shops have shut and the cars have gone, groups of boys and girls shriek and giggle outside McDonald's or Wimpy's. The lights glimmer through the windows of the half-deserted pubs. Otherwise there is no sign of life at all.

On the eve or early morning of market day the clash of metal frames as stalls are put up gives the first warning of a change. By nine o'clock in the morning, or soon after,

the transformation is complete. The square is gay with multi-coloured awnings, crammed with people, and humming with voices and the shuffle of feet. The stalls are offering fruit and vegetables, female underwear in penetrating colours, rows of gumboots or cheap crockery, piles of Sellotape at reduced prices, electrical appliances, health foods, videos and dog-eared paperbacks. Around the square and in the streets leading into it, the shops are crowded and the pavement echoes with footsteps. A babel of voices spills through the clashing swing-doors of the pubs. The buildings round the market place act as a backcloth to all this activity: eighteenth-century houses raising comfortable brick façades above new shop-fronts; stone banks embellished with turrets or tricked out with Gothic or classical arcades; the bay-windowed and stuccoed front of a hotel; a stretch of black-and-white half-timbering, not always fake; the soapy encaustic of Woolworth's or Montague Burton's; the pediment of a town hall or the Corinthian columns and busty Ceres of a corn exchange.

This waking-up of the market place is a ritual which has been going on in England for centuries. Many markets have been held in the same place for eight hundred years, and a few for over a thousand. The only centres of resort to rival them in age and importance are the churches; and the surviving markets are still full, while the churches are empty. Most English towns were created by people coming in to market to buy or sell something. Many subsequently acquired functions which enriched and enlarged them, but hundreds lived off their markets and decayed or disappeared if the market ceased.

On ordinary days the towns were even deader than market towns are today, as is made clear in many contemporary illustrations (Pl. 3). On market days they became, not just places for buying and selling, but for meeting all sorts and kinds of people. Here, for instance, are the people whom

3. The market place at Peterborough, from a painting by Theodore Fielding, *c*.1780.
4. The market square, Norwich.

Henry Purefoy, a Buckinghamshire squire living at Shalstone, near Brackley, met one market day in Brackley in 1739:

'Mr Yates, the shopkeeper, the old beggar woman, Master Fenimore senior the glazier, Mr Cooper the schoolmaster, the man who sells hats next to Mr Yates's. Mr Stranks, his man and boy, the Landlady and man and servants at the Red Lion inn, Will Loveday, the man we bought the pigs on, the Biddlesden man who drove the pigs home, Mrs Blencow the orange woman, Mr Palmer the Northampton carrier, the man I spoke to about the sheep, Mr Leaper the gardener, the little woman by the market house we bought fish on, Mrs Molly Jakeman and her apprentice, Mr Welchman senior and his wife, the man of whom we bought the chickens, Goodman Sheppard of Gretworth'.

On another occasion those he ran into included 'Mr Arnold the one-eyed butcher, Master Gill of Brackley (who gathers mushrooms and has but one leg) and a soldier man and a woman with him who showed us the alligator'.[1]

There were about 800 market towns in England and Wales in 1600.[2] There were considerably more in the Middle Ages, and there are far fewer today. Alternative forms of buying and selling were developed, improved forms of transport enlarged their catchment areas, they were got rid of as an obstruction to traffic. Many medieval markets gave up soon after they had been started, because there was no very good reason for their existence, except that a local magnate hoped to cash in on a profitable form of activity and enlarge his revenues. Such hopes were often disappointed. If a would-be market town was wrongly sited, it soon dwindled to a village or hamlet, or virtually disappeared. All that survives of the market at Stapleford in Lincolnshire is a fifteenth-century cross, rising out of the lawn of the manor house.[3]

Quite often today, towns have a market place, but no market takes place in it. It

5, 6. Transformations in the market place at Nottingham: during the Goose Fair in about 1900; and being inaugurated as a civic square in 1929, with the new City Hall in the background.

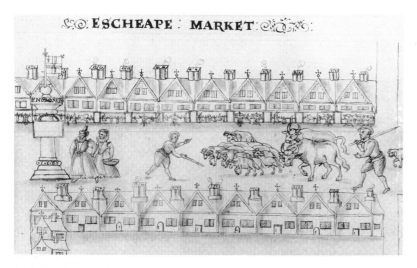

ESCHEAPE MARKET

7. The meat market in Eastcheap in 1598, as illustrated in Hugh Alley's *A Caveat for the City of London*.
8. Eastgate Street, Chester, from an engraving of *c.* 1830.

has become a permanent car-park or a sad amorphous space with a main road thundering through it. Endeavours to send it up in the world can be equally unsuccessful. The market square in Nottingham (Pl. 5) was cleared of its stalls in 1927, and laid out as a civic space (Pl. 6). Fountains, potted plants, steps, and acres of empty paving lead up to the dome of the City Hall. It is a frigid replacement for the crammed and crowded market place which for centuries had delighted all travellers who came to Nottingham. If one has to have civic grandeur, Norwich achieved it more sensibly in the 1930s: terraces lead up from the market place to the Town Hall, and down below the market (Pl. 4) remains one of the biggest and liveliest in England, as it has been since it was laid out by Ralf, Earl of East Anglia, in the eleventh century.

Nottingham and Norwich both correspond to most people's stereotype of an English market place: spacious, more or less rectangular, very much places rather than streets, and often bypassed by the main thoroughfare of the town. The market places at Ripon, King's Lynn, Newark, Chesterfield and Salisbury are other familiar examples, but there are dozens of them. Their regularity betrays the fact that they were deliberately laid out for markets, probably by the Lord of the Manor when the royal grant to hold a market was first issued.

But market places come in all shapes and sizes. They can take the form of very wide main streets, as at Marlborough, sometimes funnelling down at one or both ends, as at Yeovil; or roughly triangular at a Y-shaped junction, as at Swaffham or Hereford. Market places of this kind probably originated as unplanned markets, along one main road or at the junction of two, round which the town grew up. The fact that when the market was in progress it blocked a main road, or most of it, was acceptable in terms of the modest traffic of past centuries, but becomes less acceptable today, so that wide-street markets are likely to be abolished, as at Yarm, or to dwindle to a ribbon between highways, as at Marlborough.

In many towns with a market, including very substantial ones, there was not even an especially wide street, let alone a square, to accommodate it. The most notable example was London, where the two main markets, in Eastcheap and Cheapside (Pl. 7), were only 50

9. View of the Sheep Market in Wide Bargate, Boston, in about 1840 (detail).

to 70 feet wide.[4] There were large markets, but no proper market place, at Exeter, Worcester, Colchester, Chester, Chichester and Bath, to name but a few examples. The main streets of these towns were congested with animals or stalls on market days. In the nineteenth century this began to be found unacceptable. In 1833, for instance, Mr Folliott, of Northgate Street in Chester, infuriated by having 'pigs snoozing in their litter underneath the parlour windows', railed in the space before his house, but had to take down the railings because of complaints from the pig and cattle drovers; they had the law on their side.[5] The cattle market was finally removed from Northgate Street in 1849, and the provision market from Eastgate Street (Pl. 8) in 1863. In smaller places, main street markets survived for much longer.

Beast markets were usually kept separate, often on the edge of the town, so that the animals caused the least possible inconvenience coming in and out. The combination can be seen very clearly at Boston, where the beast market took place in the great funnel of Wide Bargate (Pl. 9), from which the relatively narrow street of Bargate proper led into the main market place in the centre of the town. The market still flourishes, but the beast market has gone, and been replaced by trees and flower-beds. No beast markets survive on their original medieval sites; they have all either been abolished, or moved out to other sites as the towns expanded — and these sites, in their turn, have become prime property for redevelopment. The closest to a survival is London's Smithfield, where the

13

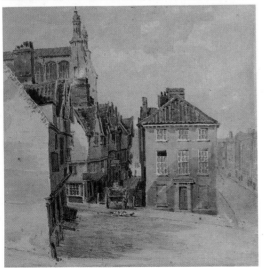

10. Looking along one of the second-floor arcades of the Piece Hall, Halifax.
11. A market island in the Haymarket, Norwich. Detail from a water-colour by John Thirtle.
12. (right) Infill at Saffron Walden. The market place in the early Middle Ages (conjectural), in 1600, and today.

beast market was replaced by a meat market in the late nineteenth century.

Some towns had specialist markets which dominated their economies, and had a far wider catchment area than that enjoyed by little local markets serving a ring of villages. The speciality could be crops or livestock. Doncaster, for instance, was famous for its wool market, at which wool from the inexhaustible flocks of Lincolnshire and Leicestershire was channelled to the clothiers of West Yorkshire. Royston and Ware had great markets for barley, frequented by buyers for the London brewers. Other markets specialized in manufactured goods. At Leeds, in the early eighteenth century, the cloth market jammed the bridge across the river, and spread up Briggate, the main street of the town. Twice a week, early in the morning, the bridge and street were filled with trestle tables and at the ringing of a bell clothiers swarmed out of adjoining shops and inns and covered the tables with their wares. For the next hour and a half, till the bell rang again, they sold cloth in grim Yorkshire silence, for resale all over England, Europe and the Levant.[6]

The cloth had to be sold on the bridge and in the main street because there was no market place; by the mid-eighteenth century the situation had become insupportable, and a covered cloth hall was built. A similar situation at Halifax led to the building of a cloth hall in about 1708, and its replacement by the much larger Piece Hall (Pl. 10) in 1774-9. This latter takes the form of a great open space surrounded by galleries giving access to cubicles, in which the clothiers of Calderdale laid out their goods. It is all still there, unlike the other West Yorkshire cloth halls, of which at best only fragments survive.

Whether or not a town had a proper market place in the first place, or whether its market place could cope with increasing demand as the town grew, was a matter of luck, or the good judgement of whoever first laid out the market place. Ipswich, for instance, grew in the later Middle Ages to be one of the largest towns in England, and its market place rapidly became inadequate. By early on it was used for selling corn and meal, but little else; the other markets crowded the narrow adjoining streets. Even the big market place at Norwich could not cater for everything, and the city acquired separate hay and madder markets in other parts of the town.

At Salisbury, on the other hand, the market place contained the mass of the town's market activities well into the nineteenth century. It represented the medieval ideal of what a market place should be. It was laid out by the Bishop of Salisbury in the thirteenth century, as part of a carefully designed new town. It originally measured about 570 by 420 feet. The layout varied a little from period to period, but every activity had its place. The corn market ran along the north side, the wool and yarn market along the east, the wheelwrights along the west, and the butchers and fishmongers along the south. The poultry market was in the south-west corner, and the cheese market, where fruit and vegetables were also sold, in the north-west corner. Pots and pans were sold to the north of the butchers.[7]

From the fourteenth century the open space of the market was progressively reduced as the stalls of butchers, fishmongers, potters and wheelwrights along the south and west sides gradually grew more substantial, and ultimately became rows of houses. A similar process reduced other market places all over England: Saffron Walden is an excellent example (Pl. 12).[8] Houses which have developed out of stalls are easily recognizable, because they have no gardens or yards. They form a little island, or two islands divided by a narrow lane, in the middle or to one side of the market (Pl. 11).

Buying or selling could also take place from the buildings around the market place. A standard arrangement was for these to erect projecting stalls on their frontage on market days. Goods could be stored in the houses, and brought out in front by the occupants on market days; or alternatively, the stalls could be let. Over the centuries there was an inevitable tendency for the stalls to become the frontage of permanent shops. An alternative development was for the houses in the market place or in the streets leading into it to build out their upper storeys over an arcade. Almost the whole of the market place at Nottingham (Pl. 13) was developed in this way, and much of the market place at Newark; there are other good examples in Broad Street, Ludlow, and the Butterwalks at Dartmouth and Totnes. These encroachments needed permission from the market authorities. Normally this was given in return for payment. When, as was often the case, the corporation owned the market, such payments were a useful way by which it could increase its income.[9]

Houses on the market place had obvious commercial advantages. They tended to become the property of the richer citizens dealing in more valuable and profitable goods, especially grocers, dealing in imported spices from overseas, and mercers or drapers, dealing in cloth. In the course of the eighteenth century, some of these began to offer banking services as well, and ultimately developed into specialist banks — but still lived above the shop, so that banks were scarcely distinguishable from the houses to either side, until they were rebuilt more pretentiously in Victorian or Edwardian days.

Another common use for the buildings around the market was as inns. Inns could offer food and refreshment to people attending the market, stabling for their horses, and accommodation for those who wished to stay the night. They were also increasingly used as places in which to make bargains privately, rather than 'in the open market'. They became especially popular for the sale of corn, by sample instead of by the sackload in the corn market. The next development, as far as corn was concerned, was the building of covered corn exchanges. They were the result of booming sales of corn to feed the fast-growing nineteenth-century cities. The great majority of them

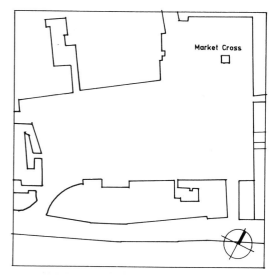

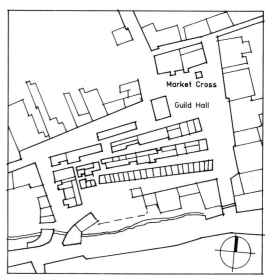

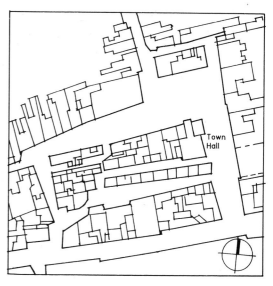

13. The market place at Nottingham, from a drawing by Thomas Sandby.

14. The corn exchange, Devizes, 1856.

were built between about 1840 and 1870, usually by private companies, who let them out for other events as well.[10] The repeal of the Corn Laws in 1846 had little effect on sales of home-grown corn until these were shattered by the import of American corn in great quantities in the 1870s. Corn exchanges were often built on the market place (Pl. 14), and tended to be ebulliently classical, and have a surmounting figure of Ceres. They were not always successful; quite often the farmers and corn-factors continued to prefer the inns. At Brigg, for instance, up till the 1950s, the Corn Exchange of 1850 remained relatively empty on market days, while the covered court of the adjacent inn was jammed to bursting.[11]

The fact that markets normally take place only on one, or at most two, days a week, leads irresistibly to their use as car-parks today, and led to their being used in the past for a variety of other activities. Parliamentary elections for the county and the borough often took place in them. They were used for open-air banquets at which hundreds of people sat down at long tables to celebrate the accession or jubilee of a monarch (Pl. 15), or the end of a war; they were used for entertainments, from balloon-ascents to bullfights. They were sometimes used for fairs; more often, however, these took place outside the town, or in another place within it, especially when the profits of the fair and the profits of the market went in different directions.[12] At Norwich, for instance, the corporation owned the market rights, but the Bishop had the profits of the fair, which took place on the great open space known as Tombland, outside the entry to the Close. At Nottingham, however, it was the corporation which had had the right to hold what became known as the Goose Fair on its market place since at least the thirteenth century. At King's Lynn a February fair has been held in the Tuesday Market since shortly after 1536, when Henry VIII gave the corporation the privilege.

The Lynn fairs, like other fairs all over the country, started as trade fairs, serving a far wider catchment area than the markets and often providing a variety of goods which enabled shopkeepers to stock up for the rest of the year. Shows, stalls for entertainment, roundabouts, and all the other paraphernalia of a fun-fair, gradually attached themselves, and often, as at Lynn, replaced the trading element altogether. At Bury St. Edmunds the great fair held on Angel Hill became more and more an amusement fair, until by the eighteenth century it was the chief social event of the year, attended by all classes, from dukes downwards, and accompanied by a theatrical season and a series of balls in the Assembly Rooms. The Lynn fair acquired a similar reputation; up till the last war young people from local country houses were still making up parties to attend it.[13]

The market place of Lynn originally had the central feature of an elaborate market cross, built in 1707 in the form of an octagonal covered market down below, and a domed storey above, possibly containing the market office. Most market places were given convenience and character by a series of buildings looked after (and usually built) by the market authority, and ranging from purely utilitarian structures to buildings of some elaboration and importance.

The selling portion of the market place was often protected from traffic by wooden railings, which kept out horses, carts and cattle. Within these railings, by no means everything was sold from stalls (Pl. 16). Much was brought into the town in carts, or in baskets, carried by the market women or slung from yokes fixed to their shoulders, and either spread out on the ground or sold direct from the baskets. But from the later Middle Ages onwards permanent stalls were usually provided for butchers and fishmongers; it was these that most often developed into houses. They were known as Shambles, a term deriving from a Saxon word meaning a bench or work-top. No functioning early Shambles survive, but one can get the feel of them in the street of open butchers' shops built by Barnstaple next to its new market hall in the 1850s (Pl. 17). At Stamford the elegant colonnaded entrance to the Shambles, built in 1804-8, serves as the frontispiece of the Public Library. At Hexham the Shambles, which dates from 1766, takes the form of a covered space supported on Doric columns; the original stalls have gone, but it is still used as a market, although not by butchers or fishmongers.

15. A banquet held in the market place at Wisbech to celebrate the coronation of George IV, 1821.

16. Market stalls in Covent Garden, London, as drawn by George Scharf in 1825.

17. The mid-nineteenth-century Shambles at Barnstaple.

In the Middle Ages all markets had a market cross. In its simplest form it consisted of a stone shaft rising from a circuit of steps, and surmounted by a cross. None survive intact (apart from the abandoned one at Stapleford) but sometimes the steps and shaft remain; at Stow-on-the-Wold these have been finished off with a Victorian cross.

In the next stage an octagonal space open at the sides was vaulted over and surmounted by a cross. In the much-restored cross at Winchester the covered space is too small for any practical use, but often it was large enough to be used for the sale of various types of goods, most commonly butter, which needed protection from the sun. Examples survive at Chichester, Salisbury and Malmesbury (Pl. 18). Sometimes, as it was at Salisbury, the cross was put up by a private donor, but if so it was normally taken over and maintained by the market authority. Buildings of this type continued to be built up to the early nineteenth century. The stylistic language changed, the octagon became a circle or a square, the buttresses and vaulting became, perhaps, a ring of columns and a dome (Pl. 19), and the cross gave way to a statue, but the type remained the same. The name 'cross' often survived too, even when there was no cross, either because of custom, or because the building replaced a medieval cross.

In the Middle Ages crosses gave markets the divine protection which was invoked for every aspect of life, secular as well as religious. Then and later they also served a practical function. The market place was the centre for news and gossip in the town, as well as for buying and selling, and the market cross was the focal point of the market, and therefore of the town.[14] Its steps created an elevated platform from which announcements could be made, new monarchs proclaimed, Acts of Parliament read out or news delivered to the surrounding crowds. At times of revolution it provided a show-place for exhibiting the severed heads of rebels. At Bungay, the classical market cross put up in 1689 still has shackles for public whippings fixed to one column; in reference to this function its dome is surmounted by an elegant statue of Justice instead of a cross.

This type of relatively small covered 'cross' could be expanded to form a larger covered market, as in the mid-seventeenth-century Yarn Market at Chipping Campden. A further stage came when a room or rooms was incorporated above the covered market, producing the buildings usually known, from their function, as market or town halls, but sometimes still called crosses. Buildings of this type had been common on the Continent since at least the twelfth century, but there are no English examples dating from before the fifteenth.

As a whole market buildings form a delightful group. The pleasure they can give is simple but satisfying. It derives from the varied treatment which can be given to a simple formula expressed on a modest scale: a covered space open on one or more sides, with or without an enclosed floor or floors above it. Sometimes variety comes from the translation of the formula into wood, ranging from the simple post and beams of the market cross at Abbot's Bromley to the gaily patterned half-timbering of the Town Hall at Hereford, long since demolished, or at Leominster, moved to the edge of the town and converted into a private house in 1853.[15] More often, it is due to its expression in the language of classicism. Endless different nuances can be expressed, or changes rung, in this way (Pls. 20-25).

Sometimes the building is incorporated into a side of the market place, as are the Town Halls at Blandford and Guildford, sometimes islanded in the middle of it, or in the middle of the broad street which served as a market, as at Yarm, Stockton and Barnard Castle. Sometimes it is surmounted by a hipped roof, sometimes by a pediment; sometimes a cupola with or without a clock rises from the roof or behind the pediment. The first floor can be supported by arches, or columns, or a mixture of the two. Sometimes there is a balcony, from which announcements can be made instead of from the steps of the market cross. An almost invariable feature is the arms of the corporation or the Lord of the Manor, an occasional one the royal arms, or a statue of Justice or a monarch.

The stylistic expression can be one of Jacobean fantasy, baroque robustness, Palladian restraint, Adamesque elegance, or neo-classical simplicity. Most often it was a local architect or builder-architect who was employed; occasionally an enterprising corporation or a powerful donor or Lord of the Manor brought in an architect of national reputation: Chambers at Woodstock, Adam at Bury St. Edmunds and High Wycombe, Wyatt at Ripon, possibly Wren at Abingdon.

The market hall at Abingdon, superbly trimmed out with a giant Corinthian order, is the most resplendent of English market buildings. But perhaps the most delightful is the contemporary Town Hall at Guildford: here an open arcade, a balcony, tall windows between pilasters, a boldly projecting clock, a pediment and a cupola, were all put together with robust directness and a gay disregard of the classical rules by an unknown provincial or a London artificer.

The different origins and variety of names of all these buildings, the fact that they are seldom used for their original purpose, and that their once open lower ground floors have often been closed in, can make them confusing to anyone who does not under-

18,19. Two stages in the evolution of the market cross. Gothic at Malmesbury (*c.*1450) and classical at Beverley (*c.* 1711).

MARKET BUILDINGS

20-22. (left) Late Gothic: the fifteenth-century Guild-hall, Thaxted; (centre) Elizabethan: the Town Hall, Woodbridge, c. 1575; (right) Artisan classical: the Town Hall, Guildford, 1683.
23-25. (facing page) (left) Palladian: the Town Hall, Blandford, by J. and W. Bastard, 1734; (centre) Palladian: the market cross, Barnard Castle, 1747; (right) Neo-classical: the Town Hall, Whitby, by Jonathan Pickernell, 1788.

stand the history of local government behind them, and its close identification with the market place.[9] Markets, like fairs, did not just happen, and did not run themselves. They could only take place by virtue of a royal warrant. Most markets were set up by the relevant Lord of the Manor, as a result of successful application to the Crown. In some cases the necessary warrant may have legalized a market which had already come into existence unofficially.[16]

Manors could belong to individuals or to bodies, such as a religious house, or the dean and chapter of a cathedral. He or it could want a market for reasons of convenience, or profit, or both. The great religious houses of the Middle Ages contained several hundred people, and so did the households of great magnates in their castles, like the Percys at Alnwick, or the Nevilles at Warwick. A market outside their gates was a convenience to them. But a successful market was also a useful source of income, derived from the rent paid by the stall-holders and the owners of the houses which grew up around it, and by the fees paid for the use of the weigh beam, which usually belonged to the owner of the market, and was the only legal means of weighing goods bought and sold in it.

A market had to be regulated, and the income from it collected. Most Lords of the Manor appointed an official to collect the rent and other market perquisites. But the actual day-to-day administration was usually the responsibility of the jury of the manorial court. These juries were permanent bodies, drawn from the most substantial residents of the manor. By use and custom they acquired a substantial degree of independence; they made their own decisions and often co-opted their own members, or were chosen by the residents of the manor rather than its Lord, and were sometimes at loggerheads with him. Running the market was by no means their only

responsibility; but it was their most important one. In addition, they were responsible for maintaining order in the market place and surrounding streets, and keeping them clean and free of obstructions, or roaming livestock. They had the power to inflict punishment for minor misdemeanours, usually in the form of fines. More serious offences were beyond their power to deal with, and had to go before the Justices of the Peace, who were appointed by the Crown, on a county basis, and often sat in another town. Since a manorial jury had little or no income, the whole system relied on a basis of unpaid jobs, working through the more substantial members of the jury by rotation.

There were hundreds of market towns administered in this way in the Middle Ages, as, to a greater or lesser extent, many of them continued to be into the nineteenth century. But the more successful a town was, the harder its leading citizens fought to increase their independence. The ultimate achievement was the fully-fledged municipal corporation, established by royal charter, represented by two members of Parliament, freed from the county Justices because it had its own courts, and from the Lord of the Manor because it owned the manorial rights, including the right to hold a market and enjoy its profits.

Some corporations developed directly out of manorial courts, but others were based, in part or whole, on medieval guilds, usually merchant or religious guilds, rather than craft guilds. Merchant guilds were associations of merchants recognized by the Crown and mostly set up in the twelfth or thirteenth centuries. Religious guilds were similar in organization, but were founded for a religious end such as maintaining an altar in the parish church, or providing deathbed comforts and memorial masses for their members. Most medieval towns had several such guilds, and one usually became especially powerful and prestigious, confined to the richest merchants of the town, endowed with land and property by successive bequests, often running a school or an almshouse, and owning its own hall (or guildhall) as well as its own chapel in the parish church. Both types of guild could easily develop into the governing body of a corporation, once a town obtained a charter. Sometimes a powerful guild and a corporation existed side by side; at York the especial splendour of the medieval Guildhall is due to the fact that the use of it, and the cost of its erection, were shared between the corporation and the Guild of St. Christopher. Guildhalls were sometimes on the market place, as at Norwich and King's Lynn, but not necessarily so: the Guildhalls of London, Bury St. Edmunds, York, Abingdon, Boston and Ludlow, all medieval in origin even if in some cases substantially remodelled, are well away from the market.

A common occurrence was for guilds to be dissolved, at the time of Edward VI's great purge in 1549, but for their property, including their guildhall, either to be handed over to the corporation, or a corporation to be specifically set up to take it over and administer it (as happened, for instance, at Louth). At Ludlow, the exceedingly rich Palmers' Guild owned property all over the town; its property was given in trust to the corporation in 1552, and its guildhall used by the corporation for their meetings, courts, and banquets. Its façade was rebuilt and the timber uprights of its hall prettily encased in Gothic columns by T.F. Pritchard in 1774-6 (Pl. 26); it is still a court-room today.[17]

Corporation privileges were never won for a town as a whole. They belonged to a smaller body within it, who were known as the freemen. Originally these were the trading element of the town, its merchants, artificers, innkeepers, shopkeepers and stall-holders — perhaps the upper third of its population. Membership came through birth or purchase and was carefully controlled. Initially, only the freemen had the right to trade in the town. Their other rights varied from place to place. Sometimes, but not very often, they elected the governing body; more often, they elected their town's two members of Parliament; they usually had the right of grazing or collecting fuel on common land belonging to the corporation. In the eighteenth century their monopoly of trade gradually disappeared, and their social make-up often became very mixed; many towns had large numbers of poor freemen, who guarded their privilege of selling their votes at election time to the highest bidder.

Technically, all the freemen were members of the corporation, but in practice the term came to be applied only to the inner governing group. This normally consisted of a mayor, a sizeable body of aldermen and councillors, a town clerk, who kept the records, and a recorder, who presided over the town's quarter sessions, and was usually a barrister. Corporation servants included a

26. (right) Inside Ludlow Guildhall (remodelled T.F. Pritchard, 1774-6).

22

sheriff, beadles and marshals, who kept order in the town and supervised public meetings. Many corporations also employed a body of musicians, known as the town waits, who serenaded important visitors, or played at festivities or in processions, and in the intervals were usually available for hire.

Corporations, in the narrower sense, sometimes formed the electorate for the town's members of Parliament, as was the case at Bath and Bury St. Edmunds. But this was comparatively rare. In most towns they had four main functions. They controlled the admission of freemen. They acted as trustees for various charities, such as grammar schools and almshouses. They kept law and order in the town, by means of their officers and courts; the mayor and aldermen were also Justices of the Peace, presided over the town's petty sessions, and sat on the bench at its quarter sessions, under the chairmanship of the recorder. Finally, they administered corporation property, including the market. Not all corporations owned the market rights, but most did; because of the markets' crucial role in the life of the town, and the income which they brought in to the corporation, running them was one of their most important functions.

From the Middle Ages onwards a good deal of state and ceremony was attached to corporations. The mayor, aldermen, councillors and recorder all had robes, of varying degrees of richness. The mayor had a sword and mace, as a symbol of office (Pl. 27). The officials had distinctive uniforms. One of the churches in the town was always the corporation church, furnished with a grand seat and sword rest for the mayor. The members of the corporation went in procession to church on Sundays, and bigger and more elaborate processions were held on special occasions.

The inauguration of a new mayor in Norwich was celebrated as follows until well on in the nineteenth century. The corporation waited on the old mayor at his house in the morning, and escorted him to the house of the new mayor who entertained them to breakfast. At eleven o'clock they all moved to the Cathedral in the following procession: first the great card and canvas dragon known as 'Snap', the mascot of the St. George's Guild, escorted by four Whifflers or swordsmen; then a band and the city beadles, escorting the blue and silver City Standard; then another beadle and the councillors in their gowns; then the city waits, playing their music, escorting the crimson and gold Standard of Justice, followed by the Mace-bearers and the Under-Chamberlain, or Havelock; then the Sword-bearer carrying the mayor's sword; then the Mayor, Mayor-Elect, Recorder, High Steward, aldermen and Sheriff, all in their robes; and finally the Sheriff's officers. After a service and sermon, they stopped before the front of the Cathedral, to listen to a Latin oration delivered by the cleverest schoolboy in the grammar school, and then processed on to a great banquet in St. Andrew's Hall.[18]

Entertainment played a major role in the life of all corporations.

It was their means of celebrating their existence, establishing their status, rewarding the services of unpaid members, and buttering up any person who could be useful to them, from the King downwards. At Boston, for instance, Sir Julius Caesar, with his wife, children and friends, were entertained to dinner in 1605: 'he being a man that may stand the corporation in great stead'. The Earl of Lincoln was entertained in 1609, the Bishop of Lincoln in 1611, Lord Rutland in 1614, Lord Exeter in 1615, Lord Lindsey and one hundred others in 1634, and so on.[12] In return, at Boston and elsewhere, the local landowners provided the wherewithal for the Venison Feasts that were a feature of corporation life. In general, corporations were ready — too ready, according to their critics — to wine and dine themselves or anybody else, on the slightest pretext.[19]

By their nature, corporations could be looked at in two ways. Were they property-owning trusts, policing and looking after their assets for the benefit of their membership, including the freemen? Or did they, as Bath corporation put it, in about 1770, take a wider view, and 'consider that the welfare of the City of Bath is entrusted to our care'?[20] On the whole, the more limited attitude prevailed, until, that is, the Municipal Corporations Act of 1835 introduced the new concept of a corporation representing, and responsible to, the rate-payers who elected it.

27. The Corporation of Worcester's sword-bearer, from an anonymous painting of *c*. 1740 in the Guild-hall, Worcester.

By then there were some 180 fully-fledged corporations.[14] The origins of most of them dated back to the Middle Ages, and, in the intervening centuries, their nature, and that of the towns they governed, often changed dramatically. The towns could grow to powerful cities, like Norwich, Bristol, Newcastle, and, of course, London, or decay to villages, like Orford in Suffolk, or Bradninch in Devon. As a result of centuries of cooperation some corporations (such as Warwick, or, to a lesser extent, Ludlow) became the preserve of the gentry living in or near the town, who excluded anyone 'in trade'.[21] Others, especially corporations in decayed towns or ones owning little property, went in the other direction. A letter written by the mayor-elect of Bridgewater in 1774, in answer to an anonymous satire, scarcely inspires confidence:

Sir,

I am creditably Informed by my friend Mr Cox That you are the author of That there epigram That was hung up against the Cross the Other night if you are So you are a impudent raskel and Durty Scoundrel besides you Have called my son in law Mr Charles Anderton the mayor capon Which is a lye as my dafter says he is No more a capon than yourself ... you had better Mind your own business and not Abuse your betters ....[22]

28. Inside Beverley Guildhall (W. Middleton, 1762-4; plaster work by G. Cortese).
29. (right) The Market House (now known as the County Hall) at Abingdon, at the time of Victoria's jubilee in 1897.

Whatever their history, size or quality, all governing bodies in towns had to have somewhere to meet and carry out their functions. A manorial court needed a room for its sittings, and somewhere to keep its records. A corporation needed space for its courts, its council meetings, its town clerk and his records, and its entertainments. Most manorial courts could get by happily enough with a single sizeable room, and a chest for records. So, at a pinch, could a corporation in a small town. One big room, furnished with a raised platform at one end for its magistrates to preside from, a table for corporation meetings, a big table for banquets, and a desk for clerks, could satisfy its needs; quite often the town clerk, who was almost always a practising attorney as well, kept his records and did his work at home. But it was common enough, from the Middle Ages onwards, for both corporations and manorial courts to have two rooms, a big room for courts and entertainments, and a small room off it, for everything else.

The big room was the archetypal 'town hall' the basic element from which the larger complexes derive their name. It was usually the only large internal space in the town, other than that available in the churches. Increasingly, from the sixteenth century onwards, it became a general-purpose room for the use of the town, as a venue for public meetings, balls, plays, concerts, lectures and so on. Its multiple functions were often reflected in its arrangement. The Guildhall at King's Lynn is said to have been equipped with movable court-room fittings, which could be removed when entertainment took over. A similar arrangement probably existed in the court-room of the Guildhall at Beverley (Pl. 28), and would explain why its baroque plaster work seems more suited for parties than judges and juries, in spite of the figure of Justice in its central roundel.

If the governing body owned the market, and had no other

building (such as a guildhall) available, it made sense to put its accommodation on the market place. There, on a site already belonging to the corporation or Lord of the Manor, and overlooking their principal asset, it could be raised up on open arcades to give dignity to the resulting building and maintain the area of lettable market space intact.

The Lord of the Manor sometimes paid for a more impressive building than a poor corporation could run to. Shaftesbury, for instance, had a corporation, and High Wycombe did not, but the little Town Hall at Shaftesbury is far more unassuming than the handsome one in High Wycombe, put up in 1757 at the expense of Lord Shelburne, the Lord of the Manor. The richer the corporation, however, and the greater its business, the bigger and more impressive the town hall, the more rooms in it, and the more specialized their uses. At the Guildhall at Bath, as rebuilt from 1775, one finds the following: a banqueting room, a council room, a court-room, a room off it for the mayor, three rooms for the town clerk and his assistants, a records room, a surveyor's office, ample kitchens, and a flat for the caretaker. It had originally been intended to have a covered ground-floor market, but in the end there was no room for the latter and a separate covered market was built on the adjacent site.[23]

Some corporations had two or more buildings, especially those which had inherited a guildhall away from the market place. In that case they often kept a presence on the market, in the form of a two-storey market house or hall, the upper storey of which could be put to various uses. Sometimes it served as a market office. At Bury St. Edmunds it was let out as a theatre. At Abingdon it was used for the county assizes; the building (Pl. 29) owes its magnificence to the fact that it was built by the corporation as a weapon in the war between Abingdon and Reading as to which should be the assize town for Berkshire (Abingdon won, but lost out to Reading in the mid-nineteenth century).[17] Ludlow corporation had four buildings (in addition to the town jail): a guildhall; a market hall, the upper storey of which was used for assemblies and balls; a butter cross at the end of the market place, the upper storey of which accommodated the town clerk and his records; and a 'tolsey' on the beast market, where tolls were collected. Only London, Newcastle, Bristol and York provided mansion houses as residences for their mayors.[24]

Few town or market buildings built between 1600 and 1800 are of more than modest scale: the Town Hall at Liverpool and the Mansion House in London are perhaps the only ones which could begin to compete with the grander country or London houses built by great landowners in the same period. In part this reflects the small size of the towns, but not entirely: towns no larger than the bigger eighteenth-century towns were to build much more grandly in the nineteenth century. Essentially it was due to the limited funds available to local government, and its unrepresentative nature.

Before 1835 corporations did not levy rates, except in a small way and for limited purposes: corporations with a quarter session, for instance, could levy a small rate to pay the expenses. Otherwise they were expected to live off income which came to them by way of their four main functions. As courts of law they drew an income from fines. As charitable trusts they dealt with sizeable endowments, but (although some corporations were accused of misappropriation) these were confined to the purposes of the trusts. As benefit societies they collected fees for the admission of freemen. As property owners they might, or might not, own the markets, the harbour, the quay and a crane on it, and common lands around the town, on which the freemen had grazing rights. They usually owned property in the town, which had come to them by way of legacies or royal grants. They owned the corporation's own buildings: a town hall, a guildhall or a market hall, and perhaps a prison. They owned the freehold of the streets and other open spaces in the town. If the town was walled, they owned the walls and gatehouses; one of the gatehouses was often used as a town prison. Some corporations had the right to charge tolls on goods or traffic passing through the gates. Chester continued to levy these until 1835, and maintained its walls and gates in consequence: for by the time tolls were abolished the walls had acquired an antiquarian value and survive today as a result.[25]

Some corporations were much richer than others. Their wealth did not necessarily bear a relationship to the size and prosperity of the town. Around 1780, Newcastle-upon-Tyne had a population of about 28,000 and a corporation income of £25,000, Norwich a population of about 30,000 and a corporation income of about £5,000. Newark corporation, in a town with a population of under 5,000, was richer than Leeds corporation, with a population of about 20,000.[26]

Taunton was a prosperous textile town, but its corporation owned very little property and the market belonged to the Bishop of Winchester. Its revenue was so minimal that it quietly expired in the late eighteenth century, leaving the town to be run by an enterprising group which had leased the market from the Bishop. Colchester was an even bigger textile town, the centre of the East Anglian baize industry, but by the early eighteenth century the corporation's finances were embarrassed, and its properties mortgaged (to, of all unlikely people, Daniel Defoe). It ceased to function in 1742, and until it was resuscitated in 1763 by the public spirit of a local attorney, Colchester did without local government.[27]

By the end of the eighteenth century Liverpool was much the richest corporation after London. It was the only one which could begin to compete in terms of patronage with the dozen or so great English landowners who had an income in excess of £50,000 a year. It had made a great, and rapidly increasing, fortune through its enterprise as a property developer and docks promoter. In 1800, its disposable income was about £40,000 a year, exclusive of about £20,000 a year from the docks, which was ploughed back into enlarging and improving them. In terms of civic building, the result was its domed and porticoed Town Hall, enclosing a suite of reception rooms of a splendour, elegance and sophistication which would have satisfied a duke.[28]

There were many town corporations much less wealthy than Liverpool, but substantially better off than Taunton, with an income of a few thousand a year, the equivalent of a comfortable country gentleman's estate, and buildings to match up with it. Boston corporation's status as a property owner is immediately made clear in the market place by an elegantly pedimented terrace of five houses, built in 1772, covered market and Assembly Rooms adjoining, built in 1822, and a cast-iron bridge across the river by the Assembly Rooms. Bridge, Rooms and terrace were all built by the corporation and are prominently blazoned with its coat-of-arms.[29]

The corporation of Newark had had substantial property left to it in the sixteenth century. In 1773 it obtained an Act of Parliament enabling it to sell off sufficient of this to build a new Town Hall (Pl.

30). The elegant building designed by Carr of York was the result. But even its comparatively modest grandeur was only achieved by making the building pay its way. The portions to left and right of the central façade were originally built as rentable houses: the great room at the back was let out for county quarter sessions and for assemblies; the space underneath served as a covered market, and was cut up by thickly spaced columns to support the pounding feet of the dancers in the great room above.[30]

A corporation that built beyond its income could get into trouble. Warwick corporation rebuilt the building known as the Court House (Pl. 31), which was in effect its town hall, in 1725-31. Almost inevitably it employed the able local builder and architect, Francis Smith, who lived in Warwick and was himself an alderman, mayor in 1728-9, and the son-in-law of a previous mayor. The resulting building was not large, but was extremely handsome. It cost £2,253. A group in the town brought a suit in chancery against the corporation, complaining that the building was unnecessary, used only for feasting and card-playing, and had been built out of revenues which should have been confined to borough charities. They won their case; the corporation was ordered to pay back £4,000, including costs and interest, into the charitable trust, and since it could not afford to do so, the building was taken over by sequestration commissioners in 1742. For nearly thirty years, until the debt was paid off, corporation meetings were held in an inn.[31]

30. Newark Town Hall (John Carr, 1773-6), seen from across the market place.
31. The Court House, Warwick (Francis Smith, 1725-31).
32. (right) The quay at Bridgwater. Detail from a water-colour of *c.* 1780 by John Chubb.

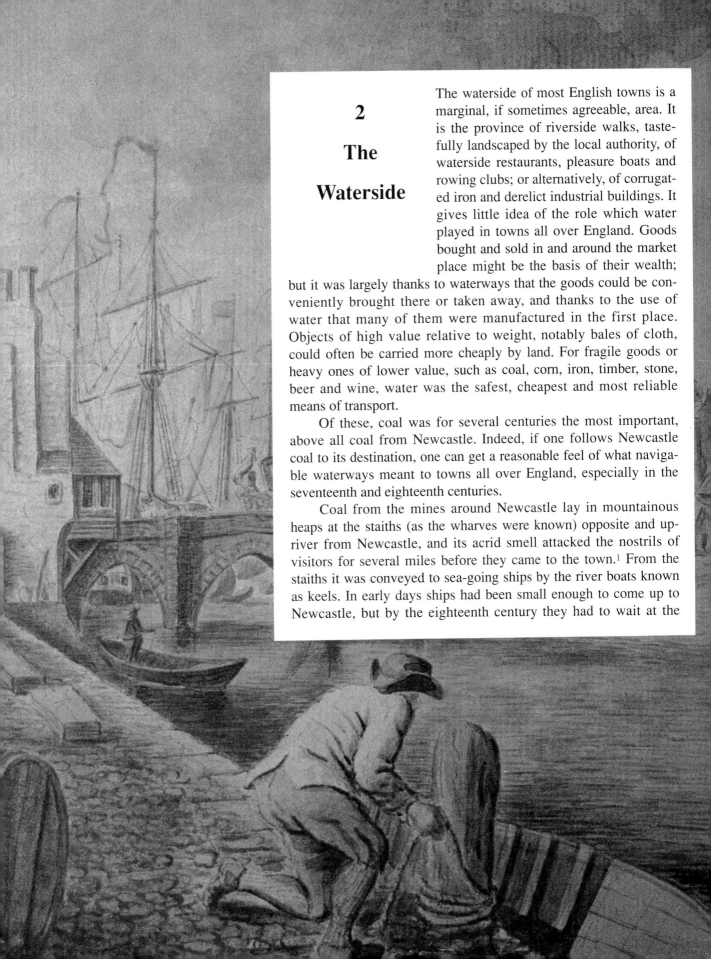

2

The

Waterside

The waterside of most English towns is a marginal, if sometimes agreeable, area. It is the province of riverside walks, tastefully landscaped by the local authority, of waterside restaurants, pleasure boats and rowing clubs; or alternatively, of corrugated iron and derelict industrial buildings. It gives little idea of the role which water played in towns all over England. Goods bought and sold in and around the market place might be the basis of their wealth; but it was largely thanks to waterways that the goods could be conveniently brought there or taken away, and thanks to the use of water that many of them were manufactured in the first place. Objects of high value relative to weight, notably bales of cloth, could often be carried more cheaply by land. For fragile goods or heavy ones of lower value, such as coal, corn, iron, timber, stone, beer and wine, water was the safest, cheapest and most reliable means of transport.

Of these, coal was for several centuries the most important, above all coal from Newcastle. Indeed, if one follows Newcastle coal to its destination, one can get a reasonable feel of what navigable waterways meant to towns all over England, especially in the seventeenth and eighteenth centuries.

Coal from the mines around Newcastle lay in mountainous heaps at the staiths (as the wharves were known) opposite and up-river from Newcastle, and its acrid smell attacked the nostrils of visitors for several miles before they came to the town.[1] From the staiths it was conveyed to sea-going ships by the river boats known as keels. In early days ships had been small enough to come up to Newcastle, but by the eighteenth century they had to wait at the

mouth of the river, at North and South Shields and Tynemouth. Here a hundred or more of them were likely to be jostling and quarrelling as to the order in which they were to be loaded. Only a few came from Newcastle; others were from London, or from Scarborough, Bridlington, Lynn, Ipswich, Ramsgate and other places along the coast, above all from Whitby (Pl. 33) and Yarmouth.[2] The coal-carrying trade played a major part in the economy of all these towns in the eighteenth century. Yarmouth's prosperity rested on coal as much as on timber and herrings; at Whitby the coal trade (with whaling and government transport in time of war, to add the icing) drove out the fishing industry and turned it from a village into a flourishing town. By 1790 it was the seventh largest port in England, in terms of tonnage of shipping belonging to its shipowners.[3]

The constellations of colliers sailing down the east coast between March and October were one of the sights of England, especially in wartime, when they sailed in convoy. In 1697, Celia Fiennes stood on the sands near Scarborough and counted seventy of them.[4] The majority started from Newcastle, but in the eighteenth century were joined by increasing numbers emerging from the Wear, with cargoes from the mines around Sunderland. Many carried passengers as well, for the sea route was the cheapest form of transport for humans as well as coal. Some dropped their cargoes

33. Boats in the harbour at Whitby. Detail from a photograph of 1880 by Frank Meadow Sutcliffe.
34. Brayford Pool and Lincoln Cathedral, as painted by J.W. Carmichael in 1858.

off at ports along the coast, to feed domestic fires, or supply the alum works of North Yorkshire. Some went up the Yare to Norwich. A few carried on to Devon and sailed up the Exe to Exeter, where their cargoes heated up the dye vats and hot-pressing furnaces of its serge industry.[5] But the majority sailed up the Thames to London.

London's coal port was at Billingsgate. Until the mid-nineteenth century coal was at least as important there as fish.[6] Most of the coal bought 'at the 'gate' stayed in London, but a small proportion continued up the Thames. It was transferred from the colliers into small lighters which could negotiate the tricky, fast-flowing passage through London Bridge, and from lighters into Thames barges, to travel up to Reading, Henley (Pl. 39) or Abingdon. At all these places the barges were likely to exchange their cargoes for corn or malt: the Thames Valley towns grew prosperous on supplying corn to London, or on using northern coal to brew malt, to be sent down to the London breweries.

As along the east coast and the Thames, other navigable waterways, both inland and coastal, conditioned the rise and importance of towns. The sea provided a route round England, as well as a route away from it. Its waterway system worked in the opposite way to road or rail systems, where trunk routes up the centre fan out into branch routes to the periphery. Instead, the main sea route ran round the outside, and from it lesser routes ran inland, like spokes from the rim of a wheel.[7]

In 1700 there were about seventy-five coastal ports of significance in England and Wales, some in natural harbours on the actual coastline, some up the tidal mouths of rivers. Approximately half their ships were engaged in coast trade, and half in overseas trade. The most important ports were at the outlets of the four main inland-waterway systems: the Trent and Yorkshire Ouse, and their tributaries, running into the Humber; the Welland, Great and Little Ouse and Cam, running into the Wash; the Thames and its tributaries; and the Severn, Avon and Wye, running into the Bristol Channel. Later in the century improvements in navigation added a fifth: the Weaver, Mersey and Irwell, running into the Mersey estuary. The five systems linked up with coastal trade at Hull, King's Lynn, London, Bristol and Liverpool respectively (Pl. 35).

In the Middle Ages seagoing vessels were so small that they could penetrate deep inland: York and Norwich, for instance, were both busy seaports; so was Lincoln, until its waterways all but silted up in the sixteenth (but were reopened at the end of the eighteenth, see Pl. 34). As the

35. Navigable waterways in England in 1660, and as extended by 1730.

36. The river and warehouses at Wisbech in about 1850, from a photograph by Samuel Smith.

33

average size of seagoing ships grew larger and they drew more water (and sometimes, as rivers silted up) these inland ports lost most or all of their seagoing traffic, in the case of York and Norwich to the benefit of Hull and Yarmouth. Even so, well into the eighteenth century sea trade was still going to places which have long ceased to be thought of as seaports, or ports of any kind: to Stockton and Colchester, Arundel and Exeter, Chester and Wisbech (Pl.36). Seaports up tidal rivers had their advantages: they were insulated from storms; ships could travel up and down to them on the tide; and the further inland they were, the bigger their catchment area. The ideal position was where the first bridge crossed the river, so that the town was a centre of road as well as river transport.

Such ports on inland waterways were points of interchange, where cargoes were transferred between seagoing ships and flat-bottomed barges, to travel lazily up and down the rivers, under the power, usually, of a single square-masted sail, or pulled by men or horses when wind was lacking. Upstream there were river ports at regular intervals (Pl. 39), but the biggest and busiest, after those at the sea end, were where the river ceased to be navigable, the terminus of the line, so to speak. Up to the late seventeenth century the terminus of the Severn was at Shrewsbury, of the Warwickshire Avon at Stratford, of the Trent at Nottingham, of the Yorkshire Ouse at York, of the Thames at Oxford.[8]

Water was also useful or essential for many industries. It provided power, or was used in industrial processes. The hammers in the iron forges of Sheffield and the Sussex Weald were powered by water. Rags were steamed and pounded into paper by water-mills along the river Medway and elsewhere. Above all, water played a critical part in the textile industry. It was used for washing the grease out of wool and cloth, for dyeing, and for fulling.

Fulling involved pounding wet cloth to form the heavy felted stuffs known as broadcloth. In the early Middle Ages human hands or feet had pounded the cloth in vats. The process had been mechanized by the invention of the fulling mill, the hammer of which could be used both for scouring cloth and felting it. From the fourteenth century onwards fulling mills proliferated and helped draw the textile industry away from the flatlands to the hills. Some cloths, especially the light cloths known as worsteds, did not need fulling, however, and their manufacture continued to flourish in East Anglia, where water was abundant but usually slow-flowing.

Industrial water, by its nature, was seldom navigable. Sea water, or salty water in tidal rivers, could not be used to wash or dye wool: few seaports, as a consequence, had a textile industry of any importance. Narrow, fast-flowing streams with a good fall were

37.   Warehouses on the river Aire at Leeds.
38.   A warehouse on the canal at Louth.
39. (right)   Detail from a view of Henley-on-Thames by Jan Siberechts, c. 1692.

40. The quay at Bristol in about 1720, from an anonymous oil painting.
41. (right) Walls and shipping at King's Lynn. Detail from an engraving after S. & N. Buck, 1741.
42. (bottom right) Navigable waterways in the canal age, 1820.

ideal for driving mills, washing wool, or taking away the waste from dye vats, but were not navigable — except, in some cases, by being dredged and supplied with locks, a technology which in England only began to be important after 1700. A few rivers and streams were famous for their value in the dyeing process, but were too small or shallow for traffic. The little Sherbourne at Coventry had been renowned since the Middle Ages for its powers as a fixative of blue dyes: hence the phrase for a faithful friend 'a true Coventry blue'. The Stroud Water, running through Stroud and the valley above it, and the streams feeding into it, were equally famous for their qualities in dyeing cloths scarlet and crimson.

The easier the link between industrial and navigable water, the more flourishing the industry, and therefore the towns which depended on it. Navigable water systems could be extended to manufacturing districts in two ways, by forming canals and improving rivers. The canal system, which was to be so important from the mid-eighteenth century onwards, was preceded by an assault on river navigation. In the decades around 1700 the Exe was made navigable to Exeter; the Avon to within two miles of Salisbury; the Aire and Calder to Wakefield and Leeds (Pl. 37), and, a little later, the Mersey and Irwell to Manchester.[9]

These improvements were made in the interests of the textile trade, and were financed by the relevant merchants or clothiers. But improving rivers benefited all kinds of industries — and antagonized others. Upstream towns lobbied for a water connection, and the towns below them lobbied against it; they did not want to see the

goods which had passed through their markets merely floating past their quays. The corporation and merchants in Nottingham, for instance, fought tooth and nail against the extension of river navigation to Derby and Burton, but without success. Both towns got their link in the 1720s (Pl. 42).[10]

From the mid-eighteenth century river improvement gave way to the construction of canals. Canals were used to connect existing towns, and only created one small new one in the eighteenth century: Stourport, where the Midland canal system linked Birmingham and the Black Country to the Severn. But the arrival of a canal, or the improvement of a river, could restore life to a decaying town or dramatically accelerate the growth of an active one. In terms of new buildings one can watch town after town springing into life or spreading its wings as the boats come in. When the Welland was made navigable to Stamford in 1673, by means of a cut in the river, it produced a spate of new building, including a row of spacious houses in St. George's Square, backing onto long plots stretching down to warehouses along the wharf; the earliest, biggest and best of them, dated 1674, was probably the home of Daniel Wigmore, a wool merchant who financed the river improvement.[11] Leominster's substantial eighteenth-century houses reflect the fact that, as Defoe wrote, the river Lun and the Wye into which it flowed had been 'lately made navigable by Act of Parliament, to the very great profit of the trading part of this country'.[12] There was now an easy outlet for the wheat and wool for which the neighbourhood was famous. At Louth the trade in wool and cloth which produced its mighty spire had dwindled away, but the little town acquired new prosperity, leading to much new building (Pl. 38), when a canal linking it to the Humber was opened in 1770; as the local historian R.S. Bayley put it in his flatulent style: 'even its Lilliputian transactions illustrate the great commercial law, that internal water-carriage and prosperity are mutually proportionate'.[13]

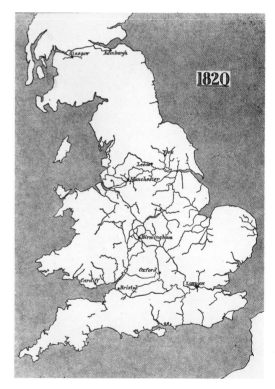

43. The world's first commercial dock. Old Dock and the Customs House, Liverpool, from an engraving of *c.* 1770.
44. (right) Prince Street, Bristol, 1825, from the water-colour by Edward Cashin, 1825.

The most substantial growth stimulated by canals was that of Birmingham. The canals did not create Birmingham; by 1700 a combination of accessible coal and iron, a river which could power mills with which to work the iron, and the absence of a corporation to discourage newcomers, had produced a town of some 8,000 people, specializing in cutlery and firearms. But its growth was restricted, owing to the lack of navigable water nearer than the Trent and Severn, and to the limited water power that its river could gener-ate. Steam and canals provided the answer; both were pioneered in and around Birmingham, and by 1800 its population was over 70,000.[14]

It is hard for a visitor to a waterside town today to visualize the extent to which ships could dominate it. In 1739 Alexander Pope was intrigued and entertained by Bristol (Pl. 40), where the river Frome ran down between quays through the centre of the city, until it was covered over in modern times to form Colston Avenue: '... you come to a key along the old wall with houses on both sides, and in the middle of the street, as far as you can see, hundreds of ships, their masts as thick as they can stand by one another, which is the oddest and most surprising sight imaginable.'[15] In Boston today the docks are well out of the centre, but in 1815 a shopkeeper could describe how 'there is ships lie within two minutes walk of the shop. Can see the tops of the mast poles of the ships over the houses as I walk the streets. There is vast numbers of ships come to Boston, they appear sometimes like a wood when the leaves are off.'[16]

Contemporary illustrations help to recreate this vanished town-scape. Buck's view of King's Lynn in 1741 (Pl. 41) looks over the town, still completely walled, to the masts in the river beyond. Depictions of Prince Street in Bristol in the eighteenth and early nineteenth centuries show masts rising above the Assembly Rooms.

Early photographs of Wisbech show the river below the bridge jammed with ships and lined with warehouses, where today there are no ships and the warehouses have shrunk to a handful.

All ports needed somewhere to load and unload goods, and somewhere to store them. In addition, at least in ports for seagoing vessels, the law required a place in which to pay customs; and for many centuries the practice of living by one's work produced houses for the merchants whose goods were in storage. The quay, the warehouses, the custom-house and the merchants' houses combined in different ways to produce distinctive riverside areas all over England. The world's first commercial dock, sealed off from the Mersey by lock-gates, was constructed in Liverpool in 1710-15,[17] but it was open to the town, and the town grew round it, so that visually it resembled earlier waterside areas (Pl. 43). Other docks followed in Liverpool, similarly open. It was not till the early 1800s that the London and Hull docks, and the later Liverpool docks, developed a separate dockland of basins and warehouses, sealed off from the outside world by mighty walls (Pl. 116).

Many English towns had very short quays. A quay running the length of a waterside was a great rarity before 1800, and not all that common after it. It is by no means clear why this was so. In walled towns it may have related to whether the walls ran along the river. This was the position at Newcastle, Bristol and Waterford. In all three places a stretch of land between the walls and river was used as a landing place, which ultimately became a quay. When the walls were taken down a long quay lined with buildings resulted.

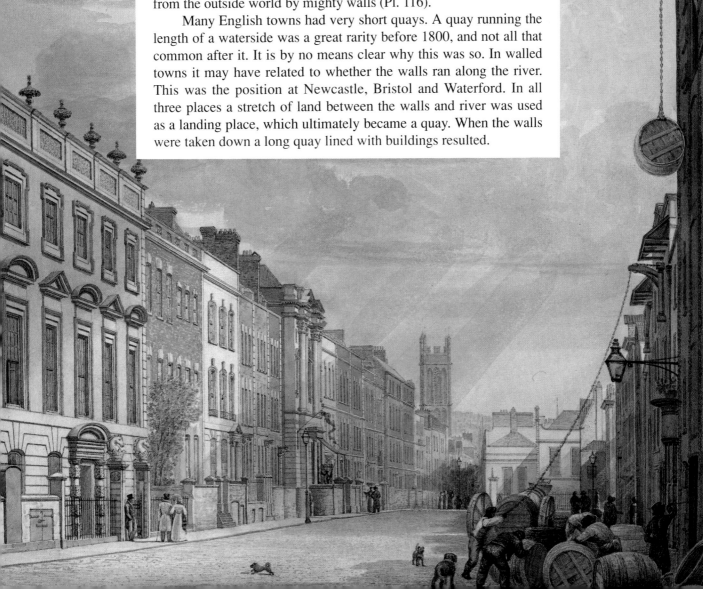

45. Looking across the Ouse to King's Staith, York.

46. Fydell House, Boston.

47. Fydell and other warehouses on the river at Boston.

At Yarmouth, on the other hand, the side of the town along the river was never walled, but even so the town acquired the biggest and best-known quay in England; travellers compared it to the even more famous quay at Marseilles.[18] It stretched (and still stretches) nearly a mile along the length of the town, and in places was over a hundred yards wide. The explanation may be that Yarmouth was built on little more than a sandbank, between the mouth of the Yar and the sea. The site had originally been used as a summer camp by fishermen who came from the south to exploit the rich adjoining fisheries. It had become a permanent settlement by the eleventh century. The safe ground for settlement must have been separated from the water by a broad shelf of mud or sand, which was levelled into a quay as the town grew in prosperity.

In all ports some merchants may originally have loaded and unloaded directly from buildings on the water's edge. From the point of view of collecting customs, however, a quay was clearly more convenient and easier to supervise. In 1558 loading and unloading was confined by law to named quays, which became known as legal quays as a result.[19]

In the Middle Ages separate warehouses scarcely existed; the familiar building type, with a flight of doors one above the other, was imported from the Netherlands in the seventeenth century. Before then goods unloaded on the quays were conveyed to be stored in merchants' homes on or near them. Storage was commonly in cellars beneath the houses. At Bristol, many of these extended under the streets. Wheeled carts were forbidden by the corporation because of the danger of heavily-loaded ones breaking through into the cellars; transport was by horse-drawn sledges, a feature of Bristol much commented on by travellers.[20]

Separate warehouses on the Dutch model first became prominent in Bristol in the early eighteenth century. In 1700-18 the marshland on a promontory between the rivers Frome and Avon to the south of the town was laid out for building, around Queen Square and Prince Street. At the same time the original quay was extended round the marsh. Buildings in the new development all followed the same formula: a house on Queen Square or the adjacent Prince Street, a yard behind it and a warehouse beyond the yard, either letting onto the quays, or onto the east side of Prince Street. Prince Street had, as a result, a row of opulent merchants' houses along one side, and of tall stone warehouses along the other (Pl. 44).

Many of the original houses survive, but only two of the original warehouses, and those much altered. They were gradually replaced by much bigger warehouses, mostly granaries, as a result of the railways coming to Bristol, the water being freed from tidal ebb and flow by the insertion of locks, and American corn in huge quantities passing through the town. The new ware houses, of which Ponton and Gough's granary on Welsh Back Quay is the supreme example (Pl. 328), towered above the houses in Queen Square; but since the ruling élite of Bristol had long since moved off to other parts of the town, the residents were in no position to stop them.

Short quays or wharves (often known locally as staiths) survive in large numbers in river towns. Many of them have origins going back well into the Middle Ages, although few, if any, have retained any medieval buildings. The King's Staith at York (Pl. 45) is a good example. It dates back to at least the fourteenth century. There are no warehouses on it; the most prominent building is the house built in about 1710 for William Cornwall, brewer, tanner and Lord Mayor.[21] This is raised up on a high cellar or undercroft for warehousing, which has its own archway opening onto the staithe. There is a second quay, the Queen's Staith, on the other side of the river. Boston has a similar arrangement: Doughty Quay on one side of the river, and Packhouse Quay on the other. Up till the early nineteenth century the rich merchants who ran Boston all lived on, or close to, these quays. At first they probably warehoused in cellars, such as the capacious one still surviving beneath Fydell House, built in 1726 by Joseph Fydell, mercer and importer of linen from Holland. The later Fydells became wine merchants and expanded their warehousing into a converted medieval building on the waterfront opposite their house. In about 1810 Thomas Fydell replaced this in its turn with the great gabled warehouse which still looks across the road to the wrought-iron gates and handsome baroque façade of Fydell House (Pls. 46, 47).[22] Many more warehouses were built at about the same time, mostly by corn merchants exporting corn from the newly drained local fens to London and the industrial cities of the north. Warehouses gradually replaced the older houses, or their presence drove the original occupants to other parts of the town. A similar development can be watched all over England.

There is a quay of a rather different nature on the river Lune in Lancaster. It is different because it was only built in 1750 and succeeding years; before that goods had to be unloaded on the river banks. It is a result of the brief but considerable prosperity which Lancaster enjoyed trading (in slaves, amongst other commodities) to Africa, America and the West Indies between about 1750 and 1800. The trade declined or collapsed soon after 1800, mainly as the result of competition from Liverpool, which benefited by being made the terminus of the convoy system in the French wars; as a result the quay and its buildings have survived as the least altered examples of this date in England. It consists of a row of stone warehouses and a porticoed custom-house (Pl. 48), designed by a local architect-builder, Richard Gillow, in 1764. The whole complex was built by the Port Commissioners, a local body set up by Act of Parliament in 1759. The development is an early example of warehouses detached from houses; there are none of the latter of any importance in the area, and never have been.[23]

The port arrangements of London, before its docks began to be built at the very end of the eighteenth century, were distinctive —

48. The Customs House, Lancaster (R. Gillow, 1764).

49. River warehouse, off the High Street, Hull.

50. An abandoned water-wheel on one of the leats at Exeter.

and also increasingly inefficient. The city walls originally ran along the river front, and the only access for trading vessels was through arches in the walls, leading into two small docks or harbours, at Billingsgate and Queenhithe. Plans for a grand City quay on the Paris model were propounded by Wren and others after the fire of 1666, by John Gwynn in 1766, and by F.W. Trench and others in the early nineteenth century. All were abortive. Billingsgate (for coal and fish) and the Queenhithe (mainly for corn, cloth and wine) remained the only legal quays. The harbour at Billingsgate has been filled in, but that at Queenhithe survives: a sad, rubbish-filled little pool, surrounded by modern office blocks.

With the growth of trade in the eighteenth century the situation became impossible, and the legal quays were supplemented by what were known as sufferance wharves, timber wharves at the end of long narrow passages leading up through houses or warehouses to the street. Finally, in spite of bitter opposition from the wharfingers, a series of Acts of Parliament initiated the docks downriver.[24]

Hull originally had no quay. It had been a new town, founded by Meaux Abbey in the late twelfth century. After a period of great prosperity as one of the principal ports for the export of wool, and later cloth, it declined when the Hanseatic merchants took over the cloth trade and preferred London to Hull. Prosperity returned in the eighteenth century as a result of the decline of the Hanseatic towns, and the rise of the West Yorkshire cloth industry and the whaling trade.

The original town was laid out where the narrow river Hull ran into the broad Humber. The main merchants' houses were in High Street, which ran parallel to the Hull, between it and the market place. The plots on the river side of the High Street ran straight down to the water. There was no town wall along the Hull, which ran inside the fortifications, but there was also no quay. Because of this, by the Act of 1558 Hull was the only town in England where ships were allowed to load and unload away from a quayside. The privilege was as much prized by Hull merchants as it was disliked by customs officials. The former's access to the water was by the narrow passages which still run down to it from the High Street. They are known as staiths, perhaps because there was once some form of wharf at the end of each lane. It may be that goods were originally unloaded only through the staiths, and taken by way of the High Street for storage in merchants' houses on either side of the street. But by at least the mid-eighteenth century warehouses on the conventional pattern were being built along the Hull, which was soon lined with them. Some backed onto houses on the High Street. Others ran through to it, and belonged to merchants living on the inland side of the street. A continuous timber walk was built along the warehouses, probably in the late eighteenth century (Pl. 49), but it was for people not goods: the warehouse cranes extended far enough to unload directly from the ships.[25]

Although Hull acquired docks from 1775 onwards, the High

Street complex survived little altered up to the 1939-45 war: ships, timber baulks, timber cranes, a long patchwork wall of four-storey warehouses, little warehouse windows in brick or timber walls, and, along the High Street, the Georgian houses of the Sykeses, Etheringtons, Maisters, Wilberforces, Blaydes and Pearces, more sumptuous than the houses of Boston merchants, and richer even than those of Bristol ones (Pl. 199). There was some destruction in the war, and more, unforgivably, after it. A few warehouses remain, and a handful of houses, including Wilberforce House and Maister House, the latter with the finest Georgian town staircase outside London. Enough survives to give some feeling of what must have been as evocative a waterside as any in England.

Early industrial waterside areas have suffered even more than the quayside and warehouse ones. This is scarcely surprising: the technology inevitably became obsolete, the buildings were often insubstantial, and many were replaced by the Babylonian lines of steam mills which are the subject of Chapter 14. Often the actual water is the most evocative surviving feature. At Bourton-on-the-Water, one can look at the clear, cold and rapid stream as it runs past guest-houses and tea-rooms, listen to the surge of its current, and contemplate how it once turned mills, washed wool, and brought the little town its name and population.

At Exeter, industrial water took the form of a series of leats or races, run off the river Exe on low ground below the main wall of the town. They were used to turn fulling mills or fill the dye vats described in 1698 by Celia Fiennes, who marvelled at the stir and bustle of the metropolis of the Devon serge industry.[26] The merchants or masters who controlled the industry lived on the higher ground, but the workmen were in cottages down towards the water. All around were expanses of cloth, lying out to dry on racks in the surrounding tenter fields. All have gone now except the leats, very narrow and fast-running, and a stretch of derelict water-wheels and workshops at the end of one of them (Pl. 50). At the mouth of this the industrial district gives way to the custom-house, the warehouses (Pl. 51) and the quayside, brought into being as a result of the Exe being fully reopened to navigation between 1675 and 1724.

At Norwich, as at Exeter, the wharves and warehouses were downstream, and the industrial waterside upstream; at Norwich, however, there was a long gap between the two, where the river went in a great loop around the Cathedral and its close. It was the

51. Looking across the Exe to the quay and warehouses at Exeter.

industrial area which, up till the late eighteenth century, made Norwich the greatest textile centre in England. The water was not used to power mills (except the New Mills, which were for corn), because the lightweight Norwich stuffs did not need fulling; it was for wash-ing and dyeing. Inland from the waterside were the cottages and tenements of the work-ing weavers. These have all gone, along with dye houses and workshops, to be replaced by later housing or factories. What is left are the occasional substantial houses of the master weavers, dyers and manufac-turers, and the Nonconformist chapels where most of the textile workers and their employers worshipped.

Although practical considerations dom-inated town watersides, people had been conscious of the potential beauty of rivers since at least the sixteenth century; in the late seventeenth and early eighteenth century house-owners who had gardens running down to rivers, and no practical use for the water, began to build gazebos or pavilions on the water's edge (Pls. 52, 53) in which they could take tea on summer evenings.

52. Eighteenth-century gazebos on the river Lea at Ware.
53. Houses and gazebos at Derby. Detail from an anonymous oil painting, *c.* 1720.
54. (right) The twilight silhouette of Lancaster Castle and parish church.

3

The Castle

And

The County

The hilltop silhouette of Lancaster Castle (Pl. 54) is one of the most dramatic and least known in England. It presides over the town of Lancaster as grandly as Windsor Castle over Windsor and Eton, or Warwick Castle over Warwick, or Belvoir Castle over the Vale of Belvoir. The visitor who labours up the steep hill comes to a different world from that of the shopping streets and abandoned mills of the town below: the church in its great wind-swept graveyard, and a circuit of eighteenth-century houses, looking over quiet greensward to the castle gatehouse and walls.

But unlike Windsor, Warwick and Belvoir, the castle has never been converted to be the residence of a monarch or great family. Nor is it preserved in aspic as a monument. Behind its portcullis the doors of its gatehouse are closed to visitors, because the courtyard into which they lead is surrounded by the barred windows of a prison. Beyond the gatehouse and prison yard are the hexagonal block, eighteenth-century Gothic windows, and separate entrance of

55. Looking towards the court room end of the twelfth-century great hall of Oakham Castle.

the Shire Hall, no longer regularly brought to life by the assizes but still occasionally used as a law court. The building as it stands today is the result of an enlargement of the medieval fabric and enhancement of its silhouette, brilliantly designed by Thomas Harrison and J.M. Gandy between 1788 and 1823. But its use as a county prison and seat of county justice and administration dates far back into the Middle Ages.

Lancaster is the last of the county castles to fulfill the double functions of court and prison. A similar arrangement was originally to be found in nearly half of the county towns of England. In some of these one of the uses may still survive, in others the buildings but not the uses. At Lincoln Castle, for instance, the county court house and prison rise out of green lawns within a circuit of medieval walls and gatehouse (Pl. 58). The courts are still in use, but the prison is converted to serve as the County Record Office. At York, the outer walls have gone, and all that survives of the medieval castle is the keep on its mound, looking down on the eighteenth-century Assize Courts, which are still in use, and the prison, which now serves as the Castle Museum (Pl. 56). At Chester, the jail has been replaced by the county offices, but the courts still sit behind the great neo-classical portico of Thomas Harrison's building, which replaces all but a fragment of the original castle. In the midget county town of Oakham the jail has long since disappeared, but the fittings of a court linger in disuse at one end of the Norman great hall, within the earthworks of the castle (Pl. 55). In the thirteenth-century hall of Winchester Castle only the ponderous Victorian Gothic of an abandoned judge's seat survives as evidence that the two assize judges used to hold their courts here, gazing at each other down the length of the hall.

Many medieval towns were built in the shadow of a castle. Some were the strongholds of feudal nobles, others deliberately set up by the Norman kings when they superimposed their new county system on the old Saxon shires, and appointed counts or earls to preside over them. Over the centuries town castles suffered a variety of fates. Many remained in, or passed into, the ownership of individual families. These sometimes abandoned them to ruin, as at Chepstow and Dudley, sometimes converted them to suit contemporary standards of style and comfort, as at Warwick, sometimes abandoned them and then moved back into them, as at Alnwick, Arundel and (much more modestly) Shrewsbury. But a number of castles remained in, or returned to, Crown possession. They became the places from which the counties were governed, by means of the sheriff's courts, the assize courts, and the courts of quarter sessions.

The important point about these courts is that they had executive and legislative, as well as judicial, powers. Up till the creation of County Councils in 1888, buildings which today shelter somewhat confusingly under the different titles of castle, county hall, shire hall, assize courts and sessions house all had one and the same function.

They were the seats both of county justice and county government.[1]

The basis of the system were the Justices of the Peace for the county. These were appointed by the Crown, on the recommendation of the Lord Lieutenant. They were substantial country landowners with an admixture (in the eighteenth century, if no earlier) of Church of England clergy. They sat in small groups at petty sessions to deal with minor offences. In larger groups at quarter sessions, they dealt with more serious crimes, but also with a mass of administrative matters. The most important of these were the maintenance or building of roads, bridges, and county buildings, the licensing of public houses, the fixing of prices, and the levying of county rates. The proceedings were quasi-judicial. A bridge or a road would be 'presented' for not being in proper repair, found, as it were, guilty, and its repair or reconstruction would be ordered by the court.

Twice a year two Crown judges, travelling on different circuits from London, came to each county for the assizes. A select group of Justices of the Peace attended these as what was known as the grand jury. One of the judges sat in the Crown Court, which dealt with criminal cases involving the death penalty, the other in the *nisi prius* court, which dealt with major civil suits. At the beginning of each assize the Crown Court judge delivered what was known as a charge, a general address one of the functions of which was to retail decisions of the central government. The grand jury, sitting separately, was responsible for finding if there was a 'true bill' in criminal cases, that is to say, whether the prosecution had produced enough evidence to make it worth while sending the case before the judge. In addition, it discussed county matters, and made pronouncements about, or decisions on them.

The sheriff (originally 'shire reeve') had his own court. It was a relic of the Saxon shire system, and its jury consisted of all men of standing in the county. By the seventeenth century the court had only one function of significance left, but this was an important one. At it the men of standing, who came to consist of the county freeholders, met under the sheriff to appoint the two members of Parliament for the county. Until a system of dispersed polling-stations was developed in the nineteenth century, the freeholders had to come to one place to vote. In the case of a controversial election and a big county like Yorkshire, this could mean long journeys and a great congregation of people. But in the eighteenth century the sheriff increasingly tended to call a preliminary meeting of a limited number of more important people to discuss the election. If they

56. York Castle: the Assize Courts (John Carr, 1773-7) and former county gaol (1701-5).

57. A sleeping figure, perhaps a Justice on the bench, sketched at Taunton assizes by John Chubb, *c.* 1780.

58. Looking down on Lincoln Castle.
59. (right) The High Sheriff driving out of Chester to meet the judges, from a drawing by William Tasker, 1845.

were sufficiently unanimous, no election contest took place. Such a small county meeting at York in 1753 was attended by 155 people.[2] County meetings, both large and small, could also be held to discuss matters of general policy and send messages concerning them to Parliament or the monarch; many such meetings were held, and exerted considerable influence.

The sheriff was responsible for seeing that the decisions of the county courts were carried out, and that the persons summoned to them attended. He also had to wait on, and entertain, the assize judges, and provide them with a suitable escort (Pl. 59). Serving as sheriff was accordingly expensive, but also prestigious. The job was often given to members of new landowning families, anxious to establish their social position, and ready to spend money in order to do so. In 1787, for instance, the sheriff for Derbyshire was the cotton manufacturer Sir Richard Arkwright. The gold, blue and scarlet liveries of his escort, the scarlet and gold of his trumpeters, and the gleaming black of his horses, were more splendid than anything provided by previous sheriffs in Derby.[3]

The assizes, county elections, county meetings, at least one of the four quarter sessions, and the county jail, were usually concentrated in one town, which became known as the county town. A few of these towns were also counties in their own right, so that the 'county of the city of Worcester', for instance, had its own assizes and quarter sessions, and jurisdiction over a small circuit of surrounding villages. In a few counties the functions were split; in Suffolk, for instance, county elections were held in Ipswich in the eighteenth century, and assizes in Bury St. Edmunds. The other quarter sessions were distributed around other towns in the county.

Where there was a royal castle available, it became the focus of county activities. County meetings and elections were held in its great hall, or outside in the castle yard, if large numbers of people were involved. Meetings in the castle yard at York, at the centre of the largest and most politically active county in England, could be especially crowded and exciting. It was there, in 1784, that little William Wilberforce got up in the teeth of a gale, spoke in support of an address condemning the government, and established his reputation. As Boswell described it: 'I saw what seemed a mere shrimp mount upon the table; but as I listened he grew, and grew, until the shrimp became a whale'.[4] York's eighteenth-century architects played up to this kind of drama; the jail with its central cupola, and the matching façades of Carr's court building and prison extension on the other side, make the castle yard a northern echo of Michelangelo's courtyard of the Campidoglio in Rome (Pl. 56). The enclave of a county castle was a separate world from the main town, legally as well as visually: the mayor and corporation had no jurisdiction over it, just as they had no jurisdiction over a cathedral close, if there was one. The feeling of this separation still comes over strongly at Lincoln: the castle, the close and the town rubbing shoulders, but each keeping to themselves, with their own walls and gatehouses, or the remains of them (Pl. 58). Where there was no castle available the county had to do as best it could, either acquiring property for its own buildings, or sharing with the corporation.

The assizes were social and ceremonial, as well as judicial, occasions.[5] The sheriff drove out in his coach to meet the judges, preceded by mounted trumpeters and javelin men, and accompanied by a crowd of Justices and county gentry on horseback (Pl. 59). The procession returned through the town to the judges' lodgings along streets lined with spectators. The judges were escorted to and from the courts with similar pomp on each day of the assizes, as well as to church for an inaugural sermon by the sheriff's chaplain. The week was celebrated with a succession of dinners, balls, and theatrical performances. The sheriffs feasted the judges, and the judges feasted the Justices and the grand jury. The grand jury had to come into town to fulfill its duties, but the rest of the county gentry and aristocracy also came in in force, to attend the festivities, and listen to the court cases. The court rooms were crowded with spectators, and the occasion fulfilled something of the function of a successful television show. The Justices had the right to sit on the bench at either side of the judge. Sometimes their wives accompanied them, as recounted in a letter written by Anna-Maria Leighton during assize week in Shrewsbury in about 1750. She was married to Charlton Leighton, the elder son of Sir Edward Leighton, of Loton Hall. 'Thank God', she wrote, 'we are all well here, only a little fatigued with three assemblies we have had this week and a great deal of good company at them, but they did not afford me half the entertainment as the trials ... at the Crown Bar ... I sat always next his Lordship who was extreme good company; and at my request reprieved a young woman who I heard him condemn to be hanged for the murder of her child.'[6]

Up till the eighteenth century the two courts of the assizes took place at either end of one large room, often the medieval great hall of the castle. The same room was used for assize dinners, and for county meetings, dinners and festivities at other times of the year, or was let out for theatrical performances. On a county level it fulfilled a multi-purpose function similar to that of the hall in a town hall, or, on a national level, of Westminster Hall in London. In the latter no less than three courts sat in different corners, up till the early nineteenth century; the rest of the hall was lined with little shops, and Londoners amused themselves strolling, gossiping, shopping, and listening in to the cases.[7]

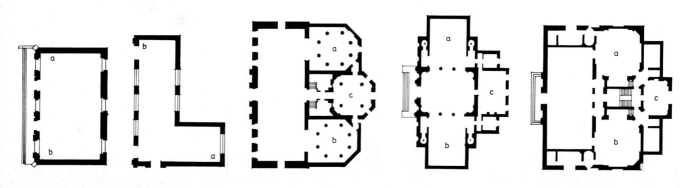

60,61. (top left and centre left) Paired doors to the County Hall, Derby (George Eaton, 1657-9), and the Sessions House, Northampton (attributed to Henry Bell, 1676-88).
62. (bottom left) Comparative plans of county buildings. 1. Derby (1657); 2. Northampton (1676); 3.Warwick (1754); 4. Nottingham (1770); 5. Stafford (1794).
a. Crown Court, b. *Nisi Prius* Court, c. Grand Jury Room.
63. Modified open plan. The court-house, Waterford (James Gandon, 1784).

In the counties this arrangement survived in some towns into the nineteenth century; at Winchester, for instance, until 1874, at Gloucester until the present Shire Hall was built in 1814-16. The change at Gloucester is said to have been sparked off by the fury of the judge in the Crown Court, where a murder case was being heard, when his jury burst into laughter at a joke being made by the judge in the *nisi prius* court at the other end of the hall. But long before then a different type of plan had been evolved in other counties, as the courts were gradually separated out from the hall.[8]

New county halls were built at Derby in 1657-9 (Pls. 60, 62), and at York in about 1673.[9] Both of them kept the traditional arrangement of one big hall, but had the new feature of two grand doorways, one at either end of the main façade. The combination allowed the Crown judge and the *nisi prius* judge to make state entrances at the same time. The next stage took place in what became known as the County Hall or Sessions House at Northampton (Pls. 61-2).[10] It was built in 1676-88, after the previous building had been burnt out in a fire which destroyed much of the town. It was originally designed as one big space, but on an L-plan, so that one court was round the corner from the other. It had no less than three entrances, two grand ones surmounted by the royal arms on the main front, and one slightly less grand one round the corner. The first two were probably reserved for the judges, the third used by the public.

A further development took place in the Guildhall in Worcester, built in 1721-3. In spite of its name, this was built for joint use by

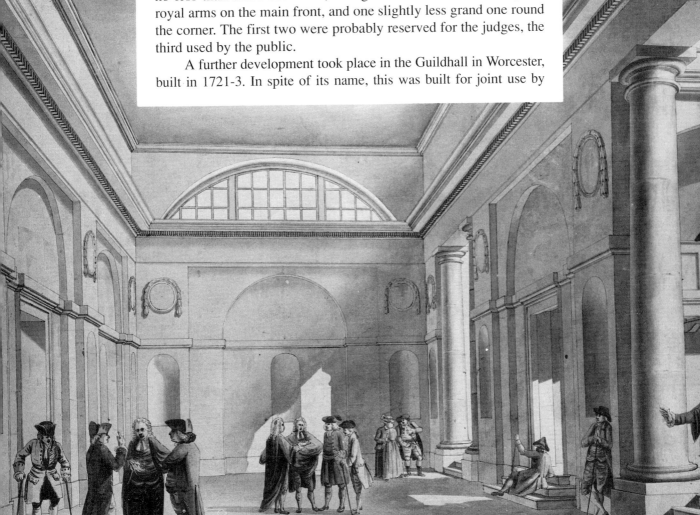

the county and the city, and was paid for by subscription raised both in Worcester and Worcestershire. Worcester, being a county as well as a city, had its own assizes, which took place on the same visit of the judges as the Worcestershire ones.[11] The joint use explains why the Guildhall is noticeably larger and grander than town halls or guildhalls built in other towns at the same time (Pl. 64).

At Worcester the double entry was given up. A single central doorway led into the middle of a great hall, beyond which was a central staircase between the Crown and *nisi prius* courts. Both these courts opened through large archways into the main hall, so that they had a degree of privacy but not total separation. The arches have been filled in, but are still visible. A room off the first landing of the staircase served as a grand jury room. The Shire Hall at Warwick, designed by Sanderson Miller and built in 1753-8, had a similar plan (Pl. 62), clearly inspired by that of Worcester; here again the courts, which, unlike those at Worcester, are still in use, have been blocked off from the hall. The hall was used for county meetings, but also as a ballroom during the annual Warwick races. At the County Hall at Nottingham (James Gandon, 1768-72), and the County Hall or Assize Courts at York (John Carr, 1773-7), the courts were to left and right of the hall, but opened into it in much the same way as at Warwick and Worcester (Pl. 62).[12] In 1784 Gandon used the Warwick arrangement at the court-house at Waterford; a contemporary drawing (Pl. 63) gives a good idea of how the courts opened into the hall in this type of plan.

The next stage can be seen at the Middlesex Sessions House on Clerkenwell Green (Thomas Rogers, 1779-82), and the Shire Hall at Stafford (John Harvey and Samuel Wyatt, 1794; Pl. 62). In plan these resembled Warwick and Worcester, except that the courts were completely separated from the hall.[13] This, or a variation on it, was to remain the standard arrangement for new county halls, or the assize courts built in big cities, throughout the nineteenth century.

The status and function of a county hall was reflected in its architecture, by the use of ornament, or the application of one of the classical orders. On average, the buildings grew larger and more impressive from the seventeenth century onwards. At Derby, York, and Northampton, decoration was concentrated on the entrances, and on the royal arms incorporated in them. Northampton, which was noticeably more sumptuous than earlier buildings, was decorated with an applied Corinthian order. Inside, the ceiling had rich plaster work, enriched with appropriate symbols: chains, leg-irons and hand-cuffs over the Crown court, and (less obviously) cornucopiae over the *nisi prius* court.

The Guildhall at Worcester (Pl. 64) has a giant order and a great deal of appropriate sculptural ornament; statues of Justice, Peace, Plenty, Chastisement and Hercules (signifying Labour) on the parapet; monarchs around the entrance; the royal arms in the main pediment, and the city arms beneath it; and, for the courts,

64. The Guildhall, Worcester, 1721-4.
65. The Crown court-room in the Shire Hall, Warwick (Sanderson Miller, 1754-8).
66. (top right) The *Nisi Prius* court-room in the Assize Courts, York (John Carr, 1773-7).
67. (bottom right) The Shire Hall, Stafford (John Harvey and Samuel Wyatt, 1794).

blindfolded faces of Justice on the keystones of the great arches and the inscription 'Fiat Justitia, Ruat Caelum' in the Crown court, and 'Audiet Alteram Partem' in the *nisi prius* court.

The exteriors of the county halls at Warwick and York have applied orders, Corinthian at Warwick and Ionic at York (Pl. 56): the York façades are designed with exquisite restraint and delicacy under the influence of French neo-classicism. In both buildings the courts take the form of rotundas, with a giant order of Corinthian columns rising through two storeys and supporting domed lanterns; there are galleries at first-floor level, behind the columns. They are lovely rooms, dignified and yet intimate: sitting up in the galleries and looking down on the judge's clerk and barristers in their wigs and gowns, one has a curious illusion of having moved back into the eighteenth century (Pls. 65, 66).

The county jail at Warwick was built a few decades after the Shire Hall, and its Doric order contrasts, without doubt deliberately, with the rich Corinthian of its neighbour. But there was a growing feeling that a sober and solemn Doric, or at least a chaste Ionic, was more suited to a place of justice than Corinthian. This was accompanied by an increasing distaste for the use of the building for balls and dinners (for which a Corinthian order was entirely appropriate). The feeling was expressed by Sir George Onesiphoros Paul in 1802, at a county meeting held at Gloucester to discuss an abortive project to rebuild the Shire Hall. The new building should have 'a grandeur arising from simplicity, and a well conceived arrangement of parts' rather than from 'an excess of costly ornament'. He rejected the suggestion that it should be convertible for balls. Why, he asked, should the rate-payers pay for 'the ornamental stucco, enriched cornices, lustres, looking-glasses and girandoles, or even for the sophas and tea-tables provided for the care and accommodation of our beautiful countrywomen'?[14]

The form of building he wanted had already been designed by Gandon at Nottingham, Harvey and Wyatt at Stafford (Pl. 67), and above all by Harrison at Chester. Gandon used a simplified Ionic order, and Harvey and Wyatt a Doric one (but the great hall behind it was still used for balls and assemblies, and decorated accordingly). At Chester (Pls. 68-71) there was money to spend, for the county had invested in improving the navigation of the river Weaver, and was enjoying growing profits from tolls; the Weaver ran through the centre of the English salt industry. Harrison used Doric for his main building and the archway to the courtyard, and Ionic for the barracks and armoury to either side of it. All this was up on a cliff-top; down by the river, linked to the main building but on a lower level, was the county jail, rusticated and without any order, but grim and grand. The whole huge complex combined grandeur with monumental simplicity.[15]

Harrison was remodelling Lancaster Castle in the Gothic style at the same time (Pl. 72). The choice of style was partly determined

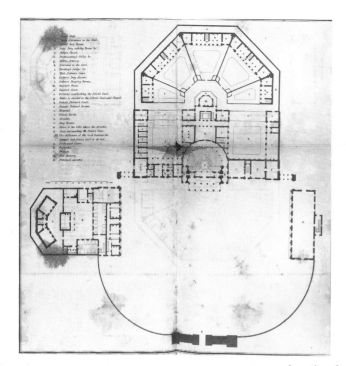

68-71 The plan, officers' mess wing, and two views of
the entrance portico, Chester Castle (Thomas Harrison,
1788 onwards).

by the fact that much more of the original castle survived at
Lancaster than at Chester. But it also reflected an awareness of the
potentialities of Gothic, as a symbol of the medieval origins of
county government, and of castle Gothic as an expression of security and authority. The County Courts at Carlisle (Robert Smirke,
1810-12) were in a similar castellated style. In the ensuing decades
Gothic was to take its place alongside Greek Doric as the favoured
style for jails and law courts. At Carlisle Smirke separated the necessary accommodation into two matching blocks and put the law
courts into massive round towers to either side of the entrance to the
main street. The result would have made a magnificent entrance to a
capital city, but the modest county town to which it leads comes as
something of an anticlimax.

Interesting and at times impressive though these county buildings are, they gave direct employment to a handful of people, in
comparison to the county bureaucracies of today. Their permanent
establishment consisted of a clerk to the Justices, occasionally a
county surveyor, the jailer of the county jail and his warders, and a
handful of janitors and caretakers. The clerk to the Justices was an
important official, but only a part-time one: he was invariably a
leading solicitor, resident in the town. County surveyors, responsible for work on bridges, roads and county buildings, were first
appointed in a scattering of counties in the early eighteenth century.
By the end of the century most, though by no means all, counties
had them; before the nineteenth century the job was invariably a
part-time one.

But the spin-off from a county hall was considerable. The peri-
odic incursions of Justices of the Peace coming from their country

houses and rectories, of litigants with business at the court, of freeholders attending elections or county meetings, and of county families coming in to enjoy the assizes, brought much business to the inns. It encouraged the settlement of lawyers and doctors, and the emergence of shops and individuals offering services, from the painting of portraits to the sale of wine. People of independent income and of gentle birth, or with pretensions to gentility, tended to settle in towns where such visiting gentry, resident professionals and good shops and services offered an agreeable way of life. Local country-house owners sometimes acquired permanent town houses, and removed to them in the winter from the chilly halls and galleries of their country seats. New schools grew up to cater for their children, or old schools acquired a reputation as places attended by children of gentle birth.

As a result, corporations were prepared to pay for new county buildings, even though county business was no concern of theirs, in the hopes of attracting the assizes and county business to the town. In 1698 Ipswich built a new session house largely in the hopes of drawing the Suffolk assizes from Bury. It failed, probably because the new building was not grand enough, but the superb so-called market or town hall at Abingdon was built for the same purpose in 1678-80, and succeeded.[16] Much later, one of the main reasons why the corporation of Leeds built a new town hall in 1852-7, and equipped it with court-rooms far in excess

72. The Shire Hall, or main court-room, Lancaster Castle (Thomas Harrison, 1788-99).

73. (right) Looking across the gardens to the Long Alley almshouses, Christ's Hospital, Abingdon.

of the needs of the town, was to win for Leeds the position of assize town for the West Riding. This was a projected new arrangement, the only Yorkshire assizes having previously been held at York. Leeds succeeded, much to the discomfiture of Wakefield, the rival claimant, which lacked the resources to build so magnificent a building.[17]

56

4

Churches

And

Charities

The beautiful and unspoilt street known as East St. Helen's leads from the market square of Abingdon to the tower and spire of the church from which the street derives its name. Beyond the church is the churchyard, enclosed on three sides by almshouses and on the fourth by the church itself. It is as peaceful a place as one could hope to find. First come Twitty's almshouses (Pl. 75). These, as an inscription in the pediment announces, were built in 1706 as the result of a legacy from Charles Twitty, deputy auditor of the Receipt of Exchequer in Westminster. The legacy was left 'of his pious inclination of the parish of his nativity', to maintain 'in meat, drink, and apparel and all other necessaries of life three poor aged men and the like number of poor aged women'. The old women lived on the left and the old men on the right; in between was a common hall, under the pediment and cupola.

Next comes the range known as Long Alley almshouses. It was built in 1446, for seven poor men and six poor women, by the Fraternity of the Holy Cross, the forerunner of its present owner, Christ's Hospital. In about 1500 a covered walk, lit through an open timber arcade, was added on the churchyard side. In 1604 the governors of Christ's Hospital embellished this walk with three

74, 75. Brick Alley and Twitty's almshouses, Christ's Hospital, Abingdon.

porches, added a cupola, and employed an Oxford painter, Sampson Strong, to cover porches and arcade with texts and depictions of almspeople and charitable activities.

The old people met for prayer in a central hall. They did not eat there; they were given a weekly allowance for clothes and food, and supplied with a brass badge, and a free haircut once a month. They either ate in the town or heated up food in the fireplaces in their own rooms. These have exceedingly tall brick chimney-stacks, which probably date from the early seventeenth century; their enfilade figures prominently in the view of this part of the town from across the Thames. The chimney-stacks are on the far side of the almshouses, facing onto a formal garden, of lawns, gravel walks, flower-beds, apple trees and clipped yews (Pl. 73). The garden was first laid out in 1580, and its original arrangement was described in 1627 by Francis Little, the then Master:

'The garden plot to the said Almshouse on the west side thereof, where before was nothing but stinking ditches and filthy dunghills, very unwholesome and noisome to the poor people. This plot they cleansed, manured, dressed and made it fruitful ground, and new ditched it about and caused fair sweet water to run by it; they fenced it with a quick mound and planted the borders with fruit trees, and allotted each of the almsfolk a portion of the ground to bear them herbs for their use and flowers for their pleasure.'[1]

The third range is known as the Brick Alley almshouses (Pl. 74). It was built by Christ's Hospital in 1718, to replace an earlier range. It originally accommodated six men and six women. Unlike its neighbours it was built on two floors: the men lived downstairs and the women upstairs. The building was fronted by a two-storey arcade, behind which ran a first-floor gallery, its white-painted balusters set off by the chequered brick of the arches. The range is given a little extra dignity by the embellishment of the central staircase projection with a framed and pedimented inscription.

A gate in the gap between the Long Alley and Brick Alley almshouses leads out onto the swans and pleasure-boats of the Thames.

The almshouses still serve their original purpose. In the hall in the Long Alley almshouses the Master and governors of Christ's Hospital meet at a carved Jacobean table surrounded by mementoes of their history. The room was panelled by Francis Little in the early seventeenth century. At the same time he built out a bay window and commissioned Sampson Strong to paint portraits of founders, benefactors, and past governors. Prominent among them is a double portrait of Geoffrey Barbour and John Howchion (Pl. 76). In the background of the picture is the skyline of Abingdon and a section of the almshouses; to the right antlike figures are busily building a bridge and a causeway leading up to it.

The picture refers to the rebuilding of Abingdon bridge in 1416-17, and the building at the same time of a causeway across the water meadows and a second bridge at Culham, over a cut of the Thames. It was an ambitious piece of medieval engineering, of importance to the town, because it diverted one of the main routes from London to the west through Abingdon. Barbour and Howchion were leading promoters of the scheme, both individually and in their capacity as members of the Fraternity of the Holy Cross.

The Fraternity and the Chantry or Guild of the Trinity were both attached to the church of St. Helen's. Like other religious fellowships and guilds at the time, they were associations of laymen concerned with the religious welfare of their members and the embellishment of the parish church. Each built an aisle of the church; the Fraternity is also said to have paid for the rood screen, and almost certainly built the room over the north porch, in which it held its meetings (and which still belongs to Christ's Hospital).

76. Sampson Strong's portrait of Geoffrey Barbour and John Howchion, in Long Alley almshouses, Christ's Hospital, Abingdon.

But whereas the Guild of the Trinity remained entirely religious, the Fraternity of the Holy Cross expanded its interests. Its members were closely involved in building and funding the bridges, and after they were completed undertook the cost of maintaining them. It established almshouses, of which the Long Alley ones were the most important. Its position was established by a royal charter granted by Henry VI in 1441. Endowments and benefactions made it rich, and all the leading merchants of the town belonged to it.

Because of its religious element, the Fraternity was dissolved under Edward VI in 1548, along with thousands of similar organizations. In 1553 much of its property (and a little more, from other sources) was given to a new body, known as Christ's Hospital. Like its predecessor, this was put in charge of the almshouses and the upkeep of the bridges; it was also given a general responsibility for charities in the town. Three years later Mary Tudor granted the town a corporation.

In effect, the two bodies ran the town for the next few hundred years. In terms of property, the Hospital was about twice as rich as the corporation, but there was no rivalry between them, because they were run by the same people. Both bodies were self-perpetuating, and anyone who was appointed Master of the Hospital almost invariably also served at some stage as the mayor of the town. In the nineteenth century the Hospital (somewhat reorganized by the Charity Commissioners) supplied funds for a free library, gave the town a park, a site for a cottage hospital, and a new site for the grammar school, and put up most of the money for the new school

77. The church porch, Cirencester, *c*. 1490.
78. (top right) St. Mary's Hospital, Chichester.
79. (bottom right) The former hospital and chapel in the Merchant Adventurers' Hall, York.

buildings. The park was named Albert Park, and has its own Albert Memorial, in the form of a statue of the Prince on a column. The land round it was developed with churches, villas, and the grammar school; it became Abingdon's select quarter, and the rent from it greatly increased the Hospital income. The Hospital is still the biggest property owner in the town. Today it owns and looks after all the town's almshouses, including Twitty's, and the delightful Tomkins almshouses in Ock Street.[2]

Tomkins almshouses have a different story altogether. In the eighteenth century Abingdon grew prosperous out of manufacturing malt and exporting it by barge down the Thames to London. The industry added to the prosperity of Christ's Hospital, which owned the only wharf in the town, next to the church and almshouses. In the eighteenth century the Tomkins family were the main maltsters, and the richest family in the town. They lived in three handsome houses, which are still the best and biggest eighteenth-century houses in Abingdon. They were Baptists and Whigs. They never served on the corporation or as governors of Christ's Hospital; both organizations were exclusively Church of England and Tory. Benjamin Tomkins, who died in 1732, lived in Clock House, Ock Street, next to one of his malt-houses (and today next to its successor, Morland's Brewery). The Baptist chapel was just across the road. In his will he left money for the building and endowment of almshouses for eight poor Baptists. These were built in Ock Street, almost opposite his house. House, chapel, malt-house and almshouses formed a Nonconformist neighbourhood.[3]

Most towns of England have a structure of churches, chapels and charities similar to that of Abingdon. The greater part of the town histories which came out by the hundred in the eighteenth and nineteenth centuries are given up to listing and describing them. From earliest times, the churches were tied into the secular as well as the religious life of the town, and the two overlapped. The market place at Cirencester, for instance, is dominated by the mighty multi-storey porch of the parish church (Pl. 77). This was probably used for meetings of the manorial courts, which ran the town under the Augustinian Abbot; the Abbey both owned the manor and appointed the rector. In the seventeenth century, by a natural progression, it became the town hall.

These charities, even if endowed or administered by laymen, almost invariably had a religious element; alms were distributed at the parish church by the rector or churchwardens; the inmates of schools and almshouses either had their own chapels and chaplains, and were required to attend the former, or had seats allotted to them in their parish church. The idea that education and the care of the poor, old, and sick were religious activities derived from the teaching of the gospel, and the doctrine that good works were essential to salvation. Founding schools, hospitals and almshouses acted as a double insurance; not only were the actions good in themselves, but

they created a continuing body of people who were required to celebrate masses and send up prayers for their benefactors, and by doing
so could shorten their time in purgatory. But even when this aspect
of charitable foundations was disallowed at the time of the
Reformation (and in fact used as grounds for dissolving large numbers of them), good works were still seen as meritorious, and the
tradition of founding and endowing charities continued unabated.

In the Middle Ages the founders could be individuals or organizations. Many charities were founded by religious fraternities and
guilds, others by merchants' or trade guilds. The distinction was not
hard and fast, because many of the latter developed out of religious
guilds. At York, for instance, the York Company of Merchant
Adventurers, which controlled the city's textile trade, developed out
of the Guild of Our Lord Jesus Christ and the Blessed Virgin Mary,
which was in existence by 1356. The Guild, and later the Company,
combined its trading, social and charitable activities in one two-
storey building, which still stands in Fossgate. The first floor was
occupied by a hall, and the ground floor by a hospital. The latter
took the form of one great room, the same size as the hall above it,
opening at one end into a chapel (Pl. 79).[4]

This was the standard plan for hospitals during the Middle
Ages. The term 'hospital' had a wider meaning than it does today. A
hospital was a refuge for people in need or trouble, including the ill,
the old, foundlings, orphans, pilgrims, and travellers. Its great room
was open to all, and the chapel at the end provided the consolations
of religion.

In the course of time hospitals began to specialize, so that one
finds, for instance, Christ's Hospital, London, educating orphans,
Christ's Hospital, Abingdon, and many others running almshouses,
and St. Bartholomew's and St. Thomas's Hospitals in London looking after the sick. The big halls, too, began to be subdivided into
cubicles. Subdivision may have started as early as the fifteenth century, but the earliest surviving examples, in the Great Hospital at
Norwich, and St. Mary's Hospital at Chichester (Pl. 78), date from
the seventeenth. In the latter the partitions date from 1680 and supply the hall with eight two-room dwellings for old people, each with
its chimney-piece and brick chimney-stack, threaded through the
hall. The hospital is still in use, and the hall still opens at one end
into a chapel.[5]

The next stage can be seen at the Hospital of St. Mary
Magdalene, Glastonbury. Here the hall became redundant, and its
roof was taken off in the sixteenth century. The cubicles developed
into two rows of little stone houses, looking onto a narrow courtyard
leading to the chapel. The resulting formula, with the courtyard a
little widened, was to become a common one for almshouses in the
seventeenth and eighteenth centuries: it is used for Tomkins almshouses at Abingdon, although there what looks like a chapel at the
end turns out, on inspection, to be no more than the entry to a garden.

80. The Clopton asylum (1730) on the edge of the Abbey churchyard, Bury St. Edmunds.
81, 82 (facing page, left, right) Inscription by the entrance to Fishermen's Hospital, Yarmouth, and retired fishermen sitting beneath it, as photographed by P.H. Emerson in the 1880s.

An alternative arrangement, involving a much more spacious court, appeared in the mid-fifteenth century, at the Hospital of St. Cross, just outside Winchester, and at the Bede House, Ewelme. The model here was the courtyards of great houses, or the courts of Oxford and Cambridge colleges; rows of external doors give access to staircases leading to separate lodgings. Ewelme had the refinement of a covered timber walk round the courtyard, a version of the stone cloister of much the same date round Founder's Court at Magdalen College, Oxford. Such a covered walk is quite often found in later almshouses, whether round a courtyard as at Bromley College, Kent, built by John Warner, Bishop of Rochester, for the widows of clergymen, in 1666, or along a single range, as at the Long Alley almshouses, Abingdon, and the Penrose almshouses at Barnstaple; the latter were built in 1627 by a Barnstaple merchant and mayor, John Penrose. Galleries serving two floors, as at Abingdon's Brick Alley almshouses (Pl. 74), are much rarer. A final stage came when almshouses were built on two or more floors approached by enclosed corridors, as at the Clopton Asylum at Bury St. Edmunds (Pl. 80), and Hosyer's Hospital, Ludlow. The former was built as almshouses by a Bury doctor in about 1744; the latter was a rebuilding of medieval almshouses put up by the Palmers' Guild, the property and endowments of which had been handed over to Ludlow corporation in 1552.[6] This kind of transfer of guild properties and responsibilities to the relevant corporation was an alternative to their refounding under separate trustees, as in the case of Christ's Hospital, Abingdon.

In addition to almshouses built round courtyards, and smaller almshouses built in the form of a single range, many were built on a half-H plan, often with the resulting open courtyard finished off by a wall and a handsome pair of gateposts. But whatever their size, origin or date, as a group almshouses form one of the most agreeable features of English towns. Their function tends to make them peaceful and unpretentious places, but the desire of their builders to leave a fitting memorial to themselves or whoever founded the charity usually gives them a modest degree of importance, perhaps in the form of a central pediment, a framed door-case, or a cupola. Almost invariable features are a tablet recording the origins of the charity, and the coat-of-arms of the founder. Occasionally the founder's statue features in an alcove; the courtyard of the Fishermen's Hospital in Yarmouth is presided over by a statue of Charity, with attendant children (Pls. 81-3).

Almshouses were always for the favoured few, who were eligible under the terms of the charity, or had a friend or patron among the trustees. They could never hope to cater for more than a small percentage of the old and sick poor in the town. The rest became the responsibility of the parish, and were looked after either by outside relief, or by being put into parish workhouses: in a few big towns in the eighteenth century parishes combined and built big 'Union' workhouses, ancestors of the Poor Law workhouses of the nineteenth century. The system of parish relief had been formalized in the sixteenth century, and was paid for by poor rates, levied parish by parish, and collected by the parish officers.[7]

83. Charity in the courtyard of Fishermen's Hospital, Yarmouth.
84. (right) Looking east to the pulpit and Cholmley gallery in St. Mary's Church, Whitby.

Parishes were in origin ecclesiastical districts, but from early days their organization had been part religious, part secular, made up of the rector or vicar, and any curates whom they might appoint, and of a body of unpaid secular officers. These came collectively to be known as the vestry, were responsible for maintaining the churchyard and the fabric of the church, and had various duties assigned to them or their appointees in the parish.

That a parish should undertake the care of the poor seems a reasonable product of its ecclesiastical nature. But its existence and availability led the central government to load responsibilities on it which were by no possible description religious. Parish vestries oversaw the repair of roads, disciplined vagrants, and maintained law and order. Many towns in which there were no corporations and where the manorial courts were ineffective, were run by the vestrymen. The London parishes outside the City were governed by their vestries, which were the precursors of the London boroughs.[8]

This mixture of secular and religious, which could lead to the same vestry meeting appointing an organist or a preacher and giving out a contract for the removal of parish sewage, could be found in other spheres. In post-Reformation days, for instance, the proving and administration of wills, and all the lawsuits that resulted from them, were under the control of ecclesiastical consistory courts, often meeting in a church or chapel; the York consistory court met in the church of St. Michael-le-Belfry, until a separate building was built for it next to the church in the 1830s.[9] Rectors and vicars, besides normally sitting as chairmen of the vestry, often served as Justices of the Peace. Clerical JPs, especially in the late eighteenth and early nineteenth centuries, could be powerful on local benches and at quarter sessions, because their attendance was more regular than that of the secular Justices, who tended to be away for much or most of the year, and did not always bother to attend when they were not. So the clergy were to some extent running the county.[10]

The actual churches were also put to secular use. The vestrymen sometimes held their meetings in the vestry, which could be a room of some architectural pretensions — although more often they met in an inn. Meetings of the whole parish were held in the church, usually attended by all who paid rates, to discuss parish business which was not necessarily, or even usually, of a religious nature.[11]

This mixing of the religious and the secular was not considered odd. Religion was seen as working through society and supporting the social and political order, just as the social and political order supported it. The religious man achieved salvation through accepting and playing his role in society, and following the teaching of the Church, not through relying on personal inspiration and a direct link with God; it was such attitudes which had inspired Nonconformist sects in the mid-seventeenth century, and all but destroyed the social and political order as a result.

Although there was room for private devotions, the essential

expression of religion was service on Sunday. This represented society collected together for worship and prayer, and it was thought only right that the way in which it assembled should express the nature of society. If one looks down from the galleries of the parish church at Whitby — a unique example of a town church still arranged much as in the eighteenth century — one sees a social map of the town as it then was (Pl. 84). The chancel arch is filled with the magnificent pew of the Cholmley family, the Lords of the Manor, in the form of a gallery supported on barley-sugar columns and carved with cherubs' heads. Other large pews, comfortably lined with red or green baize, were for the shipowners, shipbuilders, and bankers who provided the leading families of Whitby. The middle class sat in narrower pews without the baize; the poor in free seats on long benches in the back of the church or in the galleries. Whitby was not a borough; otherwise there would inevitably have been a mayoral pew, with a coat-of-arms and a stand for the mayor's sword, and the mayor and corporation would have processed to and from the church each Sunday.

Presiding over all was the rector in his high three-decker pulpit. At Whitby this was originally in the central aisle, in front of the chancel arch and the Cholmley pew; the communion table was in the chancel behind, but it was only used when the communicants moved in there to take communion, on certain Sundays during the year. The dominant position of the pulpit, and the reading desk beneath it, was to be found in churches all over the country. The sermons that most clergymen gave from these pulpits aimed to be lucid, rational, sensible, unemotional and uncontroversial. An unemotional religion is not necessarily a superficial one, and the apathy of the eighteenth-century Church of England was to be much exaggerated by the Victorians. Much care and expense went to the rebuilding, repair and embellishment of town churches, and their fitting out with organs, galleries, communion tables and rails, and reredoses — most of which, being in the classical style, were swept away in the nineteenth century.

In every town, the architectural diapason of the parish church was accompanied by the minor note of one or more Nonconformist chapels. The modest chapels of the seventeenth century, when Nonconformity was at its most radical but congregations were seldom rich, were usually replaced by handsomer buildings in Georgian days (Pl. 85). By then hard work and application had often made the Nonconformists very prosperous; but on the whole, the dynamism was fading, until John Wesley re-introduced it in new form in the second half of the century. The most active and enterprising congregations were often Unitarian; their rational religion conformed to the spirit of the times, and in places like Wakefield (Pl. 86) Unitarian families effectively ran the town.

85. Rook Lane Chapel, Frome, 1707.
86. The Unitarian Chapel, off Westgate, Wakefield, built in 1751-2.
87. (right) Burgage plots along Newbiggin in Richmond, Yorkshire. Detail from the bird's-eye view of the town by Robert Harman, 1724.

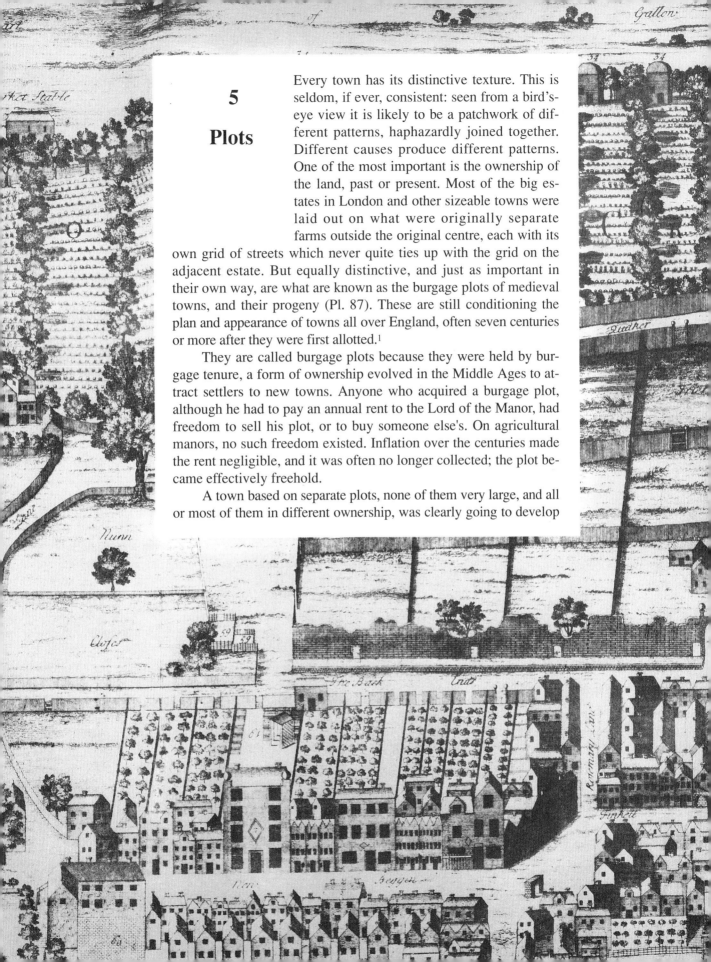

5

Plots

Every town has its distinctive texture. This is seldom, if ever, consistent: seen from a bird's-eye view it is likely to be a patchwork of different patterns, haphazardly joined together. Different causes produce different patterns. One of the most important is the ownership of the land, past or present. Most of the big estates in London and other sizeable towns were laid out on what were originally separate farms outside the original centre, each with its own grid of streets which never quite ties up with the grid on the adjacent estate. But equally distinctive, and just as important in their own way, are what are known as the burgage plots of medieval towns, and their progeny (Pl. 87). These are still conditioning the plan and appearance of towns all over England, often seven centuries or more after they were first allotted.[1]

They are called burgage plots because they were held by burgage tenure, a form of ownership evolved in the Middle Ages to attract settlers to new towns. Anyone who acquired a burgage plot, although he had to pay an annual rent to the Lord of the Manor, had freedom to sell his plot, or to buy someone else's. On agricultural manors, no such freedom existed. Inflation over the centuries made the rent negligible, and it was often no longer collected; the plot became effectively freehold.

A town based on separate plots, none of them very large, and all or most of them in different ownership, was clearly going to develop

88. Varied street pattern based on medieval burgage plots on King's Parade, Cambridge.
89, 91. Elevations of Wilkes Street, Spitalfields, London, showing pattterns of development and names of developers.

in a different way from a town or part of a town based on large blocks of property under the control of one owner.

The typical burgage plot was long and narrow. This was especially the case in the many towns based on one long main street. It resulted from the natural desire of those moving into the town to have a street or market frontage combined with a reasonable area of land. Some medieval towns were laid out from the start (or from early on) with lanes parallel to the main street, giving back access to the plots. Others had no such access, and the only way to get to the back, apart from going through the house, was either not to build up the whole frontage, or to pierce an arch through it; such arches still abound in English towns.

Plots were not necessarily all of the same width, but there was a tendency to standardize them when a town or district was being laid out. At Ludlow, for instance, the standard width seems to have been about 33 feet.[2] Over the centuries plots were often amalgamated or subdivided, leading to changing widths on the street frontages.

Tayler , joiner | William Tayler, joiner | Marmaduke Smith , blacksmith | Richard Michell | George & A
Dyer

But it was rare to get an amalgamation of more than two or three plots, especially in the centre, where property was most expensive. Out of the centre it was easier to get hold of substantial frontages: plots were cheaper, and often fell vacant in bad times; the peripheral areas in walled towns were often not laid out in plots at all, but left as orchards or fields, which were later developed field by field.

One result is the varied pattern of street frontages typical of the central areas of numerous English towns which are based on a medieval layout (Pls. 88, 90). Their variety comes from two sources. The rhythm of plot width changes because some are an amalgamation of two or more original plots; and the style of the buildings on the plot varies, because they have been rebuilt by different owners and at different dates. So on one stretch of street one may find a double-gabled half-timbered house followed by two brick Georgian houses, of different widths and height, but both with level cornices, contrasting in colour and skyline with their neighbour; then a Victorian shop, in a mixed polychromy of brick and stone; and so on. The resulting streetscape does not form an architectural unity as do the terraces of a Georgian resort, but as an expression of organic growth over the centuries it has its own quality.

Streets, squares and terraces of later date are as likely to be based on long narrow plots, often with back access, as streets of medieval origin; the advantages of such plots remained much the same over the centuries. However, the fact that many of them were built within a few years as part of one development inevitably made them tend towards uniformity. This was not necessarily complete, however. Quite often, walking in a part of a town that was developed in the first half of the eighteenth century, one comes across a street or streets that at first sight seem all of a piece, but on a closer look are made up of blocks of around two to six houses, each block a little different from its neighbours (Pls. 89, 91). The explanation is that the area was developed at the same time, and often belonged to the same ground landlord, but was let out in blocks to different builders, who were not required to conform to a unified street design, although they might be bound by certain constraints in their leases as to floor heights, cornice lines, materials, and so on.

In the later eighteenth century and during much of the nineteenth developments by one entrepreneur tended to be larger, and control by the ground landlord greater. The result were the terraces

90. Contrasting plot development in Stafford.

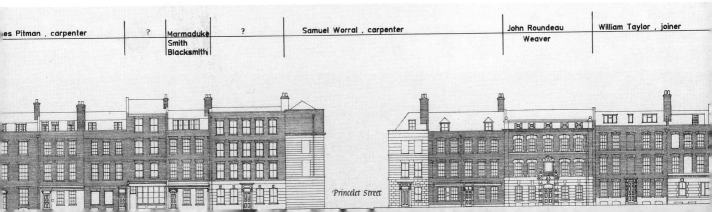

es Pitman, carpenter | ? | Marmaduke Smith Blacksmith | ? | Samuel Worral, carpenter | John Roundeau Weaver | William Taylor, joiner

Princelet Street

of unified design that were pioneered in Bath and became a feature of later Georgian and early Victorian developments, especially in the resorts. After 1850 terraces made up of identical units continued to be built in large numbers, but the prestige of the unified terrace was waning; it was found too monotonous. In residential squares like Cadogan Square in London, and new commercial streets like Corporation Street in Birmingham, individual plots were developed to different designs with the active encouragement of the ground landlord, even when several contiguous plots were built on by the same developer. The result is a variety that has a resemblance to streets based on burgage plots, even though all the buildings date from the same few years — and the plots, at any rate on new commercial streets, are usually wider.

Development of plots could lead to variety in the back lands, as well as on the frontages. Over the centuries the long strips at the back of individual buildings had varied histories. Some became gardens (Pls. 92, 93), the long narrow gardens which are a feature of many English towns — or were, until the houses became offices and the gardens car-parks. Many filled up with a mixture of back extensions, stores, stables, workshops and warehouses. A distinctive feature of King Street, King's Lynn, are the passages leading by way of openings in the street down through what used to be the backyards of houses to warehouses on the river at the end of the yards. In a few cases the warehouses survive, even though no longer on the water, since a broad quay was built out into the river in the nineteenth century.

One distinctive use of back plots was to provide courtyards for inns. These were lined, in many cases, with galleried ranges containing guest rooms on one or both sides (such as survive at the George at Southwark), with stabling beyond, all approached by way of an archway on the street frontage, but usually with back access as well. Inn courts could be extremely long, and provide tempting opportunities for redevelopment, especially in this century. In Cheltenham, for instance, the modern shopping arcade off the High Street is a redevelopment of the Plough Inn, and the long yard behind it.

Back plots were often developed as courts of houses or shops. This was usually the result of the owner of a house in the centre of a

92. (left)   Looking down the garden from a house in St. James's Square, Bristol. From a water-colour by a member of the Pole family, *c*. 1800.

93.   Garden on a double plot behind the Olde House, Dog Pole, Shrewsbury, as shown in a painting of *c*. 1700.

94. A yard off Church Street, Whitby.

town moving out, often to a new property on the edge of it. He could move because he wanted up-to-date and fashionable accommodation, or because property in the centre had become so valuable that he could not resist the profit of building on his garden, or for both reasons. The house was then likely to be let as a shop (if it was not one already) or to be cut up into, or rebuilt as, tenements, and the garden to be lined on one or both sides with new buildings. The owner moved into his new house, and drew a comfortable rental from the old one.

By the end of the eighteenth century this process had produced a labyrinth of courts in the City of London and along Fleet Street which still, in great part, survives, even if the buildings have been rebuilt several times. It was easy, but not inevitable, for courts to become slums. Samuel Johnson lived happily for many years 'in the dusky recess of a court in Fleet Street'[3] along with other literary or professional people. Other courts were lined with thriving small shops or workshops.

But courts most often accommodated working-class housing. As such, they were to be found in large numbers all over England, in towns of moderate size, as well as bigger cities: in Stamford, Yarm, Barnard Castle, Richmond, Dorchester (Pl. 95) and Whitby, for instance, as well as London, Manchester, Nottingham and Liverpool. Norwich had no less than 600. At Whitby in the later eighteenth century shipowners and shipbuilders moved out to new terraces or detached houses outside the town, and the gardens of their old houses in the centre were developed as courts (Pl. 94). By the time John Wood made his plan of the town in 1828, its centre was a teeming warren of courts, lived in by sailors, dockers and workers in ship-building yards, sail factories, and rope walks, the product of Whitby's prosperity in the whaling and coaling trades. As many of these courts had back access, the town acquired a network of pedestrian ways leading through courts up and down the steep hills which enclose the river and harbour. A good few courts survive, although more were cleared away in the 1950s and 1960s.[4]

When owners of adjacent courts each built a row of houses to either side of the dividing wall, the automatic result was back-to-back housing. The high density that resulted from this *ad hoc* arrangement of tenements on the street front and narrow courts of back-to-back houses behind them proved so profitable to landlords that it was widely copied in new developments, until it was legislated against in the mid-nineteenth century.

The filling of back gardens with courts is one way in which the texture of a town could be altered. Another came about when a much larger plot of land in or close to the middle of a town became available. Land previously occupied by a castle or religious house provides one example. At the dissolution of the monasteries, religious houses were often converted into or replaced by sizeable private residences surrounded by gardens and even fields. These in their turn could be demolished and replaced by housing. The most notable example is at Newcastle, where the buildings, fields and orchards of the Blackfriars were converted into a private house at the Reformation, and remained largely unbuilt on, while Newcastle grew round them. They were sold for development in 1834, enabling the laying out of Grey Street and its feeder streets in the centre of the town.

In Nottingham the Plumptres, merchants grown rich from the textile trade, had bought a house and ample land round it on the edge of the town in the early sixteenth century. They continued to live on the site until the nineteenth; in 1724 the house was rebuilt as a magnificent Palladian mansion, designed by Colen Campbell. In 1853 house and gardens, by now in the centre of an expanding city, were sold for development. They were replaced by the Victorian warehouse area known today as the Lace Market.[5]

95. A court behind a house in High Street, Dorchester.

Castle and city walls could also leave their mark on a town, long after they had been demolished. In Devizes the former presence of the castle bailey explains the curve of New Park Street, Slee Street and Bridewell Street, which ran outside its walls; at Richmond the market originally took place inside the bailey, and the curve of the market place follows the line of its long-vanished walls (Pl. 96). At Wisbech the castle originally sat on a circular mound on the edge of the town; the castle keep was replaced by a great house in the early seventeenth century; the house was demolished in 1815, and a double crescent of houses built round the flattened mound (Pl. 97). At Bath the city walls were demolished in the course of the

eighteenth century, but their line survives in the streets called Town Walls and Bar Walls, which originally ran inside them.

Field patterns outside a town can also be reflected in subsequent development. Brighton was originally surrounded by large open fields, known as laines, divided into big areas known as furlongs by paths running parallel to the sea, called breakways. The furlongs were divided into long narrow strips, sometimes as little as 25 feet wide, called paul pieces. When the fields were enclosed around 1800 the laine known as the West Laine went to the Lord of the Manor, Thomas Read Kemp, but the rest were mostly divided paul piece by paul piece among the copyholders. Kemp built Kemp Town on his share, but the remaining land was developed by the paul piece owners. The result was the distinctive pattern of much of Brighton: long parallel roads, very closely spaced, running, without intermediate cross streets, up to Western Road and St. James Street, which are on the line of the original breakways.[6] There is a somewhat similar development, based on former strip farming, in the area of Liverpool to the north of the original centre.[7]

Finally, a vanished river can maintain a ghostly presence in a town. In Derby, for instance, the curving façades of Victoria and Albert Streets, laid out in the 1850s, follow the line of the Markeaton Brook, which now runs under them. The biggest and best example is probably the Fleet River in London. Originally, in Pope's words, this 'rolled the large tribute of dead dogs to Thames'[8] down a steep-sided valley to the west of the City walls. It was covered over in 1737 and replaced by Farringdon Street, but the river still flows in a drain underneath it. The little street known as Sea Coal Lane, now far out of the sight of any water, marks where colliers used to unload their cargoes on the quays along its banks.

96.   Looking down into the market from the castle keep, Richmond, Yorkshire.
97.   Aerial view of Wisbech, showing the redevelopment of the site of the castle.
98. (right) Robert Adam's engraving of the façade of the Royal Society of Arts in the Adelphi, London, built 1772-4.

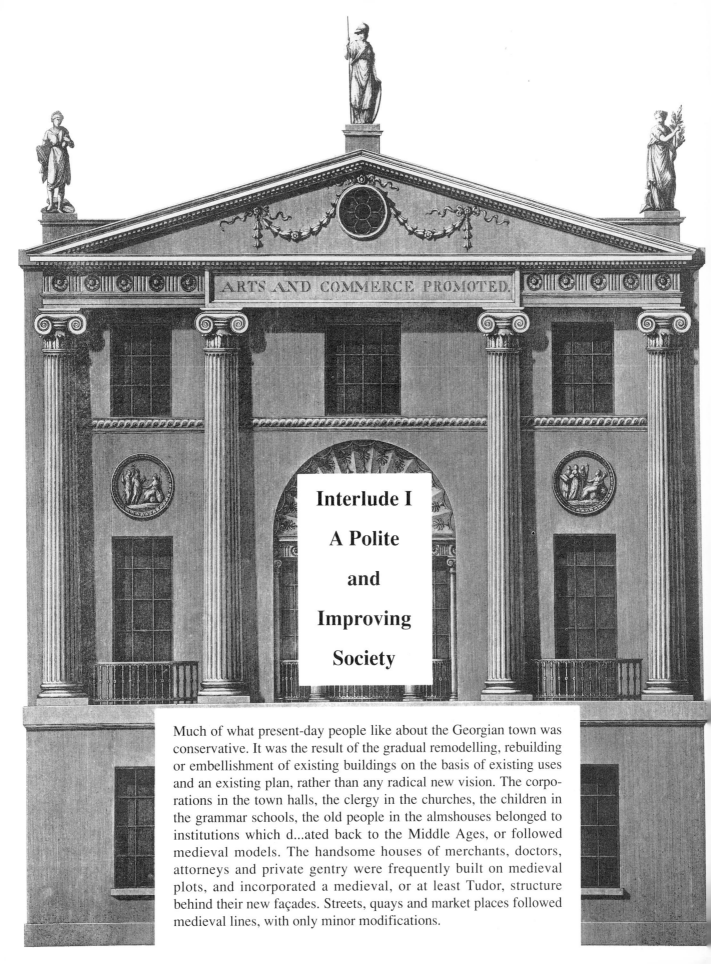

ARTS AND COMMERCE PROMOTED.

Interlude I

A Polite

and

Improving

Society

Much of what present-day people like about the Georgian town was conservative. It was the result of the gradual remodelling, rebuilding or embellishment of existing buildings on the basis of existing uses and an existing plan, rather than any radical new vision. The corporations in the town halls, the clergy in the churches, the children in the grammar schools, the old people in the almshouses belonged to institutions which d...ated back to the Middle Ages, or followed medieval models. The handsome houses of merchants, doctors, attorneys and private gentry were frequently built on medieval plots, and incorporated a medieval, or at least Tudor, structure behind their new façades. Streets, quays and market places followed medieval lines, with only minor modifications.

But the Georgians also introduced innovations which were remarkable in themselves and were to have a major effect on the towns around the world. Outside the old centres new streets, squares and crescents had a new unity and spaciousness: inside them assembly rooms and theatres supplied a range of recreation; towards the end of the century new jails, hospitals, docks, warehouses and mills provided a new vastness of scale. A new type of town grew up around mineral springs, or by the seaside. And by means of the provision of public walks, the planting of squares, and the destruction of town walls, greenery began to flow into the towns and the towns to open themselves up to the country.

Much of this was tied up with a new way of life. The people who emerged from the terraces to visit assembly rooms or theatres, promenade on the walks, or make excursions to the resorts, formed a recognizable class, similar to but not quite the same as the upper social strata of earlier centuries. They were what was known at the time as polite society.

'Politeness' was so loaded a word in the eighteenth century, and is so empty a one today, that something has to be said about it.[1] A polite man was someone polished, in the sense that he had no angularities which limited his contacts with other people. As the third Earl of Shaftesbury put it: 'We polish one another and rub off our corners and sides by a sort of amicable collision'. Fielding exhorted polite people to contribute 'as much as possible to the ease and happiness of those with whom you converse'.[2] The aim was conversation without constraint between people of different rank, religion, occupation or politics. In 1700 this was a revolutionary idea. Barriers of rank were still formidable, and for the previous half-century and more England had been torn apart by religious and political strife. Society was both formal and violent. Lords and ladies were intensely conscious that they were different from other people. They sat under canopies of state, sported a train and a page to carry it when they went visiting, and took offence if they were offered a chair without arms to sit in. Gentlemen wore swords and were quick to draw them. Catholics did not mix with Protestants, Whigs did not speak to Tories.

The eighteenth century evolved in reaction against the seventeenth. Many people felt that the traumas of the latter must be avoided at all costs; the heat had to be taken out of the system. Civilization was the result of men learning to act together in society. The polite man was essentially social, and as such distinguished from arrogant lords, illiterate squires and fanatical puritans. All in their own way were angular, rather than polished. The ruling characteristic of the last group was enthusiasm, a quality at the opposite pole to politeness, and intensely disliked by all polite people. Enthusiasm involved belief in personal inspiration, and readiness to follow it and, if necessary, break up society in doing so.

Not everyone could hope to be polite. Polite society formed a

group within society as a whole. The polite person needed sufficient property to give him the means to education, and a stake in society. The larger the group, the better, however. The polite society of eighteenth-century England was always a minority, but a large and growing one. Essentially, it was made up of the people who owned and ran the country.

Polite society needed places to meet in, and a common language with which to communicate. Much care and energy went into producing these. The main meeting places were assembly rooms, public walks, theatres, clubs and coffee-houses. The common language included more than the spoken language; it was a language of dress, behaviour, movement, art, architecture and decoration as well. *Habitués* of walks and assembly rooms learned the accepted ways of making conversation, dancing, and greeting acquaintances. In the theatres provincial audiences learned about polite dress and manners from companies on tour from London. Dancing-masters, teachers of elocution and finishing schools provided training. Books such as F. Nivelon's *The Rudiments of Genteel Behaviour*, published in 1737, taught the behaviour which would 'distinguish the polite Gentleman from the rude Rustick' (Pl. 99).

Polite gentlemen and ladies learnt how to understand the language of classical architecture, to use it correctly, and to appreciate how it could be modulated in order to express a mood or underline importance. They learnt partly from increasing numbers of books, often issued by subscription, a selection of which was to be found in the library of any polite person; partly by visiting and talking about the buildings which were admired.

Resorts and spas became important means towards the production of polite society. Politeness was to do with breaking down barriers. By their nature spas attracted people to come from different backgrounds to one place, in pursuit of health; and once away from their everyday context such people found it easier to shed prejudices, mix together and (if they were not too ill) enjoy themselves in doing so. Spas had always attracted a minority of people who were not ill at all, but had remained little more than villages. In the eighteenth century the tradition was expanded to provide a greater range of social activities, and attract far more people, turning villages into towns in the process. Spas became the prototypes of modern holiday resorts, with a resort industry to support them.

A holiday, prior to the eighteenth century, was a single day's celebration to mark a religious feast, or three or four days of carnival, in which a town or city went crazy, or a retreat into the country to stay with friends or relations. The idea of a holiday as a form of heightened and liberating social life, of large numbers of people leaving their work or normal place of residence in order to come together in one place for two or three weeks, solely in order to enjoy themselves, was pioneered in the eighteenth century.

By the mid-eighteenth century Bath had become so overwhelmingly the most important resort in England that its earlier rivals tend to be forgotten. Up till about 1720 Tunbridge Wells,

99. Figures from Nivelon's *Rudiments of Genteel Behaviour*, 1737: (left) 'Standing' and 'Dancing the Minuet'; (above) 'To offer or receive' and 'The curtsey'.

Epsom and Hampstead were more flourishing and fashionable, and influence was probably running from them to Bath, rather than the other way round.

It is worth taking a look at Epsom, in its short heyday as a spa in the late seventeenth and early eighteenth centuries. John Toland, in his *Description of Epsom*, published in 1711, described the background of the people on its walks, the first in England to be called Parades. 'By the conversation of those who walk there, you would fancy yourself to be this minute at the Exchange, and the next minute at St. James's; one while in an East-India factory or a West-India plantation, and another with the army in Flanders or on board the fleet in the ocean.' He commended the tolerance of its coffee-houses: 'A Tory does not stare and leer when a Whig comes in, nor a Whig look sour and whisper at the sight of a Tory. These distinc-tions are laid by with the winter suit in London, and a gayer, easier habit worn ... if at any times we must deal in extremes, then we pre-fer the quiet good-natured hypocrite to the implacable, turbulent zealot of any kind. In plain terms, we are not so fond of any set of notions, as to think them more important than the peace of society.'

Toland ascribed much of the responsibility for this tolerance to an individual referred to as 'the governor'. He was 'a gentle-man of our society ... esteemed for his good humour, good breed-ing and good living, who presides over the social life of the town, is the enemy of all party disputes, and the arbiter of all differences.'[3]

Toland's description of his governor is paralleled forty years later by a description of Richard ('Beau') Nash, the social arbiter of Bath. It was written by Lady Luxborough in 1755. 'Would you see our law-giver, Mr Nash, whose white hat commands more respect and non-resistance than the crowns of some kings ... To promote society, good manners, and a coalition of parties and ranks; to sup-press scandal and late hours, are his views.'[4] In the interval Bath had outstripped Epsom, and become the supreme creation and exemplar of polite society in England.

Nash had arrived in Bath as a penniless Welsh adventurer in 1702. By about 1706 he was in charge of the modest social events which were put on in the town for the people who came to take the waters, or those who accompanied them. He developed them into an immensely successful social routine. In doing so, he turned Bath from a small health resort with a social element into a large social resort with a health element. The importance of the latter must not be played down. Large numbers of genuinely ill people continued to come to Bath: 'It is impossible to walk a hundred yards without meeting some dreadful object', wrote Lady Harriet Cavendish in 1804.[5] But taking the waters provided a pretext for healthy people to take a holiday. And since Bath was a health resort, hard drinking, over-eating and late hours were discouraged. As a result everyone except the genuinely ill felt very well there.

100. (right) The old pump room, Bath, as depicted in the water-colour by Humphrey Repton, 1784.

The situation when Nash got to work is described in his biography by Oliver Goldsmith: 'General society among people of rank or fashion was by no means established. The nobility still preserved a structure of Gothic haughtiness, and refused to keep company with the gentry at any of the public entertainments of the place. But when proper walks were made for exercise and a house built for assembling in, rank began to be laid aside, and all degrees of people, from the private gentleman upwards, were soon united in society with one another.'[6]

Nash's achievement was to get different groups and types doing things together. He established common meeting-places, a common routine, and common codes of dress and behaviour. The routine had three high points: meeting at the pump room (with a band playing in the background) at nine o'clock (Pl. 100), promenading on the parade at twelve o'clock, and dancing or playing cards in the assembly room from six o'clock to eleven o'clock. Women not properly dressed for dancing, or men wearing boots or swords, were not allowed into the assembly rooms. In the pump and assembly rooms, or on the parades, it was acceptable behaviour for people to introduce themselves to each other, and 'Gothic haughtiness' on the part of the great was discouraged. 'It is difficult to imagine anything more agreeable than the easy and familiar way of life that everyone adopts', the magazine *Pour et Contre* commented in 1734. 'Duchesses walk the streets here unattended', proclaimed Lady Luxborough in 1755. Goldsmith called the resulting society a 'polite kingdom' which had escaped from the rule of 'ceremonial observance' into 'politeness, elegance and ease'. Fifty years later the guide-books were repeating what had become Bath's accepted philosophy: 'Ceremony, beyond the essential rules of politeness, is totally exploded ... everyone mixes in the room upon an equality'.[7]

Entry to this polite society was not for everyone. It was, as Goldsmith put it, for 'the private gentleman upwards'. What were called at the time 'the common sort of people' were excluded. In fact entry was available to anyone who wore the right clothes and could afford the subscription of two and a half guineas which gave access to assembly rooms and balls; as far as Bath was concerned, you were a gentleman or lady if you dressed and behaved like one. All through the eighteenth century comments were made, satires written and caricatures drawn, in mockery of the mixed background of the people who frequented Bath. But there was a deliberate

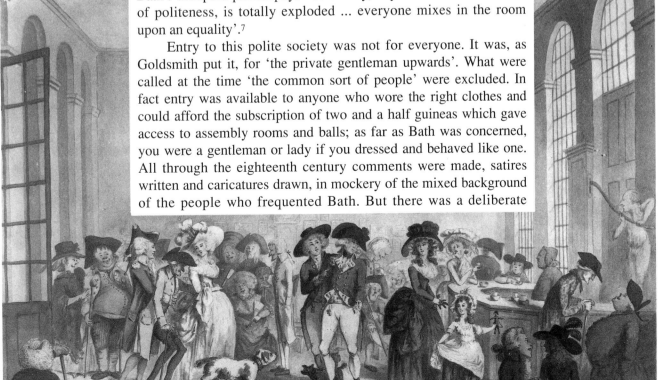

philosophy behind this mixture, the philosophy which Lady Luxborough attributed to Nash: 'to promote society, good manners, and a coalition of parties and ranks'. This was expanded in a description of Tunbridge Wells of about 1760; by then Tunbridge had become a satellite of Bath, for Nash officiated as Master of the Ceremonies there in the summer, when the Bath season was over, and had impressed his personality upon it. 'People of the greatest title, rank and dignity, people of every learned profession, of every religious and political persuasion; people of every degree, condition and occupation of life (if well dressed and well behaved) meet amicably here together.'[8] Bath was amicable too. To quote Lady Luxborough again: 'We can offer you friendly conversation, friendly springs, friendly rides and walks, friendly pastimes to dissipate gloomy thoughts'.

Visitors to Bath had a feeling of escape, that escape from social constriction, everyday life, and everyday persona, which is the essence of any good holiday. At Bath, according to a Frenchman writing in 1745, English ladies 'cast off the constraint and melancholy imposed upon them by the yoke of habit during the rest of the year'.[9] A sense of gaiety and excitement, of possible adventures and sad departures, ran through visitors and impregnated the buzz of conversation which rose from the pump-rooms, parades, and assembly rooms.

The excitement was spiced by two powerful ingredients, sex and gambling. The card room was at least as important a feature of the assembly rooms as the ball room, and unlike the latter was crowded all day long. Gambling in the public rooms was made illegal in 1745, but the law was frequently evaded, and private gambling continued throughout the eighteenth century. Women gambled as much as men. Throwing a dice, it was remarked, gave opportunities 'to display a well-turned arm, and scatter to advantage the ray of the diamond '.

There were other ways of displaying a well-turned arm in Bath. It was a marriage-market, in which mothers could show off their daughters to advantage on the Parade or in the Rooms, or widows look out for new husbands and impecunious men of fashion for rich widows (Pl. 102). It was a place for flirtations, intrigues, and love affairs. Bath prostitutes (known as 'the nymphs of Avon Street') were eulogized in a letter written to John Wilkes by his friend Thomas Potter in about 1750: 'If you prefer young women and whores to old women and wives, if you prefer toying away

101. Section of the Octagon Chapel, Milsom Street, Bath (T. Lightoler, 1766-7).

102. *A Real Scene on the Parade at Bath*, from an engraving of *c.* 1750.

hours with little Satin Back to the evening conferences with your mother-in-law, if the sprightly notes of the fiddle are preferable to the squalling of your brat; but above all, if the divinely inspired passion called lust has not deserted you, hasten to town to take a place in my post-chaise to Bath.'[10]

But Bath discovered the secret of all good resorts of the future, and offered its visitors plenty of alternatives. Religion became big business there. By 1800 visitors had a choice of eleven Church of England churches or chapels, and nine Nonconformist ones. Doing the rounds of the different services and savouring the quality of the sermons became a favourite Bath occupation. The most fashionable places of worship were built as private speculations and brought their backers a handsome income from the pew rents charged during the season. The most fashionable of all was the Octagon Chapel in Milsom Street, the best shopping street in Bath (Pl. 101). It belonged to a Bath banker, and was opened in 1767. It offered extremely comfortable pews, six open fireplaces blazing through the winter months, and a superb organ. Excellent concerts and oratorios were put on there. There were similar events at other churches, and a weekly concert in the Assembly Rooms.

The best London actors came down to play in the Theatre Royal. Gainsborough lived in Bath from 1759 to 1774, and Lawrence started his career there in the 1780s. The shops were as good as those in London. There were subscription libraries and coffee-shops, to which people came to gossip as well as to borrow books or eat and drink. Gossip was fuelled by an apparently endless supply of skits, poems, and pamphlets which rolled off the Bath presses and were handed round the coffee-shops. Saying how awful Bath was becoming was one of the favourite activities of visitors who continued to come back year after year.

Not least of the reasons for the success of Bath was its beauty. To beauty of site was added beauty of plan and architecture, perfectly fitted to the nature of the life which was led there. The united society which Nash sought to create was expressed in the integrated design of terraces, squares and crescents which acted as a backcloth to its activities.[11] The 'easy and familiar' mode of life in the town, and its status as a health resort, were reflected by another characteristic. It was an open city: there was greenery, and views into the countryside everywhere. One of the charms of spas had always been their semi-rural nature; to this day Tunbridge Wells has remained a series of little settlements, scattered in an Arcadian landscape of commons and rocks. At Bath the quality which had been natural in a village was developed to give delight to a town.

Its population increased ten-fold between 1700 and 1800, from about 3,500 to 35,000. It became, for a time, the eighth largest town in England. At first its new houses had mainly been built for visitors, as lodging-houses, or houses to let. But more and more it became a town where people settled, attracted by its beauty, the pleasures of its society — and the fact that property there was cheaper than in London. Merchants, professional people, and naval and military officers retired there. Widows and spinsters with private incomes found that these would go a long way there. A good many people settled or lingered there when they should have been elsewhere. The Revd Edmund Nelson, father of the admiral, remorselessly abandoned his icy Norfolk parish and went off there for several months every winter. Mr Custance, of Weston House near Norwich, took his wife and family there for nearly five years from 1792, ostensibly to educate his daughters. During this period he made occasional shorts visits to his family estate, but his wife never once returned there.[12]

The dual nature of Bath, as a place where some people went to visit, and others to settle, reflected a development of polite society which soon spread over the country. Other resorts flourished and grew into towns, and the more successful of them inevitably became places of settlement as well. More and more provincial towns began to cater for the needs of polite society, by acquiring the necessary equipment of assembly rooms, public walks, theatres and racecourses (Pls. 103-6).

The influence and importance of Bath was great, but it would be a mistake to exaggerate it, just as it would be a mistake to exaggerate the considerable importance of Beau Nash in Bath itself. Polite society in provincial towns began to develop at much the same time as in Bath, and, to begin with at least, probably independently of it.

London and Bath existed in tandem. Bath owed its reputation to the resort there of fashionable people from London. The squares and terraces of the West End — or, as it was known at the time, the polite end of the town — began to be developed before those of Bath. The theory of a polite society, in so far as it existed, had been evolved in London, above all by Joseph Addison, who dominated English literary and intellectual life from the London coffee-houses in the early eighteenth century.[13] Addison extolled the virtues of social life, and the importance of getting fox-hunting country squires up to town to be civilized. In his *Spectator* articles, Sir Roger de Coverley, the country gentleman, and Sir Andrew Freeport, the city merchant, learn to tolerate and appreciate each other's background and values. Similar interactions were going on all the time in the West End, as its new terraces absorbed courtiers, country gentlemen, and city merchants, who emerged from them to meet at the theatre, in clubs, in coffee-houses, at court, and on the walks. All this had its reflections in Bath; but on the other hand, from about 1730 onwards, Bath was growing in importance and independence, and influencing London itself, as well as resorts and provincial towns.

Apart from Bath, Tunbridge Wells, Epsom and Hampstead, most English resorts only became important later on in the century, even if their mineral springs may have been frequented by small

103-106. (right) Theatres at Newcastle-upon-Tyne (1789), Reading (1788), Winchester (1785), and Newbury (1802), from James Winston, *The Theatric Tourist*, 1805.

82

numbers before that. Scarborough was one of the first to get under way. Its spa was established by the 1720s, and from then on was much resorted to by the northern aristocracy and gentry; but it was too remote to grow to any considerable size before the coming of the railways. In resort terms, it was a satellite of Hampstead rather than Bath; by at least 1733 its Long Room was kept by 'Mons. Vipons, Master of the Long Room at Hampstead'.[14] Henry Skillicorne began to promote his mineral spring at Cheltenham in 1736, with a walk and Long Room which also suggest the influence of Hampstead as much as of Bath. But Buxton and the Hotwells at Bristol were first promoted in a big way in the 1760s and 1770s, clearly under the influence of Bath.

Although Scarborough owed its *raison d'être* as a spa to its mineral springs, the fact that they were down on the beach made it the first resort in which sea bathing featured (Pl. 187). Directions for 'Bathing in the Sea' were printed at the end of Peter Shaw's *Dissertation upon the Scarborough Waters* as early as 1730; even before then, in 1724, a visitor described how 'both ladies and men bathe in open sea'.[15] But it was Dr Richard Russell's *Dissertation upon the Use of Sea-Bathing* (1749), and his promotion of Brighton, which really set under way the seaside development of health resorts, which soon also became pleasure resorts. Brighton, Weymouth, Margate and Southampton became fashionable between 1750 and 1770, and all were much under the influence of Bath.

Apart from the resorts, some country towns acquired a greater reputation for polite society than others. They, too, became places where polite people came to settle, retire, or spend a portion of the year. In some places this was deliberately encouraged by the corporation or a group of people in the town. This was the case at York, which had been in economic and social decline owing to the collapse of its textile industry and the abolition of the Council of the North. 'Our races and the residence of the gentry among us', wrote Francis Drake in 1736, 'in our present decay of trade, seems to be the chief support of the city. Our magistrates take great care that families of this sort should be encouraged to live here, by allowing of all innocent diversions, and making of public walks for their entertainment.... Our streets are kept clean, and lighted with lamps, every night in the year.... We now reckon forty-two gentlemen's coaches, twenty-two hackney coaches and twenty-two hackney chairs to be in full exercise in the city; and it will be no vanity in me to say, that though other cities and towns in the kingdom run far beyond us in trade, and the hurry of business, yet, there is no place out of London, so polite and elegant to live in as the City of York.'[16]

Country gentlemen, according to Drake, 'have found by experience that living at York is so much cheaper than London, that it is even less expensive than living at their own houses in the country'. The corporation allowed 'greater liberties' to Roman Catholics, with the result that numbers of Catholic families settled in the town.

The corporation of Winchester was equally tolerant, and its polite society developed along similar lines, if on a smaller scale.[17] In general, there were certain qualities which helped make a town 'polite and elegant to live in': a decayed local industry, leading to cheap property, a good situation, plenty of country houses in the neighbourhood, the provision of assembly rooms and walks, and the existence of some local event — assizes, fair, or races — to act as a social magnet for the right kind of people. Shrewsbury, Doncaster, Richmond, Ludlow, Warwick, Beverley and Bury St. Edmunds all qualified; at Doncaster the building of the Mansion House, with its magnificent room for entertainment, and the promotion of the races, were probably as deliberate expressions of a policy to attract polite society as at York.

107. The Assembly Rooms, York, from the engraving by W. Lindley, 1759.

The inscription on the foundation stone of the York Assembly Rooms (Pl. 107) depicted them as a means, amongst other things, towards reviving the glory of the city by bringing new prosperity to it.[18] A flourishing polite society had many economic spin-offs. It needed lawyers and doctors, to look after its members, and ultimately to join them; architects, painters, sculptors, furniture-makers, framers, gilders, goldsmiths, upholsterers and coach-makers, to design and furnish their houses and stables, when they were alive, and supply their memorials when they died; drawing-masters, dancing-masters, music-masters and finishing schools for young ladies to polish them; wine-merchants and high-class grocers to feed them; and wig-makers, hairdressers and milliners to look after their appearance. London was inevitably the main centre for luxury arts and industries, but many provincial centres developed as well. At York in and around 1770, for instance, one could find John Carr, the most talented and successful architect outside London; Thomas Atkinson, an able architect much patronized by Catholic families; Philip Mercier, a gifted French artist who had, however, failed to establish himself in London; and a group of plasterers, carvers, furniture-makers and masons who had been assembled by Carr and produced work of as high a quality as anything being done in London.[19]

The qualities of 'politeness, elegance and ease' that were acquired in the assembly rooms and on the walks were not necessarily confined to them. Such places acted as civilizing agents, and led to a general improvement of manners, in the widest sense of the word. As Burke put it: 'Manners are of more importance than laws. ... Manners are what vex or soothe, corrupt or purify, exalt or debase, barbarize or refine us, by a constant, steady, uniform, insensible operation like that of the air we breath in'.[20] A code of conduct which forbade violence, drunkenness, and intolerance in the places where polite society met together, helped to reduce them in all aspects of life as lived by its members, and encouraged these to go further, and try to reduce them in society as a whole.

The attraction of politeness in the early eighteenth century had been one of contrast. It was a missionary cult, gradually extending its frontiers in a wild country, rather than the settled culture of a majority. Faction and intolerance, brutality and ignorance by no means disappeared, even within polite society. One can take as an example, a scene in the market place at Newark, early in January 1781. Over it presided the bland and beautiful façade of the Town Hall, politeness in architecture exemplified. Behind its portico local polite society regularly gathered for assemblies in an exquisitely decorated ballroom. But the same portico was now crowded for a different end: 'Monday afternoon', as a local newspaper described it, 'a bull was baited in the market-place at Newark, which afforded great diversion to many hundred spectators; the windows of every house which commanded an open view were crowded with ladies and gentlemen, who resorted thither to gratify their curiosity'.[21]

Even so, the growing refinement of polite society led to a general change for the better in manners in the course of the eighteenth century. There was a similar connection between social and practical life. The group or groups of people who were known in their social aspect as polite society were also property owners and members of a ruling class. They emerged from beneath the chandeliers of the assembly rooms, from theatres, racecourses, walks or pump rooms to run the country as JPs, members of Parliament, government officials or ministers of the Crown, or to administer their own estates and interests as landowners, merchants, or members of the professions. In their active life emphasis moved from 'politeness' to 'improvement', but the two concepts were related. One of the dominant features of the eighteenth century throughout Europe was the attitude associated with what became known as the Enlightenment, the belief that life in all its aspects could be improved by the use of the intelligence. Politeness might have no intellectual content in itself, but the tolerance which it promoted could be used as a lubricant to encourage a free trade in ideas. A nation in which the upper echelons knew how to live together and join in discussion in a civilized fashion, without tearing each other apart, without wasting their energies in political or religious feuds and factions, a society, in short, run by polite, sensible men who knew the world and whose judgement was not clouded by prejudice or enthusiasm, would be free to concentrate on improving itself.

'Improvement' was much in the air in the eighteenth century. Methods of commerce could be improved, by the provision of better quays, docks and warehouses. Manufacture could be improved, by new techniques such as the application of steam power, and that subdivision of labour which amazed visitors to Birmingham in the mid-century. Transport could be improved, by the formation of canals, the building of bridges, and the making of turnpike trusts. Agriculture could be improved, by enclosure and better methods of farming. Towns could be improved, by the paving, lighting, straightening and widening of streets, the formation of new streets, the destruction of medieval town walls, the provision of water (Pl. 108), the laying out of public walks, and the erection of public buildings. Country houses could be improved, by being rebuilt or remodelled in a purer taste, or given a new setting of idyllic parkland. The arts could be improved, by enlightened patronage and the founding of academies. The condition of the poor could be improved, by the provision of schools, hospitals, and better prisons.

An enlightened eighteenth-century man moved freely from one type of improvement to the other. He bought pictures, built temples, bred sheep, acted as governor of hospitals and charity schools, promoted canals and turnpikes, put money into docks, mines and mills, sat on improvement commissions in the towns, and as a JP supervised the building of bridges and prisons. Improvements of all types were visited with interest by the members of polite society. In the mid-century, for instance, one finds Mrs Lybbe Powys, of Hardwicke House in Oxfordshire, moving from Vanbrugh's King's Weston to the Bristol glass manufactures, and from Kedleston to the Derby silk mill — and attending local assemblies in the evening.[22] Around 1800 the Plymouth attorney, Henry Woolcombe, went from visits to the studios of Turner, Nollekens and Haydon to tours of Rennie's great breakwater outside Plymouth Sound, or Foulston's County Asylum at Bodmin; in his capacity as citizen, alderman, mayor, and solicitor to various improvement trusts, he was involved in building churches and schools, making and widening roads, organizing art exhibitions, and providing Plymouth with a theatre, an assembly room, and an Athenaeum, for lectures and meetings.[23]

Improvement could be financially rewarding. But the landowner who saw his rents double as the result of enclosure, the investor pocketing the dividends from his canal shares, was in the happy position of feeling that his improved bank balance was also improving the stock of general happiness. For the eighteenth century saw the development of a new doctrine. The welfare of all was best served by individuals pursuing their own interests. As early as 1723 the Earl of Shaftesbury had written that 'the wisdom of what rules and is first and chief in nature, has made it to be according to the private interests and good of everyone, to work towards the general good'.[24] In the mid-century Adam Smith stood Shaftesbury's doctrine on its head: it was to the general good for individuals to work towards their own private interest and good.

The doctrine worked for the poor as well as the rich — at any rate for what the rich saw as the interests of the poor. 'There must', the Bishop of Norwich told schoolchildren in 1755, 'be drudges of labour as well as counsellors to direct and rulers to preside.... These poor children are borne to be daily labourers.' Accordingly, it was in their interests to be taught, as Isaac Watts put it, 'the duties of humility and submission to superiors', and 'diligence and industry in their business.'[25] But a healthy, industrious and law-abiding working class was as much an asset to the nation as a whole as to itself.

Important though improvement was, it had to work within boundaries to find acceptance. Sensible men were not going to risk the recurrence of the troubles which had torn England apart in the seventeenth century. The country had emerged out of them with religious tolerance, absence of exclusive social barriers and a constitution which kept a balance between the powers of monarch, parliament and people. The result was an object of admiration to foreigners, and of pride to Englishmen: the constitution was gradually accepted even by the Tories and its perfection became an article of faith amongst the Whigs. Admittedly, elements in it were open to criticism, such as the existence of pocket boroughs, and the uneven spread of parliamentary representation. But any change would upset existing interests. A majority of the ruling classes held that it was better to accept

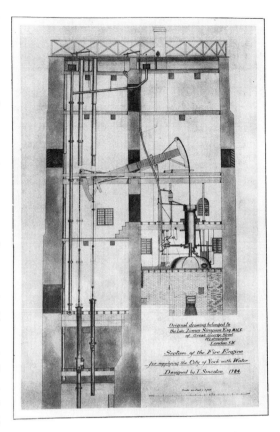

108. The engine supplied by John Smeaton to the York Waterworks Company, *c*. 1784.

the system as it was, than risk the disruption which trying to change it would cause. The one issue that was jealously watched over was whether the balance of power was changing: above all, whether the powers of the monarch and the executive were becoming too great.

Town corporations were left alone, on similar grounds. James II's endeavour to meddle with them was one of the main causes for his fall. Property rights were considered the basis of society, and corporations were thought of in their role as property owners, just as much as in their executive or judicial role. By the mid-eighteenth century most corporations, for a variety of reasons, were Tory, and since they were almost all self-perpetuating, likely to remain so. That they were in no conceivable sense representative of their towns did not necessarily worry contemporaries, but in many cases they were not even representative of the property owners in the town; it was common enough for a town the richest inhabitants of which were Whigs (many of them often Dissenters) to have a Tory corporation. Whigs and Whig politicians might have liked to change the situation, but left the corporations alone, because an attack on them would be an attack on property.

Out of a combination of suspicion of giving too much power to king or central government, and lack of confidence in corporations grew one of the most distinctive features of the eighteenth century, the improvement trust or commission. An improvement trust was set up by Act of Parliament, as the result of a local petition. Its aim could be to make or improve a road, construct a canal, a dock, or a bridge, improve navigation on a river, enclose open fields or common land, or widen streets, create open spaces, bring in water, or set up a police force in a town. The Act of Parliament gave the necessary powers of borrowing money or raising it, usually by imposing a rate or a toll, and of acquiring property, by compulsory purchase if necessary. Parliamentary ratification was needed, but Acts of Parliament setting up trusts and commissions never emanated from Parliament itself. They merely ratified a local scheme, and were passed without trouble, unless there was a sufficiently strong counter-petition from a rival group; in such a situation Parliament acted as a referee, adjudicating the strength of local feeling. Once such Acts had become law, they were administered by bodies of trustees or commissioners, which almost invariably included the original petitioners. These were usually large bodies, made up of anything from fifty to two hundred people. Under Acts passed in the early nineteenth century they were often elected, by the rate-payers or local people with a stipulated property qualification. But in the eighteenth century they were usually appointed under the Act, and filled gaps in their numbers by co-option.[26]

Improvement commissioners in schemes affecting towns usually included the members of the corporation, if there was one, but were not confined to them. Sometimes the corporation had a majority, but very often it did not. Essentially, the commissions were designed to include all those with substantial property interests in the town. By the end of the century hundreds of towns all over England, whether they had a corporation or not, were being largely run by one or more bodies of commissioners. Commissioners cleaned, maintained or improved the streets and public open spaces, lit the town, supplied it with water, and ran a police force. But judicial power always remained with the Justices of the Peace.

Town improvements often had an aesthetic aim, but the pursuit of beauty or magnificence tended to be tempered by a practical point of view which was typical of English improvement. Wide streets were handsome, but they also ventilated a town, and made it more healthy. The economic argument for grand new public buildings was put by John Gwynn in his *London and Westminster Improved* (1766): 'public works of real magnificence, taste, elegance and utility, are of the utmost consequence; they are not only of real use in point of splendor and convenience, but as necessary to the community as health and clothing to the human body; they are the great sources of invention and of ingenious employments, and are a means of stamping real value upon materials of every kind.'[27]

The charitable trusts which ran many eighteenth-century schools and hospitals were not unlike improvement trusts. They were normally supported by subscribers, and run by a committee or board of governors. No Act of Parliament was needed to set them up, because no tolls had to be imposed or property compulsorily purchased; but they were equally the result of people of substance joining together to provide a public amenity.

The movement for charity schools started before that for hospitals.[28] The initial impetus was provided by the Jesuits. In 1685, when under the protection of James II, they started up a chapel in the Savoy, and opened a free school for the poor in its neighbourhood. Its success so alarmed the Protestants that Church of England free schools were hastily started up in the parishes of St. James's, Piccadilly, and St. Margaret's, Westminster. From there the idea spread over the country (Pl. 109). The aim of doing down popery was soon supplemented by more general objectives. The extent to which the poor were becoming a burden on their parishes, and worries about the 'monstrous increase in Deism, Profaneness and Vice' amongst them, suggested the usefulness of catching them young, and training them in habits of Christian belief, industry, and acceptance of their station. It was important not to teach them too much, however; the negative need was concisely stated by the Revd George Hadley in 1788: 'The working poor are by far the most numerous class of people, and, *when kept in due subordination*, they compose the riches of the nation. But there is a degree of ignorance necessary to keep them so, and to make them either useful to others or happy in themselves.'[29]

The first subscription hospital was the result of a meeting of four individuals, including Henry Hoare, the banker.[30] They assem-

109. The Bluecoat School, Chester (1717).

bled in St. Dunstan's Coffee House, Fleet Street, on 14 January 1715, to discuss 'a charitable proposal for relieving the sick and needy, and other distressed persons'. A subscription list was set up, and led to what became the Westminster Hospital. Five more London hospitals were built, or rebuilt, on a subscription basis during the century (Pls. 110, 111). The movement spread to the provinces with the founding of the Winchester Hospital in 1738. Between then and the end of the century at least twenty-nine hospitals were built all over England, mostly on a county basis and in county towns. All provided free treatment. They were usually called infirmaries, to distinguish them from the many institutions called hospitals which were in fact almshouses or schools. Prior to this there had been no medical hospitals in the provinces (although sporadic medical treatment was given in some parish workhouses), and London had had to rely on two medieval foundations, both re-established under Henry VIII, St. Bartholomew's and St. Thomas's.

A good many charity schools and one or two hospitals were built or endowed by an individual. In London, for instance, St. Thomas's was rebuilt in 1693-1709 largely at the expense of Sir Robert Clayton, one of the richest City merchants, and the first block of Guy's Hospital was built in 1721-6 through the munificence of Thomas Guy, a publisher and printer who had sold his South Sea shares at the right time. But the majority were built and maintained by subscription. The subscribers were drawn from both the middle and the upper classes. The six main founders and supporters of what became the Greycoat Hospital in Westminster were Westminster tradesmen, including a cheesemonger, a draper and a bookseller. The supporters of the Ladies' Charity School in Highgate included a marchioness, six countesses, a viscountess, and eight baronesses. The main promoters of the General Hospital at Bath were Ralph Allan, the owner of the Bath stone quarries, Beau Nash and a group of Bath doctors and apothecaries; the scheme was inaugurated in 1723, but the building was not built until 1738-42. Pembroke, Queensberry and Radnor wards in the Salisbury General Infirmary, which was built to the designs of the younger John Wood in 1767-71, preserve the names of the three main benefactors, the Earls of Pembroke and Radnor, and the Duchess of Queensberry.[31]

The founding and maintaining of hospitals was seen as a meritorious expression of benevolence, but, as with the charity schools, there was a practical side to it. Waste of life was a waste of national resources; and hospitals could have the same effect on the morals of the poor as charity schools. The latter view was expressed in a broadsheet for the County Hospital at Winchester, published in 1737. Hospitals could help recover 'the common people' from 'that profligate state of life which is the general complaint of these times'. They removed them out of the way of bad example, 'and it may be reasonably presumed that great numbers will be insensibly reclaimed by the exact regularity of manners which is maintained in

110, 111. (top right) St. Thomas's Hospital and (bottom right) St. George's Hospital, London, painted in 1746 by Samuel Wale and Richard Wilson for the subscription room of the Foundling Hospital.

90

an Hospital, as well as by the frequency of such reflections as are naturally suggested in the House of Mourning.'[32]

Fashions for improvement tended to go in waves as far as the poor were concerned, as well as in other fields. The charity-school vogue was followed by an infirmary vogue, and that in its turn by a vogue for reforming, improving and building of prisons.[33] Schools and hospitals had been built by associations of private individuals. Any attempt by the central government to take over responsibility would have been bitterly resisted, as an undue extension of its powers; the two movements even bypassed the traditional association of relief of the poor with corporations and parishes. The provision and maintenance of prisons, on the other hand, was an accepted responsibility of government. It was county rather than national government which was involved, however; prison building in the 1780s and 1790s was controlled on a county basis by the same local men of property as supported schools and infirmaries, but in their official role as Justices of the Peace. In 1779-82 the central government attempted to set up national male and female penitentiaries in London. Their design was put out to competition, but the scheme, like most of those involving an extension of government powers in the eighteenth century, met with violent opposition and came to nothing.

Prison reform was set off by an outburst of jail fever (as typhus was then called), which killed thousands of prisoners in the 1770s and 1780s. Jail fever in its turn was caused by a great increase in the number of prisoners, leading to intolerable overcrowding of the existing prisons. Various factors contributed to this, including a general rise in population, more sparing use of the death penalty, and the fact that, thanks to the War of Independence, it was no longer possible to transport prisoners to the American plantations.

The crisis that resulted forced county Justices to embark on a massive programme

112. The bust of John Howard over the entry to the gaol at Shrewsbury (Haycock and Telford, 1787-93).
113. The former county jail, Abingdon (J. Wyatville and D. Harris, 1805-11).

of prison building, and led to a matching increase in the county rates. But it was a reforming group within the Justices, and the professionals whom its members consulted, who ran the programme in most counties. Prison building became an expression of the most advanced thinking of the time, both on the medical and the social front. The prisons were planned to eliminate jail fever, and largely succeeded in doing so. But they were also intended, in the most optimistic spirit of the Enlightenment, to reform those imprisoned in them, partly by the regime installed in them, and partly by their architecture.

The leading personalities behind the new prisons were John Howard and William Blackburn. It was Howard who, by his indefatigable tours round the British Isles and Europe, and the publications which grew out of them, drew attention to the appalling state of many English prisons, and laid down the principles on which new prisons should be built. William Blackburn turned his ideas into buildings. He had won the abortive competition for a Male Penitentiary in 1782, and became Howard's friend and disciple. Between about 1785 and his early death in 1789 he designed fifteen prisons in England and Wales, and one in Ireland, and was consulted over the design of at least three more. He died on his way to provide designs for a new jail in Glasgow.[34]

The architecture of charity schools is in the same vein as that of almshouses: modest, intimate, and often enlivened by charming statues of a boy or girl, or both, in their distinctive dress. The architecture of infirmaries was inspired by that of country houses; the resulting buildings were dignified, unpretentious, usually with a central pediment, sometimes with an applied order, sometimes with pavilion-like wings. Outside London they were relatively small, with the exception of the great Royal Naval Hospital at Stonehouse, outside Plymouth, which was a government building. But many of the new prisons were extremely large, and as a group they were unlike any buildings which had previously been seen in England.

Separation, security and ventilation were the slogans under which they were built. Separation and ventilation were adopted to get rid of the dangers of contagion and miasma, by which disease was thought to spread. The prisons were divided into separate blocks, and, in place of the communal wards of old-style prisons, each block was divided into cells. Often the blocks were raised on arcades, so that air could circulate underneath as well as around them. Confinement in cells was intended to have a moral effect. Shut up on his own in his cell, except for regular visits from the chaplain, and outings to the chapel (where prisoners sat in boxes, screened off from each other), the prisoner could contemplate his evil-doings and be brought to a condition where he was ripe for repentance and reform.

So there arose, on the outskirts of towns all over England, these worlds within worlds, often far and away the largest buildings

114. Entrance and rear elevations of Chester Castle, by Thomas Harrison (1788).

in the towns where they were erected, isolated from everyday life by their high walls, behind which rose distinctive blocks of cells, with their lines of small windows, sometimes arranged on a grid, sometimes in a star-shaped pattern around the chapel or governor's house (Pl. 68, 121). What ornament there was was normally confined to the entrance gate, unless the prison was combined with a court-house, as at Chester, and one or two other places. Chester Castle was designed by Thomas Harrison, not Blackburn, although the latter was consulted. Blackburn was a competent neo-classical designer, but Harrison was one of the most gifted architects of his generation. The architecture of Chester Castle (Pls. 69, 70, 114) symbolized to perfection the reforming spirit behind it: the cool splendour of the entrance front and the stone-domed court to which it led, redolent of the dignity, majesty and impartiality of justice; and down below, on a lower level owing to the fall of the ground, radiating blocks of cells, carved out of heavily rusticated stone, ventilated through great iron grilles, and each in view of the governor, in his house at the centre of the web.

The prison at Chester Castle was demolished to make way for county offices, and only one row of cells survives. Most prisons of this date have either been demolished, or much altered and added to. Perhaps the least altered remaining example (and much the most accessible) is a relatively small one, the former county jail at Abingdon (Pl. 113). It was built in 1805-11, with some contribution from Jeffrey Wyatville, but probably for the most part to the designs of Daniel Harris, who had been clerk of the works for Blackburn's

115. The Central Market, Newcastle-upon-Tyne (John Dobson, 1835-6).
116. (top right) The West India Docks, Port of London, from a contemporary aquatint.
117. (bottom right) The Royal William Victualling Yard, Stonehouse, Plymouth (John Rennie junior, 1828-32).

prison at Oxford, and later served as the governor there. The Abingdon building owes its survival to the fact that it ceased being a jail as early as 1868, and for years was a corn warehouse, before being adapted, ironically as a recreation centre, in recent years.[35]

Prison-building provided the first opportunity in England for creating the kind of heroic geometry which was a feature of neo-classical design on the Continent, and was only applicable to large building complexes. Hospitals, with the exception of the London hospitals and the Naval Hospital at Stonehouse, had not been large or complex. The architecture of the London hospitals was in the baroque tradition; only Stonehouse, which consisted of 15 separate pavilions linked by a colonnade, had something of the neo-classical sense of endless repetition, besides being medically advanced for its date. In the decades around 1800 further examples of heroic geometry were built: more prisons, and also docks, asylums, bridges and covered markets. In London, the West India Docks of 1800-2, Alexander's London Docks of 1801-5, the East India Docks of 1804-8, and Hardwick and Telford's St. Katherine's Docks of 1825-8, were all very large complexes, in which huge warehouses laid out on a rectangular grid around the water provided endless vistas of austere but splendid brick façades (Pl. 116). Telford's Gloucester Docks, built for the Gloucester Berkeley Canal Company in 1826, were not quite so large, but their tall stone warehouses, spread out like pavilions along the quaysides, are still impressive enough. Foulston's County Lunatic Asylum at Bodmin (1818) used the radiating plan evolved for prisons in a hospital context (Pl. 121). Foster's St. John's Market in Liverpool, Fowler's Hungerford and Covent Garden Markets in London, and Dobson's Central Market in Newcastle (Pl. 115) were on a far larger scale than previous markets.

The tradition carried on further into the nineteenth century, in the nobly simple architecture and vast scale of the younger Rennie's Royal William Victualling Yard (Pl. 117) at Stonehouse (1828-32), in the geometric layouts (but seldom the architecture) of the workhouses of the 1830s and 1840s, and above all in Jesse Hartley's Albert Docks at Liverpool (1841-7), the last and proudest product of this particular line, and still, by some miracle, surviving (Pl. 118).

One of the earliest and most impressive examples of this type of architecture was Soane's unsuccessful design for a Male Penitentiary, entered for the competition of 1782. A bird's-eye view brilliantly puts over its obsessive geometry and formidable scale (Pl. 119). The prison was to be built on the edge of London, in Wandsworth Fields, but in his drawing Soane has transported it to a setting of woods and mountains. In doing so he shows his kinship with continental neo-classicism. The more progressive European architects of the time delighted in projects for vast public buildings, of overpowering formality, often laid out on a geometric plan, but set in untouched natural surroundings, preferably mountainous. They wanted to combine and contrast the works of man and nature at their most heroic.

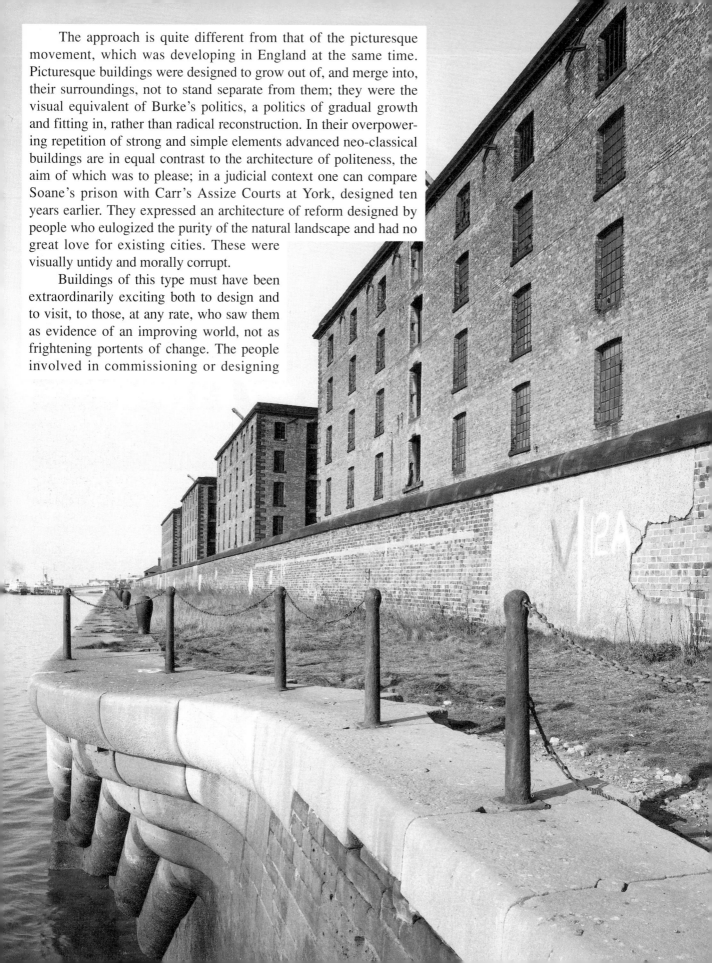

The approach is quite different from that of the picturesque movement, which was developing in England at the same time. Picturesque buildings were designed to grow out of, and merge into, their surroundings, not to stand separate from them; they were the visual equivalent of Burke's politics, a politics of gradual growth and fitting in, rather than radical reconstruction. In their overpowering repetition of strong and simple elements advanced neo-classical buildings are in equal contrast to the architecture of politeness, the aim of which was to please; in a judicial context one can compare Soane's prison with Carr's Assize Courts at York, designed ten years earlier. They expressed an architecture of reform designed by people who eulogized the purity of the natural landscape and had no great love for existing cities. These were visually untidy and morally corrupt.

Buildings of this type must have been extraordinarily exciting both to design and to visit, to those, at any rate, who saw them as evidence of an improving world, not as frightening portents of change. The people involved in commissioning or designing

118. (left) Heroic geometry realized. Albert Docks, Liverpool (Jesse Hartley, 1841-7).
119, 120. Heroic geometry unrealized. Projects by Soane for a Male Penitentiary, 1782, and by Telford for a single-span London Bridge, embankments and warehouses, 1800-2.

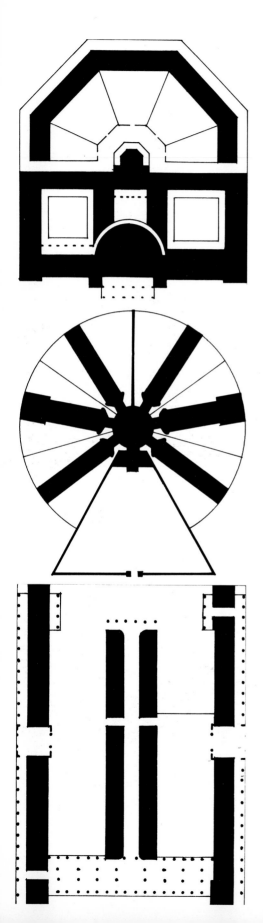

them tended to have advanced views, in architecture, science, art, philosophy, and often (though by no means invariably) in politics. In religion they were often Unitarians, that is to say, members of the intellectually most radical of the Christian sects, which was prepared to jettison the mystery of the Trinity in its pursuit of rational religion. Many were educated at the famous Unitarian academy at Warrington, or the Universities of Glasgow and Edinburgh, which were notably more progressive than the English ones. Many belonged to, or founded, literary and philosophical societies in their native towns.

In general, in traversing the world of improvement and enlightenment, one keeps meeting similar patterns and overlapping groups. On the whole they are middle-class groups, although they include upper-class members, such as the Earl of Shelburne, disciple of Adam Smith and friend of Priestley and Bentham, or his one-time colleague in government, the radical Duke of Richmond.

The leaders in prison reform repay examination. John Howard was a Nonconformist merchant from London, and a frequenter of the Warrington Academy. William Blackburn was probably a Unitarian; certainly one of the few buildings designed by him other than prisons was the Unitarian chapel in Bristol. In Gloucestershire a comprehensive programme of new prisons, all to Blackburn's designs, was pushed through by Sir George Onesiphoros Paul, whose family textile mill was one of the most advanced in England.[36] The new Sussex prisons were due to the Duke of Richmond. Prison reform in Lancashire, and the new jails in Preston and Salford (both designed by Blackburn) and at Lancaster Castle (by Thomas Harrison), were mainly due to Thomas Butterworth Bayley, son of a Manchester merchant, trustee of the Cross Street Unitarian Chapel there, graduate of Edinburgh University, member of the Society of Supporters of the Bill of Rights, founder of the Manchester Literary and Philosophical Society, admirer of Adam Smith and agricultural improver.[37]

The new jail in Shrewsbury was mainly designed by the county surveyor, Thomas Telford. Telford was a Scottish protégé of William Pulteney, born William Johnstone, a younger son, who had been educated at Glasgow University and was a friend of David Hume and Adam Smith. He took the name of Pulteney on marrying the heiress of that family. Pulteney was MP for Shrewsbury, owned great estates in Shropshire, and had Telford fit him up an elegant bachelor apartment in Shrewsbury Castle (which today serves as the Mayor's Parlour). John Howard contributed suggestions to the design of the jail, and his bust was placed over its main entrance, where it still remains (Pl. 112). Telford was also involved with the Shrewsbury Improvement Commission and abortive proposals for widening and half-rebuilding the town's High Street.[38] Pulteney owned property in Bath, and commissioned Adam to design Pulteney Bridge, and a grandiose scheme for radiating avenues of houses leading away from it. These were never built; instead,

Thomas Baldwin designed the long avenue of Great Pulteney Street, closed by the Sydney Hotel, one of the few great formal vistas in an English town.

The moving spirits behind the London Docks were William Young, a Unitarian educated at Warrington Academy, who wrote tirelessly in favour of the project, in opposition to vested interests in the City, and Edward Foster, a City merchant whose family had been friends of Locke and who brought up his children on the principles of Rousseau. The architect of the Docks' superb warehouses was Daniel Asher Alexander, friend of Flaxman and Chantrey, designer of Dartmoor and other prisons, and of lighthouses all round the English coast.[39]

Finally, it is worth having a look at the Lunar Society, the informal gathering of scientists, doctors, inventors and manufacturers living in Birmingham, Lichfield and Derby, which formed itself into a society in about 1775, and was the prototype of many literary and philosophical societies founded over the next fifty or sixty years.[40] Its fourteen members included Matthew Boulton, James Watt, Erasmus Darwin, Josiah Wedgwood, and Joseph Priestley. Although its discussions were mainly scientific, its members appear in many improving or polite contexts. Boulton and Wedgwood were enlightened manufacturers who combined use of the latest technology (including Boulton's steam engines) with patronage of architects and artists such as Adam and Flaxman. Members of the group were prominent on the improvement trust which constructed the Grand Trunk Canal, the committee which established the General Hospital in Birmingham, and the Birmingham Improvement Commission. Dr William Small, one of the Society's most active members, was largely responsible for the building of combined Theatre and Assembly Rooms in Birmingham in 1774; Erasmus Darwin founded the Derby Literary and Philosophical Society in 1783.

To begin with, members of the group had advanced political views, but the French Revolution split them in two. Towards the end of the century the ideal of a consensus of polite enlightened men of property was coming under strain. It was an ideal that had been widely accepted, even if less often realized. But Toland's view that 'we are not so fond of any set of notions, as to think them more important than the peace of society' was growing less palatable. The free interaction of ideas had produced reformers who found polite society's distaste for extremes inhibiting rather than liberating, and wanted to push their ideas for reform further than most men of property would accept.

In 1774 a plate was attached to the foundation stone of the new Assembly Room in Newcastle, bearing the following inscription:

In an Age
When the Polite Arts
By general Encouragement and Emulation

121. (left) Heroic geometry realized. 1. Chester Castle (Thomas Harrison, 1788). 2. The County Lunatic Asylum, Bodmin (John Foulston, 1818). 3. Covent Garden Market, London (Charles Fowler, 1828-30). 122. Neo-classical purity. The Nelson Column, Yarmouth (William Wilkins, 1817-20).

Have advanced to a State of Perfection
Unknown in any former Period:
The first Stone of this Edifice,
Dedicated to the most elegant Recreation
Was laid by William Lowes, Esq.

It was immediately satirized in a much longer inscription, published by James Murray in his *Freemen's Magazine*. This read in part as follows:

In an Age
When the tide of corruption,
By Royal encouragement, deluged the land;
... When a stagnation
Of trade, and the high price of provisions
Had reduced the poor to the greatest extremity;
... To their everlasting disgrace, the gentlemen of Newcastle
Continued to waste their time
And spend their substance
In celebrating the rites of Venus, and the ceremonies of Bacchus.
Five thousand
Pounds were raised by subscription
Through a vicious emulation to excel in politeness.[41]

Murray was a Nonconformist clergyman in Newcastle, and a bitter critic of the Church of England. He believed 'that no man could be a real Christian, who was not a warm and zealous friend to civil and religious liberty'. He had supported the Newcastle freemen in their fight to stop the corporation enclosing the common land of the Town Moor. He stood, in fact, for reform in religion, politics, and local government, three issues which had been blocked by vested interests.[42] Other interests blocked such different issues, all supported by the enlightened, as the abolition of slavery, the freeing of trade, and the building of a proper system of docks for London. For a time, in the prosperous and optimistic 1780s, it seemed as though obstacles were beginning to crumble. But the French Revolution produced a violent reaction among the greater part of the upper and middle classes, and in the ensuing wars advanced ideas of reform were ruthlessly repressed in the name of national security. When reformers re-emerged as a power to be reckoned with after the wars, they were more aggressive, and also more powerful; they were able to set in train a more radical restructuring of society which finally overturned the settlement of 1688.

123. (right) View of Broad Street, Ludlow, by Samuel Scott, *c*.1765.

6

Houses

And

People

'There is no more beautiful street in England.' This was Christopher Hussey's reaction to Broad Street, Ludlow, as expressed in *Country Life* in 1946.[1] Over the centuries the street has been admired, described and illustrated, never better than in a painting by Samuel Scott (Pl. 123), who lived in the street between 1760 and 1768. The picture captures to perfection its spaciousness, the gentle contrasts in scale and character of the houses which line it, and their felicitous progress up the hill to the portico and cupola of the Butter Cross, and the tower of the parish church on the skyline.

Scott's street is full of people. They are clearly portraits of actual individuals, resident in the street or connected with it. Thanks to the work done by local historians many can be identified; and since most of the houses and buildings shown by Scott still exist, it is possible to stand there today and move back gently 220 years to the street as he painted it, and the people who lived in it.[2]

In the foreground Scott's neighbour, William Toldervy (Pl. 124), stands and leans over the balustrade in front of his house towards their landlord, Martin Dunne of Gatley Park, who has drawn up his horse to talk to him. The houses in which Scott and Toldervy lived, and the raised walk in front of them, with its Chinese-style railing, had been built in or around 1757 by Martin Dunne's father, on the basis of a larger sixteenth-century house. Only one is shown by Scott, for his own house is out of the picture. They were smart little buildings, with pretty, matching door-cases. The Dunnes alternated between letting them and living in them themselves. In the mid-1760s both were let, No. 35 to Scott, No. 36 to Toldervy, a London attorney who had just moved to Ludlow, which was probably his

native town. In 1770 Martin Dunne moved into No. 36, and practised there for the next forty-four years as a doctor.

The adjacent house belonged to another country-house family, the Pooles of Stretton, and was occupied by the Revd Mr Poole, rector of Stretton Grandisand, who is no doubt the man standing with a child in front of it. Like many country rectors of the time, he installed himself comfortably in the nearest town for much or most of the year, and rode out to his parish church for services.[3]

Beyond him John Thomas, the landlord of the Seven Stars, is sitting with his wife outside his inn, talking to a woman holding a baby — possibly a beggar. To sun oneself outside one's front door in this way was a mark of social class: people with pretensions to gentility did not do it. The days of the Seven Stars were in fact numbered. In 1768 it was bought by William Toldervy, who replaced it by a bigger house, and moved into it from No. 36.

Across the road, a gentleman in a cocked hat is leaning out of his window to talk to a lady standing outside her front door in a pretty print dress (Pl. 125). The man is Captain Alexander Stuart, late of the 11th Dragoons. He had served as ADC to General Lord Mark Kerr at Culloden in 1745, and then retired to be governor of Ludlow Castle. The duties were scarcely onerous, for since the Council of the Marches and the office of Lord Warden had been abolished in 1689, the castle had been abandoned, and by the 1760s was already in ruins. Stuart probably owed this comfortable sinecure to the good offices of Lord Mark Kerr, or his own powerful kinsmen, the Dukes of Argyll. He himself owned a small property in Fife, and alternated between it and Ludlow. By the 1760s he was a widower.

The lady next door is either Mrs Price, one of approximately ten widows living in the street, or, more probably, her daughter, Harriet. The latter and her neighbour were good friends, as Scott's painting suggests. When Stuart died in 1782 he left her £100 'as a grateful acknowledgement of her long invaluable friendship, and very kind and friendly attendance on and during my long confinement'.[4]

The much larger house above Mrs Price's modest residence belonged to John Aingell. He was a currier, that is to say he treated the leather used in Ludlow's glove industry. He stands in his doorway, a little old man in fusty brown, who clearly has no pretensions to fashion or gentility. He lived in his big house with his wife and a maid, one of whom is looking out of the window above him.

A much more elegant couple are about to walk past the door of this homespun household. It can be surmised that they are going to visit the widowed Mrs Sprott, who lived in the gatehouse where the town walls crossed Broad Street just below Martin Dunne's two houses. Scott's view of Broad Street was taken from in front of her windows. The gatehouse had been adapted and enlarged to make a comfortable house by her husband, Samuel Sprott. He had owned a small country house and estate at Much Wenlock, but practised as a doctor in Ludlow.

Broad Street residents, as depicted by Scott:
124. (top left)   Mr Toldervy talks to Martin Dunne.
125. (bottom left)   Harriet Price talks to Captain Stuart.
126.   Somerset Davies emerges from his new house.

Up past the the walking couple, another innkeeper, one John Toldervy, is sitting on a stool by his front door, under his inn sign. He was, perhaps, related to William Toldervy, the attorney, but had done less well in the world. His inn was only a small one and, like the Seven Stars, was not to survive for long; it had been rebuilt or re-fronted as a private house by 1768.

Beyond John Toldervy on his stool is a more portentous silhouette (Pl. 126). Big-bellied, frock-coated, cocked-hatted Somerset Davies has emerged from his front door and is about to set sail from his new house, the biggest and best in Broad Street. Every Georgian town had its equivalent to Davies: the town's leading attorney, with a finger in every pie, prominent on the corporation and on dining-out terms at the surrounding country houses. The Davieses had been active in the town since the sixteenth century, mostly as mercers. Somerset Davies served three times as bailiff, Ludlow's equivalent of mayor. For twenty-nine years he enjoyed the profitable office of collector of the Land Tax, as well as doing well as an attorney. In the mid-1760s he gave up his practice, and moved from his house in Old Street to the much grander one in Broad Street. He lived there with his wife, children and five servants. The social ascent of the family climaxed when his son grew up to buy Croft Castle, a few miles out of Ludlow, and to serve briefly as MP for the town.[5]

The Broad Street house features in an account of a visit to Ludlow made by Mrs Lybbe Powys in September 1771. She had been staying with cousins near by, and spent two nights in Ludlow to attend the races and the festivities that went with them. The amusements of her second day included a play in the morning and a ball and assembly in the evening. In between 'all the gentlemen in town' dined together at an inn, probably the Angel, at the top of Broad Street. At the same time 'every lady of any consideration is invited to a Mr Davis's, a gentleman of large fortune in Ludlow, and having been formerly an eminent attorney, of course acquainted with the surrounding families. She is a very clever, agreeable woman, and we had everything in the highest elegance.'[6]

The cross-section revealed by Samuel Scott's picture corresponds reasonably closely to a cross-section of Ludlow society as a whole: doctors, attorneys and clergymen; widows (in large numbers), local gentry and retired professional military or business men; and tradesmen or manufacturers. A number of houses in the town belonged to landed families living in neighbouring country houses. Some of these may have moved into Ludlow for the winter, but the houses were more often rented, or occupied by widows or elder sons, or lived in most of the year by the owner of a modest estate who was increasing his income by practising as a doctor, like Martin Dunne or Samuel Sprott.

Broad Street was in a state of change. In the sixteenth century it had been a street of inns, artificers, and merchants, who made or warehoused their goods in or behind their houses. By the 1760s it was beginning to polarize: shops and large inns at the top, near the market place; private houses and professional people down below. The distinction grew stronger in the course of the century, as the remaining inns in the lower part of the street closed down, and John Aingell and his like moved out or died. By the 1780s Ludlow was roughly divided into a polite end to the south of the market place, made up of most of Broad Street and its neighbours Mill Street and Dinham, and a commercial end, where Corve Street ran north from the market area through the substantial houses of rich glovers and curriers down to the tan-yards along the river Corve.

The change was a product of Ludlow's history. In the sixteenth and early seventeenth centuries it was thriving and important, for two reasons. Since the Middle Ages it had been a busy commercial town, mainly engaged in the cloth industry but with profitable sidelines, such as the making of arrows and gloves. The wealth derived from trade had lined the streets with substantial half-timbered houses, and paid for schools, almshouses, and the noble parish church. Then, in 1536, the Lord President of the Marches and his Council had been set up in the castle. Ludlow became, in effect, the capital of Wales and the Welsh border. Local landowners sitting on the Council or working for it, and attorneys getting their living from its courts, acquired or built houses in the town, visitors were continually coming in and out, and the inns and shopkeepers flourished.

The Council of the Marches was abolished in 1689. At much the same time the textile industry collapsed, put out of business by more enterprising or better-positioned textile centres in other parts of the country. By the 1720s Daniel Defoe found Ludlow in decay.[7] It recovered for two reasons. Glove-making developed into the town's main industry, and to some extent took the place of cloth; and the town became the place of residence for the kind of polite society shown in Scott's picture. Of the two the latter was the more important. Ludlow had opted for gentility.

As early as 1732 Macky reported: 'I saw abundance of pretty ladies here, and well dressed, who came from the adjacent counties, for the conveniency and cheapness of boarding; provisions of all sorts are extremely plentiful and cheap here, and very good company'.[8] By 1784 John Byng thought Ludlow 'one of the best towns for a genteel family of small fortune to retire to I have ever seen, for it is cheap, well built, and clean, surrounded by a charming country, and river; and affords a theatre, public walks, an assembly once a fortnight, and annual races.'[9]

Politically and socially early Georgian Ludlow was dominated by the Herberts, Earls of Powis. They lived at Oakley Park, a few miles outside Ludlow, and until 1771 had no town house there. But by sedulously courting the corporation, which ran the parliamentary elections, and by organizing the 'out-voters', freemen of the town who lived outside it but had the right to vote, the family made Ludlow into a Herbert borough. Then, in 1770, Oakley Park was sold to

the great Lord Clive. An amicable arrangement was entered into, and ultimately cemented by marriage. Lord Powis nominated one member of Parliament for the borough, and Lord Clive the other. To maintain their presence the Powises rented a house in the town, spending a few weeks there every year. At first they took a house in Broad Street, but in 1780 moved to Dinham House, the biggest in Ludlow. It had been the house of Richard Knight, a rich ironmaster who owned a good deal of property in the surrounding countryside but continued to make Dinham House his main residence.[10]

In 1761 the Earl of Powis presented the church with a Snetzler organ. In 1771 the family took the ruins of Ludlow Castle on lease from the Crown, planted walks of trees around it, and maintained it as an amenity for the town.[11] Whenever Lord or Lady Powis came to Ludlow peals of church bells announced their arrival. Herberts, and later Clives, were elected in increasing numbers onto the corporation, and brought in their friends and supporters, until, by the 1780s, only a handful of tradesmen were left on it. The election of a new bailiff every October was celebrated by a dinner and ball, which ranked with the festivities of Race Week as one of the climaxes of Ludlow's social year:

> The Corporation, both wealthy and great,
> Invite all their friends to their annual treat
> Nice jellies are put upon each glass stand,
> With puddings and pies on every hand
> Numberless bottles of good wine are there,
> a sumptuous and delicious fare ...
> Others go home to prepare for a ball,
> where the respectable families all,
> With Lords and Ladies far and near,
> Honour the Bailiffs in every year.

So wrote Joseph Bullock in his poem *The Beauties of Ludlow,* published in 1818; he was a Ludlow weaver, who is also thought to have played in the band at the Bailiff's Ball.[12]

Georgian Ludlow was reasonably prosperous, but never prosperous enough to expand more than marginally beyond its old boundaries. Much of the town was remodelled, but on the basis of its medieval framework. Although on plot after plot half-timbered façades gave way to new brick ones, the change was often superficial, and the original timber frame survived behind the new front. Some of the new building was the work of two interesting architects, William Baker and Thomas Farnolls Pritchard. Baker designed the Butter Cross, at the top of Broad Street, in 1743-7; No. 52 Broad Street in 1746, and possibly also No. 18 Broad Street in 1738. Both houses were for the Salwey family who had a country house at The Moor, a little outside the town. Baker was a small landowner living near Audlem in Cheshire, who practised both as an architect and a surveyor and was widely employed in Shropshire, Staffordshire, and adjoining counties.[13]

Pritchard was an able builder-architect, who lived in Shrewsbury but did a good deal of work in Ludlow, as well as in country houses all over Shropshire. It was he who designed Somerset Davies's house on Broad Street. Its restrained but handsome Palladianism was typical of his work. But he was also prepared to design in the rococo or rococo Gothic styles. He worked at the Ludlow Guildhall in 1774-6; and it was probably he who provided Gothic trimmings for Dr Sprott's house over the gateway in Broad Street, and a Gothic gazebo (Pl. 127) for the Somerset Davieses to take tea in, in the garden of their new house.[14]

Baker and Pritchard may have been involved elsewhere in the town. On stylistic grounds, however, most of Ludlow's Georgian houses are likely to have been the work of Ludlow craftsmen working from contemporary pattern books and producing safe, sensible façades like hundreds of others all over England. Only once did one of them go over the top. No. 39 Broad Street was occupied in 1753-64 by Thomas Sheward, a mason. Sheward probably designed its façade, which is made up of no less than eight Venetian windows. Alec Clifton-Taylor called this high-spirited solecism 'a prize example of over-egging the pudding'.[15] By 1768, however, an inevitable widow had taken Sheward's place.

A social mix similar to that of Ludlow was to be found in towns all over England. The proportions varied, depending on whether the town was predominantly polite, commercial, or something in between the two. In towns where the commercial element was in decline, or had never been important, the gentry often took over politically as well as socially, as they had done in Ludlow. In Warwick gentlemen began to move into the corporation in the mid-century, and dominated it by about 1780; by 1799 the Earl of Warwick, looking down from his castle, was deploring 'the very narrow and illiberal policy of excluding tradesmen'.[16]

But in thriving commercial cities like Norwich, Hull, Bristol, or Newcastle, or smaller but still prosperous textile towns like Bradford-on-Avon, Frome and Trowbridge in the west, or Wakefield and Leeds in the north, merchants, clothiers and brewers ran the town, and presided over its social as well as its economic and political life. Many of these families had been rich for several generations; they lived in style, built handsome houses (Pl. 128), intermarried with county families, and ultimately joined their number.

William Wilberforce, looking back from his Evangelical old age, described the siren charms of Hull in his youth, dominated by

127. (top left) Somerset Davies's gazebo, Ludlow.
128. (bottom left) The staircase, Maister House, Hull, 1743.

129. The Thorpe Water Frolic, Norwich. Oil painting by Joseph Stannard.

merchant families such as the Sykeses, Wilberforces, Maisters, and Etheringtons. 'It was then as gay a place as could be found out of London. The theatre, balls, great suppers, and card parties were the delight of the principal families in the town.... No pious parent ever laboured more to improve a beloved child with sentiments of piety, than they did to give me a taste for the world and its diversions.' In 1795 Wakefield had seven carriages-and-four and fifteen carriages-and-two. Three of the former and one of the latter belonged to the Unitarian Milnes family, the leading clothiers of the town; each branch lived in a handsome house on the main street, one of which was as grand as any Earl's house in London.[17]

At Norwich, one can take a quick look at the Pattesons and the Harveys. In 1764 John Patteson, a well-to-do wool-stapler, employed the London architect Robert Mylne to build him a coolly elegant house in Surrey Street (Pl. 132), set between its own forecourt and spacious landscaped grounds: 'it cost him so much that he is said to have burned all the bills, so that no one should ever know how extravagant he had been'. Patteson sent his nephew and heir, also named John, to Leipzig, to learn German for the sake of the business, and to Italy, as part of the education of a gentleman. In Italy John the younger met up with the architect John Soane, and travelled with him to see Greek temples in Sicily: on his return he employed Soane to design chimney-pieces for the Surrey Street house, and got him commissions from Norwich corporation, and the Norfolk gentry.[18]

The Harveys had been established in the Norwich textile industry since the seventeenth century. In the eighteenth and early nineteenth centuries they were probably the richest family in the town, and served repeatedly as mayors. At first they lived in big houses in the centre, but towards the end of the eighteenth century they moved out to villages around Norwich, which were becoming the fashionable places of residence for rich Norwich merchants. Thomas Harvey, who moved to Catton, had a collection of paintings, including Dutch landscape paintings, which influenced Crome and other painters of the Norwich school. John Harvey owned a big brick house in St. Giles, Norwich, and Thorpe Lodge, outside it. Besides being active in Norwich politics, industry and banking, in 1821 he instituted the Thorpe Water Frolic (Pl. 129), a river festival based on a gondola which he had bought in Venice.[19]

Many of the finest Georgian town houses were built by commercial families (Pls. 130-5). Handsome clothiers' houses line the streets of the textile towns. The best Georgian house in Chichester, with its forecourt entered by gate piers surmounted by heraldic dodos, was built by Henry Peckham, a wine merchant, in 1712. John Castle, an apothecary, remodelled the Great House in Burford in about 1700, and gave it a castellated parapet and chimney-stacks, as a pun on his name. St. Catherine's Close, on All Saints Green, in Norwich, with its elegant semicircular porch, was built by John Morse, a rich brewer with fox-hunting interests, in about 1783. Stanford House, on Castle Gate, the best Georgian house in Nottingham, was built in 1775 by William Stanford, one of the leading silk merchants and silk throwsters in the town (Pl. 133). In Whitby resident gentry were unimportant; the Cholmleys, Lords of the Manor, had abandoned their big house next to the Abbey by the mid-century, and the town was run by shipowners and shipbuilders. John Yeoman, pioneer of the Whitby whaling industry, and John Addison, shipowner, built houses as handsome as any belonging to country-house families in York (Pl. 131); in the late eighteenth century other shipowners and shipbuilders, and the occasional prosperous sea captain, moved into St. Hilda's Terrace and Bagdale, parallel rows of spacious houses approached through long front gardens on the edge of the town.[20]

Attorneys provided another important element in Georgian towns. Barristers were a comparative rarity outside London; their main function in the provinces was to provide the recorder or deputy recorder who presided over the borough quarter sessions, and the proctors, who ran the ecclesiastical courts. But virtually every town had its attorney, and the larger towns were likely to have half a dozen to a dozen of them. They had featured in provincial towns since at least the sixteenth century, but became more numerous and important in the eighteenth. At the beginning of that century they tended to

be despised as pushing, pretentious and common; by its end they were firmly ensconced as leading members of the professional gentry.[21]

They flourished because their legal skills were needed in a range of new fields, because they adventured into non-legal activities which were later to be taken over by specialists. They had always had an important role drawing up wills, marriage settlements and leases. Town clerks and clerks to the county Justices were inevitably also leading attorneys in the town, and often wielded great influence in local affairs. In addition attorneys got much work from local Acts of Parliament, setting up improvement trusts in the town, turnpike trusts out of them, and authorizing enclosures and the building of bridges and canals. Around ten thousand of these were passed between 1700 and 1845, exclusive of enclosure acts. Local attorneys played an essential part as the link between interested parties in the towns or the surrounding areas and the lawyers in London, who supervised the progress of the bills through Parliament.

Attorneys also provided an important new service for country-house families. In addition to doing legal work for them, as they had always done, they now often ran their properties. Till well on in the seventeenth century, this function had been carried out by a member of the relevant household. Any big landowner employed a group of upper servants, gentry by birth and often related to him, one of whose functions was to run his estates. In the seventeenth century households began to shrink, partly for reasons of economy (owners preferred to spend their money in other ways), partly because gentlemen were no longer prepared to work as servants. Estates were increasingly looked after by attorneys in the local town, rather than by stewards or other upper servants living in the country houses. They filled a gap until the development of a new class of land agents, working for individual landowners, and usually living on or near their estates, but not in their households.

In addition attorneys served country-house families by acting as their election or constituency agents. This function became very important with the increasing power of the House of Commons. Totally corrupt boroughs were comparatively rare: most boroughs needed careful management by the families who had acquired a sufficiently dominant interest to appoint one or both of the members. It was the attorneys who were the managers.

They also filled a gap before the development of country banks. These were a rarity outside London until the late eighteenth century. Attorneys, with their many clients and contacts, were ideally suited to put people with money to lend in touch with those who needed to borrow it. It was a function which they retained into the nineteenth century, but it grew less important with the increase of provincial banks — some of which were started by attorneys as a development of their business.

130-135. Who lived where?
(top) Master baker, Warwick: Job Lea, 1714.
(centre) Shipowner, Whitby: John Yeoman, *c.* 1760.
(bottom) Wool-stapler, Norwich: John Patteson, 1764.

The career of one leading country attorney can be followed in detail, owing to the survival of his papers.[22] He was John Ashby of Shrewsbury, who was born in 1722 and died in 1779. He became an influential figure both in a city context, in Shrewsbury, and in a county context, in Shropshire, Denbighshire and Montgomeryshire. The two spheres interacted, because Ashby owed much of his status in Shrewsbury to his position as attorney to Tory landowning families, especially the Clives at Walcot and Oakley Park, the Earls of Powis at Powis Castle, and the Foresters at Willey Hall. He acted as their parliamentary agent, and carried out the innumerable services needed to keep corporation and electors happy, from laying on dinners and fireworks at election time to improving the racecourse at Shrewsbury and supplying its coffee-house with free newspapers. He bought and sold farms for them, looked after their mining interests, encouraged improved farming methods among their tenants, bought uniforms for their hunt servants, and even went up to London to buy books and underwear for Lady Clive and to sell her diamonds.

In Shrewsbury he was inescapable. Even the turnpike roads by which the town was approached owed their existence to his activity in steering the turnpike acts through Parliament. He was mayor in 1759, and town clerk from 1767 until his death. He was a member of the Shrewsbury Hunt, the most select club in the town, more concerned with giving dinners and balls than hunting. He owned the Lion Inn, the best inn in Shrewsbury, and built out onto the back of it the exquisite assembly room which became the centre of the town's social life. He lived next door to the inn, in a little house remodelled for him by T.F. Pritchard in the Gothic style in 1766 (Pl. 136), and filled with books, Nanking china and mahogany furniture. He had inherited a small manor-house a few miles outside the town at Yockleton, and bought a bigger one at Benthall, a few years before his death, along with six hundred acres.

A few attorneys made great fortunes. Peter Walter, who probably started life as an attorney in Burton-on-Trent, went on to run estates for great people all over England, move to London, make a fortune of £282,000, buy the Earl of Cork's great house at Stalbridge in Dorset, and be pilloried by Pope for his rapacity, sharp practice and avarice.[23] The Lamb family started as attorneys in Southwell, and ended up in the inner circles of the Whig ascendancy. But attorneys more often resembled Ashby; they made small, comfortable fortunes, and acquired modest estates in the neighbourhood of the town where they practised.

Attorneys' houses survive in large numbers in towns all over England. If, in a small town, there is one eighteenth-century house bigger and more stylish than the rest, the odds are that it was built by a local attorney; in larger places there are always a handful of them, and they are amongst the best houses in the town. Stamford, for instance, which was surrounded by rich countryside and large

(top) Silk merchant, Nottingham: William Stanford, 1775.
(centre) Architect, Derby: Joseph Pickford, *c.* 1770.
(bottom) Clergyman, Rochester: cathedral canon, *c.* 1740.

estates, was particularly well stocked with the houses of the attorneys who looked after them: in particular, the Denshires, whose monuments line their chapel in All Saints Church, and who lived at Nos. 2 and 3 Broad Street and No. 3 All Saints Place; the Curtises, who were Lord Gainsborough's attorneys and lived at No. 13 Boar Hill; and the Wyches, who acted for the Earls of Exeter, served for three generations as town clerks and lived at Nos. 5-6 Boar Hill and No. 2 Broad Street. In Burford, the luscious pilastered façade of the Methodist chapel on the High Street was built in about 1720 as a private house by John Jordan, an attorney. In the 1760s, another attorney, Jonathan Midgley, built Norwood House (Pl. 137), the most stylish eighteenth-century house in Beverley. The grand neo-classical Watergate House in Chester was built in 1820 by Henry Potts, the leading attorney in the town and for many years clerk to the county Justices. He had been closely connected with Thomas Harrison in the rebuilding of Chester Castle; Harrison designed his Chester house and his modest country house in Flintshire.[24]

It was common enough for a town family to acquire a secondary house in the country and later, when they no longer needed or wanted to make money in the town, to develop into country gentry, use their town house less and less, and ultimately sell it. A case in point is that of the Gisbornes. They were one of the richest families in Derby, where they had established their fortunes in the seventeenth century, apparently as tanners. In 1767 John Gisborne

built the grandest provincial town house in England, St. Helen's House in King Street (Pl. 138). He had no known links with trade, but was powerful in Derby through looking after the political interests of the Cavendish family. In addition to his town house, he acquired a modest country retreat called Yoxall Lodge, in Needwood Forest. His son was the Revd Thomas Gisborne, a bookish friend of William Wilberforce. Yoxall Lodge, as Shaw Stebbing put it in his history of Staffordshire, was 'well suited to the placid and studious mind of its present ingenious and worthy owner ... who has enlarged and greatly improved the house, making it his principal residence, in preference to the superb mansion erected by his father in Derby'. Gisborne sold the 'superb mansion' to William Strutt in 1803.[25]

Widows and spinsters provided another element in polite society. Mrs Gaskell's description of Cranford where 'all the holders of houses above a certain rank are

women'[26] was based on her girlhood experience in Knutsford in the 1820s: it was an exaggeration, but not an absurd one. Such ladies could be the widows or unmarried daughters of country-house owners, merchants or professional people, who had been left with an annuity charged on their husband's or father's estates, rent from town property or a holding in the funds. In the sixteenth century, particularly in the country-house world, widows and spinsters often lived on in their old home, a portion of which was sometimes reserved to them in the marriage settlement. Such extended families remained commonplace on the Continent, but went out of fashion in England. Retirement to cottages or small houses in the country only began to take place in the late eighteenth century. Single ladies preferred to congregate in the towns.

As early as 1695, there were at least twenty-one genteel single ladies living with their own servants in Shrewsbury, as the census taken under the Marriage Duties Act in that year reveals.[27] The choice of town depended on a mixture of income, tastes, and family connections. The richer and more fashionably-inclined ladies tended to gravitate to London or Bath; those with small incomes or strong local connections went to one of the other resort towns, or to towns like Ludlow, with a reputation for good society and cheap living. In about 1709, for instance, Swift's friend Anne Long, the sister of a Wiltshire baronet, left London for King's Lynn 'to live

136. (top left) John Ashby's house and the Lion Hotel, Shrewsbury.
137. (bottom left) Attorney's splendour, Norwood House, Beverley, c.1765-70.
138. St. Helen's House, Derby (Joseph Pickford, 1767).

139. St. Edmund's College, Salisbury, *c.* 1770.
140. (right) Yorke House, Richmond, from a water-colour of *c.* 1770.

cheap, and pay her debts'.[28] Society there, however, turned out not to be all that polite, to judge from an entry in Swift's *Journal to Stella* of 11 December, 1710: 'I had a letter from Mrs Long, that has quite turned my stomach against her; no less than two nasty jests in it with dashes to suppose them. She is corrupted in that country town with vile conversation.'

In 1776 Boswell visited Lichfield in the company of Samuel Johnson, and found it nearly as much dominated by single ladies as Cranford. Mrs Cobb was living with her niece, Mrs Adye, in the Friary. The two daughters of Sir Thomas Aston, of Aston Hall, Elizabeth Aston and her widowed sister Mrs Gastrell, each had 'a house, garden and pleasure ground, prettily situated upon Stowhill' just outside the town. Dr Johnson's stepdaughter, Mrs Lucy Porter, 'was now an old maid, with much simplicity of manner. She had never been in London. Her brother, a captain in the navy, had left her a fortune of ten thousand pounds; about a third of which she had laid out in building a stately house, and making a handsome garden, in an elevated situation in Lichfield.'[29]

What, then, of country-house owners? It is a widely-held belief that many country towns in England owe their Georgian character to the owners of country houses, especially the less well-off ones, whose custom it was to spend the winter in their local town, just as richer owners wintered in London. Although this type of ownership existed, its importance has been much exaggerated. The houses, when investigated, frequently turn out not to have been built or inhabited by country-house families at all. Others were inhabited by widows or children rather than the head of the family. Others were 'town seats', effectively country houses which happened to be in or on the edge of the town, or were owned for political rather than social reasons, or were the main residences of families who had a secondary house in the country.

Some seats of powerful families and centres of great estates, such as Petworth House, Cirencester Park, or Warwick or Alnwick Castles, were on the edge of a town and effectively dominated it. But there were many less obvious examples. A sizeable group occupied the sites of religious houses, which had been granted to lay owners at the time of the Reformation. Such organizations not only occupied large sites, but were likely to own estates outside the town which passed with the buildings to the new owners. Many of these houses of religious origin have disappeared, like the great house on the site of the Blackfriars at the edge of medieval Newcastle,

demolished to make room for Grey Street in the
nineteenth century. But many survive:
St. Edmund's College in Salisbury
(Pl. 139), for instance, on the
site of a medieval college of
the same name, which
became the seat of a
branch of the Wynd-
hams; the Comman-
dery, on the site of
the medieval hospi-
tal of St. Wulstan's
in Worcester, later
the seat of the
Wyldes; Christ-
church Mansion in
Ipswich, on the site
of the Augustinian
priory of the Holy
Trinity, which was acquired at the Dissolution by a
London mer-chant, Paul Withi-
poll, and passed from his descendants
into the Fonnereau family. All these
families owned substantial estates and were
accepted as equals by the county. The Commandery at Worcester
had a deer park running up behind it; Christchurch Mansion at
Ipswich still provides the town with its main public park.[30] But they
were all within a few minutes' walk of the centre of the town. The
concept that a country house ought to be approached by lodge gates
and a long drive through a park only began to become current in the
second half of the eighteenth century, and dominant in the
nineteenth; then, one by one, the owners of houses of this type
acquired country properties and moved off to them.

140. Yorke House, Richmond, from a water-colour of
c. 1770.

Families who controlled, or hoped to control, the parliamentary representation of a borough often found it politic to own a
house in the town. Sometimes this was their main residence, sometimes a secondary one. Sir Charles Hotham, MP for Beverley, had a
country house near the town, and, probably, a town house in London
as well, but also employed Colen Campbell to design him a handsome house in Beverley in 1724.[31] At Bury St. Edmunds the corporation were also the electorate, and the Earl of Bristol's diary shows
how sedulously he wooed them, in order to attach one of its parliamentary seats to his family. In 1736 he built a big house in the centre
of the town, ostensibly for his wife, but probably also for political
reasons. As a house it was scarcely needed, for he lived just outside
Bury, at Ickworth, and had a London town house in St. James's
Square.[32]

115

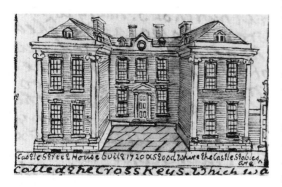

141, 142. Town and country residences of Thomas Ward. Castle House, Warwick, built by him *c.* 1720, and Barford Manor, near Warwick. Both from drawings by his descendant, the Revd. Thornton Ward.

143. (right) Provincial splendour: the staircase of Lord Fairfax's house, York (John Carr, 1765).

At Richmond in Yorkshire, parliamentary votes were tied to the ownership of individual houses, known as burgage houses. Whoever owned the majority of the houses effectively controlled the borough. Up to the 1760s the biggest owners were the Yorkes and the D'Arcys. Neither had an outright majority, and by mutual agreement each family appointed one member. The Yorkes lived in a town seat (Pl. 140), down by the river on the edge of the town; the D'Arcys had a country house at Aske, a few miles outside Richmond, but also owned and occasionally occupied Hill House, a sizeable house in Richmond. In the 1760s the D'Arcys acquired a majority of the burgages, and the arrangement collapsed. The Yorkes lost all political power in the town; in the early nineteenth century they moved off to a country house, and their Richmond house was demolished, although the Gothic tower which they had built on the hill above it to celebrate the battle of Culloden still survives. In 1762 the D'Arcys sold Aske and all their Richmond properties to Sir Laurence Dundas; he lived at Aske, and saw no need to occupy Hill House, which was let over succeeding generations to a variety of tenants.

For examples of town houses with secondary country houses attached to them, one can turn to Warwick. Landor House, in South Street, is a handsome house built in 1692-3 for a doctor, William Johnston. In about 1760 it was acquired by Walter Landor, also a doctor, the father of the poet Walter Savage Landor. Landor owned estates in Staffordshire and Warwickshire, and two country houses. But he never lived properly in these houses, or spent money on them; Warwick, where his work was, remained his principal place of residence. Elsewhere in the town Thomas Ward built a fine house on the site of the present Warwick Castle stables in 1720. He filled it with a 'noble library and number of choice valuable manuscripts and a large cabinet of ancient curios' (Pl. 141). Ward also owned Barford Manor (Pl. 142), a half-timbered house a couple of miles from Warwick, which had been in his family since the eleventh century. But he spent no money on it; the Warwick house was clearly his principal residence. Both Ward and Landor either preferred town life to the life of a country gentleman, or lacked the income to live in fitting style on their country properties: in 1732 Macky remarked that Warwick provided 'a pretty retirement for gentlemen of small means'.[34]

Shrewsbury and York, on the other hand, are examples of provincial towns which had a winter season patronized by country-house owners. Country gentry owning houses in Shrewsbury in the mid-eighteenth century included Sir Baldwyn Leighton of Loton, Sir Richard Corbett of Longnor Hall, Sir Edward Smyth of Acton Burnell, and Jasper More of Linley Hall, in addition to John and Richard Rocke, who lived in a town seat, the Abbey, across the river from the main part of the town, with two hundred acres attached to it. Such families met and mixed with the town gentry to

form Shrewsbury's polite society. One can savour the mixture in the membership of the Shrewsbury Hunt: country-house owners, or their sons, join with the lawyers Charles Bolas and John Ashby, with members of old Shrewsbury wool families, living in the town but no longer engaged in trade, and also with Mr Sandford, the surgeon, and Mr Blakeway, the draper.[35]

In York, if Francis Drake is to be relied on, the corporation deliberately set out to make the city a social alternative to London, and succeeded. And so one finds Lord Fairfax, of Gilling Castle, with a house in Castle Street (Pl. 143); Abstrupus Danby, of Swinton Hall, John Bourchier of Beningborough, and Edmund Garforth of Wiganthorpe Hall, with houses on Micklegate; and Thomas Duncombe, of Duncombe Park, with a house in St. Saviourgate. But as at Shrewsbury, these families meet and mingle at the Assembly Room with a town gentry of clergymen, lawyers, merchants, widows, and rentiers.[36]

But at Shrewsbury, too, it is worth looking at William Harrold, who had a cutler's shop in the Cornmarket, moved from his shop to a house on Swan Hill, which he built in 1740-1, and then, in 1762-6, perhaps after he had retired from trade, built three medium-sized houses on leasehold ground on St. John's Hill, in what had become the most fashionable area of Shrewsbury. He lived in one, and leased the others to a doctor and a clergyman. He was a dissenter, clearly a substantial citizen, but unlikely to have featured in polite society.[37] Houses with a similar background survive in large numbers. Many were built in pairs by successful tradesmen; paired doorcases, a common feature in Georgian houses all over England (Pl. 148), can be a sign of this kind of investment

In Bridgwater different ends of the social range were both catered for by the Duke of Chandos. He bought the manor in 1721, set out to promote the town, and built a street of grand houses lining either side of a new Castle Street (Pl. 149), and a row of artisans' houses in a back street behind it (Pl. 349). At Bridgwater one can also have the rare treat of actually seeing the social range visually. John Chubb, the son of a wine and timber merchant with a house on the quay, was an amateur artist, who in the intervals of dabbling in radical politics, drew charming water-colour portraits of people of all types in the town (Pls. 144-7).

*   *   *

Three main problems have always had to be solved when building a town house: how to fit the required accommodation on the site, what materials to build it of, and how to style it.

When there was a large enough site available, the house could

144-147. Bridgwater people, as depicted by John Chubb in the late eighteenth century: (top left) George Cass, printer and bookbinder; (top right) John 'Pussy' Woodham, barber; (bottom left) Samuel Thomas, schoolmaster; (bottom right) George Beale, merchant.

148. A double doorcase in Scarborough.

149. Looking along Castle Street, Bridgwater.

be free-standing. Unless it was a cottage on the outskirts a free-standing house was almost by definition one of the grander ones in the town, and in plan and appearance resembled those of an equivalent house in the country. But by the fifteenth century most town houses shared at least one party wall with their neighbours. In a house of more than modest size the problem of how to get adequate light to the rooms became a major factor in the design.

A small house on a narrow plot could be I-shaped: one room to the front and one to the back. On a wider plot the 'I' could be placed with the long side to the street; for a larger house, variations on an L-shape became common: two rooms or more on a floor across the street front, and a wing at the back lit from one side. On a still wider plot a proper courtyard could be fitted in, having buildings round three, or very rarely four, sides, and access by an archway on the street.

Until the eighteenth century town houses usually followed the fashions set in the country. In the fifteenth and sixteenth centuries the most prestigious form of country house was built round four sides of a courtyard, with entrance to the great hall from the court. Town houses with pretensions and the available space followed that example as best they could (Pl. 150). In the late sixteenth and early seventeenth centuries a new status symbol developed, probably because security became less of a priority: the compact, outward-looking, often high house with no internal courtyard. In the mid-seventeenth century its plan was standardized in the form of what is called the double-pile house, rectangular, two rooms thick, two or three storeys high under a hipped roof lit with dormers. As a model this was so convenient, cheap to build, easy to heat and handsome to look at that it swept the country.

In the town enclosed courtyards lost all status. The double-pile house, sometimes enlarged by a narrow wing at the back, became the standard type for a person of means. Where space was available it was often set back behind a forecourt (Pl. 151). The resulting arrangement is still often found in English towns, and is always a delight when one finds it: high iron railings, handsome gateposts enclosing wrought-iron gates, and a vista across a paved court to steps rising up to a pedimented doorway between rows of small-paned sash windows.

The conflict between available space and the desire for size produced another refinement: the top-lit staircase. This first appeared in the second half of the seventeenth century. Placing one or more top-lit staircases

150. The medieval courtyard of Stranger's Hall, Norwich.
151. Baroque dignity. The Jacob House, the Close, Salisbury.

between ranges of rooms to front and back enabled more accommodation to be fitted on a plot, without lowering standards of daylighting. It was a device which could equally well be employed in very modest houses and extremely grand ones.

At all times the standard rooms to be found in town houses are much the same as those found at the same period in equivalent houses in the country. In early town houses, large and small, a combination of two storeys of lower rooms and a hall rising the full height of the house was the normal one. The two-storey hall more or less disappeared in the course of the fifteenth century. The commonest arrangement then became a one-storey hall, parlour and kitchen on the ground floor, and chambers on the floor above. The number of rooms per floor could be expanded, and in houses of more pretensions one of the first-floor chambers served, as in comparable country houses, as a 'great chamber'. It was the main reception room, and was used especially for grand formal dinners. Bigger town houses had a withdrawing-room off the great chamber, and sometimes off one of the parlours.[38]

This type of arrangement continued well into the eighteenth century, the only change being that the great chamber became known as the dining-room. It was not until the second half of the eighteenth century that dining-rooms disappeared from the first floor, which was given over to double drawing rooms.[39] The change reflected a change in styles of entertaining in towns. When a seventeenth-century family wanted to make a splash they invited people to a grand dinner. By the end of the eighteenth century the equivalent family would invite considerably more people to a rout or a ball, after dinner. A rout was the descendant of the early eighteenth-century assembly and involved the company playing cards, taking tea or drinking wine in the drawing-rooms; a ball involved cards and dancing in the drawing-rooms, and supper in a downstairs dining-room.

This was for polite society: plainer people lived in downstairs parlours. A typical ground-floor arrangement is shown in plans for houses in Prince Street, Bristol, made in about 1725 by an unidentified architect (Pl. 152). The houses were for merchants. The two smaller ones have front and back parlours, and a 'compter', that is, a counting house, in the back extension; across the 'back court' are a kitchen and warehouse, with access to the quay. The bigger house fills a wider plot and contains three parlours and a bigger hall; but the basic arrangement is the same. The first and second floors would have had bedchambers only.[40]

A similar plan, with the 'compter' replaced by an office, served equally well for an attorney. In the house of a prosperous shop-

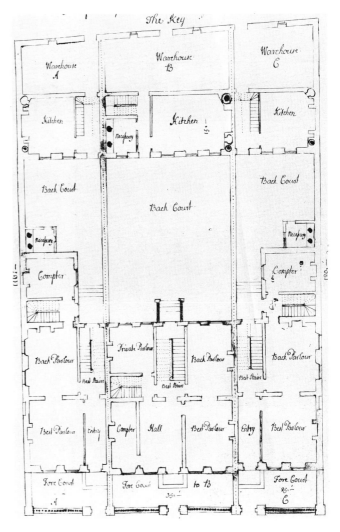

152. Plans for new merchants' houses in Prince Street, Bristol, by an unidentified architect, c.1725.

153. The Elizabethan High House, Stafford.
154. (right) Georgian brick on medieval half-timber. The former Tayleur house in Belmont, Shrewsbury.

keeper, on the other hand, the shop was likely to fill the ground floor, and the living accommodation was on the floor above.

It is in the eighteenth century that one first finds a divergence between town and country fashions. In the country, even in grand houses, reception rooms on the first floor had virtually disappeared by the mid-eighteenth century: families wanted to go straight out from their living rooms into the park or garden. In suburban houses, or country towns where more space was available, there was a similar move of living and reception rooms downstairs. But in fashionable London houses first-floor drawing-rooms become standard, and remained so until the late nineteenth century. The main reason was financial: space in central London was too expensive for any other arrangement to be possible. Instead, the greatest ingenuity was devoted to packing the necessary accommodation into houses five storeys high built on deep narrow sites.

Medieval town houses were seldom more than two storeys high. Pressure on space in the centre produced houses like the four-storey High House in Stafford (Pl. 153), apparently built in 1595. A few early seventeenth-century houses in central Bristol and the City of London were piled up five storeys, with sensational effect when each storey jutted out above the one below it. But these were exceptional; in eighteenth-century London the five-storey house became standard.

One of these storeys was produced by putting the kitchen and servants' hall into a basement. Basement kitchens had appeared at Covent Garden as early as the 1630s, and were a standard arrangement by the late seventeenth century in London. By then the French apartment system was coming into fashion, and it became common to stratify different sections of the family into separate floors above the basement: husband on the ground floor (which was the floor for business), wife on the first floor (which was the floor for entertaining), children on the second floor, and servants in the attic. In 1712 Jonathan Swift described a visit to the Duke of Ormonde's house in St. James's Square in his *Journal to Stella*: 'Today in the morning I visited upwards; first I saw the Duke of Ormond below stairs and gave him joy of his being declared General in Flanders; then I went up one pair of stairs and sate with the Duchess; then I went up another pair of stairs and paid a visit to Lady Betty; and desired her woman to go up to the garret, that I might pass half an hour with her, but she was young and handsome, and would not.'

In Lord and Lady Strafford's house in the same square in 1711 Lady Strafford was using her husband's apartment on the ground floor to economize, while he was abroad. 'I don't intend', she wrote, 'to furnish either the dining room nor drawing room above stairs, which will make the expenses every way more easy, for there must be a great many more candles and sconces to put them in above and on the staircase, which will now all be saved.'[41]

Houses of this type grew less compartmentalized in the course

of the eighteenth century, except in resort towns where they were
well adapted for lodgings. But husbands still tended to have their
dressing-rooms or studies on the ground floor and express their taste
in the dining-room, and wives to have their boudoirs or bedrooms
on the first floor, and express their taste in the drawing-rooms. In
smaller houses two drawing-rooms often filled the first floor and
bedrooms only started on the second floor. What remained for 150
years the standard type of medium-sized terrace house, with communicating L-shaped drawing-rooms wrapped round a staircase lit
from the back, seems first to have been evolved by the elder John
Wood in Queen Square, Bath, in the 1730s.

For bigger houses the ultimate of compressed grandeur was
worked out in and around Grosvenor and St. James's Squares between about 1720 and 1770. Like icebergs (Pl. 155), the resulting
houses sat on a service basement which covered the entire plot and
extended under the pavement in front of the house in the form of
coal-cellars. Above this the front portion of the plot contained three
floors for the family and an attic for servants' bedrooms, wrapped
round a grand staircase and a back stairs, both top-lit. A wing behind this main block looked onto a garden court, built over the basement. At the back of the site stables and laundries connected with
the basement and had access to mews running parallel to the street
or the side of the square.

In country towns where growth was slow, land cheap, and
houses built or remodelled piecemeal on older plots or on the edge
of the town, wide-fronted houses only two or three storeys high
continued to be built. But although the extreme form of 'iceberg'
house never spread outside London, versions of it appeared wherev-
er land was expensive or developed in large units. It was encouraged by convenience, compactness, economy and fashion. It had its
disadvantages, however. Prince Pückler-Muskau, on a visit to
Brighton in 1827, savoured the kind of entertainment for which it
was designed, and was not impressed.

'There are now private balls every evening; and in rooms to
which a respectable German citizen would not venture to invite
twelve people, some hundreds are here packed like negro slaves....
A ball without this crowd would be despised; and a visitor of any
fashion who found the staircase empty, would probably drive away
from the door.... At one o'clock a very 'recherché' cold supper is
served, with 'force champagne'. The supper-room is usually on the
ground floor, and the table of course cannot contain above twenty
persons at a time, so that the company go down.'[42]

Till well into the seventeenth century, the majority of town
houses were timber-framed — or, for the poor, built of mud with a
little stiffening. Even in stone districts, stone-built houses were
usually reserved for the rich. Brick town houses appear in the early
sixteenth century, but they are a comparative rarity until the second
half of the seventeenth century. From then on, timber-framed houses

123

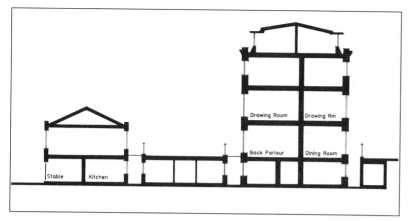

were increasingly replaced by ones of brick or stone, or were encased in whole or part with those materials (Pl. 154); inside the shell of new houses, however, timber partition walls remained standard.

The reason for the change was part fashion, part precaution against fire: following on the Great Fire houses with external timber framing had been banned in the City of London by the Building Act of 1667. They remained legal in Westminster, however, and the many brick terraces that were put up there in the later seventeenth century were probably built as much to follow fashion and continental models as to lessen risks of fire. The Building Acts of 1707 and 1709 extended increasingly vigorous controls over Westminster as well as the City, and a further comprehensive Act in 1774 covered the whole built-up area. External timber framing was prohibited by the Acts of Parliament under which some other towns, such as Warwick, were rebuilt after fires. Elsewhere ground landlords imposed conditions on builders, and fashion, fire precautions and, probably, increasing shortage of timber got rid of external timber framing in provincial towns all over England.[43]

Up till the end of the seventeenth century there was much local variety in town houses. Half-timbered houses in Bristol were noticeably different from half-timbered houses in Shrewsbury or Newcastle, stone houses in Cotswold towns from stone houses in Yorkshire; the elaborately modelled plaster pargetting (Pl. 157) which concealed timber frames in Ipswich, Colchester and other East Anglian towns evoked amazement from foreign visitors. In the course of the eighteenth century one architectural language was established, with such effectiveness that it is virtually impossible, given a photograph of an eighteenth-century town building, to guess what town it is in, unless its materials betray it.

The language spread from London, and to a lesser extent from Bath. Its spread was made possible by various means. Provincial

155.   The 'iceberg' house. Based on 16 Grosvenor Street, London (Thomas Ripley, 1724).

156.   East Anglian pargetting. Sparrowe's House, Ipswich, *c.* 1670.

157, 158. (right) Two stages in the eighteenth-century house; (top) robust Queen Anne, at the Red House, York, *c.* 1701; and (bottom) cool late Palladian, at the Georgian House, Bristol, 1789.

124

artificers worked for a time in London. London-trained artificers settled in the provinces, followed (but very rarely, before the nineteenth century) by London-trained architects. London architects designed buildings in provincial towns or, more commonly, designed country houses near them: in both cases the buildings were likely to be built in whole or part by local men, who learned a new vocabulary in doing so. Changing inflections in the classical language worked their way to the provinces in the same way — but also through the use of pattern books (Pls. 156, 158).

Before the 1720s these had been a rarity, unless imported from the Continent, and often were not up-to-date: sixteenth or early seventeenth-century editions of Serlio were in circulation into the early eighteenth century. The change started with Colen Campbell's publication of his three volumes of *Vitruvius Britannicus* in 1715, 1717 and 1725, and, on a popular level, with William Halfpenny's *Magnum in Parvo, or the Marrow of Architecture*, published in 1722. At least twenty publications by the same author followed over the next forty years.[44]

The system continued into the early nineteenth century: grand folios by leading (or would-be leading) architects, published by subscription and bought by country-house owners, architects, and the more prosperous artificers; and small-size pattern books, published in large numbers by Halfpenny, Batty Langley, Abraham Swan, Robert Morris and others, illustrated by engravings which often derived from the bigger books, and circulating throughout the building industry.

In eighteenth century London the idea of an architectural profession slowly evolved. It was made up of men trained in schools of architecture or by apprenticeship to other architects, earning their income by taking a commission on the cost of executing their designs, and free of any involvement in building speculation or estate development. Little of this

159. Gothic gazebo in a Colchester garden (James Deane, *c.* 1760).
160. (right) The Upper Assembly Rooms, Bath (John Wood junior, 1769-71).
Detail from the aquatint by Thomas Malton, *c.* 1777.

penetrated to the provinces before 1800.

In 1753 Robert Brettingham announced in the *Norwich Mercury* that as 'he is leaving off his business of mason, he intends on the character of an architect in drawing plans and elevations, giving estimates, or putting out work, or measuring up any sort of building, for any gentleman in the county'.[45] He failed to make a living and became a house and estate agent. In the second half of the eighteenth century a few provincial builder-architects took articled pupils who seem to have subsequently practised as architects only; the first professional architect of any standing to settle in the provinces was Thomas Harrison, who had studied with distinction at the Academy of St. Luke at Rome, came to Lancaster in the early 1780s, and spent the rest of his life in Lancaster and Chester.

Some provincial builder-architects did little more than copy from the pattern books; others became competent and even outstanding designers. Francis Smith of Warwick and John Carr of York are the best known, but lesser men produced capable work, like T.F. Pritchard of Shrewsbury, who featured at the beginning of the chapter, or Joseph Pickford, the architect of St. Helen's House in Derby, who was trained in London, settled in Derby in 1760, and built up a large practice (Pls. 134, 138). Pritchard, like Carr, trained up a competent body of craftsmen to work on his buildings: a book of designs for details by him survives, covering houses all over Shropshire and adjacent counties, and giving the names of the craftsmen who executed them.[46] Even a very minor builder architect like James Deane of Colchester owned a sizeable library of architectural books; little remains of him except two pretty garden pavilions (Pl. 159) and his books, which are now in Colchester Public Library.[47]

7

The

Assembly

Rooms

Let us attend an assembly in the Upper Rooms at Bath in the 1770s (Pl. 160). The evening starts at six o'clock, when it is dark, or getting dark, during most of the two Bath seasons, which run from October until early June. The high façades of Bath stone and their rows of pedimented windows come and go in the fitful light of a few oil lanterns bracketed out from the building, and of the flambeaus which escort the arriving company. The men arrive on foot, the women in sedan chairs; few if any come by carriage, for Bath is a pedestrian city. Some arrivals pay an entry fee at the door, but most have taken out a subscription for the season. They hand their coats or cloaks, if they have them, to attendants in the lobby, and pass straight on into the ballroom — except for a few older or staider couples who make for the card room and spend the evening there.

The huge ballroom is a crowded and splendid sight. It is also chilly at first on winter evenings, in spite of fires blazing in four fireplaces, 200 candles coruscating from the crystal tentacles of five double-tiered chandeliers, and another 80 or so winking into mirrors from wall brackets around the room. The rich, but not brilliant, light which this produces lights up the enfilade of columns round the walls, the statues and cameos in the niches between them, and the *trompe-l'oeil* counterparts which echo them from the window blinds across the room. The musicians tune up in the music gallery. Down

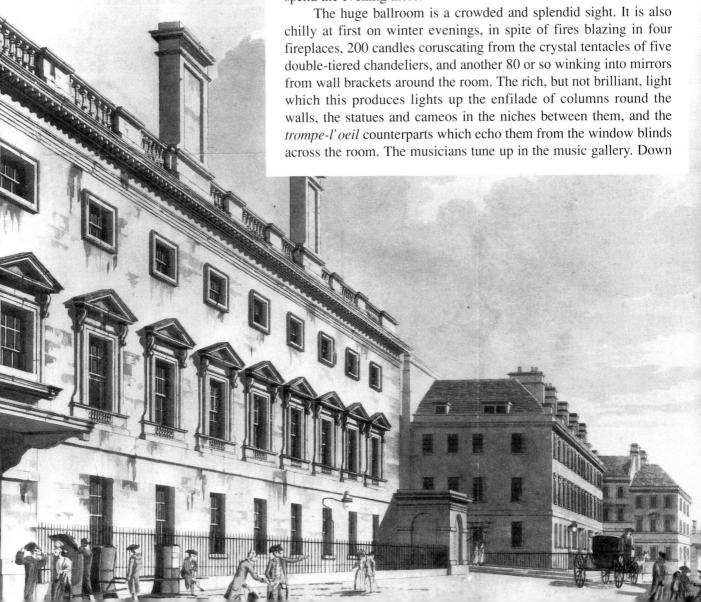

161. Captain William Wade, Master of the Ceremonies in the Upper Rooms, Bath, 1771. From the portrait by Gainsborough.

below the perimeter of the room is banked up with three tiers of benches (Pl. 173). These form a barrier round the room, and soon fill up on a busy evening. An attendance of 500 to 600 is common enough, and numbers can rise to over 800 on special occasions. Late arrivals find, like Mrs Allen and Catherine Morland in *Northanger Abbey,* that they see 'nothing of the dancers but the high feathers of some of the ladies'.[1]

At six o'clock the eleven musicians strike up from their gallery. For two hours minuets only are danced. Each involves a single couple, advancing and retreating like boxers in a boxing match, and watched with as much concentration by the spectators. The dancers are splendidly dressed. Although a certain latitude is allowed to others in the rooms, strict regulations are laid down for those dancing minuets. Ladies have to wear 'a suit of cloths, a full-trimmed sacque, or full-trimmed Italian night-gown, and petticoats, with lappets and dressed hoops', men 'a full-trimmed suit of cloths, or French frock, hair or wig dressed with a bag'.[2]

At eight o'clock minuets give way to country dances. These are danced by pairs arranged in long columns; the successive pairs at the head of the column weave their way down to the bottom, until every pair has performed. F. de la Rochefoucauld, who was in England in 1784 and was in general scornful of English standards of dancing, found country dances especially boring: 'You dance for five minutes and then stand still for half an hour to watch the others dance, and to act as pillars for them'.[3] Faulkland, in Sheridan's *The Rivals*, presented a different view (and Sheridan was an *habitué* of the Bath rooms):

'Country-Dances ... to run the gauntlet thro' a string of amorous palming puppies! — to shew paces like a managed filly! ... If there be but one vicious mind in the set 'twill spread like a contagion — the action of their pulse beats to the lascivious movements of the jig — their quivering, warm-breasted sighs impregnate the very air — the atmosphere becomes electrical to love, and each amorous spark darts thro' every link of the chain.'[4]

During country dances the spectators gossip and peer from the benches, the participants flirt, and there is time to look around the company. It is very mixed. There are duchesses and countesses, ministers and members of Parliament, but also Bath shop attendants, and Bristol manufacturers and tradesmen of all kinds, from tobacconists to sugar-bakers. The wives of the band are there too:

Nay more — there were some this grand ball to adorn
Whose husbands were puffing above at the horn.[5]

The Nash gospel of the open society is still dominant: anyone who wears the right clothes and behaves is let in. Only one exception is made, and that not very effectively: successive Masters of the Ceremonies try to stop subscribers who are not coming from sending their servants in their place.[6]

The Master of the Ceremonies lays down standards of dress, and politely ejects those who do not comply with them. He arranges the order in which those dancing minuets perform, and those dancing country dances line up. He finds a partner for anyone who needs one. He needs knowledge and tact to make up suitable couples and decide who takes precedence over whom. The absurd, grotesque, extravagant and lovable Nash is dead: his successors are smooth and splendid creatures (Pl. 161) but usually, like Nash, in debt and in trouble with women. They are elected by the subscribers, and are not paid a salary: they live off benefit balls, at which all receipts go to them. There are four of these a year, two each in the Lower and Upper Rooms. The receipts for the benefit ball in April 1767 were expected to be about £150.[7] The combined total was considered to make the job a lucrative one, but seldom sufficed for the expensive tastes of those who filled it.

At nine o'clock the dancing stops, the card tables are abandoned, and everyone crowds into the tea-room (Pl. 162). Tea, coffee and light refreshments are served from a counter behind a splendid screen of columns, and brought by waiters to the tables. Then the company returns to the ballroom, where country dances continue. The rooms by now are very hot, the dancers are flushed, excited, and sweating, the dancing gets more boisterous. But at eleven o'clock sharp the evening ends. Nash had disapproved of late hours, for Bath was after all a health resort: his hours are still kept, although in ensuing decades they are to edge a little later. The chairmen, who have been stamping and shivering in the covered arcade to one side of the building, queue up by the entrance. The dancers collect their coats or cloaks, and stream out into the cold night air. Philip Thicknesse, in his *New Prose Bath Guide* of 1777, warned against the dangers of this sudden change of temperature; in 1783 the death at Bath of Horatio Nelson's sister Anne was 'occasioned by coming out of the ball room immediately after dancing'.[8]

The evening described was for a dress ball. There were two of these a week, one in the Upper and one in the Lower Rooms, and two less formal cotillion or fancy balls, at which no minuets were danced. The rooms were also used for subscription concerts, and could be hired for private parties. During the day, they were open for cards, strolling and conversation. The system had been evolved by Nash, during his fifty-odd years as Master of the Ceremonies, and was imitated all over the country.

By the 1770s all but the smallest towns had assembly rooms.[9] They ranged from the assembly rooms at York and Newcastle (Pls. 163, 175), which vied with those at Bath, to plain rooms attached to country inns, where ten or a dozen couples danced, watched by their mothers sitting on a single bench running round the wall. The seasons varied too. Bath's eight months were unique, and evolved gradually from a two-month season in the early summer. Until Brighton started a winter season in the 1820s, all the other resorts had summer

162.   The tea-room in the Upper Rooms, Bath.

163. The ballroom in the Assembly Rooms, Westgate, Newcastle-upon-Tyne (William Newton, 1774-6).

seasons only, usually running from June until September. Bath's Masters of the Ceremonies were thus able to move off to other resorts in the summer, as Nash did to Tunbridge Wells, and increase their income by presiding over other assemblies.

All resorts of any pretension had a professional master of ceremonies. Assemblies elsewhere were run by amateurs. A local gentleman acted as master of ceremonies, if there was one; often there was not. Some assembly rooms had a committee of local ladies, one of whom was selected as Queen or Governess of the Assembly. The normal arrangement was to have a winter season, of varying lengths, and a concentrated week or two of balls in the summer or autumn, to coincide with race or assize week; at Bury St. Edmunds the big week was that of the Bury Fair, in late September or early October. In the winter season balls varied from once a week to once a month, depending on the size of the town; if monthly, they usually took place at full moon, so that families could drive in from their country houses for the evening, and return by the light of the moon. Minuets were seldom, if ever, danced at winter assemblies in country towns. All assemblies tended to start later than in Bath, and go on into the small hours of the morning.

The summer balls were much bigger, more prestigious affairs. At Bury St. Edmunds (Pl. 164), for instance, the winter balls were attended by about 70 to 100 people, whereas up to 400, including all the grand people of the county, came to the balls during the Bury Fair. Grandest of all were balls during race week in York. Dukes, marquesses and earls took lodgings in the town and came thundering in in splendid coaches escorted by running footmen, the lesser aristocracy and gentry moved into their town houses, the orchestra was doubled from five to ten, burgundy, champagne, white wine and claret flowed in the tea-room, and tickets were sold to those who wanted to watch the brilliant sight from the gallery.[10]

For ordinary assemblies, tea, coffee and light refreshments only were provided. Wine, and sometimes supper, were reserved for the big events, which could include election and King's Birthday balls, as well as those already mentioned. Supper at an assembly during race week at Wisbech, in about 1778, was described by Joseph Baretti: 'The men sit all in a row on one side, and the ladies all in a row on the other, so that each has his lady opposite him ... everyone eats and drinks, and deals and laughs and jokes, all with propriety and infinite modesty. He would be esteemed very clownish, who should offend, however slightly, female ears with any improper discourse, even with the lightest of those equivocations so much in use in our rude Venezia.'[11]

During most winter seasons a series of card assemblies were also held, at which there was little or no dancing.[12] The rooms could also be let out for private balls, or used for concerts, lectures or exhibitions; their ballroom was often the only big public room in the town.

The fashion for assemblies started between 1710 and 1720. At first they were meetings for conversation, cards and tea. They could be given as private parties or public ones. Public assemblies were soon expanded to include dancing. In the 1720s, they were still a new craze, as popular and controversial as bicycling in the 1880s, or jazz in the 1920s. Daniel Defoe was suspicious of them. In writing about Winchester, in the 1727 edition of his *Tour of Great Britain*, he commended the number of gentry and rich clergy living there, but went on to talk in darker terms of one result of this: 'As there is such good company, so they are gotten into that new fashion'd way of conversing by Assemblies. I shall do no more than mention them here; they are pleasant and agreeable to the young people, and sometimes fatal to them, of which in its place. Winchester has its share of the mirth; may it escape the ill consequences.' He expanded a little on this elsewhere. The ladies in Dorset 'do not want the help of Assemblies to assist in match-making; or half-pay officers to run away with their daughters'. He discussed the 'assemblees' held during fair week at Bury St. Edmunds, and the insinuations of another writer that 'the daughters of all the gentry of the three counties come hither to be picked up ... a way of speaking I never before heard any author have the assurance to make use of in print.'[13]

Macky, on the other hand, approved of them. 'These assemblies', he wrote in 1721-2, 'are very convenient for young people; for formerly the country ladies were stewed up in their fathers' old mansion houses and seldom saw company, but at an assize, a horse race or a fair. But by means of these assemblies, matches are struck up, and officers of the army have had pretty good success, where

164. The ballroom in the Assembly Rooms, Bury St. Edmunds (Francis Sandys, 1804).

165. (above and right) Assembly people. Details from William Lindley's engraving of the York Assembly Rooms, 1759.

ladies are at their own disposal; as I know several instances, about Winchester, Shrewsbury, Chester, Derby and York.'[14]

Assemblies were one of the main manifestations of polite society, and a means of education in its ways. The 'ladies and gentlemen' of a town were visibly on show at them. They trained young people in the social virtues, and older people too, if they were anxious to acquire them. Lady Mary Wortley Montagu wrote about this in 1756. 'The frequency of assemblies has introduced a new enlarged way of thinking; it is a kind of public education, which I have always thought as necessary for girls as boys.'[15] Boys had the universities and the Grand Tour; but assemblies were important for them too.

In spite of fears that assemblies would lead to intrigues, immorality, or marriage to the wrong sort of young man, they led often enough to marriages of the right sort to become acceptable. At a period when arranged marriages were on the wane, and private parties for members of both sexes relatively rare outside London, they provided a means of bringing suitable couples together.

One can watch an early example of matchmaking in operation at York. In about 1715, Lady Mary Wortley Montagu described how Sir John Vanbrugh was looking for a wife at the York assemblies: 'and for those that don't regard worldly muck, there's extraordinary good choice indeed. I believe last Monday there were two hundred pieces of woman's flesh (fat and lean); but you know Van's taste was always odd; his inclination to ruins has given him a fancy for Mrs Yarborough; he sighs and ogles that it would do your heart good to see him; and she is not a little pleased, in so small a proportion of men among such a number of women, a whole man should fall to her share.'[16] 'Mrs Yarborough' was the daughter of Colonel Yarburgh, of Heslington Hall, just outside York; Vanbrugh married her in January 1719.

The constellations of girls emerging from the schoolroom to look for young men must have given an atmosphere of excitement and anticipation to a good assembly. But they were also means to other kinds of meetings. In 1719, when Lady Bristol was trying to get her son elected MP for Aldeburgh, she wrote to her husband, at the time of the Bury Fair: 'the coming of the High Suffolk gentlemen to Bury happens very lucky upon this occasion, and 'tis the only one that could make me wish you to be at the Assembly'. When Walter Spencer Stanhope was canvassing at Hull in 1784, he was advised to attend the assembly and 'be all things to all the women'. At assemblies, visitors to resorts could get to know each other, new arrivals in a town could meet local society, and local society learn about new arrivals. In 1722 Macky found the York assemblies 'great helps to strangers, for in a week by their means you become acquainted with all the good company, male or female, in the place'. In 1797 Jane Austen's cousin, Eliza de la Feuillade, wrote gloomily from Lowestoft: 'This place still contains a good

132

many families, but as there are no Rooms, there is no opportunity of getting acquainted with them.' The reception of a new face in the rooms at Hull was described in the *Gentleman's Magazine* of December 1734:

No sooner entered in the room
But whispers fly — whence does he come
Who or what is he? Can you guess?
Or what estate does he possess?
Who introduced or brought him here?

Jane Austen created a similar scene when describing Mr Darcy's first appearance in the assembly room at Meryton, and how he 'soon drew the attention of the room by his fine, tall person, handsome features, noble mien — and the report which was in general circulation within five minutes after his entrance of his having ten thousand a year'.[17]

Dedicated though they were to polite society, assembly rooms and their *habitués* were not always polite; and in spite of Nash's catholic approach, some were riddled with snobbery or exclusiveness. When Savile Cust was standing for a parliamentary election at Stamford in 1734, his house was attacked by a rival political mob and thirty of his household and friends were injured; the mob was led by Askew Kirk, dancing-master and manager-cum-proprietor of the assembly rooms, who was described as 'in liquor' at the time. The annual ball given by the town's dancing-masters in the York assembly rooms sometimes got out of hand; in 1754 the alcoves around the walls were damaged by the company jumping in and out of them. At an election ball held in the rooms at Derby in 1780, Sophia Curzon described how all the county were there and 'the men were all quite drunk'. There was clearly a point in confining refreshments at ordinary assemblies to tea.[18]

Samuel Derrick, Master of the Ceremonies at both Bath and Tunbridge Wells, died on 28 March 1769. Two principal candidates lobbied to take his place at Bath. William Brereton, a dashing Irish gambler, had the backing of the Irish and Scots subscribers; Mr Plomer, master of ceremonies in the Bristol rooms, had the Bristol vote. Both candidates claimed to have been elected, and officiated as Master of the Ceremonies on rival evenings. At one of these a Brereton supporter came up to Plomer and pulled him by the nose. A meeting held to resolve matters ended in such disorder that the mayor and town clerk had to be called in to read the Riot Act. In the end, as at a papal conclave, William Wade (Pl. 161) was elected as a compromise.[19]

According to Beau Nash's philosophy, assemblies were open to 'people of every degree, condition and occupation of life, if well-dressed and well behaved'. It did not always work that way. At York in the 1720s, Whig families patronized the Thursday assemblies in

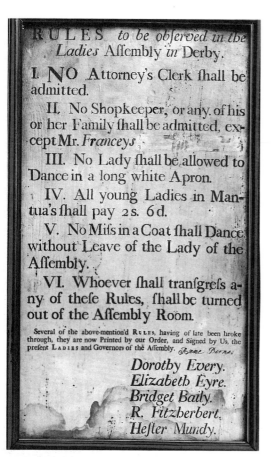

I. NO Attorney's Clerk fhall be admitted.

II. No Shopkeeper, or any of his or her Family fhall be admitted, except Mr. *Franceys*.

III. No Lady fhall be allowed to Dance in a long white Apron.

IV. All young Ladies in Mantua's fhall pay 2 s. 6 d.

V. No Mifs in a Coat fhall Dance without Leave of the Lady of the Affembly.

VI. Whoever fhall tranfgrefs any of thefe Rules, fhall be turned out of the Affembly Room.

Several of the above-mention'd RULES, having of late been broke through, they are now Printed by our Order, and Signed by Us, the prefent LADIES and Governors of the Affembly. *Anne Barnes*

Dorothy Every.
Elizabeth Eyre.
Bridget Baily.
R. Fitzherbert.
Hefter Mundy.

166. Rules for Derby Assembly Rooms, *c.* 1745.
167. (top right) The former Assembly Rooms and Theatre, Truro, 1772.
168. (bottom right) A fancy-dress ball in the County Assembly Rooms, Lincoln, in 1850.

one house, and Tories the Monday assemblies in another. Lord Carlisle set out to get rid of this distinction, and it finally vanished when new rooms were opened in 1732. In general, political exclusiveness is not found in assemblies after this date. Snobbery remained, however. In Derby in the 1740s the rules of the assembly (Pl. 166) specified that 'no attorney's clerk be admitted' and 'no shopkeeper or any of his or her family shall be admitted except Mr. Franceys'. This was Henry Francis, a rich apothecary who entertained lavishly at his big house on the market place. A second assembly was started up, for those who were not admitted to the first. When Mrs Barnes, who ran the more exclusive one, handed over to Lady Ferrers in 1748, she described how 'I told her that trade never mixed with us Ladies'. At Lincoln (Pl. 168) the assembly rooms built at the top of the hill in 1744 were patronized by the county, those built at the bottom of the hill in 1757 by the city. John Byng, staying in the George at Knutsford in 1790, was told of the assemblies there, 'at which the maid bragged that none but gentility were admitted: but *on no account* any tradesmen'.[20]

Standards varied according to the nature of polite society in each town. Resort assemblies were always less exclusive, whether out of policy or because it was harder to establish the background of applicants for tickets.[21] Some provincial towns were more catholic than others. The names of the subscribers for the winter season at York in the 1730s and 1740s are known; they include the families of prosperous apothecaries, innkeepers, stationers, master weavers, mercers, and wine merchants, as well as Philip Mercier, the portrait painter. The snobbery of the Derby ladies was clearly considered ridiculous by at least one county lady, Lady Jane Coke of Longford Hall, not least because it led to ladies having to dance together, for lack of male partners. As at York, the two assemblies were amalgamated into one when big new rooms were built in the 1760s.[22]

In country towns the bread-and-butter of assemblies was provided by the town gentry, the polite society of attorneys, doctors, clergymen, prosperous merchants, and people of private means whose main house was in the town. The local aristocracy came to the summer balls and caused excitement in the ballroom by putting in an occasional appearance in the winter; a sprinkling of lesser country-house families drove in for winter balls or had a house in the town; but it was the town gentry which organized the assemblies, was usually responsible for starting them up in the first place, and provided most of the subscriptions.

The building of assembly rooms could be financed in a number of ways. Some were built as private speculations, most commonly by the owner or landlord of an inn or hotel, either as part of a new building, as at Weymouth and Buxton (Pl. 176), or as an addition to an existing one, as at Shrewsbury (Pl. 177). At Buxton the hotel and its assembly rooms were in the Crescent, and were built along with the rest of the Crescent by the Duke of Devonshire, the ground landlord of the town. They were an element in his campaign to launch Buxton as a Midland rival to Bath.[23] At Birmingham and Truro (Pl. 167) assembly rooms were combined in one building with a theatre. For similar reasons of promotion or amenity, assembly rooms were quite often provided by corporations in one of the town buildings, or by the county in the county or shire hall, as at Chelmsford and Stafford. Such rooms were also used for corporation entertainments, and occasionally as courtrooms. The splendid ball-room in the Town Hall at Newark doubled up for quarter sessions. The even grander room in the Mansion House at Doncaster (Pl. 172), and the adjoining rooms, accommodated winter assemblies and the much bigger assemblies held during Doncaster race week.[24]

An ambitious set of corporation assembly rooms on the first floor of the Town Hall (originally the Exchange) at Liverpool have been destroyed without record by fire and remodelling. At Winchester, the assembly rooms were in St. John's House or Rooms, a medieval hospital handed over to the corporation by Henry VIII and used by it for entertainments and public functions. The corporation did not pay for the conversion, however: the great

room was remodelled from a bequest of £800 left for that purpose by George Bridges, MP for Winchester, and redecorated again in the 1770s at the expense of the then MPs, Henry Penton and Lovell Stanhope.[25]

A number of assembly rooms were paid for by subscribers. Each subscriber took out one or more shares, and became part-owner of the resulting building: in effect, they formed a joint-stock company. Subscriber owners were quite distinct from subscriber users, who paid a seasonal subscription for the right to attend the assemblies. The latter provided the basic income which, in theory, would maintain the rooms and give the subscriber owners a return. In fact the receipts

169. (above)   The Assembly House, Norwich.
170. (below)   Detail from William Hogarth's so-called *The Country Wedding.*

seldom did more than, at most, cover the costs.

One hundred and ninety subscribers paid for the Assembly Rooms in York (1730-32), around 120 for those in Bristol (1754-5), 27 for those in Norwich (1754-5), 39 for those in Derby (1763 *et seq.*), 72 for the Upper Rooms in Bath (1769-71), 128 for those in Newcastle (1773-5), and 12 for the remodelling of those in Bury St. Edmunds (1802-3). At Plymouth a combined hotel, assembly rooms and theatre was built partly by tontine subscription opened in 1810. A tontine was a form of lottery; at Plymouth subscribers were divided into grades, according to age, and each was paid an annuity; as each member of the group died, his annuity was divided among the survivors, until all were dead, when the annuities lapsed. But the building remained the property of the corporation.[26]

The initiative to build assembly rooms by subscription more often came from the town than the county. At York, as Francis Drake put it in 1736, 'The design was first set on foot by a set of public-spirited gentlemen, for the most part resident in the city'. They included Thomas Fothergill, of a York legal and mercantile family, Bacon Morritt, a leading York attorney, and Henry Thompson, a rich wine merchant. At Norwich, it was 'several gentlemen of the city' who, as reported on 1 October 1753, were negotiating to buy land on which 'to build a great fabric both for an Assembly Room and a play-house'. There were seven of them, all but one on the corporation and most of them involved in the city's textile industry. In the end they accomplished 'their merry purpose' by leasing Chapel Field House, an old house where assemblies were already taking place, and rebuilding its centre to provide new assembly rooms only, without a theatre (Pl. 169). To raise extra capital they recruited twenty further 'proprietors', ten from the city and ten from the county; the latter, who included the Earl of Buckinghamshire, the ground landlord,

171.   Lindsey's Rooms, Bath (John Wood senior, 1728).

172.   The original design for the ballroom, Doncaster Mansion House (James Paine, 1745).

173.   The ballroom, Upper Rooms, Bath, as arranged for dancing, *c.* 1842.

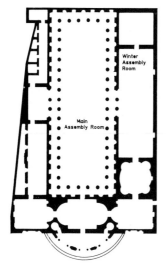

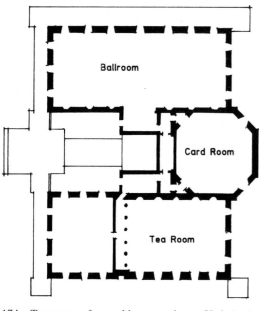

174. Two types of assembly-room plan, at York (top) and the Upper Rooms, Bath (bottom).

were no doubt brought in to give the undertaking the sanction of county approval. At Bath subscribers came from a variety of backgrounds, but the leading spirits were all Bath residents, headed by Benjamin Colborne, a Bath apothecary who lived in the Circus and served for many years as treasurer of the General Hospital. At Newcastle the county subscribed generously (the Percy family provided £900 of the total cost of nearly £6,000), but the impetus to build came from William Lowes, a recently-retired Newcastle attorney.[27]

At first public assemblies were held in any large available room or rooms. Houses which had lost their original use, or were seldom occupied by their fashionable owners, provided one venue. At York the Thursday assembly for Whigs was held in the King's Manor, the former seat of the Council of the North, and the Monday assembly for Tories took place in a big Jacobean house by the Minster, belonging to Lord Irwin. In Norwich they were held in Chapel Fields House, a similarly old and unfashionable house belonging to Sir John Hobart, but occupied by a Mr Catherall, who also let lodgings and gave cookery lessons there. Other early assemblies took place in public buildings, at Hull, for instance, in the grammar school, at Shrewsbury in the Jacobean town hall. A painting by Hogarth (Pl. 170) seems to show an assembly in a Jacobean public building, with the royal arms over its oriel window, and one casement open to show the full moon. The big room in the Guildhall at Boston is still as it was fitted up for assemblies in 1722, with sash windows, a music gallery, and benches round the walls.[28]

Purpose-built assembly rooms inevitably followed. The earliest to survive are the one at Stamford, built in about 1726, and the far grander one at York, built to the design of Lord Burlington in 1728-30. But perhaps the most influential of early purpose-built assembly rooms were Lindsey's Rooms in Bath (Pl. 171). These were named after their first manager: they were built as a private speculation by Humphrey Thayer, a London apothecary, designed by the elder John Wood, and opened in 1728.[29]

Assembly rooms had to satisfy a number of requirements. The basic accommodation was specified in a letter written to Lord Burlington by his building committee in 1730: a ballroom, a cardroom, and a room for refreshments — usually called a tea-room.[30] The ballroom had to have sufficient space for dancers and spectators, accommodation for musicians, good artificial lighting, adequate means of heating for the beginning of the evening and sufficient height and ventilation to prevent too much heat at the end of it. A particular difficulty faced country towns, assembly rooms in which had to cater for the different needs of summer and winter balls. Assembly rooms of all types needed appropriate architecture and decoration. As the foundation-stone inscription of the Newcastle rooms put it, they were 'dedicated to the most elegant recreation'. They needed to suggest both elegance and enjoyment. Few assembly rooms could be expected to go very far along this path, because of lack of money. Only in the more prosperous or fashionable country towns, and the more successful resorts, was there enough donated capital or income from subscriptions with which to finance buildings that could in any way rival the country-house architecture of the day.

A number of assembly rooms were decorated with a single order running from floor to ceiling, of Palladian sobriety at Lincoln, and Adamesque delicacy at Chelmsford and Newark. But in the ballroom at Lindsey's Rooms at Bath, John Wood evolved a more elaborate formula that was to have considerable influence (Pl. 171). It combined the scale and architectural disposition of a great hall with something of the gaiety and glitter of a drawing-room. The orchestra was placed in its traditional position in a first-floor gallery. This provided a scheme for the room. It was divided into two architectural zones — or three, including the cove of the ceiling. The lower zone was embellished with fireplaces, festooned overmantels, and mirrors. The zone above was dominated by a recess for musicians, which was bracketed out over the central entrance in the form of a balcony, and rose up to break into the cove with an arch. Three splendid chandeliers marched down the length of the room.

Many later assembly rooms were similarly divided. The formula was most closely followed by Paine for the Great Room in the Mansion House at Doncaster (Pl. 172), and by the younger Wood for the Upper Rooms at Bath (these, incidentally, killed his father's Lower Rooms, which closed down immediately after the Upper Rooms were opened). Paine varied the proportions, and devised sumptuous decorations, which were only partly realized. The younger Wood increased the scale, and enriched his upper zone with a Corinthian order (Pl. 173). Both rooms were lit by crystal chandeliers. These became an essential status symbol for assembly rooms of all sizes.

At the Upper Rooms at Bath, ballroom, card-room and tea-room were designed in sequence on a half-H plan (Pl. 174); the ballroom was the grandest room, but all three were of the same height and had related schemes of decoration. The assembly rooms at Norwich were built on similar lines, but the three rooms were in enfilade. At York, Lord Burlington adopted a different approach (Pl. 174). He made the ballroom the dominant element. It rises above the rooms to either side and is lit by a clerestory; it resembles the nave of a basilica, with lesser rooms in the equivalent of the aisles. A similar plan was followed at Derby and Newcastle, and in the now demolished rooms at Beverley. At Derby and Newcastle, unlike York, the main rooms were up on the first floor, allowing an impressive ascent by staircase, and a handsome external silhouette.

The big room at York (Pl. 175) was a recreation of an 'Egyptian Hall' as described by Vitruvius. The superb result was not especially practical. The room originally had no music gallery,

and no form of heating. The spectators were placed behind the columns, where they could not get an adequate view of the dancers. In 1751, a row of benches was built inside the columns. As embellished in 1755 these were handsome examples of rococo design (Pl. 107), but made the space for dancing too narrow. A big assembly room needed space for two parallel sets of country dances as well as for spectators. The best width for this seems to have been between 35 and 40 feet; the width between the columns at York is 28 feet. On the other hand the plan dealt very adequately with the problem of winter and summer assemblies. The winter assemblies were held in the lower rooms to one side of the big one, the biggest of these being used for dancing. In race and assize week the great room became the ballroom, and the winter ballroom became the card-room. A similar system may have been adopted at Newcastle.[31]

At assize week in Norwich the double doors between ball-room, card-room and tea-room were opened up, and country dances danced along the length of all three rooms. This is said to have been a splendid sight, but must have interfered with other activities. At Warwick the problem was solved by using two buildings. Winter assemblies took place in the Court-House, using the big room on the first floor there as a ballroom. Race week assemblies used the much larger room in the Shire Hall. The stone floor of its great hall was boarded over to serve as a ballroom, and the two octagonal courts converted into card-rooms, or card-room and tea-room. As a contemporary guidebook put it: 'the pillars are encrusted with wreaths of lamps; and the whole solemn appearance of a court of justice is changed into the brilliant and sportive scene of gaiety and fashion'.[32]

Towards the end of the eighteenth century orchestras began to move down from the gallery, and be placed on a raised platform at one end of the ballroom, as at Newcastle, or a recess to one side of it, as at Bury St. Edmunds. At Newark Town Hall the band probably sat on a raised platform in the apse behind a screen of columns at the end of the great room there — alternating with the bench of Justices who occupied the same position at quarter sessions. There was a similar arrangement (without the Justices) in the same architect's Assembly Room at Buxton.[33]

All these rooms were decorated in the delicate neo-classical style associated with Adam — in contrast to the chaste Palladian of York and Bath, or the Palladian-cum-rococo of Doncaster and Norwich. Adam himself designed assembly rooms at Glasgow in about 1790, and the beautiful interior of the assembly rooms at Derby in 1774. Both have gone, the latter as late as 1963 after damage by fire. The style was particularly fitted to a ballroom, especially one not of enormous size. The rooms at Newark and Buxton are lovely examples, and that at Buxton has been sensitively redecorated and retains its chandeliers (Pl. 176), the crystal drops of which echo the festoon of the plaster work. There is a similar relationship

175. (left) Inside York Assembly Rooms (Lord Burlington, 1731-2).
176. A detail in the Assembly Rooms, Buxton (John Carr, c. 1780-90).

in the assembly room at the Lion Hotel in Shrewsbury (Pl. 177) where the chandeliers are reflected in oval and lyre-shaped mirrors, set in delicate plaster work. The room was added on to the Lion in about 1777, perhaps to the designs of T.F. Pritchard.[34] It survives more or less intact, down to the paintings of dancing muses on the door panels (Pl. 178). The much bigger rooms at Bury St. Edmunds and Newcastle retain their chandeliers, but their decoration is a little thin for their size — though the ballroom at Newcastle is so large that it cannot but be impressive. Bury has the delightful and unusual feature of a double flight of stairs, climbing up from the dance floor to the tea-room and card-room, which were on the floor above.

It is hard to judge of the quality of the elaborate ballroom added on to the Castle Inn at Brighton in about 1776, for only a shadow of it survives (Pl. 179a). It was said at the time to have 'united simplicity with grandeur, and elegance with propriety'. It was one of a suite of rooms designed by John Crunden, the architect of Boodle's Club in London, and was embellished with paintings of the story of Cupid and Psyche,

as well as with other painted decoration and plaster work. In 1822 it was absorbed into Brighton Pavilion and became George IV's Chapel Royal; Cupid and Psyche disappeared, but even so its unecclesiastical appearance was satirized by Pugin in his *Contrasts*. In the 1880s it was demolished and reconstructed, with further simplifications, as St. Stephen's, Montpelier Place. This in its turn became a furniture warehouse.[35]

Oddly enough, only two known paintings from the Georgian period show an assembly ballroom with an assembly in progress: Hogarth's so-called *Country Wedding,* which is possibly of an imaginary scene, and Rowlandson's satirical and highly inaccurate view of the Upper Rooms at Bath, which is designed to make the occasion seem ridiculous rather than 'a splendid sight', as Jane Austen put it in *Northanger Abbey*. Other views show assembly rooms empty, or occupied by a few strollers, or, at best, by the company preparing for the evening, as in Rolinda Sharples's view of the ballroom in the Clifton Assembly Rooms (Pl. 180), painted in 1817-18. The room survives today, fitted with leather sofas and armchairs, as the main room of the Clifton Club.

Although a good many assembly rooms were built during the

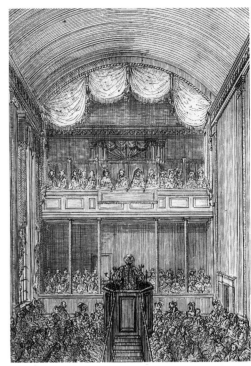

177. (top left) The assembly room at the Lion Hotel, Shrewsbury (probably T.F. Pritchard, 1777).
178. (bottom left) A muse on one of the doors in the Lion.
179a. (above) The assembly room at the Castle Inn, Brighton (John Crunden, *c.* 1776) and 179b (top right) converted as the Chapel Royal.
180. *The Clifton Assembly*, by Rolinda Sharples, 1817-18.

first half of the nineteenth century, few flourished for more than a few decades, and in the second half of the century they were closing down all over England. At Clifton the club took over in 1855; the Norwich Rooms were sold up in 1865; the Bury Rooms became the Athenaeum club in 1853; the Bath Rooms staggered on until 1914.

Their demise was due to a combination of snobbery and changing social habits. Jane Austen's description of the Eliots neglecting the Rooms at Bath 'for the eloquent stupidity of private parties',[36] is as accurate as all her social observations. When assemblies first started up a ball in a private house was a rare event. During the eighteenth century more and more private balls took place, and houses in both town and country were designed or altered accordingly. Assembly rooms had set the example, but their successful indoctrination of the public helped to make them redundant. Every town house of any pretensions now had its big double drawing-room, with balconies for sitting out on and a sweep of stairs down to the supper room. The crush, as Pückler-Muskau complained, could be appalling, but ladies could be sure that the shoulders they rubbed were not those of the 'shop-assistants who they had met across the counter that morning'.[37]

Assembly rooms fought back by becoming more exclusive. In Bath, Nash's doctrine was abandoned in 1816, when the committee running the Upper Rooms resolved that 'no Clerk, hired or otherwise, in this city or neighbourhood — no person concerned in retail trade — no theatrical nor public performer by profession, shall be admitted'. As a result, separate assemblies or balls for Bath trades-people were started up in the Guildhall. The division became a common one: at Abingdon, in January 1833, for instance, a ball in the Council Chamber of the Guildhall (where assemblies had been held since at least the 1770s) was attended by 'the ladies and gentlemen of the vicinity', and in the same week 'the sons and daughters of the respectable tradesmen of this borough, and their country friends, had a ball in the Red Lion Inn'.[38]

The clientele, thus limited, proved in the end inadequate to support the assemblies.[39] Rooms survived, if they did, either by offering extra facilities, such as a billiard room, a newspaper room and a subscription library, or by becoming ordinary public rooms, let out to anyone who wanted to hire them. On 22 April 1881, for instance, the rooms at Stamford were let out for a performance by 'twenty unrivalled lady artistes representing the armour-clad Amazons, from Niblo's Grand Opera House, New York'. The result may have been, as the posters promised, 'a grand, gorgeous, glorious, glittering, gigantic and unique entertainment', but it was not what the rooms had been built for.[40]

181. Two ladies at a Weymouth assembly, 1775.
182. The lion on top of the assembly rooms at the Lion Hotel, Shrewsbury.
183. (right) Detail from *The Mall*, by Thomas Gainsborough, 1783.

8

The

Walks

The parades and promenades of England are not what they used to be. Brighton's three miles of promenade, like sea fronts all over England, has become a bypass for cars, rather than a place for people. The Mall in London, in the intervals of providing a ceremonial route for royalty or visiting heads of state, is little more than a traffic hazard separating the West End from St. James's Park. The North Walk at Barnstaple, once famous throughout the west of England, has vanished beneath a ring road and a railway. Nobody walks on the Grand Parade in Bath. The Broad Walk in Kensington Gardens is crowded enough, but an English face on it is almost as rare as on the Mall in Simla. The English have lost the habit of social walking, once as common in Britain as on the *passeggiatas* or *paseos* of Continental Europe. But in the eighteenth century malls, parades, walks, promenades or esplanades were the outdoor counterpart of assembly rooms, the place where polite society came 'to see and be seen'.

The London Mall was the first in England. It was laid out by Charles II in 1660, under an avenue of trees. It was used for pall mall, a mallet-and-ball game which came to England from Italy, by way of France. The king and his courtiers played there, and other fashionable people came to watch them, or to stroll up and down under the trees. By the early eighteenth century the game had been given up, but fashionable people still came to walk there. In about 1720, the Mall was described as follows: 'Society comes to walk here on fine, warm days, from seven to ten in the evening, and in

184. Promenaders on the Mall, St. James's Park, London, from an engraving after Boitard, 1745.
185. (right) The Grand Parade at Bath, from a drawing of *c*. 1780.

winter from one to three ... the park is so crowded at times that you cannot help touching your neighbour. Some people come to see, some to be seen, and others to seek their fortunes; for many priestesses of Venus are abroad, all on the lookout for adventure.'[1]

A painting of about 1740 shows it jammed with fashionable people, including Frederick, Prince of Wales, and his courtiers. A satirical print of the same period (Pl. 184) shows a 'priestess of Venus', lifting up her skirt to attract a vapid young man. But to Sir Richard Phillips, writing in 1817, when no one promenaded there any more, and looking back nostalgically to the days of his youth, it was all unadulterated glamour. 'My spirits sunk and a tear started into my eyes as I brought to mind those crowds of beauty, rank and fashion which used to be displayed in the centre Mall of this park on Sunday evenings. How often in my youth had I been a delighted spectator of this enchanted and enchanting assemblage! Here used to promenade, for one or two hours after dinner, the whole British world of gaiety, beauty and splendour. Here could be seen, in one moving mass, extending the whole length of the Mall, 5,000 of the most lovely women in this country of female beauty, all splendidly attired and accompanied by as many well-dressed men.' Something of this glamour is put across in Gainsborough's picture of the Mall, painted in 1783 (Pl. 183).[2]

Public walks spread quickly all over England. Outside London they were especially popular in spas and resorts, although by no means confined to them; any place with pretensions to having a polite society almost inevitably also had a place where its members walked together. Tunbridge Wells had, in fact, anticipated the Mall in London. What became known as the Walks, and today are called the Pantiles, were first laid out as early as 1638, in the form of a levelled green bank, and a double row of trees. The company walked here in the intervals of taking the waters, and tradesmen set up stalls of trinkets with which to tempt them. By the 1680s the walks had been paved and the stalls had become a row of permanent shops behind a colonnade. By 1700 a Long Room for dancing, gambling and taking tea had been added to the shops. A lower walk was occupied by a market, where the servants of those promenading above could buy provisions. In about 1760 the company was described as 'quite beautiful and noble, in the daytime moving along the parade, like a walking parterre, and at night, in the room, like a galaxy of stars in a bright nocturnal sky'.[3]

When Celia Fiennes was in Shrewsbury in 1698 she visited a garden off the churchyard of the Abbey (which had been converted as a parish church at the Dissolution). Here were 'several fine grass walks kept exactly cut and rolled for company to walk in; every Wednesday most of the town, the Ladies and Gentlemen, walk there as in St. James's Park and there are abundance of people of quality live in Shrewsbury'. In the eighteenth century these were replaced, as the fashionable venue, by walks in the Quarry. This great open space, between the town walls and the bend of the Severn, had been common land and a place of public resort since the Middle Ages. In 1719 an attorney, Henry Jenks, who was mayor that year, planted a walk of trees along the river, and a linking walk to join it to the town. Henry Jones, in a poem published in 1769, compared the company in the Quarry to that on the London Mall, to the advantage of the former:

> See, Severn, on your banks your daughters move,
> Daughters of virtue, elegance and love;
> Such blended charms the soul can never pall,
> Where all Arcadia mingles with the Mall,
> Where courtly grace with rural vigour joined,
> Reigns o'er the heart, and captivates the mind,
> Where taste, and dress, and attitude, and air,
> With thee, St. James's, may with joy compare.
> Salopian maids (the muse's happy theme)
> Disdain the rich deceit, the poor extreme,
> With native charms their cheeks alone shall glow
> And to *themselves* they all their conquests owe.[4]

The first public walk to be called a parade was in Epsom. A row of trimmed elms and a paved Parade were laid out on the south side of its main street sometime between 1707 and 1711, 'for visitors to exercise on after taking the waters'. A similar New Parade was formed on the opposite side of the street between 1711 and 1718. Previous to this the term had only been applied in a topographical sense, to exercise grounds for soldiers.[5]

Bath followed Epsom with a projected parade in 1729, and an achieved one in 1740. The first formal walk in Bath had been laid out in about 1708, arguably at the instigation of Beau Nash. It was in Orange Grove, by the Abbey. It consisted of a paved walk, 200 feet long and 27 feet broad. Next to this 'three rows of tall sycamore trees lined out two other alleys, parallel to the former, which were spread with gravel, for the use of the common sort of people'.[6]

In 1729 the architect John Wood projected something much more ambitious in Queen Square. This was intended to form an architectural

whole, like the forecourt of a palace. The pavement on one side was planned to be a hundred feet broad, to make 'a grand place of parade before the whole front of our supposed palace'.[7] This parade never materialized, because Wood could not raise the money to extend the site or level the ground. But in 1740 he succeeded, on another site down by the river. Here, between 1740 and 1743, two parades were built, one to the north and one to the south, each backed by a row of houses. The principal of these was the North Parade, soon known as the Grand Parade (Pl. 185). It was on a raised terrace, looking over an existing bowling green to the Assembly Rooms. Unlike the projected Queen Square parade it had a view, across the river to hills and woods. Wood hoped to embellish his terrace with Corinthian columns, but failed to raise the money. But 'notwithstanding this, the Grand Parade still deserves its name; it is the principal place of polite resort in the city, as the paved alley on the south side of Orange Grove was formerly; and the building of this parade, with the country before it, reflects a beauty to each other which has the power of charming and delighting the eye of almost every beholder.'[8] For the next forty years or so, it and the Mall in London were the most renowned promenades in England. Views from a promenade to country, park, or sea, became fashionable in British towns, with a radical effect on their nature.

In the mid-century promenades proliferated. In York the corporation, as part of its campaign to attract the right sort of people to the city, laid out the New Walk (Pl. 186) along the river in 1733-4, and extended and widened it in 1739-40. 'Our friend Mr Etty says that he does not know any public walk in Europe superior, if equal

to it', wrote Robert Davies in 1818. Richard Taprell was equally enthusiastic about the North Walk at Barnstaple, first laid out along the river Taw in 1759, and gradually extended until by 1812 it was two furlongs long. It was, he wrote, 'the famous North Walk, the boast of Barnstaple and her public ornament'.[9]

At Norwich the open space known as Chapel Fields, on the south-west edge of the city, was planted with walks of elms in 1749,

at the expense of Thomas Churchman, a rich master weaver. By 1754 it was reported that 'this place will in a few years most probably be the Mall of Norwich'. In Liverpool the corporation laid out Mount Sion, or St. James's Walk, in the 1760s, on a hilltop overlooking the Mersey, where the Protestant cathedral now stands. In 1785 Leicester corporation laid out the New Walk on the edge of the town, looking over to the hills of Charnwood Forest.[10]

Town walls or churchyards were sometimes used as a place of promenade. Walks were planted as an extension to the churchyard at Ross-on-Wye by John Kyrle (Pope's 'Man of Ross') in about 1696, and in the churchyard of St. Mary-at-the-Walls, Colchester, in 1714; the latter were described in 1748 as 'much resorted to by people of the best fashion'. In Presteigne in 1825 walks in the churchyard (Pl. 188) and on the site of

189, 192. (top and top right) The sea front at Sidmouth, from a panoramic view by Hubert Cornish, published by John Wallis, 1815.
190. (centre left) The Steine, Brighton, 1806.
191. (bottom left) Royal Marine Library, Brighton.
193. (bottom right) The Chain Pier, Brighton. Detail from a gouache of c. 1830.

the castle were 'often paraded by no inconsiderable portion of the gay and fashionable'. A picture in the church shows the gay and fashionable already walking in the churchyard a hundred years or so previously. At King's Lynn walks were planted along part of the line of the demolished medieval walls, probably in the early eighteenth century. At Dorchester the town was surrounded with walks of limes, sycamores and chestnuts, except for a section where the town ran along the river. The corporation planted these along the line of the Roman fortifications in two phases, one in about 1700-12, and the second in 1743-4. The end result was to turn Dorchester, perhaps deliberately, into a copy in miniature of Paris, where boulevards were laid out along the line of the city walls from 1670 onwards.[11]

In the late eighteenth century it became fashionable to promenade along the sea. At Scarborough the mineral springs were on the beach, and people taking the water were already walking or driving up and down the sands by the 1690s (Pl. 187). At Weymouth a seaside parade probably started developing about 1772-3, when what became the Royal Hotel was built to face the sea, perhaps the first building in England to do so for amenity rather than practical reasons. A walk along the sands was supplemented by a surfaced walk in about 1786. The result became known as the Esplanade: technically an esplanade was an open area to allowing a free field of fire around a fortification, and the Weymouth esplanade may have been so called from forts built along the beach in the Civil War, and still in use in the 1780s. It was the ancestor of seaside esplanades all round the world.[12]

At Brighton, the original place of promenade was the Steine (Pl. 190), an open space at the edge of the town, used by fishermen to lay out their nets. Visitors promenaded around it, looking at the company and the fishermen while a band played. The sea was only visible in the distance. The space was gradually surrounded by fashionable houses, including the Prince of Wales's Pavilion, and the fishermen moved elsewhere. By about 1780 visitors were also walking along the cliff between the town and the sea. In the 1790s, a Marine Parade was formed, running east from the Steine above the beach, and houses were gradually built along it. This was extended bit by bit, until by 1840 the sea front of Brighton and its neighbour Hove stretched for two and a half miles of houses and terraces.

A sea-front promenade became a necessary status symbol for a resort of any pretensions. Most started in a modest way. Here, for instance, is the Revd Edward Butcher describing the sea front of Sidmouth in 1805. Along the 'shingly rampart' of the shore: 'a broad commodious walk, which is called the Beach, has been constructed, and furnishes a delightful *promenade*. It is nearly a *third* of a mile in length, is kept well rolled, and furnished at the extremities, and in some other parts, with convenient double seats, from which either the land or the sea may be contemplated with every advantage. Close to the walk, and about the middle of it, is a tolerably spacious covered retreat, called *The Shed*, in which, as it is benched all round, and open only to the sea, a most convenient view of that sublime object may at all times be obtained.' Here (Pls. 189, 192) were to be found large parties busily chatting, and the 'weak invalid' inhaling the healthy breeze. Within a few years the Shed had been remodelled as Wallis's Marine Library.[13]

A library was a common feature of seaside promenades;[14] it was a place of social resort as well as one in which to buy or borrow books, and its owner usually published local guidebooks and sedulously puffed his resort. Wallis, for instance, published guides by Butcher and others, a series of views of Sidmouth, and a roll-out panorama of the sea front. Brighton's equivalent was the Royal Marine Library (Pl. 191), on the Marine Promenade.

From the 1820s piers provided an additional place for promenading. They were not originally intended for this purpose; as their name indicates, they were designed as landing places for ships. Many resorts had no harbour, and the only means of joining the town to deep water was by building out a causeway from the sea front to a jetty. This was the reason for the Chain Pier at Brighton (Pl. 193), the first seaside pier. It was built by a private company in 1822-3. It soon became used as a promenade, and a similar development took place in other resorts. At Cromer in the 1840s, for instance, the fashionable time for promenading on the pier was in the evening, to watch the sun setting into the sea. As a local guidebook put it: 'Servants in livery and all common persons are not allowed at this time ... Smoking is not allowed on the jetty until

152

after nine o'clock in the evening, at which time ladies usually retire from their evening promenade ... On Sunday the jetty is, with just consideration, resigned to the inhabitants of the town.'[15]

What was it all in aid of? Promenades fulfilled many of the functions of assembly rooms, but out of doors. They were places in which polite society exchanged news, developed social or sexual relationships, and established its identity. In the days before radio, television and telephone, a promenade was an important means of dispensing news; if anyone had been away, and wanted to advertise his or her return, the way to do so was to promenade in the right place at the right time. A promenade was also a useful place in which a visitor could be given a quick run-down of local society. John Byng, walking with a Mr M. in the Quarry at Shrewsbury in 1793, describes how 'Mr M. had to bow to everybody, and then to relate their histories to us'.[16]

Celia Fiennes described the company on the Abbey walks in Shrewsbury as consisting of 'most of the town — the ladies and gentlemen'. This is like saying 'everyone was there', meaning 'everyone who mattered'. By showing oneself on a town's walk one affirmed one's status as a lady or gentleman; if one was doubtful about it, one could test it out by seeing who did, or did not, bow to one.

Promenades, like assembly rooms, were a means towards marriage. Mothers showed off their daughters on them. Adventurers picked up rich widows on them. But they were also places for flirtations, intrigues and assignations. 'Priestesses of Venus', if sufficiently well turned-out, were in evidence on the Mall and the resort parades, even if not on the walks of country towns — just as, in the nineteenth century, Skittles and other courtesans rode round the Ring in Hyde Park, along with duchesses and countesses. Such ladies presumably did not acknowledge them, but they did not object to them either. The male half of polite society wanted them there.

Above all, promenades taught the social virtues. Taprell expressed this in execrable blank verse, writing about the North Walk at Barnstaple:

> ... Public Walks, in certain
> Circumstances, productive may be of
> Certain evils. But of all good effects
> Destitute they are not. The
> Civilities of social life by their
> Means facilitated are, and increased.
> Here friends together meet and their friendship
> Pure improve and heighten. Here neighbours their
> Neighbours see, and smile for smile exchange, with
> Words as soft and gentle as the breath of
> MORN — or make more distant bows and pass on.
> But even this an advantage is. For
> Those who meet never, strangers are.[17]

194. A view along the New Walk, Leicester.

195. The entrance to the shops along Montpellier Walk, Cheltenham.
196. (right) Beach and terraces at Weymouth.

A promenade often helped to create a neighbourhood. At Norwich, the planting of walks on Chapel Fields in 1749 was followed by the remodelling of the Assembly House, in 1753, and the building of a theatre in 1757, all in the same small area. At Shrewsbury the planting of the Quarry walks helped to move the most fashionable residential neighbourhood from the east to the west end of the town. At Brighton, the town's most desirable residences were built round the Steine; and when T.R. Kemp sought to develop Kemp Town as a select neighbourhood, the provision of parades was an essential part of his plans. At Leicester the New Walk (Pl. 194), and the terraces and crescents that grew up around it, became the most select area in the town; others came in the course of the nineteenth century, but they followed the thrust to the south-east, inaugurated by the Walk.

At Cheltenham one can watch the development of the polite part of the town around rival walks. Up till the mid-eighteenth century it was a market town almost confined to a long High Street. There were mineral springs in the neighbourhood, however. In 1739 Henry Skillicorne, who owned one to the south of the High Street, planted a walk of trees, known as the Well Walk, leading up to it, and built a Long Room, for cards, tea, and dancing. In 1788 George III visited Cheltenham, promenaded on the Well Walk, and established the town as a fashionable resort. Other springs were developed, each with garden, walk, and pump room. To the east of the Well Walk Henry Thompson developed the Montpellier Promenade, Pump Room and Gardens between 1802 and 1825, and the Harward brothers the Sherborne Spa, walk and gardens in 1818. The Montpellier Gardens specialized in evening promenades. 'There are few scenes more animated and improving', as a guidebook put it, 'than the Montpellier Promenade ... between eight and ten, with the presence of the lovely, the titled and the fashionable, as they parade up and down the grand walk, to the sound of music.'[18]

All these were south of the High Street. In 1825 a Cirencester banker, Joseph Pitt, acquired a mineral spring to the north, and set out to develop the Pittville Spa. He equipped it with an even grander pump room, walk, and garden. The competition from the southern spas was too strong. Pittville was slow to catch on, Pitt overstretched himself and went bankrupt, his architect was convicted of forgery, and sentenced to transportation.[19] The buildings and gardens survive as one of the most agreeable areas of Cheltenham.

All these amenities were originally in open country, but the terraces and crescents of Regency Cheltenham grew up round their walks and gardens without destroying them (the Well Walk was the only casualty). The Sherborne Spa was replaced by the Queen's Hotel, and the walk of trees leading up to it from the High Street became the Promenade, today the main street of Cheltenham. A row of fashionable shops, separated by cast-iron caryatids, was built along one side of the Montpellier Parade (Pl. 195). The end result was today's Cheltenham, proudly, if not altogether accurately, presented in its promotional literature as the 'first garden city'.

9

Terraces,

Squares,

And

Crescents

The idea of a row of dwellings all of the same design was not a new one in eighteenth-century England. Buildings of this nature had been built since the Middle Ages, and were the natural outcome of any situation where one entrepreneur was providing dwellings for a number of people. Almshouses were the most obvious example. The ranges which lined the courtyards of great houses or university colleges, with their rows of doors letting onto staircases, were effectively terraces, even if made up of lodgings rather than individual houses. Another group consisted of official residences, such as the Vicars' Close at Wells (Pl. 198), built in the mid-fifteenth century for the Vicars Choral at the cathedral, and the half-timbered row put up for a similar purpose and at much the same time at Windsor Castle.

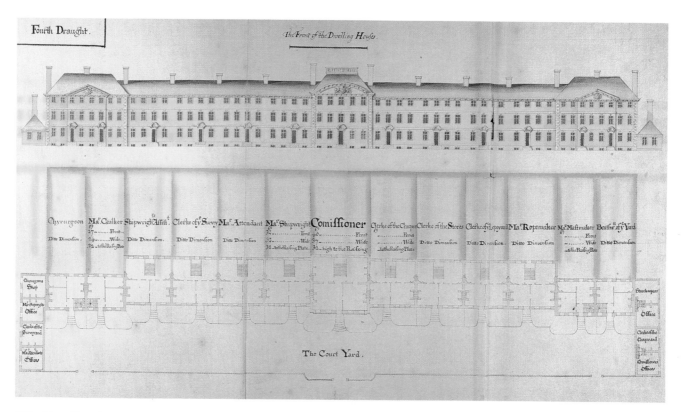

197. The officers' terrace, Plymouth dockyard (attributed to Robert Hooke, c. 1690-1700).
198. (right) The mid-fifteenth-century Vicars' Close, Wells.

Other types of terrace were not all that common, owing to the fragmented nature of property ownership in medieval town centres, and the piecemeal growth of housing outside them; those that were built were likely to be put up on the cheap, for occupation by the poor, and not to have survived. But there are interesting examples still in existence at York, Coventry and Tewkesbury.[1] At York a row of half-timbered houses was built in Goodramgate in the early fourteenth century, alongside the graveyard of Holy Trinity, in order to endow a chantry in the church; in Tewkesbury, a row of half-timbered shops was built along the edge of the Abbey churchyard in about 1450. Churchyards in city centres had a potential for development which was taken up comparatively seldom, perhaps because of the pressure of demand for graves. All these buildings were unpretentious; any architectural elaboration was confined to the hall or chapel which completed the courtyards of almshouses, colleges and private houses. In contrast the town houses of richer people were often detached, and invariably of individual design, even if they were one of a row.

A new situation arose at Covent Garden in the 1630s.[2] The rapid growth of London, an owner with a sizeable plot of land on the edge of the town, and that owner's decision to develop it as a residential area for aristocratic or upper-class families, combined to produce something previously unknown in England — and barely known on the Continent. The owner was the fourth Earl of Bedford, the land that originally occupied by a garden belonging to the Abbey

156

or Convent of St. Peter, Westminster, the result the open square of Covent Garden, the church of St. Paul's looking onto it, the houses built over arcades around it, and four streets of smaller houses leading into it. The resulting symmetry was impressive, even though compromised by the presence of the garden of Lord Bedford's own house on the south side of the square. Inigo Jones was the architect, and his models were the piazza of Livorno, which was in fact a commercial square surrounded by shops, and the Place des Vosges in Paris, a residential square with occupants as prestigious as those who moved into Covent Garden.

The architecture of Covent Garden had little influence in England. The arcades proved inconvenient, except for prostitutes in the eighteenth century, and the treatment of the façades was barely imitated. But, after the Civil War, the idea of the residential square with attendant streets caught on in London, far more so than it ever did in

Paris. St. James's and Bloomsbury Squares were developed from 1662, Golden Square from 1676, Devonshire Square from 1678, Soho Square in about 1680-1, Red Lion Square from 1684. Most of these were developed with attendant streets, and several of them centred round a church or large house, in the manner of Covent Garden. York Street, running north out of St. James's Square, connected it axially with the main entrance (since moved) of Wren's St. James's Church; the north side of Bloomsbury Square was filled by the house of the fifth Earl of Bedford, its ground landlord and developer, the south side of Soho Square by the house of the Duke of Monmouth.

The squares catered for upper-class or substantial middle-class residents. The houses ranged from large ones in St. James's Square, which soon overtook Covent Garden as the most fashionable address in London, to more modest ones in Golden and Red Lion Squares. But the architecture of all of them was unpretentious. The houses were built of red brick with timber trim, in a vernacular classical style which derived from Holland. A similar style was being used for the numerous terraces which were springing up along the new streets of a rapidly expanding London. But the streets seldom had a consistent architectural treatment: they were let out for development in blocks, and the contractor who filled a block usually provided his own design, which was seldom exactly the same as that in the next block. In the squares the architectural treatment, however modest, was usually more of a piece.

To begin with there was no obvious use for the centres of the squares, except to produce a sense of space. Open areas in towns had previously developed in order to accommodate an activity — most commonly a market or, on the Continent, public sports, entertainments and meetings. A market soon appeared along one side of Covent Garden, expanded until it filled the square, and ultimately all but drove out the residential element. The centre of the square was surrounded by wooden rails, to keep out carts and carriages. A similar system was adopted at St. James's and Bloomsbury Squares. The resulting spaces were gravelled, so that the residents could walk up and down on them. In contrast, the centre of Soho Square was filled with a garden, and closed in by railings and gates (to which the inhabitants had the key). A garden in a square seemed an obvious feature, once it had been installed, and was to become an essential element of English residential squares; but it had not been thought of before. The Soho Square garden centred round a statue of Charles II. This use of a royal statue as a feature was to be copied in a number of other squares, in and out of London, during the eighteenth century.

Up till the end of the seventeenth century only London was rich enough, and growing fast enough, to need residential squares. Out of London even terraces were a rarity, and perhaps only built in the form of official residences, such as the rows of clergy houses in the Close at Rochester, or the row of officers' houses built in the 1690s in the dockyard at Plymouth (Pl. 197). The latter (probably designed by Robert Hooke) had more architectural pretensions than the buildings in any square or terrace in London. It was articulated with pavilions, in the manner of Hooke's Bethlehem Hospital.The central and grandest pavilion was the residence of the dockyard Commissioner; the whole range was clearly intended to have a dignity suited to its official function.[3]

Bristol — then the second largest town in England — was the first provincial town to acquire a residential square. Queen Square and the adjacent Prince Street were planned in 1699, and mostly built between 1700 and 1718. The land belonged to the corporation; it had previously been marshy ground in a bend of the river outside the walls, and been used by Bristol citizens for exercise and recreation. The square was very large, larger than any London square except Lincoln's Inn Fields. The corporation let out plots to individual developers, mostly substantial Bristol merchants who built houses for themselves, and sometimes an extra house or two for letting. The leases laid down standards and conditions, which resulted in most of the houses having the same cornice line, but otherwise there was no uniformity. The stylistic language was close to that of London terraces, with an occasional provincial extravagance or aberration. In 1716 the centre was laid out with gravel walks lined with lime trees; an equestrian statue of William III followed in 1742, and is still there. The development had a commercial element;

there was a custom-house on the north side, and most of the houses in the square and in Prince Street had backyards leading to warehouses, on the quays or close to them. A second, smaller, square, known as St. James's Square (Pl. 199), was built on the other side of the town, as a private development, between about 1707 and 1716. It was in similar style but more homogeneous.[4]

Peckwater Quad in Christ Church, Oxford, was built at almost exactly the same time, between 1707 and 1714, and enclosed a similar, but slightly smaller area of ground. There the resemblance ended. With the architecture of Peckwater one hears, for the first time in an urban and residential context, the language of polite society. It was designed by Henry Aldrich, Dean of Christ Church, *bon viveur*, composer of glees and catches, but also a collector, a classical scholar, and an amateur architect who had travelled in France and Italy. The foundation stone was laid by the Earl of Shaftesbury, the leading writer on art and architecture of the day.[5]

199. St. James's Square, Bristol. From a water-colour by a member of the Pole family, *c*. 1805.
200. Peckwater Quad, Christ Church, Oxford (Henry Aldrich, 1707-14).

There was nothing quite like Peckwater anywhere in Europe (Pl. 200). It was built to contain lodgings, and ringed with doorways opening onto staircases, in the traditional manner. But Aldrich designed it like the courtyard of a palace. Three of its sides were adorned with two-storey Ionic columns and central pediments. The

fourth was intended to be filled with an even grander range, fronted by a giant order and containing rooms for dons rather than undergraduates; instead, it was completed after Aldrich's death by a building of similar form, designed by his friend George Clarke as the college library.

By the 1720s the architecture of London squares and terraces was much despised by the *cognoscenti*. The views expressed by James Ralph in 1734 reflected informed taste. Of Soho Square he wrote that 'the buildings round it are not scandalous, 'tis true, but they have not the least pretensions to taste or order'. As for St. James's Square, it had 'an appearance of grandeur superior to any other plan in town, and yet there is not any one elegant house in it ... if the houses were built more in taste, and the four sides exactly corresponding to each other, the effect would be much more surprising, and the pleasure arising from it more just.'[6]

An opportunity to produce such an effect had arisen nine or ten years previously. From 1720 Grosvenor Square and a grid of surrounding streets were laid out to the north of Piccadilly, on farmland brought into the Grosvenor family by marriage with an heiress. In 1725 Colen Campbell published a design for 'seven new intended houses on the east side of Grosvenor Square' (Pl. 202). The houses formed one magnificent whole, fronted by a two-storey Corinthian colonnade above a rusticated ground floor. It is not known who, if anyone, commissioned this design, but it was never built.

Instead, Grosvenor Square ended up almost as much of a mixture as Queen Square in Bristol. Three houses on the west end of the north side were designed by Edward Shepherd as a single unit

with a central portico; the east side was built to a unified scheme, but its architecture was unpretentious; elsewhere the houses went their own way. The most interesting aspect of the development was its planning. Mews ran parallel to the main streets and contained the stables and outbuildings of the houses. Such a system of back access had appeared in embryo in other London developments, but it was first comprehensively applied on the Grosvenor estate and soon became the standard plan in London (Pl. 203).[7]

The opportunity missed in Grosvenor Square was taken up in Queen Square in Bath (Pl. 201). This was built between 1729 and 1736 to the designs of John Wood, who was also the developer. Wood was born in Bath, worked as a builder in the streets around Cavendish Square in London, moved for a time to Yorkshire and returned to Bath in 1727, attracted by the prospects in the growing city. He produced a number of plans (known only from his own descriptions) for enlarging or rebuilding Bath on a grand scale, as a re-creation of a Roman city, but got nowhere with them. In 1728 and subsequent years he leased land from Robert Gay, a London surgeon and ex-MP who owned a substantial estate on the northern edge of the town. On it he built Queen Square.

At Queen Square and elsewhere Wood devised a setting to reflect the polite society, with its common standards of dress and behaviour, which had grown up under the aegis of Nash. Queen Square was built mainly to provide fashionable lodgings, or houses to rent, but its rows of houses were designed, as Wood himself explained, to look like the courtyard of a palace. The grandest façade, on the north side, was decorated with a Corinthian order and a central pediment in a fashion reminiscent of, and probably inspired by, Peckwater Quad. Twenty-five years later Wood used the same device in a different way in the Circus (1754-8), another collection of prestigious houses, but built on a circular plan, like the Colosseum turned inside out. The design harked back to Wood's reincarnated Roman-cum-Ancient-British city, which was to have included a 'Grand Circus for the Exhibition of Sports'; but the paved centre of the circus was never, in fact, put to public use.[8]

As described in chapter 8 the unified architecture of Queen Square was intended to provide the backcloth to a parade, and when this proved abortive, the project was revived in North and South Parades, in cut-down form. The idea, even if never fully realized, was a brilliant one, and makes one wonder whether Campbell had similar intentions for his projected east side of Grosvenor Square.

201. (top left) Queen Square, Bath (John Wood senior, 1729-36).
202. (bottom left) Unexecuted design by Colen Campbell for the east side of Grosvenor Square, London, 1725.
203. (above) The mews behind Torrington Square, London, from a drawing by George Scharf, c. 1850.

What in the end made the Parades a success was less their architecture than the novelty of their setting, looking out to gardens and across the Avon to woods and hills. As Fanny Burney put it when staying in lodgings on the South Parade in 1780: 'We have meadows, hills, Prior Park, the soft-flowing Avon — whatever nature has to offer, I think, always in our view.'[9]

It seems unlikely that this relationship was originally of much importance to Wood. His Queen Square and Circus had been designed as formal enclosed spaces, on the continental model. The centre of Queen Square was laid out as a formal garden, but Wood's remark, when describing it, that 'the intention of a square in the city is for people to assemble together',[10] looks back to continental precedents. The Circus was all hard surfaces. The Parades were built where they were because building land was available there. Wood was probably more interested in their conjunction with a proposed 'Royal Forum', another, in this case abortive, resurrection of his Roman city, than in their relationship with river and countryside. However, by the time he came to write about the Parades in 1742 he recognized the importance of the relationship; and his son John Wood the younger and other Bath architects were to develop it as a dominant characteristic of Bath.

The idea of *rus in urbe* was not entirely new. John Sheffield, first Duke of Buckingham, had had the words inscribed on the frieze of his London residence, Buckingham House.[11] This was built in 1702-5, and looked along the Mall and over St. James's Park, on what was then the edge of London. Almost all the London squares had open country to one side; as early as 1708 the north side of Queen Square was left open, to give it a view to the hills of Hampstead and Highgate. Between about 1728 and 1750 the modest houses on the west side of Arlington Street were rebuilt on a much grander scale, and the street became as fashionable as St. James's and Grosvenor Squares. The reason was the outlook over Green Park; in 1734 James Ralph described a house being built there by Gibbs for the Dowager Duchess of Norfolk as having 'one of the most beautiful situations in Europe, for health, convenience and beauty; the front is in the midst of the hurry and splendour of the town, and the back in the quiet and simplicity of the country.'[12]

But at Bath the relationship was exploited more creatively. A triumphant second stage after the Parades came with the Royal Crescent (Pl. 204), designed by John Wood the younger, and built between 1767 and 1775. Wood took the concept of his father's Circus and opened it to the outside world. Art and nature were consummately brought together, and nothing went wrong for lack of money. A great sweep of columns looked out over grass slopes to the hills; sheep and horses grazed on the grass while the cream of Bath promenaded before a backcloth of splendid architecture. The Royal Crescent took over from the Grand Parade as the fashionable promenade, just as the Grand Parade had taken over from Orange Grove. It became immediately and justifiably famous. 'The beautiful situation of the Crescent cannot be understood by any comparison with anything in any town whatsoever', wrote Elizabeth Montagu, one of the best-known hostesses of her day, in 1779. Fanny Burney was equally in raptures a year later: it was 'the exquisite crescent, which to all the excellence

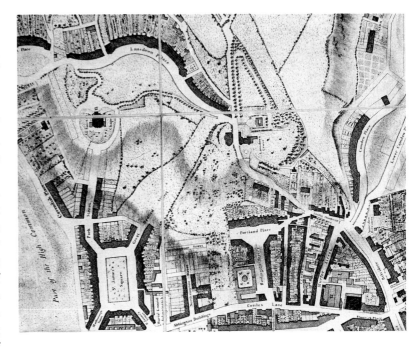

204. (left) Royal Crescent, Bath (John Wood junior, 1767-75), from an engraving of 1801.
205. Lansdown Crescent, Bath, and its surroundings. Detail from the plan of Bath by C. Harcourt Masters, 1794.
206. Looking up to Lansdown Crescent.

of architecture that adorns the Circus, adds all the delights of nature that beautify the parades'. In *Northanger Abbey* Jane Austen made the Thorpes and Allens leave the Pump Room and 'hasten away to the Crescent to breathe the fresh air of better company'. In 1819 Egan described its appearance at the time of the promenade on Sunday: 'crowded with fashionables of every rank ... with the addition of the splendid barouche, dashing curricle, elegant tandem, gentlemen on horseback and co.'.[13]

With Royal Crescent the Bath style reached maturity. The pursuit of a civilized society and the pursuit of health and nature were fused together. The town spread up the steep slopes on both sides of the Avon in a series of terraces and crescents in which façades of sophisticated elegance looked out to trees and greenery. The healthiness of this open layout, in contrast to the narrow streets and lack of green spaces of almost all towns then in existence, including the centre of Bath itself, was much commented on at the time. So was the enjoyable contrast which resulted from its fusion of city and country; as Nash's successor, Samuel Derrick, put it 'you may, in a quarter of an hour, change the most romantic solitary scene into crowd, bustle, splendour, music, dancing ....'[14]

The Bath mixture survives today, only a little adulterated by the growth of the town, which has spread across some of the prospects. It reaches its apogee in Lansdown Crescent, high on the hill above Royal Crescent, and approached from it by way of St. James's Square and the steep

207. Lansdown Crescent, Bath (John Palmer, 1789-93).
208. (top right) Sheep in Cavendish Square, from the title-pages of John Stewart's *Critical Observations on London*, 1771.
209. (bottom right) The view from Lansdown Crescent.

slope of Park Street (Pls. 205-7, 209). This is more exquisitely fitted to the slope of the land than Royal Crescent. Its houses follow the contours in long S-shaped curves; their architecture has none of Wood's grandeur, but is of extreme elegance. Each house has the lovely feature of an arch of delicately curving wrought iron, supporting a wrought-iron lantern above the steps and entrance. From the broad sweep of road and pavement before the houses two fields framed by trees drop very steeply away to more trees and a tree-lined walk, also on an S-curve, from which one can look through a framing of branches to the long façades above the grass slopes; a little to one side, until it was destroyed in the war, a Gothic chapel on an eminence was poised as an accent in the view, like a temple in an eighteenth-century park.

Lansdown Crescent, St. James's Square, Park Street and All Saints' Chapel were designed by John Palmer between 1789 and 1794. It is not known who laid out the ground below the Crescent or designed the naturalistic planting of St. James's Square; it may have been Charles Harcourt Masters, a Bath architect who was also a landscape designer and laid out the Sydney Gardens there in the late 1790s. The Lansdown slopes, St. James's Square, and Sydney Gardens are the first examples in Bath of the layout of public spaces in the naturalistic style. There was no landscaping below the Royal Crescent, just railings and open turf.

In fact the landscaping of public spaces seems to have started in London. Even the Royal Crescent's arrangement of sheep grazing behind the railings may have been anticipated in Cavendish Square, where it was to be found by 1771 (Pl. 208). The formal layout of Grosvenor Square was replaced by naturalistic clumps of bushes in, or shortly after, 1774; Portman Square was similarly arranged by 1792, and its planting may have dated back to its first laying out in the 1770s.[15] Other squares followed their example.

The development of Bath, and the gradual transformation of the London squares, was the urban counterpart of the landscape movement in the parks and environs of English country houses (which in its turn owed much to Kent's laying out of the London garden of the Prince of Wales in 1734, 'with the appearance of beautiful nature').[16] The sheep grazing almost up to the houses of the Royal Crescent were paralleled by sheep, deer or cows grazing almost up to the windows of country houses all over England. The S-curves of the roads serving Lansdown Crescent, and the views

from it down to the lower town, had been paralleled as early as 1758 by the contour-hugging curves of the great terrace at Rievaulx, and the tree-framed views down from it to Rievaulx Abbey.

The idea of bringing the country into the town was not found acceptable by everyone. Even in Bath the streets laid out by Thomas Baldwin express an alternative concept of town planning. In 1771 *rus in urbe* was attacked in a London context, even before it had got fully under way, in *Critical Observations on the Buildings and Improvements of London*, attributed to John Stewart. The author poured scorn on the sheep in Cavendish Square. 'To see the poor things starting at every coach, and hurrying round their narrow bounds, requires a warm imagination indeed, to concert the scene into that of flocks ranging in fields, with all the concomitant ideas of innocence and a pastoral life' (Pl. 208). He found almost all London squares 'tinctured with the same absurdity ... they are gardens, they are parks, they are sheep walks; in short, they are everything but what they should be. The *rus in urbe* is a preposterous idea at best; a garden in a street is not less absurd than a street in a garden.'[17]

But the buildings of Bath were universally admired. In 1766 John Gwynn made the sweeping statement that 'in this age of mistaken refinements there is not in the kingdom one city, town or village wherein any regularity is observed, or attempt made towards magnificence or elegance, except the city of Bath.'[18] Sixty years or so later, the charge could scarcely have been sustained, but it was the example of Bath (sometimes coming by way of London) which was responsible for the change. By 1830 its influence could be seen everywhere: in squares, terraces, crescents and occasional circuses, of unified design held together by the use of the order or, more subtly, by proportions dictated by an order which was not used; and in terraces and crescents looking out over gardens and prospects, and often providing a backcloth for the promenading of fashionable, or would-be fashionable, people.

The speed of development was slowed by the American War of 1776-83, and the intermittent French wars between 1793 and 1815; the latter caused a slump in the mid-1790s, which bankrupted builders and left unfinished carcasses of terraces all over the country. The real building boom came in the 1820s, with widespread residential developments on the Bath model, set in motion by postwar prosperity, and the realization that, thanks to the development of stucco as a facing material, the absence of a good local building

210. Looking down Royal York Crescent, Bristol.
211. Design by C.A. Busby for Brunswick Terrace, Brighton, *c.* 1825.
212-214. (top right, far right, centre) Terraces at Scarborough (*c.* 1830), Wakefield (*c.* 1790) and Louth (*c.* 1800).
215. (bottom right) A house in Colleton Crescent, Exeter (*c.* 1805).

stone was no bar to producing buildings that at least looked as magnificent as the best of Bath.

In London the Adam brothers' Adelphi of 1768-72 and their Portland Place of 1776-80 pioneered the use of stucco, and introduced delicate and decorated variations on the orders that offered an alternative to Palladianism, and were to be imitated in towns all over the country, Bath included. Bedford Square, built in the mid-1770s and possibly designed by Thomas Leverton, was, as it were, Queen Square translated into the Adam language. In Bristol there was much building, in fits and starts, all through the eighteenth century, until the crash in 1795. Queen Square was followed by five more squares and numerous terraces, in which Bristol's comfortable vernacular or robustly ignorant baroque gradually succumbed to the influence of Bath — helped along by the arrival of Bath stone and, on occasion, Bath architects in the 1780s.

But the most exciting Georgian terraces in Bristol were built in the 1780s and 1790s on Clifton Hill. From the slopes of this steep-sided circular hill to the east of the old city superb views could be enjoyed, down to the Hotwells and into Clifton Gorge, or across to the centre of Bristol. It was an ideal context in which to combine art with nature, in the Bath manner but even more dramatically. A succession of curving and snaking terraces were connected by boldly curving roads and raised up on a mighty superstructure of cellars and retaining walls, to give them a footing on the steep slopes. The most ambitious were probably built in deliberate emulation of Royal Crescent and Lansdown Crescent at Bath: the 1,100-foot-long Cornwallis Crescent lower down the hill, and up above it, above green-planted slopes, the 1,300-foot-long Royal York Crescent (Pl. 210), fronted by a wide stone-flagged promenade on which residents or visitors could parade and enjoy the view.

At the time of the financial crisis, most of the terraces were half-finished and some barely begun; but after 1805 carcasses were

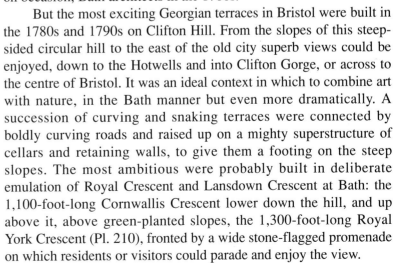

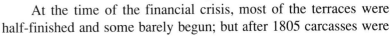

completed, gaps were filled, and Clifton was firmly established as at once a spa, a desirable place for retirement and the West End of Bristol for its richer merchants and manufacturers.

The influence of Bath was felt just as sharply, if in a different way, in the great schemes promoted in London between 1813 and 1830 by John Nash. Echoes of Bath were to be found over and over again in Regent Street and Regent's Park; in Park Crescent and the two Circuses (and the great abortive circus planned to look inwards and outwards in the centre of Regent's Park); in the colonnades of the Quadrant and Park Crescent, reminiscent of the colonnades of Bath Street; in the rich but varied architecture and fashionable shops of Regent Street, a bigger metropolitan version of Milsom Street in Bath; in Regent's Park, a bigger and more elaborate version of Sydney Gardens and its intended terraces; in the use of the Regent's Canal to make a feature in Regent's Park, just as the Bath and Avon Canal had been made a feature in Sydney Gardens; in the picturesque landscaping of Regent's and St. James's Parks, as a man-made alternative to the wooded prospects around Bath. Even Nash's stucco was originally marked out and coloured to imitate Bath stone.

The almost equally ambitious stucco terraces and squares of Kemp Town and Brunswick Town (Pl. 211) at either end of Brighton were built at much the same time as the Regent's Park terraces, from 1823 onwards, and provided an influential variation: a promenade for the fashionable backed by grand classical façades but looking out to sea instead of to the countryside or onto parks. Their grandest feature was the composition made up by Lewes Crescent and Sussex Square in the middle of Kemp Town, looking across richly planted sea-blown pleasure-grounds to the sea itself, and connected to the beach and lower promenades by a tunnel and triumphal arch facing the sea.

Late Georgian terraces, squares, circuses and crescents were built all over the British Isles, but especially in the more rapidly expanding towns: the successful resorts, the two wonder cities of Liverpool and Birmingham, the ports of Bristol and Hull, the naval centres of Portsmouth and Plymouth, the newly prosperous manufacturing town of Manchester and the long-established industrial centre of Newcastle. A good deal in such towns has been effaced by later development, war damage and the holocaust of the 1950s and 1960s, but a good deal survives, especially in resort towns. A speciality of these were the bow windows, built in long enfilades as little observatories from which visitors could gaze out to sea (Pl. 212).

Once terraces, squares and crescents had been established as desirable and fashionable, most smaller or slower-growing towns acquired at least one example (Pls. 213-7). Sometimes the upper crust of the town moved into it, more often its members stayed in one-off houses and new development catered for the next social layer: the lesser professional families, widows and the like. Such

216. (top right) The Crescent, Wisbech, *c.* 1820.
217. (bottom right) Rutland Terrace, Stamford, 1829-31.

168

developments were mainly respectable rather than grand, usually built of brick, with pretty door-cases and not much else. A typical and pleasing example is at Wisbech (Pls. 97, 216). Here the seventeenth-century building known as Wisbech Castle, standing in the centre of the town in its own grounds, was bought in 1793 by Joseph Medworth, a charity school boy from Wisbech who had made his fortune as a builder in London. Medworth offered to sell the house to the corporation as its town hall, and, on being refused, demolished it and developed the site. The debit result of this was the loss of a very interesting house, the credit a pleasing development of modest brick terraces enclosing an egg-shaped space on which Medworth built a house in the Gothic style for himself.[19]

Other provincial towns had their own transplant from Bath or Cheltenham. Stamford was essentially a town of independently designed houses, but in 1829-31 J.C.Wallis, a veterinary surgeon, acquired a bowling-green on the edge of the town and developed it as Rutland Terrace. The result was a long, mainly stone-faced terrace of twenty houses, enriched with balconies, verandas, and pilasters (Pl. 217). On the other side of the road Wallis provided a communal landscaped enclosure, running the length of the terrace; the houses looked out across this to open country.[20]

This is one of the many variations on a central landscaped square which are to be found all over England and form one of the pleasantest features of terraces of this date. In an arrangement especially common in Cheltenham, the terrace is set back from the public road behind a communal garden, through which a private road gives access to the houses. The garden may be reduced to a narrow strip, or enlarged to what amounts to a little park, as in Park Crescent in Worthing. Another variation appears in embryo in Cornwallis Crescent at Clifton (Pl. 218). Here there is a long raised terrace running along the back of the houses. It is separated from the houses by an area, crossed by bridges, and joined by steps at the other side to a communal garden. There are store rooms under the terrace; the area passage gives access to these and to the back doors of the houses.

The next stage came when the terrace was replaced by small individual gardens, all letting out onto the communal one. In London the arrangement had been shown in unexecuted plans for a double circus on the Eyre estate in St. John's Wood, made by John Shaw in 1803 (but involving villas not terraces), and a similar and equally abortive

project for the Ladbroke estate in North Kensington, made by Thomas Allason in 1823. It was actually carried out on the north side of Gillespie Graham's Moray Crescent in Edinburgh (1822-30) and in Amos Wild's Park Crescent in Brighton (1829). Along with variants on Cornwallis Crescent, it became quite common in early Victorian London, especially in Maida Vale and on the Ladbroke estate as it was finally laid out between 1840 and the early 1850s. Here a rich variety of squares, terraces and crescents back onto long communal gardens, often elaborately landscaped (Pl. 219). It was, and is, both an attractive arrangement and a highly practical one, as the communal gardens are more accessible to residents than ones isolated by roads in the middle of a square. But it makes back access and mews stables impossible; it was emphatically designed for modest middle-class families who did not own a carriage.[21]

218. Communal garden and terrace, Cornwallis Crescent, Clifton (1791-4).
219. Looking into the communal garden between Elgin and Lansdowne Crescents, Notting Hill, London.
220. (right) Looking down Bath Street, Frome, towards the market square.

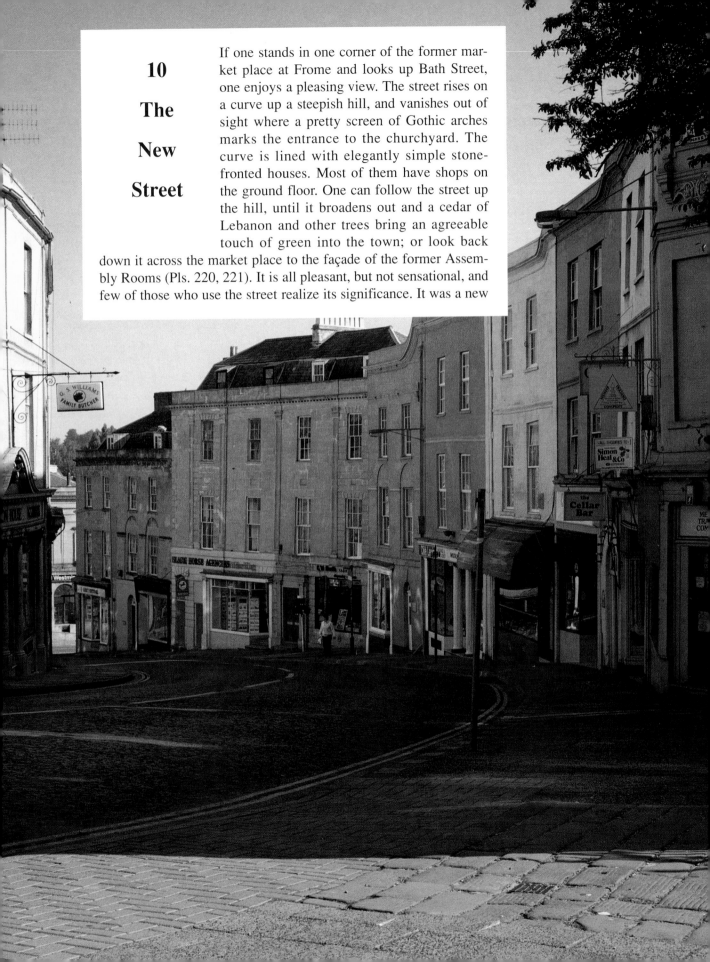

10

The

New

Street

If one stands in one corner of the former market place at Frome and looks up Bath Street, one enjoys a pleasing view. The street rises on a curve up a steepish hill, and vanishes out of sight where a pretty screen of Gothic arches marks the entrance to the churchyard. The curve is lined with elegantly simple stone-fronted houses. Most of them have shops on the ground floor. One can follow the street up the hill, until it broadens out and a cedar of Lebanon and other trees bring an agreeable touch of green into the town; or look back down it across the market place to the façade of the former Assembly Rooms (Pls. 220, 221). It is all pleasant, but not sensational, and few of those who use the street realize its significance. It was a new

221. Looking down Bath Street, Frome, to the Assembly Rooms, from a late-nineteenth-century photograph.

street, a brave piece of town planning for a small town, cut through its centre as the result of an Act of Parliament passed in 1810 — three years before the act that led to the building of Regent Street in London.

The 1810 Act was the third of three acts involving Frome, and the only one to entail demolition in its centre. All were administered by a body of trustees which had been set up under the first act in 1757, and subsequent gaps in which were filled by co-option. The 1757 Act was concerned with repairing and widening the approach road to the town. A second Act, passed in 1797, enabled the town to be lit and paved, and created a new road, known as North Parade, which led in a straight line out of the town, from Frome Bridge to North Hill. North Parade was soon lined with terraces, for Frome at the end of the eighteenth century was prosperous from textiles. Bath Street was the counterpart to North Parade. It took traffic out to the other side of the town up a wide street and an easy gradient, instead of the steep and narrow lanes which had been the route before. At the end of the day Frome had some handsome new terraces, an attractive piece of planting, and a convenient route through the town, at a time when the resulting traffic was sufficient to give an agreeable clatter and sense of life to the streets, and not heavy enough to make them unpleasant. It is ironic that in recent years the existence of this route has delayed the building of a bypass, and enabled a stream of lorries and heavy traffic to hurtle through the town centre.

The name Bath Street is apposite, for the width of the street's carriageway and pavements was modelled on those of Union Street in Bath, and the architecture of the houses which lined it followed Bath models, and may well have been designed by a Bath architect. But in fact it was named after the Marquess of Bath, rather than Bath itself. He was a major property owner in Frome, and a trustee under the Act. He co-operated in the destruction of a huddle of cottages, mostly belonging to him, in order to open up a view of the church from the new street. His architect, Jeffry Wyatville, designed a Gothic screen to frame this view, and a new front for the church. In the market place further improvement was due to the Earl of Cork, who lived nearby at Marston House, and was another trustee. By replacing two houses which belonged to him with assembly rooms above a covered market, he provided amenities for the town, and a pleasing termination to the view down Bath Street.

Co-operative though these local magnates were, the leading force behind the new street was almost certainly a Frome attorney called Thomas Bunn. The Bunns were Nonconformists, and active in the life of the town. In or before 1784 Thomas Bunn's mother and sister had founded one of the first Sunday Schools in the country in Frome. In 1789 Bunn himself became a trustee under the 1757 Frome Act, and from then until his death in 1853 he was involved in constant projects. Not all were successful. His failures included projects for a crescent, a park, and a South Parade, to align with North Parade and provide an axial vista from the crescent through the town. One of his last successes was the founding of the Frome Literary and Scientific Institute in 1844; the building put up to house it in 1868 still presides over the entry to the town, as a small but handsome symbol of enlightenment.[1]

Frome is one of a number of towns where eighteenth-century ideals of improvement were applied to town centres. Examples are not all that common. It was easy enough to lay out new streets on the edge of a town, as long as the ground landlord was willing and the town sufficiently prosperous and growing to make raising the necessary capital no problem. To carve out any significant new space in the centre was far more difficult. It involved the purchase and demolition of property in areas where land was both much more expensive than open land on the outskirts, and usually fragmented into plots belonging to different owners.

For centuries this meant that no new streets were built in town centres. Even after a destructive fire, such as occurred in London in 1688, Warwick in 1694, Northampton in 1675, and Blandford in 1731, the problem of dealing with property owners resulted in the destroyed areas being rebuilt on the old street lines, with minor adjustments and improvements.[2]

It was not till the mid-eighteenth century that a number of new factors led to significant change. The growth of wheeled traffic made conditions in many existing thoroughfares unendurable. The increasingly sophisticated use of improvement trusts and local Acts of Parliament enabled property to be compulsorily purchased and money to be borrowed or raised by imposing a rate. The general taste for 'improvement' made the remodelling of a town centre a praiseworthy rather than an interfering exercise. Even so, the difficulties were still considerable.

The first new streets were the consequence of new bridges — themselves another result of increasing traffic. A new town bridge on a new site had to be approached by new roads, a new bridge on the site of an old one usually made necessary the widening or alteration of the existing approaches. A number of short new streets came into existence, predictably if unimaginatively called Bridge Street. They provided the approach to Charles Labelye's Westminster Bridge in London (1739-50), to James Bridge's Bristol Bridge (1763-8), to John Gwynn's English Bridge in Shrewsbury (1769-74), and the same architect's Worcester Bridge (1771-80). All these required Acts of Parliament,[3] which set up bodies of commissioners

222. Bridge Street, Worcester, from the bridge.
223. (right) Market Square, Taunton, from an early- nineteenth-century engraving.

and gave them the necessary powers of buying property and raising money. The new streets which resulted were lined with terraces of houses, of a fairly modest nature. Most of these have long since been demolished; but a complete street of elegant medium-sized houses survives at Worcester (Pl. 222). Although the relevant Act was passed in 1769, the houses were not built until after 1782, when T.R. Nash described the project in his county history: 'On the city side is intended an entire new street of forty feet width, letting in a beautiful view of Malvern hills with the adjacent country; this, I doubt not, will render the town much healthier.'[4] This combined appreciation of beauty and health is typical of contemporary views on town improvement.

But well before Bridge Street was built in Worcester, a pioneering improvement of a town centre had taken place at Taunton. It was largely due to a body known as the Market-House Society. This was founded in 1763 by a group of 'sensible and public-spirited' Taunton residents. They had the ingenious idea that the money wasted on election contests in the town could be diverted to its improvement. They patched up an agreement between the prospective candidates, and used their election budget as an improvement fund. They then rented the right to run the market and collect its revenues from the Bishop of Winchester, who had owned it since medieval times. In 1768 they brought about the passing of a Taunton Market Act, and were themselves appointed trustees.

The aim of the Society was to clear out the market place and build a new market-house on it. As happened in the market squares of so many towns, much of its centre had become obstructed by a huddle of lanes, houses, and no less than eleven inns. As Toulmin's history of Taunton put it in 1791: 'a spot of ground, so crowded with buildings, in the centre of the town, besides obstructing the free circulation of air, could not but be attended with many inconveniences and nuisances, by the filth lying in its narrow passages, and the receptacles for idleness and vice, which many of its buildings, from their situation, became.'[6]

The buildings were bought up and demolished. The resulting open space (Pl. 223) was railed in with posts and chains, to define the market. One side was filled with a new market-house, designed by a local amateur, Coplestone Warre Bampfylde, who was one of the trustees. It had arcades for market stalls to either side of a central building, which contained a reading-room and a meeting-room for the trustees on the ground floor, and assembly rooms on the floor above. Through the market place, and on the axis of the market-house, ran 'a large pavement of broad flag stone, two hundred and sixteen feet in length, and eighteen feet in width, called the Parade'.[7] Here the polite society of Taunton could promenade (but perhaps not on market days).

The part played in Frome by Bunn was filled in Taunton by Sir Benjamin Hammet. He was born in Taunton, in about 1736, reputedly the son of a serge manufacturer or a barber. As a young man he is said to have worked as a porter in a London bookshop, and then made his fortune as an insurance broker, merchant banker and shipowner. He divided his time between the City of London, where he became an alderman, and Taunton, which he represented in Parliament from 1782 to 1800. He was knighted in 1786.[8]

224. Looking down Hammet Street, Taunton, to the tower of the parish church.

Besides being active on the Market Trust, Hammet was involved in at least three other schemes for the improvement of Taunton. He was a trustee under various Turnpike Acts, and the leading spirit behind the paving of the town. In 1785 there was a possibility that Taunton would lose its status as the assize town for Somerset, owing to the dilapidated condition of the castle, where the assizes were held; Hammet leased the castle from the Bishop of Winchester and restored it, partly at his own expense and partly by subscription. Finally, in 1788, he embarked on his own development. In that year he obtained an Act of Parliament which enabled him to buy up property and demolish houses in order to lay out what became known as Hammet Street (Pl. 224). The new street opened a vista from the market place to the medieval tower of the parish church, and was lined with terraces of elegantly simple houses. 'The effect produced does honour to the taste that designed it', commented Toulmin. Moreover, 'the town, by these improvements, now affords what for many years it wanted, houses for the reception of genteel families out of trade'.[9]

Today, the market place has become little more than a traffic roundabout, with the market hall, lopped of its wings, at its centre; but the view down Hammet Street is still as dramatic as when it was first opened up. The market improvement was a pioneer; Hammet Street takes its place among a clutch of improvement schemes of the late 1780s, inaugurated by the Newcastle-upon-Tyne and Liverpool Improvement Acts of 1786, and the Bath Improvement Act of 1789.

The Newcastle improvements (Pl. 234) were the least ambitious.[10] They were modest but interesting precursors of the great Grey Street development of the 1830s. They involved the making of a covered market and cutting of two new streets, Dean Street, leading up the hill from the Guildhall to Mosley Street, and Collingwood Street, linking Mosley Street to Westgate. Mosley Street was also a new street, laid out by the corporation in 1784-5; most of the ground needed was corporation property and no Act had been necessary.

Dean Street and Mosley Street were the result of intelligent exploitation of Newcastle's dramatic but difficult geography. The town was on two levels, down by the river and on a plateau above it; communication was made difficult by the steep slopes from one to the other, and the deep gulleys which scored the plateau and ran down to the river. The two main streets of the upper town, Pilgrim

Street and Newgate Street, were divided by one of these gulleys. Mosley Street was built to join them together on land obtained by bridging across the head of the gulley. Dean Street ran up the gulley, and provided a link from riverside to plateau, on a steep gradient but much more negotiable than the precipitous lanes which had formerly joined them.

The 1786 Act did not set up a commission, or authorize a rate; the work was to be done by the corporation at its own expense. Newcastle was one of the richer English towns; in 1780 its income was over £25,000 a year. It could afford it. Even so, at first only half the scheme materialized; Collingwood Street and the markets were not built until 1806-12. The streets built under the Act were lined with modest brick houses. Mosley Street had more pretensions; a theatre was built there in 1787-8, and it became the best street in central Newcastle. The theatre was designed by the Newcastle architect David Stephenson, who was also the surveyor for the new streets, and may have designed the houses on them. Only a few survive. The theatre made way for Grey Street in the 1830s.

In December 1785, Liverpool corporation set up a committee 'to consider of the best methods of improving the town'. It sat weekly in the Exchange, its meetings were advertised in the papers, and anyone was allowed to bring plans of suggested improvements for inspection. The result was the passing of an Improvement Act in 1786, and the setting up of an Improvement Committee. The main achievements under the Act were the widening of Castle Street and Dale Street, and the formation of Brunswick Street. Castle Street was widened on the west side to become a broad street, about 100 feet wide, closed, not quite axially, by the Town Hall at one end and St. George's Church at the other (Pl. 225). The new side of Castle Street was lined with brick and stucco terraces, articulated by an applied order. They were designed by James Wyatt, who in 1788-9 also made designs for enriching the Town Hall with a dome and portico, to form a fitting termination to the street.[11]

Liverpool corporation was the most enterprising of pre-Reform-Act corporations. From 1709 it was developing the first commercial dock system in the world. In 1672 it had made a deal with the Molyneux family, and acquired a clear title to an enormous stretch of common land on its eastern boundary, ultimately all to become built-up land. By 1786 only three docks had been formed (and a fourth was on the way), the common land was only partly built over, but the resulting income already made it the second richest corporation in England, through its own good management. A second Improvement Act in 1825 led to the widening of Lord Street, other street widenings, and the formation of a crescent around a rebuilt St. George's Church. In 1828-35 an exceedingly grand custom house was built on the site of the filled-in Old Dock, to close the southern vista at the end of an extended Castle Street. Crescent, church, Custom House, and new terraces in Lord Street.

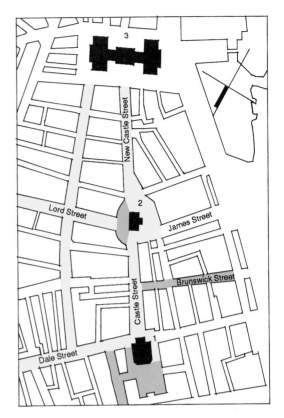

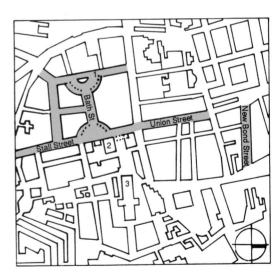

225. Improvement in Liverpool, 1786-1830. New streets shown red, widened streets yellow. 1. Town Hall. 2. St. George's Church. 3. Customs House.
226. Improvement in Bath, 1789-1810. New streets shown red. 1. Cross Bath. 2. Pump Room. 3. Abbey.

227. A view along one of the colonnades of Bath Street, Bath (Thomas Baldwin, 1791).

were designed by John Foster junior, the corporation architect. By 1831-2 street formation and widening, and new buildings, including a new jail and market, had left the corporation with a debt of £792,000. The debt was entirely serviced by the corporation, mainly out of its income from property and the docks; none of it was put on the rates.[12]

The improvements inaugurated at Bath by its own Act, passed in 1789, involved a more modest expenditure of £64,000. But the results are all still to be seen, and very beautiful some of them are; whereas, although the generous width of the streets in central Liverpool is mainly due to its 1786 and 1825 Acts, all the buildings that resulted from them have gone, with the exception of the additions to the Town Hall. The Bath Act was preceded by an earlier one of 1766, the main achievement of which had been the building of a covered market (since demolished) and the new Guildhall. The 1789 Act followed on the presentation of a plan to the corporation by Thomas Baldwin, the City Surveyor, in 1788. It led to the formation of Bath Street and the streets off it, of Union Street, perhaps of York Street and New Bond Street, and to the building of a new Pump Room (Pl. 226). The money was raised by selling bonds, the interest on which was serviced by additional tolls on the turnpikes belonging to the Bath Turnpike Trust. The Act was administered by commissioners, made up of the corporation, including the town clerk, and of twenty-two named individuals; the corporation had a small majority. Even so, the minutes of the commission make clear that in its first and most active years it was dominated by two non-corporation members, John Morris and Zachary Bayly, who chaired most of the meetings. Baldwin was appointed architect to the commission.[13]

The Act estimated the value of the property which would have to be purchased and demolished at £73,367, £42,203 of which could be recouped from resale of building plots. In fact the final cost was £64,233, and the receipts were £50,512. The improvement was nearly self-financing. Its progress, however, was interrupted by the financial panic of 1792-3, which led to Baldwin's own pecuniary embarrassment, dismissal and bankruptcy, and the failure in 1793 of the Bath City Bank, in which Zachary Bayly was a partner.[14] Only the Pump Room and the Bath Street end of the improvement were built in the 1790s, mainly to Baldwin's designs; the rest was not completed, and perhaps not even started, until after 1804.

Baldwin produced a brilliant piece of town planning. Bath Street joined remodelled Cross Baths to new Private Baths, both of which dated from just before the 1789 Act. The new street was lined with colonnades (Pl. 227), widening out into little crescents to form open spaces before the two baths. The view down the resulting vista was closed at either end by their exquisite façades. To one side of the Private Baths a double screen of Ionic columns, topped by sphinxes, linked them to the end façade of the new Pump Room, and was repeated in a similar screen on its other side. This gave access to a court in front of the main entrance to the Pump Room. The result was, and is, very formal. Baldwin had little feeling for the mixture of art and nature developed by the younger Wood and John Palmer; perhaps he would have agreed with John Stewart that *rus in urbe* was an absurdity.[15]

He seems, in fact, to have been more than a Bath builder turned architect. In 1782, he had entered the competition for a National Penitentiary. In 1786 (and again, after a fire, in 1807) he designed Hafod for Thomas Johnes, a true son of the Enlightenment, whose attempts to create an aesthetic and agricultural Elysium in North Wales came to a tragic end in death, fire, and financial collapse. John Morris, the most active of Baldwin's commissioners, was a protégé of Lord Shelburne, who was in touch with all the most advanced ideas of the day.[16] This background may explain the flavour of continental neo-classicism which merges with Adamesque delicacy to give a distinctive character to Baldwin's work for the commissioners in Bath.

The recession which interrupted the improvements could be paralleled all over England. The years around 1800 were a slack time for schemes for urban improvement, or indeed building development of any kind. The economy started to pick up in about 1805. Over the next forty years a number of urban improvement schemes took place. They differ in scale and background, but all were distinct from the schemes for laying out residential terraces which were taking place at the same time.

Huddersfield was given what amounted to a new centre between about 1802 and 1823. The formation of Bath Street in Frome was paralleled by the formation of Regent Street in Yarmouth; both developed from Acts of Parliament passed in 1810. Yarmouth had suffered from having no communication between its quay and main street, except a series of narrow lanes; Regent Street joined the two together, and anticipated by several years its far more ambitious namesake in London.[17] London's Regent Street was the result of an Enabling Act passed in 1813. It was followed, between

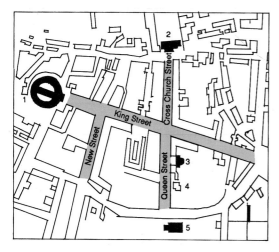

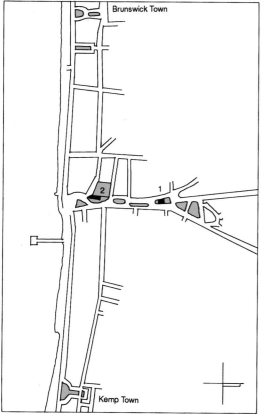

228. Improvement in Huddersfield, 1802-30.
Principal new streets shown in red. 1. Cloth Hall. 2.
St. Peter's Church. 3. Methodist Chapel. 4. Sessions
House. 5. St. Paul's Church.
229. Improvements in Brighton, 1810-40. 1. St.
Peter's Church. 2. Pavilion.

1823 and 1839, by ambitious development in the City and South-wark, resulting in the creation of a widened Borough High Street leading over a new London Bridge to a new King William IV Street and a new Moorgate. Robert Smirke was the architect for this for-gotten piece of town planning, the buildings, though not the spaces, created by which have been effaced by later development.[18] Mean-while, between about 1819 and 1828 Brighton was being remod-elled and enlarged to a coherent plan. Finally, the creation of Grey Street and adjoining streets in Newcastle, from 1834 onwards, car-ried Georgian concepts of city planning into Victoria's reign. Grey Street, along with the work in Huddersfield, London's Regent Street, and Brighton, deserves closer examination.

The development of a new centre for the growing textile town of Huddersfield was started in about 1802, and substantially com-pleted by about 1825 (Pl. 228). The practical problems were less than in other places, because the ground was owned by one land-lord, Sir John Ramsden, and much of it was not yet built on; no Act of Parliament was needed. It is not known whether a surveyor or ar-chitect was employed; the principal contractor involved was Joseph Kaye, who built most of the new buildings in Huddersfield in this period. Development was based on two intersecting streets, King Street and Queen Street; the latter continued as Cross Church Street. The upper end of King Street was closed by the façade of the earlier Cloth Hall, that of Queen Street by the parish church; the lower end of Queen Street was later closed by the tower of St. Paul's Church (1828-9). A covered market was built off King Street, and the streets were lined with simple but pleasing classical terraces.[19]

Half-way along Queen Street a little formal square opened up to reveal the looming classical façade of Queen Street Chapel, which at the time it was completed in 1819 was the biggest Wes-leyan chapel in England. The demolition of the Cloth Hall in the 1930s destroyed the terminal feature of King Street; in the 1960s a crushingly insensitive car-park smashed one side of Queen Street. Even so it is still a satisfying experience to stand in Queen Square below the proud façade of the chapel and look to the right to the handsome east end of the parish church, rebuilt in 1834-6, and to the left to the slender spire of St. Paul's (Pl. 230).

Nash's Regent Street is the best-known of the new streets, has been much written about, and is deservedly famous. But it needs to be put in its context: not a unique creation, or a revolutionary new departure, but the culmination of a process which had been going on for at least fifty years. It drew on methods and motifs which had already been used. It was made possible by an Act of Parliament which set up commissioners with special powers of purchase and borrowing. Much of the expenditure was recouped by selling long leases of the plots to either side of it. Many motifs and ideas came from Bath, including the circuses, the colonnades of Park Crescent and the Regent Street Quadrant.

There were differences, however. The work was on a much larger scale than any previous scheme and more closely connected with the central government. The commissioners under the 1813 Act were in fact the three Commissioners of Woods and Forests, government appointees in charge of the lands which George III had handed over to the state in return for a civil list. George IV had less to do with the scheme than is generally believed; as was so often the case at the time, an enlightened Scotsman had been at work in the background, in the person of John Fordyce, Commissioner of Woods and Forests from 1786 until his death in 1809. The principles which lay behind both Regent Street and Regent's Park were laid down in his reports.[20]

Moreover, Nash created a remarkable synthesis between the ideals of neo-classical grandeur and the picturesque. The Quadrant in Regent Street, the colonnades of Park Crescent, and axial vistas to the spire of All Saints, Langham Place, the façade of Carlton House (later replaced by the Duke of York's column), and the portico of the Haymarket Theatre were examples of the former; but Nash faced the exigencies of finding the cheapest practicable route and dealing with recalcitrant landowners or independent developers, and turned them to picturesque advantage, in the form of a route which weaved to and fro, and was lined most of the way by blocks of contrasting design. Grandeur and variety were brilliantly mixed together.

Equally ambitious improvements were in train in Brighton, and are especially interesting for two reasons: as the only successful example in nineteenth-century England of town planning applied on a large scale to give a basic structure to an entire town; and as an example of enlightened co-operation by a number of bodies and individuals, stimulated by the vision and enthusiasm of one man, Thomas Read Kemp. The cast involved were as follows: the Brighton Improvement Commission, set up by Act of Parliament in 1810, which was responsible for law and order in the town, controlled the maintenance and formation of roads and streets, and was effectively the local government body; the Brunswick Square Improvement Commission, set up by Act of Parliament in 1830, which filled a similar role in much of the adjacent parish of Hove; the jury of the court leet of the manor of Brighthelmstone (the full name of Brighton), which controlled the common lands on the manor; the committee set up to build the new church of St. Peter's; the shareholders of the proposed Chain Pier; and a number of

230. Queen Street, Huddersfield, looking past the Sessions House to the spire of St. Paul's Church.

181

Brighton residents including the builder-architect Amos Wilds, his partner Charles Busby, his son Amos Henry Wilds, the botanist Henry Phillipps and Thomas Read Kemp, Lord of the Manor and ground landlord of much of the town. Kemp was omnipresent. He was a member of the Brighton Town Improvement Commission, and chairman of the St. Peter's Church committee; his steward presided over the court leet jury; it was probably he who brought the Wilds family to Brighton from Lewes, where Kemp's uncle had made a fortune in the textile trade.[21]

The starting point was what was already there: a T-shaped open space made up of the Steine, running down to the sea; the Marine Promenade, fronting the sea to the east of the Steine; and the cliff walk, running in front of the old town to the west. The improvements expanded the small T to a much larger one. The upright stroke of the T took the form of a grand approach, by way of the Level, the North Steine and the Steine, by which the London and Lewes roads could descend to the sea front; and a promenade running on two levels along the sea front for nearly two miles formed the crossbar (Pl. 229). The whole framework was enriched with lavishly planted gardens, and terraces of splendid stucco architecture.

The Level and the North Steine had been common-land; the Level had been used for sheep fairs and cricket matches, the North Steine had been 'long the receptacle of filth'.[22] By agreement of the court leet both areas were put under a trust, run by seven managers; between about 1822 and 1824 they were landscaped, laid out with walks, and planted with trees, to the design of Amos Wilds and Henry Phillipps, and the North Steine was surrounded by railings. With the agreement of the Improvement Commissioners the road was split and diverted to form an island on which St. Peter's Church was built in 1824-8 (to the designs of Charles Barry), looking down the North Steine towards the sea (Pl. 231). The churchyard was planted to an elaborate symbolic scheme perhaps devised by Henry Phillipps. The end result, as Wallis's *Brighton* put it in 1828, was 'a striking and appropriate entrance from the London and Lewes roads, well calculated to fill the mind of the visitor with pleasing anticipations'.[23]

Improvements on the front had started in a small way between 1811 and 1812, when the Improvement Commissioners expended a little over £1,000 on building a seawall of flint before Marine Parade. The formation of King's Road in 1819-22, and Grand Junction Road in 1829, put a road between the sea and the old town, and made possible the formation of a continuous sea-front drive, running from Kemp Town to Hove. This was widened into a broad promenade, and protected from the sea by the construction of a new wall, built of concrete, all the way along the sea front between 1825 and 1838. Owing to the lie of the land it rose from a few feet at the west end of Hove to a height of sixty feet in front of Kemp Town

(Pl. 232). A lower walk, called the Esplanade, was constructed on the sea side of the wall below the main promenade.[24]

King's Road was built by subscription, with the help of £500 from the Commissioners. Grand Junction Road was built entirely by the Commissioners, at the cost of £1,000. The sea wall and Esplanade in front of Kemp Town were built at the cost of £8,400 by the Kemp Town residents. But the great bulk of wall, Esplanade and attendant works was paid for by the Commissioners, and their successors the corporation. By 1841 around £150,000 had been spent, raised by debentures and serviced by rates. As Granville put it in his *Spas of England*, published in that year, 'an expense that would have appalled even the Government' had produced 'one of the finest, indeed the finest marine promenade in the world ... such results, I say, and at such an expenditure of money may well be considered as a Roman work.'[25]

The building of the terraces of Kemp Town and Hove was going on at the same time as the construction of the wall and promenades. Most of the terraces were designed by Busby and Wilds. The landscaping of Lewes Crescent and Sussex Square in Kemp Town, and Brunswick Square, Adelaide Crescent, and Palmeira Square in Hove, brought greenery onto the parades (Pl. 233). The terraces were, of course, a commercial speculation. The cost of the public works was great, but on the other hand they needed little if any purchase of land: the improvements were on common land or the foreshore, and not a single house had to be demolished. The results were splendid, but had two main defects. The sea front had all the prestige, and the terraces along the Level and the Steines were never grand enough for the scale and dignity of the approach. Moreover, Brighton needed a street of fashionable shops, its own equivalent to Bath's Milsom Street or London's Regent Street. The function was to some extent fulfilled by the shops along Western and Eastern Roads, parallel to the front; but these never acquired a glamour and glitter sufficiently in keeping with the character of what had become the most fashionable of English resorts.

The first grand scale scheme for improving the centre of Newcastle dates from much the same time as the projects for London and Brighton, but, unlike these, it was abortive. The key to the

231. Looking up the North Steine, Brighton, to St. Peter's Church.

183

scheme was the property known in its last days as Anderson Place. This was a Jacobean house with later wings, and had been built by Henry Anderson, a Newcastle merchant who made one of the city's first great coal fortunes. Anderson replaced the medieval Blackfriars by what was in effect a country house set in an ample demesne on the edge of the town.

By the early nineteenth century Anderson Place still occupied thirteen acres of open ground, and Newcastle was spreading round it. By buying and developing it in combination with its own extensive property holdings, the corporation would have been able to provide the town with a new centre, without being burdened with the wearisome procedures of an Act of Parliament. No other town of its size in Great Britain had a comparable opportunity. The first person to explore it was the Newcastle architect, John Dobson. In 1824 he presented a scheme to the corporation for buying the Anderson Place estate, and laying it out in a series of squares and broad tree-lined streets, all centring on a porticoed Mansion House. To judge from descriptions, it was a formal neo-classical scheme, rather than a picturesque one. The corporation were scared of raising the capital, and nothing came of it.[26]

232. (left) Part of the sea wall, Brighton.
233. A view in the gardens of Lewes Crescent, Kemp Town, Brighton.

An inspired builder-developer, Richard Grainger, brought the scheme to fruition, though not to Dobson's original plan (Pl. 234). He seems first to have become interested in 1831. In 1834 he bought Anderson Place and its thirteen acres, for £50,000. His scheme was outlined in a plan of 'projected improvements' drawn up for him by the Newcastle architect, Thomas Oliver, and dated 8 July 1834. It envisaged two main and related developments: that of what became Grey Street and the east end of Grainger Street, along with subsidiary streets and covered markets, which was to be undertaken by Grainger; and an equally large development to the west which needed further finance and a considerable degree of compulsory purchase, and was to be undertaken by a joint stock company following on an Act of Parliament. This was passed in 1837, and the subsequent development carried out on lines somewhat different from those envisaged by Grainger. But it is on his own development, built in and around Grey Street between 1834 and 1837, that his reputation is based.[27]

Grainger's Newcastle was the result of a partnership between

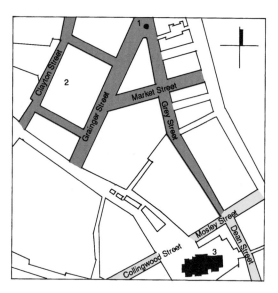

234. Improvement in Newcastle-upon-Tyne. New streets of 1784-1812 shown red, new streets of 1834-40 shown yellow. 1. Grey Column. 2. Markets. 3. St. Nicholas's Church.

developer and local authority. It was a creative partnership, unlike the destructive ones which have too often taken place in recent years, and which in Newcastle itself have destroyed much of the city's character and Dobson's own best work. The viability of Grainger's scheme was compromised by the existence of the corporation markets, built in about 1810, as a result of the 1786 Improvement Act. Grainger agreed to build new markets on another site, in return for permission to demolish the existing markets and extend his development over them.

The deal was made possible by the relationship which developed between Grainger and John Clayton, who was both the town clerk, and one of the most successful attorneys in the town. Clayton smoothed Grainger's path in his dealings with the corporation, and helped him with his finances. Grainger raised the necessary money to buy Anderson Place by mortgaging his existing properties in Newcastle, Eldon Square, Leazes Crescent and Leazes Terrace, successful new developments which he had built between 1825 and 1835. Clayton helped him with these and subsequent mortgages, besides putting money of his own into the development.

As Grainger's memorial in St. John's Church puts it: 'A citizen of Newcastle upon Tyne does not need to be reminded of the genius of Richard Grainger'. His work transformed the town, and still dominates it. Although Dobson designed some of the buildings in the new development, its planning bore no relationship to his grand neo-classical scheme. It was more closely related to Nash's *ad hoc* approach in Regent Street. Essentially, it was based on the line of the upper reaches of the valley which had already been used to form Dean Street and the cross-street of Mosley Street. Grainger filled in the head of the valley, and built what became Grey Street along it, as a continuation to Dean Street, and following the curve of the contours (Pls. 235, 236). Dean Street and Grey Street work organically together, on the basis of the town's geography, the steep curve of Dean Street rising up from the river to merge at Mosley Street into the gentle curve and ascent of Grey Street.

The intended opening of Grey Street was blocked by Stephenson's Theatre Royal in Mosley Street. Grainger did a deal with the theatre proprietor whereby the old theatre was handed over to him and a much grander one built towards the top of Grey Street (Pl. 237), by Grainger and partly at his expense. The silhouette of its great portico projects into the street at the top of the curve, and combines with the Grey Column to form a culmination to the street, based on picturesque rather than formal principles. The Grey Column was an addition to the original plan. The idea of creating such a column, as a tribute to the hero of the 1834 Reform Act, was initiated by a body of admirers after the street had been projected. Grainger took it over, and used it to make the keystone of his street, and to give it its name.

The buildings along the street follow the Regent Street formula:

186

235, 236. Successive views in Grey Street, from engravings in M. Ross and W. Collard, *Views in Newcastle-upon-Tyne*, 1841.

the blocks are related to each other in that they are all of the same scale and of classical design, but each block is different, and the resulting variety within unity is increased by the way the buildings drop and curve down the hillside. The street contained a mixture of shops and financial buildings, in the form of an exchange and a number of banks and insurance offices, the façades of which acted like pavilions to vary the street façades. Functionally, Grey Street was, as a result, a mixture of Nash's Regent Street and Smirke's King William IV Street and Moorgate — but expressed in magnificent northern limestone, rather than stucco.

New streets continued to be made in the central area of towns all through the nineteenth century. Corporations continued to use the local Act as a tool for compulsory purchase and raising of money, and their finances were eased by the power to impose rates (and issue bonds) given them by the 1835 Corporation Act and its successors. In London, New Oxford Street was formed in the 1840s, Victoria Street in the 1850s and 1860s, Southwark Street in 1862, Shaftesbury Avenue and Charing Cross Road in 1877-86. Out of London, the 1860s saw the creation of Boar Lane in Leeds and Victoria Street in Liverpool; Albert Square in Manchester and Chamberlain Street in Birmingham followed in the 1870s. In many resorts large sums were expended on the creation of seaside promenades, and sea walls to support and protect them.[28]

On some of these streets handsome new buildings were built; most of them answered the dual purpose of easing traffic and getting rid of slums, but visually the end result was disappointing. The art of composing a street had been lost; for the Victorians the priorities lay elsewhere, and the idea that a street should have a consistent character, or be in any way composed, had become suspect. Victorian cities were remarkable places, but for different reasons.

237. Looking down Grey Street past the portico of the Theatre Royal.
238. (right) Looking along the shed at York Railway Station (Thomas Prosser, 1877).

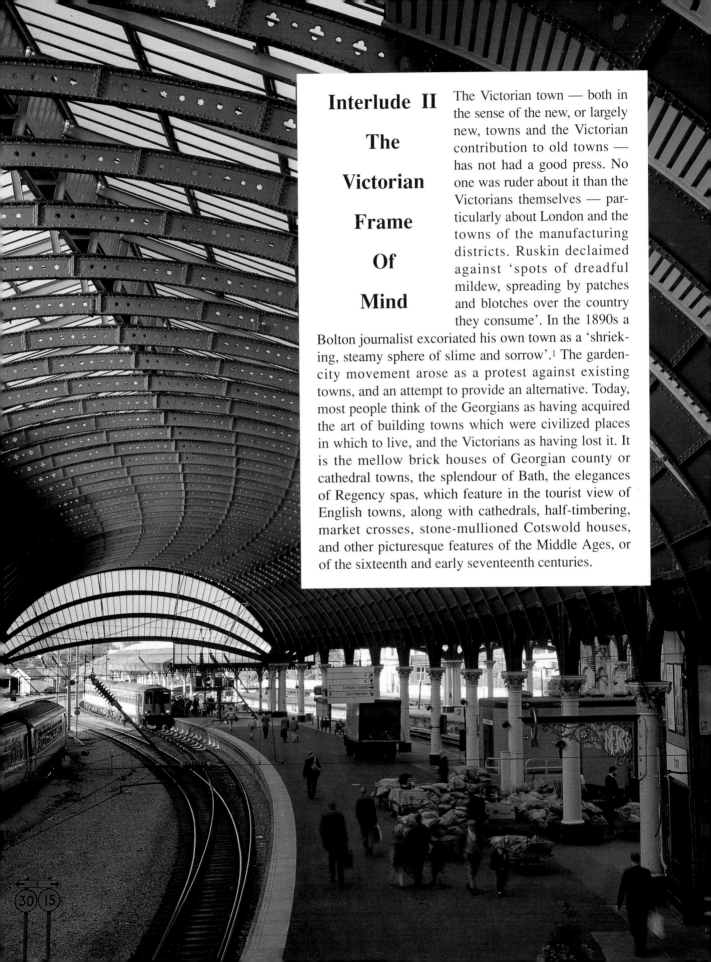

Interlude II

The

Victorian

Frame

Of

Mind

The Victorian town — both in the sense of the new, or largely new, towns and the Victorian contribution to old towns — has not had a good press. No one was ruder about it than the Victorians themselves — particularly about London and the towns of the manufacturing districts. Ruskin declaimed against 'spots of dreadful mildew, spreading by patches and blotches over the country they consume'. In the 1890s a Bolton journalist excoriated his own town as a 'shrieking, steamy sphere of slime and sorrow'.[1] The garden-city movement arose as a protest against existing towns, and an attempt to provide an alternative. Today, most people think of the Georgians as having acquired the art of building towns which were civilized places in which to live, and the Victorians as having lost it. It is the mellow brick houses of Georgian county or cathedral towns, the splendour of Bath, the elegances of Regency spas, which feature in the tourist view of English towns, along with cathedrals, half-timbering, market crosses, stone-mullioned Cotswold houses, and other picturesque features of the Middle Ages, or of the sixteenth and early seventeenth centuries.

And yet anyone who approaches Victorian towns without prejudice cannot fail to find them, not only exceedingly interesting, but also exceedingly enjoyable. A northern mill town has every bit as much character as a Cotswolds wool town. In spite of the carnage wreaked in the 1950s and 1960s in almost every Victorian town of any size, in spite of tawdry new shopping centres and ring roads, roundabouts and subways, a walk round a town like Bradford is still as worthwhile an experience as a walk round Bath.

It is also a very different experience. The Victorian town was a world apart from the Georgian one. To state this does not mean that there were no resemblances and continuities. There was no pantomime transformation scene, in which Georgian towns suddenly turned into Victorian ones. The origin of much that happened or was built in Victorian towns is inevitably to be found in previous generations. Similarly, the Victorian town is not a monolithic entity; there were towns of all kinds, and development and changes within towns over the decades. Even so, the towns have common characteristics which add up to something which has its own distinctive and undeniable flavour.

Georgian towns are based on an ideal of consensus. Of course there were disagreements or tensions in them. There were bread riots; there were duels; there were violent and punitively expensive election contests; there were feuds within corporations, and flaming rows amongst the subscribers to assembly rooms. At many levels the towns were brutal and violent places. But the upper and middle classes in them were supported by the belief that, if only sensible educated men of property would act together, all problems could be solved. The best kind of election was one that was fixed by sensible men beforehand, so that no contest took place: in fact that was how most borough elections were held. Educated men knew what buildings should look like: there was an accepted tradition, which could be developed but not abandoned. Differences between religious sects existed, but the resemblances were more important; the differences were not crucial enough to do battle over. Even the problem of the lazy, improvident, lewd and profligate poor could be solved by the right application of firmness, help, education (of the right kind) and medical care. Today, when the problems and the people have all gone, and only the buildings remain, the consensus shines out in them as an achieved ideal, and gives the towns their serenity and charm.

A Victorian town was a battlefield. Liberals fought against Conservatives. Dissenters fought against the Church of England. Protestants fought against Catholics. The middle classes fought against the upper classes. The workers fought against the employers. Protectionists fought against free-traders. The drink interest fought against the temperance interest. The pulpit fought against the stage. Goths fought against classicists. The godly fought against the ungodly. One shop fought to win custom from another. Yet Victorian towns were not physically violent places; they were less violent

239, 240. (right) Two details of the Royal Albert Bridge, Saltash (I.K. Brunel, 1852-9).

190

241-244. The Four Seasons, over a shop front in Frome.

than Georgian towns. They had accepted conflict and learned how to confine it. The battles of Victorian towns were fought in newspa-per columns, in speeches and meetings in public halls, in monster rallies and processions — and in their buildings. The gin palace on one corner, blazing through its engraved glass windows, the Non-conformist chapel blaring out hymns on another, the soaring spire of the Anglican church on a third, the piled-up windows of a board school on a fourth, were all fighting, in their different ways, for the allegiance of the people in the terraces around them. Allegiance was won by change of heart, not by weighing up pros and cons. People were converted to temperance in as full a sense as they were converted to Methodism. They were even converted to Gothic architecture: G.G. Scott, in his autobiography, described the 'moral awakening' which came to him from reading Pugin: 'Pugin's articles excited me almost to fury, and I suddenly found myself like a person awakened from a long feverish dream.... I was in fact a new man.'[2]

Intellect alone no longer seemed enough to deal with the problems of society. Characteristics which polite and enlightened people had regarded with deep suspicion in the eighteenth century were once again admired. Life was a battle, and those who had to fight it needed interior fire. Enthusiasm was once more acceptable.

The sense of drama which derives from this conflict was accentuated by another kind of drama, that of contrast of scale. The heroic geometry which had been inaugurated by pursuers of Enlightenment at the end of the eighteenth century continued to be produced by their heirs: more and bigger complexes of asylums, docks, markets, hospitals and jails were joined by huge workhouses cast in the same mould. There were new building types: the mighty engineering of great railway sheds, bridges and viaducts (Pls. 238-40); monster hotels and department stores; water towers and gas works. Established types such as town halls, hospitals, breweries, mills, and even terrace houses grew vastly bigger. Much of this was only to be found in the bigger towns; but even in quite small ones, mills and breweries towered and viaducts strode above the little houses.

Size was an expression of money and power. For fifty years England was indisputably the most powerful country in the world, the basis of its power were the goods being made and the services being provided in the towns, and the money earned by these goods and services, albeit unevenly distributed, poured back into them. It was not only the scale that changed, but the richness of individual buildings. The solidity and wealth of ornament lavished, for better or worse, on Victorian town architecture separates it dramatically from the town architecture of the eighteenth century. Never has there been such a wealth and ebullience of stone carving, ornamental brickwork, ironwork, tiles, carved woodwork, mosaics, and stained or decorated glass as is to be found on Victorian buildings at almost all levels, from town halls and railway terminals to small-town shops, public urinals and suburban villas (Pls. 241-4). Partly this

192

was the result of mechanically powered cutting and carving, of mass-produced and therefore cheaper ornament, of improved transport which enabled products from all over the country to converge on one building site far more easily and cheaply than before. Partly it was because the cost of labour, although it was rising in real terms with the wages of those who provided it, was rising more slowly than the income of those who commissioned the buildings. But at the back of it all was a steady, cumulative and — in its visual expression — sensational increase in wealth.

By the end of the century this increase had spread down to the working classes. It contributed to the boom in the consumer and entertainment industries of which something is said in later chapters. But in the first half of Victoria's reign, working-class belligerence petered out after the debacle of Chartism in 1848. It was the middle classes, steadily getting richer and larger, who made the running, and who used their power to agitate for change.

They by no means spoke with a united voice, however. There were, for instance, rational reformers and moral reformers. The former were utilitarians, or influenced by the utilitarians, convinced, in the tradition of the Enlightenment, that the problems of society could be solved by rational analysis. They believed in extension of the franchise, political representation for new towns, elected local government, the growth of commerce as a result of free trade, the control of poverty by a national workhouse system, drainage and improved housing in the interests of public health, the spread of education, and entry to universities, civil service and armed forces by means of examination, not purchase or patronage. They attacked the upper classes because their vested interests stood in the way of these reforms.

The moral reformers believed in the individual regeneration of Christians as a result of study of the Bible, leading to hard work and pure living, without drink, gambling or illicit sex. They wanted legislation to control, reduce, and if possible abolish all these vices. They attacked the upper classes because they were immoral.

The two groups overlapped; sometimes they supported the same ends for different motives; rationalists could hold to their beliefs with as much fervour as moralists. But the extremes were clearly irreconcilable: a man who believed in the divine inspiration of every word of the Bible was not going to get on with someone who subjected it to critical analysis, still less with one who did not believe in God at all. The middle classes did not have a monopoly of reform, nor were all the members of the middle classes reformers. None the less, a dominant feature of the first half of Victoria's reign was the struggle between the reforming spearhead of the middle classes and the conservative bulk of the upper classes.

At a local level this contest broke out in the form of Nonconformist refusal to pay church rates (Pl. 245), and attempts to break the control of local great families over parliamentary boroughs. In

1835 CARTOON
On the Bungay Church Rates Dispute
in which John Childs of the Press
became a prominent figure

THE CHURCH IN DANGER FROM HER SUPPORTERS.
Nº 2 of Illustrations of the Bungay Church Rate Persecution — Take no Bail

245. Supporters of church rates in Bungay march against the Nonconformists, from a cartoon of 1835. 246-248. (right) Buildings erected by Richard Newcomb in Stamford: (top) Rock House, Scotsgate (1842); (centre) cottages in Rock Road (1844-5); (bottom) Rock Terrace, Scotsgate (1841).

Stamford this took architectural form, which survives to the present day. Since the sixteenth century the two members of Parliament for Stamford had effectively been appointed by the Cecils, Earls and Marquesses of Exeter. They lived just outside Stamford at Burleigh, were Lords of the Manor, and owned much of the town. In the 1810s an attempt to break this hold had been made in the traditional eighteenth-century way, by a rival landowning family, in the person of Sir Gerard Noel of Exton Park. The architectural survival of this is the columned façade of the Stamford Hotel. Noel built it in the centre of the town in 1810-13, as headquarters for his campaign, and crowned it with a statue of Justice, as symbol of his desire to bring justice to the people of Stamford. His campaign failed, he lost the election of 1812, and went all but bankrupt as a result.[3]

In the 1840s the assault was renewed in a different context, by a different kind of person. Richard Newcomb, a self-made man from Grantham, moved to Stamford, bought the town's principal newspaper, the *Stamford Mercury*, was elected mayor of the reformed corporation, and set out to lay siege to the Cecil empire. As a preliminary gesture he built a house for himself, Rock House in Scotsgate (Pl. 246). Its scale and heavyweight classicism could not begin to compete with Burleigh, but at least made it the grandest house in the town.

In his newspaper campaigns and public speeches Newcomb used the language of Liberalism; but some of his methods belonged to old-fashioned power politics. Above all, he bought up houses whenever he could in the town, and built new houses on any vacant plot he could acquire — all in order to control or influence votes. His new buildings include a terrace of ten imposing houses in Scotsgate (Pl. 248), opposite his own house, four cottages perched on arches at the back of a former quarry near by (Pl. 247), and two elegant shops marking the beginning of a projected new street on the site of a former inn yard. The street never got finished because Newcomb's campaign failed, as Noel's had, with even more catastrophic effect on his own finances. The shift in power which was taking place easily enough in the new industrial towns of the north was harder to bring about in a small country town, bound by long-standing ties of deference, loyalty, and economic dependence to one family.[4]

Whatever their politics, all Victorian towns, but especially London, and the growing industrial and commercial towns, had serious problems. Urban populations increased as well as urban wealth. Between about 1810 and 1850 the increase seemed likely to overwhelm many towns. In those decades not only were more and more mills and manufacturers eager for workers, but the population

194

of both England and Ireland (for reasons which are still debated) was increasing very rapidly. The overspill from both countries poured into English towns — that from Ireland in especially large numbers after the potato famine of 1845-9. Many of the Irish immigrants were diseased, or destitute, or both.

At first the towns were unable to cope with this increase; the necessary expertise and the administrative system were lacking. Their problems were accentuated by the fact that periods of boom in the manufacturing towns were interrupted by shorter but savage periods of depression, when thousands of people were put out of work; basically, the mills were overproducing.

The result, in many towns, was appalling poverty, overcrowding, bad housing, lack of drainage, and resultant misery, disease and death — above all, death from cholera in the great epidemics of the mid-century. All this was accentuated because, as in all human situations, there were individuals who were prepared to exploit the defenceless: landlords prepared to build housing to the lowest possible standards and to rack-rent the tenants who crowded into it; employers prepared to force down wages and force up hours; parents, in too many cases, prepared to exploit their children.

A major part of the drama in Victorian towns comes from the story of how these problems were attacked and — not solved, but certainly partly solved, during the course of the nineteenth century. To tackle them it proved necessary to make a radical alteration in the balance of urban society and accepted scales of value. *Laissez-faire*, at least in its crudest form, had to be abandoned; the powers of government had to be increased. Voluntary associations remained extremely important, but one of the most significant features of Victorian towns was the growing power of government in them — national government, but, since the idea of state control was still regarded with deep suspicion, more especially local government, by corporations, by local boards of health, and by poor-law commissioners, school boards and hospital boards. All these were locally elected by an electorate the size of which was steadily increased by a succession of laws passed throughout the century.

The campaign for health loomed large in Victorian towns; it was as important a factor as any in their development. Its foundation had been laid by the pioneering doctors, at county infirmaries and elsewhere, in the eighteenth century, but the Victorians waged it with increasing knowledge, fervour, and powers of enforcement. Much of the new energy and authority of local government in Victorian days grew out of health. Corporations spent far more on the provision of drainage, sewerage and a good water supply than on anything else; they paved and cleaned the streets and laid out cemeteries; and a large part of their local legislation was concerned with laying down standards for new housing, or regulating potential health hazards, such as slaughter-houses. Apart from corporations, local boards of health were set up in smaller towns from 1848

onwards, and given wide powers which in effect made them the local government authorities.

When streets and open spaces were formed or widened in Victorian towns, it was as much in pursuit of health or convenience as aesthetic effect or public magnificence. Similar considerations had, as we have seen, carried weight in the eighteenth century, but in Victorian towns they tended to preponderate. Take, for example, St. George's Square in Huddersfield. This is the main square of the town and the central feature of a grid of streets laid out next to the railway station from 1849 onwards. It is a handsome enough space, because of its size, the long and splendid façade of the railway station, and the solid classical buildings on its other sides. But anyone who visits it must wonder why it is such an odd and unsatisfactory shape, like an irregular T, with the crossbar set at a slope to the upright. The crossbar follows the line of the station, and the railway behind it, which runs at approximately 60° to the street grid.

The reason for the shape of the square is that it was not planned at all. When the scheme for the new development was published by the Ramsden estate, the ground landlord of most of Huddersfield, it was attacked in a series of articles on 'The Sanitary Movement' in the *Leeds Mercury*. The main point of the attack was that the development ran against good sanitary principles, and repeated the mistakes of earlier Ramsden developments in Huddersfield: back-to-back housing, over-narrow streets, lack of back streets for refuse disposal and no 'open space, or square, to serve as lungs, or breathing place, for the inhabitants of the enlarged town'. It was also attacked because its tight grid of buildings almost completely blocked out the view of the new station.[5]

The Ramsden estate responded to this and similar attacks by making a number of changes in the plan. Most notably, it provided the required 'lungs, or breathing space' and preserved the view of the station by the simple expedient of knocking out one of the blocks of buildings from the grid. St. George's Square was the result. The adjustment satisfied the critics, and there was no subsequent move, by the estate or anyone else, to attempt to give the square architectural unity by the design of the new buildings round it, or the layout of the open space. That was not the way Victorians worked.[6]

The pursuit of knowledge was as important to the Victorians as the pursuit of health, and the results were as obvious in the towns. It led to buildings of many types, catering for all classes: schools, colleges, universities, museums, art galleries, and institutes of various kinds, including Mechanics' Institutes.

Mechanics' Institutes were founded and built in large numbers between about 1825 and 1850; so, in much the same period, were buildings for literary and philosophical societies, or similar bodies. The latter had first appeared in the late eighteenth century, but the half-dozen or so eighteenth-century foundations were followed by several dozen more after the French wars (Pl. 249). They formed collections of books or specimens, which often provided the basis of future museums, put on concerts and conversaziones, and held regular meetings to listen to papers and discuss literary, historic or scientific subjects (the 'philosophy' in their name would today be called science).[7]

Literary and philosophical societies were supported by the professional classes and the more intellectually-minded bankers, merchants or manufacturers in their towns. In effect, this meant the upper crust of the town. In the more earnest Victorian atmosphere, their buildings and the events put on in them took a somewhat similar position to that of assemblies and assembly rooms in Georgian days; indeed, assembly rooms could often only survive financially by imitation, and the provision of libraries and lectures.[8]

Mechanics' Institutes grew out of a related background, but were more controversial.[9] They were based on the assumption that the kind of deliberately limited education provided in the charity schools was not good enough for intelligent artisans. They set out to educate them further by the provision of a library, lectures and exhibitions. Working-class men were always represented on the committees which ran them, but much of their backing and almost all their money came from middle-class Liberals, usually Nonconformist. These saw serious educated artisans as potential allies in the battle against the upper classes and the Church of England; moreover, they thought that they should have a parliamentary vote, and therefore needed to be educated in order to use it responsibly.

Although the education provided in the Institutes was intended to be non-political and non-controversial, they were often opposed by local Conservatives and Anglicans. They were also frequently regarded with suspicion by working men, as being too much under the wing of the manufacturers. Because of these and other problems many Institutes failed to survive more than a decade or two, or changed their membership and catered for clerks and shop assistants, rather than artisans. Others flourished, however, until the provision of other forms of education made them redundant; their libraries were often taken over by corporations as the basis for public libraries. Because of the considerable amount of middle-class money involved in them, their buildings could be very handsome. The Mechanics Institute in Burnley (Pl. 250), which was built in 1855, is an Italianate *palazzo* almost as grand as a club in Pall Mall.

Until the Education Act of 1870, primary education remained the responsibility of religious denominations. New schools were built in very considerable numbers, but by the mid-century it was becoming clear that a system of voluntary education was unable to cope. The Nonconformists gradually accepted the idea of state-funded primary education, but it was strongly resisted by the Church of England. In the end, in spite of Nonconformist opposition, the 1870 Act included provisions for state subsidies to existing Church of England schools. To supplement these, however, new

249. The building and museum of the Literary and Scientific Association, Frome (1868).
250. A corner of the Mechanics' Institute, Burnley (1855).

board schools were built in large numbers by locally-elected school boards. Many were built on constricted sites, and had to be several storeys high as a result. The cliff-like façades and high multi-paned windows of their classrooms, rising above the little houses, became a new feature of the townscape — inspiring Sherlock Holmes, in a railway carriage between Clapham Junction and Victoria, to apostrophize them to Watson as 'Light-houses, my boy! Beacons of the future! Capsules, with hundreds of bright little seeds in each, out of which will spring the wiser, better England of the future'.[10]

The pursuit of health was, relatively speaking, uncontroversial — except for opposition from the considerable forces of inertia and self-interest. The pursuit of education was a highly inflammable subject because it got caught up with religious issues, and the powerful emotions which these invoked. The strength of religious feeling was a third inescapable and intensely important factor in the development of Victorian towns. Like most other aspects of Victorian life, the religious revival was in fact riddled with conflict: but whatever the beliefs, they resulted in buildings. These are still with us, in spite of much demolition: an enormous number of churches, chapels, schools, convents, and other religious buildings erected in towns during the Victorian period. Between 1840 and 1876 1,727 new Anglican churches were built in England;[11] the number of Nonconformist or Roman Catholic places of worship built in the same period has not been established, but was certainly considerably more. Religious buildings of one kind or another were to be found in every few streets, often several in the same street. They were built in poor districts as well as rich ones. The churches built for the poor, many by individual donors, were often at least as impressive architecturally as the churches in the prosperous new suburbs (Pl. 251).

Some of the money for churches in poor districts may have been subscribed by people who felt that religion would make the poor less of a threat to their own security. Some suburban churches may have been built mainly to give a seal of respectability to new

251. St. Agatha's, Sparkbrook, Birmingham (W.H. Bidlake, 1899-1902).

neighbourhoods. Many of the issues which so bitterly separated Anglicans from Nonconformists and Protestants from Catholics, or split the denominations apart within themselves, seem in the twentieth century (as they would have done in the eighteenth) to have generated far more heat than they were worth. Much Victorian religious literature was mawkish, sentimental or verbose, much religious architecture was crude or derivative, many ostensibly religious Victorians were narrow-minded, self-satisfied or hypocritical. None the less, nothing can explain away the dedication, deep seriousness and intensity of feeling which made the Victorian era the last great religious age in English history.

The resulting architecture was completely different from that of the eighteenth century. No longer did unimpassioned divines read their sermons from tight little pulpits, occasionally raising a hand to make a point. The excitement which the eighteenth century had tried so hard to take out of religion (and had so disliked when it was re-introduced by Wesley and Whitfield) was back in force. It took different forms with different denominations (although each tended to borrow from the other). Anglicans and Roman Catholics went back to the Middle Ages to bring back the mystery of the altar, raised above the congregation and set back at the end of a deep and richly decorated chancel. The Salvation Army fought their campaigns like soldiers, brass bands and all. The Nonconformists transformed the function of choir and pulpit; the pulpit was in effect blown up into a stage, on which the preacher gave a dramatic performance intently watched and listened to by a tense and crowded audience; in intervening acts the choir, raised rank after rank above the pulpit beneath an enormous organ, became a mass chorus, leading the congregation (Pl. 252).

The resemblance between many Nonconformist chapel interiors of the mid- and late nineteenth century and a theatre auditorium is unmistakable, and was deliberately contrived at the time. Chapels were competing with theatres for custom, and adopted similar methods. The resemblances worked both ways: a pub at night with lights glowing through windows of embossed or stained glass, music playing from the penny-in-the-slot polyphon, and porches enticingly decked out with mosaic, marble and tiles, was taking hints from churches and chapels.

A further feature of Victorian life was the importance given to the home. In the eighteenth century a man was judged by his ability to get on with other people, whether in his work or in the society of the walks and the assembly rooms. Something of Georgian social life survived: 'church parade' on Sundays, for instance, remained a major event on into Edwardian days, especially in the resorts (Pl. 254). But for most people, home and the family came first. Home was at once a temple of the domestic virtues, and a haven from stress, where, for instance, 'the busy tradesman ... throws off at intervals the cares of life, and gathers fresh health and energy to

252. Nonconformist grandiloquence. The Upper Independent Chapel, Heckmondwike (Arthur Stott, 1898-9).

253. A villa in the Taunton suburbs.
254. Church parade at Eastbourne, *c.* 1910.
255. (right) The Town Hall, Todmorden (John Gibson, 1870-5) with the Yorkshire moors behind it.

pursue its struggles'. The aim of the successful Victorian citizen was not a house embracing its neighbours in a terrace, but one standing apart from them in a garden (Pl. 253).

So much for the conflict in the Victorian age. But sixty years were bound to see changes. Just as consensus was breaking down towards the end of the eighteenth century, conflicts were being resolved towards the end of the nineteenth. One solvent was provided by the idea of the gentleman. The middle and upper classes stopped fighting each other (or fought each other less) because attendance at the new public schools gave them common values. Victorian gentlemen became as cohesive and important a group as polite society had been in the previous century.

More generally, the aggressiveness of the high Victorian years began to give way under the influence of what Matthew Arnold called sweetness and light.[12] There was a growing and widespread belief that differences of creed, politics or style could be resolved by increased knowledge combined with increased aesthetic sensibility. Everything could be reconciled with everything else. Liberals and Conservatives met happily at dinner together; Nonconformists smiled at Anglicans; Goths became a little classical, and classicists a little Gothic. People found it easy to enjoy themselves, and a rich crop of new buildings dedicated to amusement rose up to cater for them. More will be said about this in Chapter 18.

11

The

Town

Hall

Newark Town Hall, designed by Carr of York in 1773, looks like a country house which has strayed into a Nottinghamshire market place. When Alfred Waterhouse remodelled Eaton Hall for the Duke of Westminster a hundred years or so later, the result was like a town hall, transplanted clock tower and all to the flat Cheshire plain.

In between there had been a change in the balance of patronage. Carr of York's reputation and fortune came from designing country houses; buildings in towns were a sideline for him. Country houses had dominated English architecture; it was by them, and to a lesser extent by London houses designed for their owners, that architectural fashions were set and ideas introduced; the patronage of country-house owners was essential to the career of any ambitious architect.

Before 1800 no town corporation, outside the City of London, could dispose of an income approaching that of a great landowner. The grandest provincial town hall was that of Liverpool, as remodelled to James Wyatt's designs from 1789 onwards; but it was a cockle-shell compared to Wyatt and Wyatville's Ashridge, as rebuilt for the Earl of Bridgwater in 1808-17.

By the end of the eighteenth century the weight was shifting from country to town, and by the time Eaton Hall was built the balance had changed completely. Eaton Hall (Pl. 257) was the most lavish country house of the Victorian era. It cost about £600,000. Waterhouse's Town Hall in Manchester (Pl. 256) cost a round million. Waterhouse designed a number of country houses, but he was not a country-house architect. The bulk of his practice, which earned him the biggest architectural fortune of the nineteenth century, just as Carr made the biggest one of the eighteenth, came from banks, offices, warehouses, chapels, museums, law courts, town halls and other public buildings in the towns. There was still money to be made in a specialist country-house practice, but there was more to be made in a town one.

The shift reflected a straightforward shift in population. In 1801, by one estimate, only 21.3 per cent of Englishmen lived in towns with populations of 20,000 or more; by 1891 the figure had reached 61.7 per cent. But, as far as town halls were concerned, it also reflected a change in the nature and ambitions of corporations.

The change was set in motion by the Municipal Corporations Act of 1835. This followed on the Reform Act of 1832 as the second of the two reforming acts passed by Earl Grey and the Whigs. It led to 178 existing corporations being remodelled. Their town councils, instead of being self-perpetuating, as they had been in the great majority of cases, were now elected by the rate-payers. This change by no means produced a democracy. The rate-payers qualified to vote varied between about 3 per cent and 10 per cent of the adult male population, until the Municipal Franchise Act of 1869 raised the proportion to about 20 per cent. Until 1882, only those who owned property worth £1,000, or occupied property of a rateable value of £30, were eligible for election. In terms of Victorian money values this meant that middle-class electorates produced middle-class mayors, councillors and aldermen. The immediate result of the Act was most commonly that corporations run by middle-to-upper-class Church of England Conservatives were replaced by corporations run by middle-class Nonconformist Liberals. The Grey administration had been well aware that this would happen.

The reformed corporations had less power than their predecessors. They took over existing corporation property, with one major exception. The charities which the unreformed corporations had administered as trustees were moved to the supervision of newly-formed charity commissioners. The corporations no longer ran almshouses and grammar schools, or appointed clergy to livings, with all the powers of patronage that this had involved. The centuries-old combination of executive and judicial powers went too. Aldermen and councillors ceased to sit on the bench in the town courts. The courts remained, but they were presided over by JPs and a recorder appointed by the Crown. Only the mayor survived, as chairman of the bench for petty sessions.[1]

The numerous bodies of independently appointed or elected commissioners which had been set up alongside the old corporations, to pave, drain, light, water or police the towns, survived intact, with one important exception. Policing the towns, which had sometimes been carried out by the old corporations, sometimes by commissioners, sometimes by both bodies, was made a statutory duty of the new corporations; they had to set up a paid police force (Pl. 258), and a watch committee to supervise it.

The new corporations, in short, were given a comparatively modest role: to look after corporation property and run a police force. The Act was intended to break the power of Conservative corporations and improve standards of public order, rather than to bring about a sweeping reform of local government. But in fact it set in motion a process which did produce such a reform.

The new town councils were representative as their predecessors had not been. They were also endowed with new powers of increasing corporate income; when the income from corporation property was insufficient, they could levy a rate. The new councillors brought aggressive new blood into town government, and used their powers and their backing from the electorate to increase their functions. They became empire-builders — or just builders. They took over the powers of local commissioners. They bought up gas companies and water companies, increased their efficiency, and extended their operations. With the encouragement of the central government they imposed health and building regulations, installed

256. (top left) Manchester Town Hall, from a drawing by Alfred Waterhouse, 1869.
257. (bottom left) Eaton Hall, Cheshire (Alfred Waterhouse, 1870-82).

258. Entry to the original Police Department, Wakefield Town Hall.

drainage, tramways and electricity, built hospitals and public baths, and opened parks, cemeteries, art galleries and public libraries.

This process was not confined to the corporations reformed under the 1835 Act. The Act also encouraged non-corporate towns of sufficient size to apply for incorporation — something which had not happened since Leeds was incorporated in 1626. By 1903 a further 135 municipal boroughs had been created, mainly in the industrial north; the list included Birmingham (1838), Manchester (1838), Huddersfield (1868), Bradford (1847), Halifax (1848) and Rochdale (1856). These new corporations started life without any inherited property, and were dependent on rates or their own enterprise. In most of the towns involved the market had belonged either to the Lord of the Manor or to private companies. Many corporations bought them out, often at considerable expense: but at Sheffield, the Dukes of Norfolk continued to own and run the markets until 1899.

The flamboyant character, gift for publicity and subsequent fame of Joseph Chamberlain, who inaugurated a policy of expansion during his mayorship of Birmingham in 1873-6, has given that city an undeserved reputation as the pioneer of what became known as 'municipal socialism'. In fact, the northern corporations anticipated it, often by several decades. Liverpool took over the waterworks in 1846, Bolton and Manchester in 1847, Bradford in 1854, Rochdale in 1866, Birmingham not until 1876. Gas went public in Rochdale in 1844, in Halifax in 1853, in Burnley in 1854, and in Birmingham in 1874. Birmingham's Corporation Street, inaugurated in 1876, was the most ambitious of the new streets cut through provincial English towns, but it had been anticipated by Victoria Street in Liverpool, the remodelling of Boar Lane in Leeds, and the Deansgate improvements in Manchester, all achieved or inaugurated in the 1860s.

To pay for their improvements, towns borrowed on a scale which would have terrified even the biggest corporations or bodies of commissioners of the eighteenth and early nineteenth centuries. The rates soon ceased to be a supplement, and became the basis of borough finance. Between 1860 and 1900 Bradford corporation spent £1·5 million on street-widening and town improvement, £300,000 on drainage and sewerage, and £3 million on water supply. Liverpool corporation spent £1,345,969 on water supply between 1880 and 1892, and £1,652,767 on town improvements between 1837 and 1871. Birmingham's Elan Valley water supply cost it £6,000,000 between 1892 and 1904. Even Rochdale, a considerably smaller town, borrowed over £2·5 million between 1856 and 1902, about 60 per cent of which went on its water supply.[2]

The sums spent on water supply were the direct result of the cholera epidemics of the 1830s and 1840s; it became clear that water was literally a matter of life and death as far as towns were concerned, and it was felt that such a matter should not be left to private companies. Nevertheless some corporations managed to run their water boards at a profit. Gas was less obviously vital, but also more attractive financially: the outlay on setting up a system was much smaller and in many cases corporations drew a handsome dividend from gas (and later electricity) which they used to subsidize other activities. It was for this reason, as much as through a desire to improve a public amenity, that existing gas companies were often taken over, usually as the result of a local Act.

The creation of new streets, or the widening of old ones, produced less obvious and immediate returns, but corporations had the example of Haussmann's Paris to show them how new streets increased rates, and property values. Birmingham corporation, for instance, followed compulsory purchase with seventy-five-year leases on cleared sites, a process which in the long run brought it great wealth as a property owner.[3] A number of corporations combined the formation of new streets with slum clearance; by natural evolution, the areas where new streets were useful means of reducing traffic congestion were also areas of old property, which had often decayed into slums. In London New Oxford Street, and later Shaftesbury Avenue and Charing Cross Road, were driven through the rookeries of St. Giles. Corporation Street in Birmingham and Victoria Street in Liverpool ran through slum areas. The Shaftesbury Avenue improvements of the 1880s were the first in which the principle was accepted that dispossessed occupants had to be rehoused; the cost of doing so was one of the reasons for the meagre nature of the new streets.[4]

The half-century between 1850 and 1900 was the golden age for municipal corporations in England. They were kings in their own domain, running their affairs with minimum interference from the central government. The numerous local government Acts passed by Parliament were 'permissive', that is to say, their adoption was left to the discretion of individual corporations. These were increasing, decade by decade, in power, income and enterprise. There was little bureaucracy and much initiative. Not everything was golden, of course. Some corporations had a better record than others. Virtually all of them alternated between periods of expansion and periods of economy, sometimes short-sighted and disastrous. The problems which many towns faced were appalling, and only some of them were solved. Nevertheless what was achieved was remarkable, in terms of reform, legislation and public works. Visually, the most prominent, though not necessarily the most expensive, elements of this achievement were the town halls. The half-century was their golden age as well.[5]

The function of a town hall was complex. It involved three main elements: the hall itself, reception rooms for the mayor and corporation, and rooms for corporation business, including a council chamber and a court-room. The division, as we have seen, had developed over the centuries from the original nucleus of a hall for courts and entertainments, combined with a smaller room for business.

259. The Town Hall, Devonport (J. Foulston, 1821-3).

260. The Town Hall, Birmingham (J.A. Hanson and E. Welch, 1831-5).

261. (right) Statue of Disraeli, before St. George's Hall, Liverpool.

The hall had originally been the preserve of the corporation, but by at least the seventeenth century it was becoming a public room for the use of the town, available for plays, balls, and meetings as well as for corporation banquets and entertainment. This use continued through the eighteenth century, although, as far as the public was concerned, the beneficiaries tended to be confined to the polite end of the town, which used the hall, and sometimes the rooms off it, for assemblies and subscription concerts. Sometimes the great room doubled up as a court-room. An eighteenth century alternative to town halls also appeared, in the form of privately funded assembly rooms, which became the main public rooms of the town, and could be hired out for functions other than assemblies, or used by the mayor or corporation for their entertainments. In 1753, for instance, when Bristol corporation gave a lease to a body of private subscribers for a plot of ground on which to erect assembly rooms, the lease specified that the corporation should have the free use of them for six days a year — but only if it needed to entertain royalty.[6]

Another strand was added when commissioners or trustees of Improvement Acts began to acquire their own public rooms. The first example of this was probably the Market House at Taunton (1772), with its assembly room above and meeting room for the trustees below. At Devonport, following on the town's 1814 Improvement Act, a handsome little Town Hall (Pl. 259) was built by subscription in 1821-3. It took the form of a Doric temple; the commissioners' offices, the police, the fire-engine and cells, were in the base, and there was a hall 70 foot by 40 up above. This was leased out to the county justices for petty and quarter sessions, but was also available for hire.[7]

The most ambitious of commissioners' town halls were at Manchester (1822-5, demolished), Brighton (1830-2) and Birmingham (Pl. 260).The last was built in 1831-5, after a competition held in 1830. A petition from the rate-payers resulted in an Improvement Act in 1828, and levying of a special rate. The resulting building was an adaptation of a temple, on the Devonport model; as at Devonport the commissioners had their committee room on the ground floor, and the upper portion was filled with the hall. But Birmingham was much richer and bigger than Devonport, and its Town Hall was correspondingly larger, with a free-standing Corinthian order all the way round instead of a Doric order on the entrance front.[8]

More important, as far as the town hall of the future was concerned, the great hall contained an enormous organ. Its presence was due to the fact that the hall was intended from the start to accommodate the triennial Birmingham Music Festival. This had been inaugurated in 1768, to raise funds for the General Hospital. Like other music festivals of the eighteenth century, it had taken place in a church, in this case the church of St. Philip. The church had become too small, but an organ had become an essential feature of the festival. A new one was built by subscription, and presented to the Hospital for installation in the Town Hall. It was a monster, but a splendid monster, claimed to be one of the biggest organs in the world. It could play a carillon of handbells from the keys of the swell-organ, and incorporated the world's first tuba mirabilis, based on its designer, William Hill's experiments in making high-pressure train whistles for his friend Hudson, the railway king. Mendelssohn was one of the first to play on it, and found the experience exhausting.[9]

Birmingham Town Hall set a precedent. An organ became an essential status symbol for all similar buildings. Next in line came a far bigger hall and an even better organ, in St. George's Hall, Liverpool, designed in 1840 and built in 1841-54. The hall had originally been planned as a subscription hall, but few subscriptions came in, and in 1840 the project was amalgamated with a separate one for new assize courts, and later taken over by the corporation. In 1836 the first election held since the 1835 Act had replaced the unreformed Conservative corporation with a Liberal one. The new corporation was anxious to announce its arrival with a grand gesture, and since it had taken over the docks and town property of its predecessor it was in a position to do so. It was extremely rich and getting richer. It could build St. George's Hall almost entirely out of its own resources, at an ultimate cost of £300,000, and in doing so set a new standard of magnificence for civic buildings which poorer corporations and towns had to do their best to keep up with (Pl. 261).[10]

St. George's Hall in Bradford followed in 1851-3. Bradford was not yet incorporated, and its commissioners were less expansive than those in Birmingham. Its hall belonged to the alternative tradition of public rooms built by subscription. Architecturally it followed the model set by Birmingham

262. The organ, Leeds Town Hall. From the original design by Cuthbert Brodrick.

and Liverpool, organ and all. Almost immediately a campaign was started to build a similar subscription hall in Leeds. As in Liverpool, subscriptions were disappointing, and in the end the hall was built by the corporation between 1853 and 1858. Again, as at Liverpool, courts were incorporated into the building. At Leeds there were three, one for borough quarter and petty sessions, and two built on speculation, as part of a successful campaign to make Leeds the assize town for the West Riding. Brodrick's winning competition design was clearly inspired by St. George's Hall in Liverpool. It did not incorporate a dome, but a dome was ultimately added, following the prototype of Liverpool Town Hall and the suggestion of Sir Charles Barry, the assessor for the competition. A portico led under the dome into the hall, and at the end of the hall was one of the most magnificent of all town-hall organs (Pl. 262).[11]

Leeds Town Hall set the style that was to be followed by town halls all over the British Isles: a dome or tower, complete with clock and peal of bells; a great hall and an organ; and much pomp, pride, and sculptural enrichment in the architecture. All this did not have much to do with the functional needs of expanding corporations; their expansion was anyway mainly in the future and it was the, in terms of municipal functions, unnecessary hall and (at Leeds) dome which dominated the buildings. St. George's Hall, Liverpool, incorporated no municipal offices at all; at Leeds there was a council chamber and suite for the mayor in one corner, but the other offices remained scattered over the town until the Municipal Buildings were erected in 1877-84.

The town halls expressed civic pride, combined with a desire to improve and instruct. Spiritually and architecturally, as well as musically, the organs set the tone. Their vast size, and the serried ranks of benches for choirs or orchestras beneath them expressed the changed nature of town halls or public rooms: no longer for polite society but halls for mass meetings and massed choirs, truly public halls for the whole town. At the same time the concerts of which these organs formed the core were designed to improve the taste of audiences, as well as to entertain them, by introducing them to the world's great music. They were to be expressions of art, but art made popular by a process of inflation, much as Handel's

Messiah was inflated in the same period by massed choirs and huge orchestras. This inflation of classical motifs was transferred from the musical to the visual world, starting with the caryatids, allegorical sculpture, massed squadrons of pipes, polychromatic decoration and sumptuous carving of the organs, and spreading out over the whole building. Architecture, like music, was seen as a means of raising taste. J.D. Heaton, one of the main protagonists of Leeds Town Hall, saw it as 'a noble municipal palace', which would become 'a practical admonition to the populace of the value of beauty and art, and in the course of time men would learn to live up to it'. The editor of the *Leeds Intelligencer* agreed with him: 'It is not, we think, anticipating too much to look forward to a greater appreciation of art among that portion of the inhabitants — the great bulk of the population — whose daily pursuits do not tend to encourage such a taste'. But the architecture (and, for that matter, the organ) also reflected civic pride. It was, as Heaton put it, 'intended to present an appearance worthy of the wealth and prosperity of the town'.[12] This was a new concept, and an important result of the 1835 Act. Before this town halls had expressed the wealth and prosperity of the corporation; now they were to stand for the whole town, and become, as Charles Barry put it in connection with Halifax, 'the exponent of the life and soul of the city'.

The demands of civic pride, and the desire to instruct and improve, continued to inform town halls for the rest of the century, although the latter element grew less important. Town halls acquired an unmistakable aura, which was not necessarily a matter of size: the sense of importance comes across just as strongly in Godwin's little Gothic Town Hall at Congleton, built in 1864-6 for a small reformed corporation, or even, as interpreted by an eccentric architect, at Eye in Suffolk, designed by E.B. Lamb in 1857 for an even smaller one. On the whole, new town halls in unincorporated and mayorless towns had less pretensions. Such towns continued to be run by manorial courts or commissioners until the Health Acts of 1848 and 1858 put more and more of them under local boards of health. Occasionally, however, special circumstances produced something more ambitious, as in the case of the local board town halls at Todmorden and Burslem. John Gibson's Town Hall at Todmorden (Pl. 255), built in 1870-5, is a sumptuous miniature version of the Birmingham formula, and was paid for by the Fieldens, the main local manufacturers.[13] The Town Hall at Burslem (Pl. 263) was built in 1852-7, to the design of G.T. Robinson; contributions from rich local potters enabled it to concentrate a monstrous dose of civic self-importance into one small building.

Occasionally, corporation town halls were paid for by individuals. G.S. Gibson, the Quaker maltster whose family dominated the economy of Saffron Walden, replaced its modest Town Hall on the market place by a more ponderous Gothic one (Pls. 264, 265), designed by Edward Burgess; resplendent in top hat and mayoral

263. Burslem Town Hall (G.T. Robinson, 1852-7).

264, 265. Before and after. The Georgian and Victorian town halls, Saffron Walden.

robes, Gibson stands at the head of his corporation before his new building in a photograph taken to celebrate its completion in 1879.[14] The much larger Town Hall at Lancaster was built in 1906-9, at the expense of Lord Ashton, the local king of the linoleum industry.

On the whole town halls grew bigger to keep up with the population of their towns and the growth of their responsibilities. A corporation which, in 1840, had departments for town clerk, police, rates, and the borough surveyor, could find by 1900 that it had acquired at least twelve more, for gas, water, streets, sewers, parks, health, baths, markets, libraries, electricity, museums and finance; and in 1902 corporations took over local schools from the school boards as well. Municipal offices, instead of being appendages tacked onto halls and council chambers, became the largest constituent of large buildings; sometimes these were built without a hall, either because a hall already existed in another building, or because it was considered unnecessary or too expensive; in that case the council chamber often took its place as the focal point of the plan. The resulting building was often called the municipal building or the municipal offices, although quite often, as at Bradford and Sheffield, it continued to be called the Town Hall, even though it had no hall.

All corporations had their different histories, and it is worth looking at two of them to get some idea of the complexities and pressures involved.

Halifax was incorporated in 1848. The corporation occupied temporary quarters for a year or two, but the necessity for a new building soon became clear.[15] Two sites were canvassed, backed by two of the richest and most powerful men in Halifax. The Conservative third-generation Church of England mill owner and philanthropist Edward Akroyd, MP, favoured a site on the edge of the town and commissioned George Gilbert Scott to design a Gothic town hall to go on it. The Liberal first-generation Nonconformist carpet manufacturer, Alderman John Crossley, preferred a site in the town centre, which he happened to own, and produced a classical design by the Bradford firm of Lockwood and Mawson. He offered to build the hall and sell it to the corporation, site included, for £11,500; he would pay for the tower himself. His generosity was not entirely disinterested, for the site was part of a larger one which he was in the process of clearing and developing. A town hall would clearly help to establish the neighbourhood. War was waged in the local newspapers, but in the end Crossley won, perhaps because he was on the council and the building committee, and at the time Akroyd was on neither. But the architect chosen was not Lockwood and Mawson, but Sir Charles Barry (Pl. 266).

A memorandum presented by Barry deserves quotation: 'A Town Hall should, in my opinion, be the most dominant and important of the Municipal Buildings of the City in which it is placed. It should be the means of giving due expression to public feeling upon

all national and municipal events of importance ... in short, it should be, as it were, the exponent of the life and soul of the City, and should therefore be as much as possible in the heart of it. To fulfill these conditions effectively, the building should occupy a central and elevated position and be isolated from all surrounding buildings, it should be a lofty structure having a Tower of commanding importance, having a Clock which should be seen from all parts of the Town, to mark the time both by night as well as by day, and also a peal of Bells, and means should also be provided for occasional displays of flags, illuminations, fireworks, &c., as well as for communication, at all times, with the several districts of the Municipality by the aid of electric wires. The building should be fire-proof throughout, and have a terrace upon the top of it, for commanding a view of all parts of the City. ... The Design of the Building should be so arranged as to afford the means of holding public meetings within it, and of addressing public gatherings of the people around the exterior.'[16]

Barry also criticized the 'serious error' committed in earlier town halls of 'partly devoting these buildings to the recreations, rather than exclusively to the serious business of life, whereby a

266. (left) The Town Hall, Halifax, (Charles Barry, 1859-62).
267. (right) The Prince of Wales driving through Halifax to open the Town Hall. From the engraving in the *Illustrated London News*, 15 August 1863.

needlessly lavish expenditure has been incurred'. He was presumably alluding to great halls with organs; his own plan had a top-lit hall, but it could only accommodate 1,200 people, had no organ, and as it was the main circulation route to other parts of the building was not suitable for regular use as a public hall. Even so, the building cost far more than had been envisaged. The borough surveyor had thought that £17,000 (site included) would cover the cost of a suitable building; Barry's building was costed at £33,000; in the end the bill was around £50,000 (Pl. 266).

This included £2,592 for the 'expenses of opening'. All Victorian town halls were opened in style, especially when a member of the royal family was involved. Crossley, who was suitably mayor for the year of the opening, had persuaded the young Prince of Wales to perform the ceremony. The resulting jollifications were far more lavish than anything which could conceivably be envisaged for a similar ceremony today, and touched with that element of the ridiculous which tended to haunt municipal self-importance. The guard of honour of the Volunteers which assembled at the station to greet the Prince presented arms by mistake to a gaily decorated excursion train; a royal salute pealed out prematurely from cannon on Beacon Hill; when the train finally came in, it stopped short of the benches of local ladies assembled to greet the Prince, who got out and left the station without their realizing that he had arrived; he alighted, too, on bare flags, missing the Crossley carpet which had been woven for his reception. During almost the whole of his visit, as on so many similar occasions in England, torrential rain damped the spirits of all involved.[17]

None the less, it was a remarkable occasion (Pl. 267). One hundred and sixty-four special trains brought 66,000 people to Halifax to see it. Ten thousand Sunday School children and teachers, and a choir and orchestra of five hundred, assembled in the Piece Hall to sing to the Prince on his way to the Town Hall. Six thousand, three hundred and seventy freemasons and members of other secret orders lined the route, wearing white gloves and rosettes. A triumphal arch, designed by Barry, was erected across Princess Street. There were banquets, fireworks, illuminations, and a balloon ascent. The Prince sat, upright and genial, in his open carriage in the rain. Inside the Town Hall, the central hall was packed; the mayor made a speech; the Prince declared the building open. The mayor, in his speech, emphasized that 'the cost of building and furnishing the present structure will not entail any serious burden on the inhabitants of the borough, being met mainly by funds accruing by judicious

268. Rochdale Town Hall, from a painting of *c*. 1870, probably by W.H. Crossland.
269-272. Rochdale Town Hall: four corbels showing (above) W.H. Crossland; (facing page, top left) G.L. Ashworth; (top right) Edward Taylor; and (bottom right) W.A. Scott.

management of the local revenues and resources'. Cost was clearly a sensitive issue, but 'mainly' was an exaggeration; £13,000 of the £50,000 total came from profits from gas and markets, but the remaining debt was not finally paid off until 1933-4.[18]

Almost any town hall cost more than it was expected to, and the case of Halifax was in fact less extreme than that of Rochdale, a town of about the same size, where the initial budget was £30,000 and the final cost £154,755 — considerably more than the cost of Leeds Town Hall, although Leeds was five times its size.[19] At Rochdale, too, the Town Hall reflected the enthusiasm of one particular member of the council, George Leach Ashworth. The town had been incorporated in 1856; the question of building a town hall was raised in 1858 but the economizing wing of the council delayed action until 1863. Ashworth had been against the idea of having a town hall at all, but he had been put on the building committee, and grew increasingly enthusiastic. The building was put out to competition, which was won in 1866 by W.H.Crossland, of Leeds. Over the next ten years the idea of a 'neat and elegant' building gradually gave way to one that would be 'a handsomer town hall than is possessed by any of the great boroughs of the north'. The building grew more and more elaborate (Pl. 268), and correspondingly expensive, as the architect enthused Ashworth and the building committee, Ashworth egged on the architect, and both were ridiculously optimistic about costs.

There were heated debates in the council, reported word for word in the *Rochdale Observer*. In its initial stages the project was attacked by Alderman Edward Taylor, who thought that the money would be better spent on drainage, parks, and sanitary improvements. Crossland, Ashworth, and Taylor are depicted on corbels in the vestibule to the Mayor's Parlour. Ashworth holds a replica of the Town Hall; Taylor shakes his fist; Crossland looks resigned but exhausted. On a fourth corbel, Councillor W.A. Scott, proprietor of the *Rochdale Observer*, has the impartial air of a referee (Pls. 269-272).

In fact, by the time the Town Hall opened in 1878, controversy had been replaced by self-congratulation. Rochdale had been rich and fast-growing enough to pay for Taylor's public improvements and Ashworth's fantasies without an increase in the rates. The *Rochdale Observer* sounded a typically Victorian note: 'amidst this dense and money-getting population, over whom King Cash reigns supreme, and among whom the love of art has yet to be developed, the sculpture and decoration stand forth as a substantial assertion that there are higher pleasures than mere animal indulgence — the gratification which springs from the contemplation and love of the beautiful.'[20]

Rochdale Town Hall was Gothic. A sizeable minority of Gothic town halls were built in the 1860s and 1870s, when the Gothic Revival was at its peak. Scott's abortive project for Halifax, in 1857,

273. Looking up the tower of Stockport Town Hall (A.B. Thomas, 1904-8).
274. (right) A reception on the staircase of Hull City Hall (Russell, Cooper & Davis, 1906-14). From an Edwardian photograph.
275. (top facing page) The old Town and Market Hall, Penzance (W. Harris 1836-7).
276. (bottom facing page) The Town Hall, Bolton (W. Hill, 1866-73).

was perhaps the first; he adapted its design for that of Preston Town Hall, which was built in 1862-7, just after Godwin's Town Hall at Northampton, which owed something to the Halifax design, and was built in 1861-4.[21]

Whatever the style, town halls had to have certain common qualities. They had to express the importance and prosperity of the town; they had (as the Halifax building committee put it, and unless the economizing party was in the ascendancy) to 'be the dominant and most important building in the municipality'. This was not easy, given the increasing pretensions of Victorian commercial buildings. If one looks down Princess Street to Halifax Town Hall, and takes in the lavish *palazzo*-style façade of the White Swan Hotel on the way, one can appreciate how Halifax, and for that matter almost any town hall, had to have a tower or dome, the bigger the better; such features, combined with size and opulent detailing, were necessary to lift it above the banks, warehouses, offices and hotels which surrounded it.

Gothic town halls could be made as impressive as classical ones, as Rochdale and Manchester made clear, and could also suggest, rightly or wrongly, that the roots of a town went back into the Middle Ages; as the needs and accommodation required grew more complex it was perhaps easier to fit them into an irregular Gothic envelope than a regular classical one, and they could provide all that was needed in the way of towers and dramatic skylines.

But the classical style remained the favourite one for town halls through into the twentieth century (Pls. 275, 276). Their classicism was, however, inevitably changed, partly in reaction to the Gothic revival. Architects became more eclectic and adventurous. The mullioned and transomed windows of the Elizabethans, the quirkiness of Italian mannerism, Wren's church towers, the red-brick vernacular of the later seventeenth century, the grandiloquence of both English and continental baroque, the sinuous lines of the rococo, the cool perfection of French neo-classicism, provided a rich repertoire, elements from which were put together with little regard for historical correctness, a readiness to abandon symmetry at any time for convenience or picturesque effect, and a facility in devising new motifs. The results were not always successful; they could be inept, or whimsical, or as pompous as municipal life at its worst. But at their best they could be both enjoyable

277. Inside the Pannier Market, Barnstaple (R.D. Gould, 1853-5).

278. (right) Inside the Market Hall, Bolton (G.T. Robinson, 1851-5).

and approachable, suggesting a combination of dignity, innovation and friendliness that was appropriate to the style which many corporations were setting out to achieve.

Finding a site for a new town hall was often a difficult business. Possible central sites were often too small, or dismissed as too expensive. The little Town-cum-Market Hall of Penzance, built on the site of its predecessor in 1836-7, stands beautifully on the top of a hill at the head of the main street, and its dome (Pl. 275) floats over the town like a miniature St. Paul's; but its island site was too constricted, and new municipal buildings were needed as early as 1864.[22] Many corporations compromised with sites that were large enough but badly placed, or too far out ever to become the pivot of the town. Few towns were as successful as Bolton. Here the large market place (itself a relatively new creation, laid out on the site of a bowling-green in 1826) was cleared out in the 1860s, and the Town Hall (Pl. 276) built in the middle of it; Town Hall and square became, and remain, the dominant central features of Bolton.[23]

Town halls represented only a small proportion of corporation building. This included market halls, exchanges, courthouses, police stations, water towers, pumping stations, bridges, aqueducts, museums, art galleries, libraries and schools, many exceedingly impressive as examples of architecture or engineering, many very large scale — in addition to gardens, parks and cemeteries, as discussed in chapter 16.

The long-standing connection between corporations and markets has already been described. Nineteenth-century corporations or local authorities always did their best to acquire local market rights, if they did not own them already, and usually succeeded. Many corporations built covered markets. These were by no means a nineteenth-century invention, but the nineteenth-century ones far exceeded their predecessors in size and pretensions. The earlier markets invariably had timber roofs. The huge timber-roofed market hall designed by John Foster for Liverpool corporation in 1820-2 has been demolished; so has Fowler's Hungerford Market in London (1831-3), which was built by a private company. Dobson's almost equally large Central Market in Newcastle (1835-6; Pl. 115) has been mutilated, though not beyond hope of recovery. The noble hall of the Higher Market at Exeter (Dymond and Fowler, 1835-8) has been cut up by shops, although the arcade and fine arched roof

survive. Among the least spoilt survivors of timber-roofed market halls are that in Oxford, and the Pannier Market in Barnstaple (Pl. 277). The latter's multitude of arches were probably inspired by the roof of Higher Market, Exeter. It was part of an ambitious scheme inaugurated by the Corporation through a local Act passed in 1852. It included the Pannier Market itself, approached by an archway leading through the Guildhall, a corn market under a Music Hall beyond it, and a Shambles (Pl. 17), in the form of a row of butchers' shops covered by a pentice, across the road to one side.[24]

The Pannier Market marks the end of a tradition, for in the 1850s glass and iron sheds replaced glass and wood ones as the dominant form. Market halls were not pioneers in this field, unlike conservatories and railway buildings, but they followed close behind and produced perhaps the most impressive groups of glass and iron buildings in England after the great railway sheds. One of the first to be built was the Market Hall at Bolton (1851-5), heralded by the Vicar of Bolton as 'a market house which Europe herself might admire and emulate'.[25] His pride was justifiable (Pl. 278). Most of the timber halls had been enclosed by stone walls of handsome classical design, but the wooden structures behind them were of necessity substantial enough not to offer a striking contrast to the stonework. After the ponderous classicism of Bolton market as seen from the street, the soaring delicacy of the iron and glass structure concealed inside comes as a deeply enjoyable surprise. There is a similar contrast between the exterior and interior in Horace Jones's Smithfield Market in the City of London (1866-8) and the much later Kirkgate Market in Leeds (1903-4). But market halls were not always wrapped round with masonry; there are fine examples of completely iron and glass ones at Manchester and Huddersfield. Whatever the combination, they can seldom be described as utilitarian. Indeed, the great expense of the Market Hall of Bolton led to T.L. Rushton, the Conservative local politician who was largely responsible for it, being thrown off the council in 1852, and contributed to the Liberals taking over from the Conservatives in the following year.[26] In general, civic pride almost always led to a greater or lesser degree of embellishment; the arms or other devices of the corporation were prominently displayed and the gates and lights could be of magnificently robust design.

Similar ornamental ironwork is often to be found on the bridges that were built as a result of corporation traffic improvements. The grandest is Holborn Viaduct, built in the City of London in 1863-9, to save traffic negotiating the steep sides of the valley of the Fleet. The stone and cast-iron bridge was marked at each of its four corners by office blocks like Italianate *palazzi* (two of which survive), and the whole was embellished with statues of symbolic ladies, City worthies and winged City of London lions.

The cast-iron bridge built across the old High Street by Stockport corporation in 1864-8 was smaller, but even more drama-

tic (Pls. 279, 280), owing to the narrowness of the street at the bottom of its steep valley, and the way the bridge looms above it. At Halifax, one can walk down from the cast-iron and terracotta corporation market (by Leeming and Leeming, 1895) to the turrets and Gothic ironwork of the North Bridge across the river, built by the Corporation in 1869-71. In 1875 the bridge was embellished by the statue of Edward Akroyd, which has been re-erected next to the great church he built near by on Haley Hill. Though he failed to get the town hall he wanted, Akroyd had been chairman of the council improvement committee which was responsible for the bridge; the plinth of his statue (Pl. 281) is decorated with panels showing him building his church and bridge, and commanding the local Volunteers.[27]

Waterworks and sewerage were frequently the corporation departments that absorbed most money and produced most in the way of public works. Because of their role in the fight for public health, they were rightly the objects of corporation pride. But much of what was built was inevitably outside city boundaries. To appreciate the massive scale of Birmingham's involvement in its water supply it is necessary to drive up into the Welsh mountains, and see the towering dams, pumping stations, ancillary buildings and lavish surrounding landscaping of the Elan valley reservoirs. All this dates from 1896-1902; in this, as in most other municipal activities, Birmingham was a late starter. Cities were proud of their waterworks, and aware of the achievement which they represented. In 1866, for instance, a local historian celebrated Bradford's achievement as follows: 'The New Bradford Waterworks ... constitute one of the mightiest triumphs of this engineering age, and surpasses the greatest of the famous aqueducts which supplied Imperial Rome with water ... the works extend twenty-four miles, intersecting deep glens, crossing high mountains, and piercing the hills by many miles of tunnel.'[28]

279, 280. (left) The bridge across the High Street, Stockport, and the adjacent steps.
281. Episodes in the life of a local worthy. Details from the plinth of the statue of Edward Akroyd, Halifax (J.B. Philip, 1875).

219

The embellishment of pumping stations was one way in which towns could show their pride, but these, too, were often outside the city, so that it is in unexpected country localities that one comes across a great Gothic or Italianate hall with a campanile chimney next door. Some of these were built by private water companies; for example, the amazing Gothic pumping station at Bestwood was built in 1871-4 by the Nottingham Waterworks Company, the equally lavish classical pumping station at Papplewick (Pl. 282) by the corporation after it had taken over the waterworks in 1879. Until 1902, London's water was supplied, in spite of mounting criticism, by private companies, but its sewerage system was the creation of the Metropolitan Board of Works and its engineer, Joseph Bazalgette. Its pumping stations include Abbey Mills (Pl. 284), a semi-Gothic semi-Byzantine cathedral of sewage built in 1865-8 in the marshes by the river Lea.[29]

A water system often involved a water tower. At Liverpool this was built as early as 1853, next to a pumping station, on one of the many hills above the town. It is a structure of Roman grandeur, two circuits of brick arches piled up one within the other (Pl. 283). But one has to make an outing from the town centre to find it.[30] Colchester is dominated by its brick-arched water tower built in 1882, in the same vein as the Liverpool one, if displaying considerably less finesse. Pevsner, in his *Buildings of England*, described it as 'a painfully assertive composition', but the town would be the poorer without it.

The Baths and Wash-Houses Act of 1846-7 allowed corporations to charge a rate to pay for the building of public baths, and William Ewart's Museum Act of 1845 did the same for museums. Ewart's two Public Libraries Acts of 1850 enabled towns with a population of over 10,000 to charge a 1/2d. rate to start a public library; his 1855 Act increased this to a 1d. rate, and reduced the population limit to 5,000.

Response to these Acts was slow; between 1850 and 1855, for instance, less than twenty public authorities established libraries. But it picked up, until by the end of the century, most towns had them.[31]

One disadvantage was that the penny rate was not enough to provide a decent library, or a building to contain it; there was a similar situation with museums. Some towns took over the libraries of declining Mechanics' Institutes. But many owed their libraries and museums to private benefactors: sometimes these provided an endowment, but more often they paid for the building, and the local authority undertook its running and upkeep. This was the arrangement with the most munificent endower of libraries, Andrew Carnegie. He endowed his first library in 1882, and ultimately paid for 380 buildings, all over the British Isles.

Buildings put up by local philanthropists are numerous, and of every kind and size. The little Chadwick Natural History Museum in the park at Bolton, erected from a legacy left for that purpose by Dr S.T. Chadwick in 1876, has been demolished. The library and museum at Derby, erected in 1878 by Michael Thomas Bass, brewer and MP for Derby, survive, as do the great congeries of museums and libraries in Liverpool, including the Walker Art Gallery, paid for by a rich Conservative brewer. Museums and art galleries were often erected in parks (Pl. 285), partly because these were seen as having an educational function, partly because a park provided a free site, belonging to the corporation.

In Birmingham, however, as in Liverpool, they were mainly in the centre, around Chamberlain Square. Until two thirds of the buildings were swept away in the great holocaust of the 1960s, they formed part of the most powerful, concentrated and evocative example of Victorian municipal and civic pride in England — even if one which had developed in an *ad hoc* manner that was typically Victorian (Pl. 286). Around

282. (top left) Inside the pumping station, Papplewick (Ogle Tarbotton, 1881-5).
283. (bottom left) The water tower, Everton, Liverpool (Thomas Duncan, 1853).
284. The Abbey Mills pumping station, London (Bazalgette and Cooper, 1865-8).

221

the Town Hall's rich Corinthian colonnades stood the Council House, Museum and Art Gallery, all designed by a Birmingham architect, W. Yeovil Thomason, and built in two sections between 1874 and 1885; the Central Library (E.M. Barry, Martin and Chamberlain, 1863-82), and Birmingham and Midland Institute (E.M. Barry, 1855-7); the pinnacles and spires of Mason's College, forerunner of the University (J.A.Cossins, 1875-80); the School of Art; and the magnificent Liberal Club (J.A. Cossins, 1886), where the Liberal plutocracy which ran the town could lunch before crossing the square to council meetings. The spaces in between were littered with monuments to distinguished sons of the city, or those whom Birmingham wished to honour: Queen Victoria, Peel, Priestley, Watt, Mason (of the College), Wright, and above all Chamberlain and Dawson. A lofty Gothic fountain was erected to honour Joseph Chamberlain in 1880. Next to it, George Dawson, Baptist minister and prominent citizen, stood under a Gothic canopy, at once an echo of the fountain and a miniature Albert Memorial. It was Dawson who proclaimed, at the Free Reference Library in 1866, that the public library movement was the largest and widest church ever established, and enunciated the doctrine that 'a great town exists to discharge towards the people of that town the duties that a great nation exists to discharge towards the people of that nation.'

285. The Cartwright Memorial Hall, Bradford
286. Chamberlain Square, Birmingham, from an engraving of *c.* 1900.
287. (right) Street advertising in London in the 1820s and 1830s, as drawn by George Scharf.

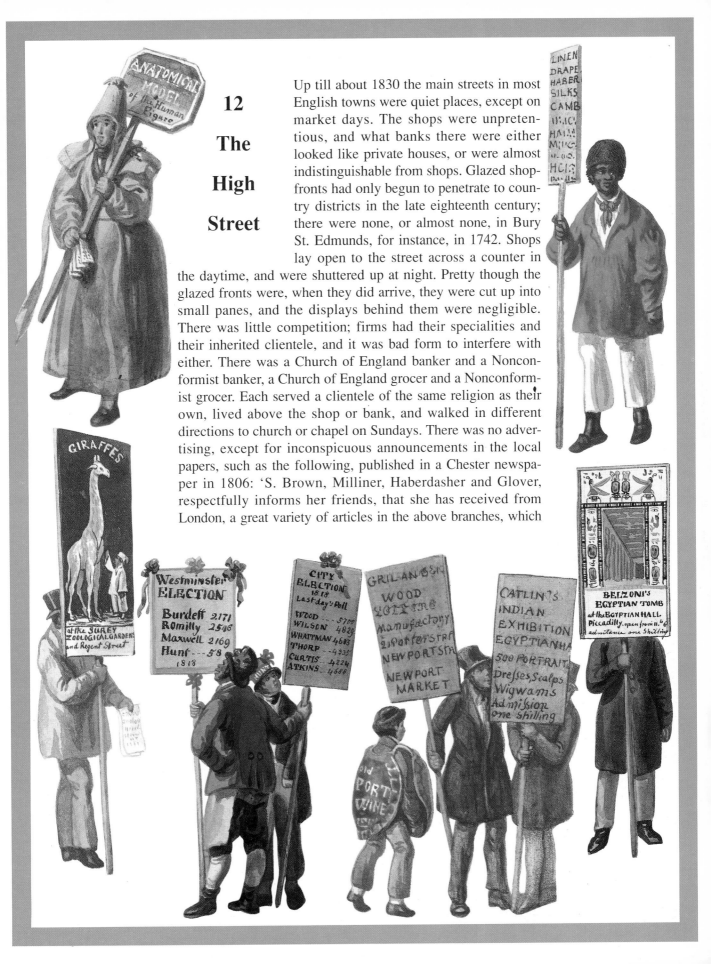

12

The

High

Street

Up till about 1830 the main streets in most English towns were quiet places, except on market days. The shops were unpretentious, and what banks there were either looked like private houses, or were almost indistinguishable from shops. Glazed shopfronts had only begun to penetrate to country districts in the late eighteenth century; there were none, or almost none, in Bury St. Edmunds, for instance, in 1742. Shops lay open to the street across a counter in the daytime, and were shuttered up at night. Pretty though the glazed fronts were, when they did arrive, they were cut up into small panes, and the displays behind them were negligible. There was little competition; firms had their specialities and their inherited clientele, and it was bad form to interfere with either. There was a Church of England banker and a Nonconformist banker, a Church of England grocer and a Nonconformist grocer. Each served a clientele of the same religion as their own, lived above the shop or bank, and walked in different directions to church or chapel on Sundays. There was no advertising, except for inconspicuous announcements in the local papers, such as the following, published in a Chester newspaper in 1806: 'S. Brown, Milliner, Haberdasher and Glover, respectfully informs her friends, that she has received from London, a great variety of articles in the above branches, which

will be opened for public inspection on Monday next; and she flatters herself, that for elegance, neatness and fashion, they will meet their kind approbation.'[1]

Change got under way with the development of methods of advertising in London in the 1820s. A new competitiveness appeared, which was to reach unprecedented heights in the course of the next hundred years. In the process high streets all over England were substantially changed; in some more prosperous towns they were completely rebuilt (Pls. 288, 289).

In visual terms three main methods of selling goods were evolved, by window displays, by advertisement, and by architecture. The first was tied up with the development of the shop-front. The basic form of this had been established in the mid-eighteenth century, as a result of a creative use of the language of classicism. There is no better example than the shop-front erected in Artillery Lane, Spitalfields, in about 1756 for a silk mercer, Samuel Rybot (Pl. 293). Its façade is based on a Doric order, and the spaces between the columns are filled by shop windows and by entrances to the shop and to Rybot's residence above it. The shop windows are divided up into numerous panes, each measuring about 12 by 15 inches.

Later in the eighteenth century, the frieze of shop entablatures began to be inscribed with the name of the shopkeeper. The columns, following the taste of the time, became spindly and elegant,

288, 289. The east side of Bradshawgate, Bolton, Lancashire, before (above) and after (below) rebuilding as a result of street widening in 1914.

dwindled to pilaster strips, or disappeared altogether; delicate fan-lights appeared above the doors, and sometimes above the windows. Occasionally the formula was translated into Georgian Gothic (Pl. 290). Around 1830, taste changed again, and substantial columns and heavier detail came back into fashion.

By then a new wind was blowing through the retail world, stimulated by improved techniques of glass-making and the arrival of gaslight. By the early nineteenth century shop-window panes had increased to about four times their size fifty years previously. Gas lighting on any scale first appeared in London with the founding of the Gas Light and Coke Company in 1812. Shopkeepers were one of the first groups to take advantage of it. A shop with an attractive front lit up by gas standards in the street in front of it, and with gaslight blazing out through the glass, was in a strong position to attract custom, especially if it had a striking display in the window. J.B. Papworth, an able architect who worked almost exclusively for London manufacturers and tradesmen, designed a series of London shop-fronts in the 1820s and 1830s which brilliantly exploited the potentialities of the new developments (Pl. 291).[2]

But a gas-lit shop-front was only one form of advertising. The period saw the first large-scale exploitation of more prominent adver-tisements, whether printed in newspapers or magazines, handed out as broadsheets, or displayed on sandwich-boards (Pl. 287). Façades

could be plastered with advertisements, too, or be made into a form of advertisement by lavish architectural treatment. All these devices were exploited to the full by London gin-palaces of the period, but they were only doing in slightly more blatant form what everyone else was doing.

From London the improved style of shop-front spread to the provinces, along with improved techniques of window display. An 'old draper', whose reminiscences were published anonymously in 1876, gave a vivid picture of what happened in Bristol when he moved there in about 1825 from London. 'Before I went to Wine Street they had never been in the habit of displaying any quantity of goods in the windows, and my style of window-dressing was looked upon as a decided innovation. A roll or two of cloth, with a few men's hats in paper in the background, would constitute all the show that was originally made. People seemed to depend more upon their connexion and usual customers than to seek for new ones. But when I came to open shawls in rows, one behind the other, commencing with a low height, and gradually filling the window into the back, people did not quite know what to make of it. Many of the drapers of the town and their assistants were attracted by the display, and I learned afterwards that I

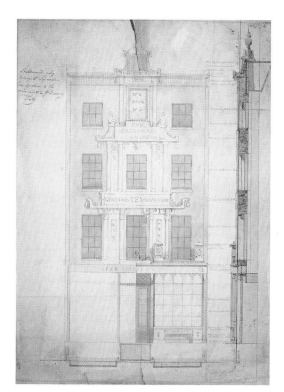

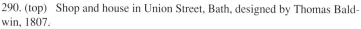

290. (top) Shop and house in Union Street, Bath, designed by Thomas Baldwin, 1807.

291. (centre) Design by J.B. Papworth for Sparrow's Tea Warehouse, Ludgate Hill, London, 1822-3.

292. (right) The Family Linen Warehouse, Ludgate Hill, (J.H. Taylor, 1841), from John Tallis, *London Street Views* (2nd edn., 1847).

293, 294, 295. (facing page) Three stages of the shopfront: (top left) in Artillery Lane, Spitalfields, 1756; (top right) in Stonegate, York, *c.* 1800; (bottom right) in Stonegate, York, *c.* 1860.

226

had caused some merriment by the anxiety I displayed in looking at what was being done by backing on to the edge of the pavement, and surveying it from various points of view, so as to get the goods to my mind. But the plan answered admirably; and we not only sold the goods we showed in the windows, but we made new customers every day.'[3]

But even the modish front of his former shop in Ludgate Hill, which 'was thought so handsome in that period', seemed to him 'but a poor shabby sort of affair ... when compared with the immense sheets of plate glass that are now commonly to be found in even the second-rate drapers' shops'.[4] One of the first of these new fronts appeared, in fact, on Ludgate Hill, next door to the most famous of Papworth's shops of the 1820s, his Chinese-style Sparrow's Tea Warehouse (Pl. 291). The new front was designed by John H. Taylor in 1841, for John Harvey's Family Linen Warehouse (Pl. 292). Its curving glass shop windows rose up some 18 feet through the equivalent of two storeys of Papworth's façade, in tall sheets of glass divided vertically by slender cast-iron mullions. The glass curved boldly to a central door, and by doing so increased the frontage and provided a vestibule. Thin pilaster strips, surmounted by consoles, and a vigorously modelled cornice acted as a frame to the glass. The cornice was finished off by a palisade of cast-iron ornament.[5] Curving glass, consoles, and cast-iron trim were to become favourite elements of Victorian shop-fronts.[6]

Harvey's shop-front must have caused a sensation, especially when lit up at night. Other shopkeepers were encouraged to install similar fronts as a result of the abolition of excise duty on sheet glass in 1845, which approximately halved its price. Comparison of the editions of strip panoramas of London streets published by John Tallis in 1838-40 and 1847 shows how quickly the fashion spread through London; in the first edition few shops have glass sheets of any size, but in the second they are everywhere.

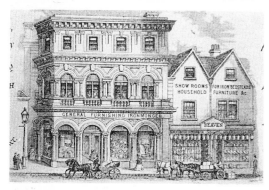

MAIN ENTRANCE, 22 & 23, MARKET PLACE.

From London the fashion spread to the provinces, until by 1870 small-paned shop windows survived only in back streets, or in commercially stagnant or old-fashioned towns. Sometimes the new big panes continued to be framed by wooden columns or pilaster strips, but often iron was used instead of wood and the columns shrank to a diameter of 2 or 3 inches (Pl. 295). Sometimes installation of a new shop-front was accompanied by rebuilding or re-fronting of the premises, but more often the old façade survived above the shop window. Sometimes it was given a little extra adornment, or a coat of stucco was slapped on top of it; very often it was profusely covered with lettering, announcing the name of the shop and everything that it had to sell. This abundance of lettering was the corollary of abundance of goods in and around the shop-front; not only were the shop windows, especially in country towns, often crammed to bursting, but the outside of the shop-front was festooned with goods as well. It was an attitude to display which is still to be found in the poorer shopping streets of some northern towns.

In most towns at least one shop did especially well, and expanded as a result; and in bigger towns there were inevitably several of them (Pls. 296-9). Expansion usually took the form of absorbing the house next door, and continuing the shop window across it; an especially successful concern could run through a string of houses. At some stage the resulting conglomeration might be rebuilt or remodelled as a single design, but very often this never happened. A splendid example of the process survives at Asprey's in Bond Street. Here the shop-front originally installed in about 1860 runs across the front of three late eighteenth century houses, and continues through a later extension. The windows rise up through two storeys, and are an early example of extension of display to the first floor, which was to become increasingly common in the last decades of the century.

Very often these expanding concerns were drapers' shops. Some moved into other lines of goods in the course of expansion, and gradually became department stores, or something not far removed from them. England was a little behind France and America, and when department stores did come they were pioneered in the north rather than in London. Bainbridge's in Newcastle and Kendal Milne in Manchester were selling a wide variety of goods as early as 1850; and the numerous Co-operative Society shops which sprang up in Yorkshire and Lancashire, starting in Rochdale in 1844, soon developed into what were essentially department stores. The northern equivalent of William Whiteley, London's self-styled 'universal provider', was David Lewis in Liverpool. Lewis was the more enterprising of the two. Not only did he start branches in Birmingham, Manchester and Sheffield, but he also embarked on a vigorous and inventive campaign of advertising (Pl. 300), culminating in 1885 with the bringing of the abandoned *Great Eastern*, the biggest ship of the day, from Gibraltar to Liverpool, for exhibition to the public. Moreover the big London shops (with the single exception of Marshall and Snelgrove in 1875) were not rebuilt until around 1900; Lewis built big department stores to a unified design on Bull Street, Birmingham, in 1885, and on Market Street, Manchester, in 1880.[6]

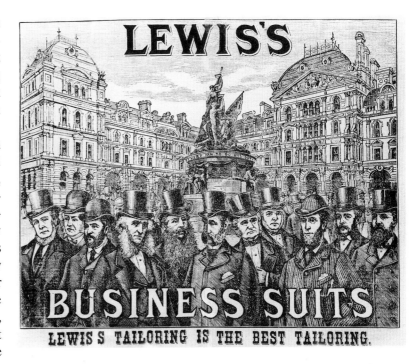

Apart from their shop-fronts, Victorian shops in England form an architectural *melange*: there is no unified building type, such as is to be found in banks or warehouses. Shopkeepers concentrated on their shopfronts, and the rest of the building usually tagged along behind. The great glass fronts were, in fact, much criticized in their day by architects and the architectural press for their effect on the façades above them. 'We have been called a nation of shop-keepers', wrote George Gilbert Scott in 1857, 'yet there are few things in which we fail more signally than in our shops.... The very idea of its being necessary to the satisfaction of the eye to see how a building is supported is utterly ignored, and fronts of towering altitude are erected with no apparent substructure but plate-glass! Surely no age but our own would have endured such barbaric building.'[7]

Perhaps the most interesting shop buildings were those which had a display front on the first floor as well — or had lavishly glazed upper floors, for the better lighting of their showrooms (Pl. 301). In the resulting buildings the masonry acted as a framework for two or more storeys of glazing, or as a scaffolding through which the glazing appeared. Numerous combinations were possible, and the material used could be stone, brick, terracotta, wood, iron, or different combinations of the five. Buildings of this type are very much in a minority among Victorian and Edwardian shops, but they are nearly always enjoyable, and sometimes exciting.

One way of developing the potentialities of a shopping district was to exploit the back lands and build an arcade leading out of a main shopping street. The shopping arcade[8] was invented in Paris in the late eighteenth century, stimulated by the fact that shopping on most streets in Paris was an unpleasant occupation, owing to their narrowness and lack of pavements. In England, arcades appeared in two main batches, between 1816 and the early 1830s, and again between about 1870 and the early 1900s; for some reason, few were built in the mid-century. The first batch were built in masonry, glass and wood, the second in masonry, glass and iron. Both in their materials and their style they relate to the covered markets of the same period, but whereas the markets were mostly built by corporations or other local authorities, the arcades were built, with rare exceptions,

296, 297. (top and centre left) Coxeter's shop, Ock Street, Abingdon, in *c*. 1845-50 and *c*. 1880.
298, 299. (centre and bottom left) James Beaven, Trowbridge, later Burgess and Co., in 1860 and the 1890s.
300. (above) One of David Lewis's advertisements of the 1880s, with Liverpool Exchange and the Nelson Monument in the background.
301. Upper-storey display window in Scarborough.

by individual speculators or by companies set up for the purpose.

Land became available in various ways. Several arcades exploited the long narrow plots typical of the property pattern of English towns. Others, like the long since demolished Lowther Arcade in the Strand, or the surviving Barton Arcade in Manchester, formed part of development on land bought up by Act of Parliament as a result of street-building projects. The magnificent Great Western Arcade in Birmingham was built in 1875-6 over the line of the railway, which had been cut at low level from the new Great Western station. The even grander County Arcade in Leeds (Pl. 302), and its transverse Cross Arcade, were built in 1898-1900 by a company which had purchased the site of the Beast Market off Briggate. Not all arcades were a financial success. To succeed, they had to join two streets which were already busy, or provide a convenient route to and from the centre. Dobson's Royal Arcade in Newcastle (1831-2) was architecturally one of the most splendid, but was never a success, because it was off the main shopping routes. Even so, its demolition in 1966 was unforgivable, and its later re-erection in mangled form offers little compensation.

Being designed all of a piece, arcades had an architectural unity which is only occasionally found in open-air shopping streets: shop frontages, flooring, top-lit roofs, entrances, lighting and the gates which close the arcades after hours all hang together. The early arcades can have an enchanting intimacy of scale, but the great age of the English arcade was after 1870, when glass, iron and terracotta were used with a boldness of structure and a fertility of ornament to provide as gay and colourful an ambience for shopping as one could hope for (Pls. 302-3).

Multiple stores were comparatively late arrivals. The great amorphous mass of London was the first to acquire them. The ABC (Aerated Bread Company) opened its first shop in the Strand in 1861, and gradually acquired branches all over London. Lyons Tea Shops followed in 1894. Neither firm opened branches outside London, and both have disappeared in recent years. Boots was the first shop to establish a national chain; the original store was opened in Nottingham in 1877, and Jesse Boot, its proprietor, began to open stores in other towns from about 1890.

Michael Marks opened a market stall in Leeds in 1884, and took Thomas Spencer into partnership ten years later. Spencer

302, 303. County Arcade, New Briggate, Leeds (Frank Matcham, 1898-1900); Central Arcade, Newcastle-upon-Tyne (J. Oswald and Son, 1904).

brought in capital which enabled Marks to open stalls in other towns, and he soon moved on to stores. Woolworth's opened its first English store in Liverpool in 1909. W.H. Smith had begun to acquire railway bookstall rights as early as 1848, but did not open stores until the 1920s. By then Montague Burton was also beginning to spread its network. It was in the decades between the two wars that the multiples really established their hold on provincial high streets; and the same decades saw the emergence of the 'big five' banks. These developed as a result of the amalgamation of several hundred smaller banks, spread all over the country, and today largely forgotten. If, in a provincial town, one comes across an especially pretentious or imposing bank sailing under the colours of one of the 'big five', the odds are that it was originally the headquarters of a local bank, whether private or joint-stock.

The development of advertising began to affect banks and insurance companies at much the same time as shops. But since the former needed to give the impression of being places in which it was safe to deposit money, rather than enjoyable to spend it, their methods were different: they went in for architectural importance, rather than seductive flashiness.

To begin with, it was not the private companies which did so, however, but the joint-stock ones, which had more capital behind them. At first only insurance companies were involved. Joint-stock banks (except the Bank of England) were forbidden by law until 1826, and until 1833 were only allowed outside a sixty-mile radius from London. The prohibition was the result of the Bank of England's jealous and effective attempt to keep its monopoly. It was broken by Act of Parliament after many private banks with limited capital had gone bankrupt in the financial crises which followed the Napoleonic wars.[9]

Perhaps the first joint-stock insurance company to promote itself in a big way was the County Fire Office. This was founded by a lively opportunist, J.T. Barber Beaumont. He had started life as a history painter, moved on to finance, assembled an impressive board of titled or wealthy directors to attract shareholders, and made use of architecture to help his promotion.[10] In 1817 he took a lease of the best site in the Regent Street development, at the end of the Quadrant looking onto Piccadilly Circus. On this (to the designs of Robert Abraham) he built an insurance office more palatial than any existing commercial building in London, other than the Bank of England. It was surmounted by the company's crest, a figure of Britannia sitting on her lion. 'County Fire Office' was proudly and prominently inscribed on the parapet. Below, the frieze was equally prominently inscribed with the name of the Provident Life Insurance and Annuity Office, which Beaumont had founded at the same time. Engravings of the building featured largely in the notices of annual general meetings which Beaumont published in the advertisement columns of both London and provincial newspapers (Pl. 304).

County Fire Office,

AND

PROVIDENT LIFE OFFICE,
Regent-Street, London.

PRESIDENT AND TRUSTEES,

The DUKE of NORFOLK,
The DUKE of RUTLAND,
The MARQUIS of NORTHAMPTON,
EARL GREY,
LORD BRAYBROOKE,
LORD KING, &c. &c. &c.

AND SIXTY DIRECTORS.

Managing Director, } J. T. Barber Beaumont, Esq. F.A.S.

AT an ANNUAL GENERAL MEETING of the Members of the COUNTY FIRE OFFICE, held at the Society's House, in REGENT-STREET, on February the 14th, 1822,

The Hon. WASHINGTON SHIRLEY in the Chair,

The following *Resolutions were carried unanimously:—*

That this Meeting is highly gratified in observing that the Association continues to proceed in uninterrupted harmony, and unexampled prosperity.

That of SIXTY-FOUR THOUSAND PERSONS, who have committed their security to the protection of the County Fire Office, *none have been disappointed*—CLAIMS having been paid to *One Thousand Three Hundred and Fifty Sufferers*, and not a SINGLE LITIGATION having occurred with *any Claimant!*

That the accumulated Funds of the Association, amounting to *Upwards of Half a Million Sterling*, and the Provisions in its Act of Parliament and Deed of Settlement, render the Security of the Policy Holders ample and indisputable.

That in the equal Distribution of the Surplusses or Profits, RETURNS of 25 and 20 *per Cent.* have been INVARIABLY paid to all Persons, who have continued insured in the Office Seven Years, upon ANNUAL as well as *Septennial* Policies, which Returns, during the LAST EIGHT YEARS, have exceeded £36,000!

That the Thanks of this Meeting are given to J. T. BARBER BEAUMONT, Esq. Managing Director, for the unabated Zeal, great Attention, and valuable Services, which he continues to render this Office.

That the Thanks of this Meeting are given to the Hon. WASHINGTON SHIRLEY, for his impartial Conduct in the Chair. (Signed)

WASHINGTON SHIRLEY, *Chairman.*

304. Advertisement in a Plymouth newspaper for the County Fire Office, London, 1822.

231

Over the next thirty-five years London acquired increasing numbers of imposing insurance buildings. By 1854 they were described as 'among the architectural ornaments of the metropolis'.[11] Meanwhile, in the provinces, insurance buildings and banks were putting on airs. In both cases it was the joint-stock companies which set the pace. The more impressive buildings were usually put up by provincial firms, rather than as branch offices of London ones.

After a comparatively slow start joint-stock banks came into existence in increasingly large numbers. Their emergence was much resented by the private banks, justifiably so, in their own terms, for by the end of the century the majority of private banks had either been absorbed by joint-stock ones, or turned joint-stock themselves in self-defence. The founding of the Leicestershire Banking Company, for instance, in 1829, provoked an angry correspondence in the local papers, probably inspired by private bankers. One correspondent called the new bank a project 'as quixotic and utopian as an attack upon windmills or a visit to the moon'. Another suggested that its promoters were 'men engaged in trade, and consequently had an object in knowing the pecuniary situation and connection of their competitors in business'. But the bank flourished and grew, as epitomized by its proudly Gothic headquarters, built to the designs of Joseph Goddard in 1870-2 (Pl. 305).[12]

Joint-stock banks tended to have more pretensions than private ones, partly because, as new arrivals, they needed to make themselves conspicuous, partly because they had share capital behind them, partly because they had different functional requirements. Up till the 1830s private banks were still essentially private houses, in which one of the partners lived, with a banking hall incorporated in or attached to them. The hall could take the form of an appendage to one side, or form part of the ground floor of the main building; its presence was usually, but not invariably, marked by a shop window. Like shops, banks normally had two doors, one giving access to the bank, and the other to the residence.

Until at least the mid-nineteenth century, the head office of a joint-stock bank usually incorporated a residence for the manager. But in addition to the banking hall it had to contain a room of some size and dignity to act as a boardroom, and an even bigger room for shareholders' meetings. It was a public building with a private element, whereas a private bank was a private building with a public element. Moreover, private banks usually developed as an ancillary to some other form of business, which had already generated a flow of capital and a network of potential customers; they were offshoots of textile firms, or breweries, or law businesses. Joint-stock banks had to generate their capital from their investors. A handsome building, exuding success, could be a means to this end.

In the 1830s the architecture of joint-stock banks was already noticeably different from that of private banks, although modest

305. The former head office of the Leicestershire Banking Company, Leicester (Joseph Goddard, 1870-2).
306. The former Yorkshire and Agricultural Bank, Nessgate, York (J.B. and W. Atkinson, 1839).
307. (right) A detail of the former West of England and South Wales Bank, Corn Street, Bristol (W.B. Gingell, 1854-6).

compared to what was to come. The former Yorkshire and Agricultural Bank in Nessgate, York, built in 1839 to the designs of J.B. and W. Atkinson, is an example (Pl. 306). In its case architectural pretensions failed to win success: the bank had only been founded in 1836, but 'excessive expenditure on new buildings in York and Whitby' is said to have contributed to its failure in 1842.[13]

The rebuilding of Grey Street, Newcastle, between 1835 and 1840, established the joint-stock bank as a vehicle for architectural display. The columned and pilastered pavilions which punctuated the plainer façades along the street were occupied by hotels or banks: the latter included the nine-columned front of the Bank of England, the smaller, but handsome, building of the Newcastle Joint Stock Bank, and the premises of the Northumberland and Durham District Banking Company (Pl. 309). This was described in 1842 as 'the most highly ornamented building which has yet been executed in any part of the town'.[14]

When provincial joint-stock banks were allowed in 1826, the Bank of England was given a *quid pro quo* in the form of permission to open its own branches outside London. A number were opened in the next ten years, but it was not until the 1830s that they began to become architecturally ambitious. The building in Grey Street, built in about 1836, was followed by branches in Manchester, Bristol and Liverpool, built to C.R. Cockerell's design in 1844-9. Their design developed from his earlier Westminster British Fire and Life Office, in the Strand in London, which was built in 1831. They were a brilliant expression of the dual function of contemporary bank buildings. The bank occupied two storeys behind a giant order, and the manager's residence had a range of windows opening onto a balcony, under a mighty pediment above.[15]

Although Cockerell's banks found no imitators, they must have helped establish the concept of banks as monumental buildings, and set up standards of grandeur for competitors to equal or excel (Pl. 310). In 1854-6, nine years after the completion of the Bristol branch of the Bank of England, the West of England and South Wales Bank built a new head office in Bristol, to the designs of W.B. Gingell (Pl. 307). It outdid Cockerell's bank in splendour, however far it fell short of it in subtlety. Its design was based on that of Sansovino's St. Mark's Library in Venice, one of the most opulent of Italian Renaissance buildings. It was a measure of high-Victorian self-confidence or extravagance that Gingell produced something even more opulent. His building had no residential accommodation and is made up of two mighty storeys, each marked by an applied order; within the major order is a minor order, articulating arched openings which run the length of the façade; and out of the cracks, so to speak, ooze more cherubs, foliage, and allegorical figures of doubtful purport, than one would have thought possible to cram into a relatively short, two-storeyed façade.[16]

The private banks had to react as best they could; and the more

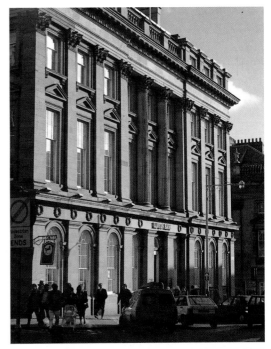

308. (left) Becketts Bank and Park Row, Leeds, from the painting by Atkinson Grimshaw, 1882.
309. The former Northumberland and Durham District Bank, Grey Street, Newcastle-upon-Tyne (*c.* 1840).
310. The Birmingham Joint Stock Bank, New Street, Birmingham (*c.* 1880).

successful entered with ebullience into the fray. A series of new joint-stock banks founded in Manchester in the 1820s and 1830s were followed, in 1848, by the rebuilding of Heywood's Bank in St. Anne's Street; the result was a dignified and charming composition, designed by J.E. Grogan, in which the bank building (including accommodation for a manager) was echoed on a smaller scale by the residence of Sir Benjamin Heywood, the senior partner. Heywood's Bank was reticent, however, compared to the grandest private banks of the 1860s and 1870s: in Leeds, the Gothic *palazzo* designed by G.G. Scott for Beckett's Bank (Pl. 308); in Manchester, the equally ebullient Brook's Bank, designed by G. Truefitt in 1870; and the smaller but imposing bank designed in 1864 by Waterhouse for the Backhouses, one of the Quaker families which dominated nineteenth-century Darlington. This, unlike the other two, survives, as does one of the last really grand private bank buildings, the former Foster's (now Lloyds) Bank in Cambridge. This was built, also to Waterhouse's design, in 1891, and its huge banking hall is lined with brilliantly detailed faience decoration.

Head offices of both private and joint-stock banks were inevitably grander than branch offices, but branch offices could be imposing too, especially when they were built by a London bank in a big provincial town. The most notable nineteenth-century examples are the banks designed by John Gibson for the National Provincial Bank in the 1860s and 1870s: a central bank in Bishopsgate, almost as lavish as Gingell's bank in Bristol, and handsome branch offices in the West End, Southampton, Newcastle, Middlesbrough, Stockton-on-Tees and Sunderland.[17]

Insurance buildings (Pl. 312) were often at least as imposing as banks, and followed much the same chronological pattern; as in London, insurance buildings were perhaps a little in advance of banks. Purpose-built offices for building societies came later, but by the end of the century were joining banks and insurance offices along the high streets. The smaller branches in the smaller towns often did no more than remodel the ground floor of an existing building, but new buildings were built in very large numbers. They occupied a corner site, if possible. Some variation of the classical style remained the most popular, as expressing the note of reliable prosperity that was needed; but there were many exceptions, especially towards the end of the century, when eclecticism was running rampant.

Specifically office areas were, and still are, a rarity in English towns. Although the first purpose-built office buildings were put up in the City of London in the 1850s, it was not until well into the twentieth century that office elements drove out warehouses, houses and shops from significantly large areas. A few other big towns followed the City, and acquired office districts in miniature, such as Mosley Street in Newcastle (Pl. 312), or Castle Street and the streets off it in Liverpool; in the latter district the bank and insurance buildings of the early twentieth century vied with the City in splendour (Pl. 311).

311. The former Martin's Bank, Liverpool (Herbert Rowse, 1927-32).
312. An insurance building in Mosley Street, Newcastle-upon-Tyne.
313. (right) Detail of a warehouse of the 1870s in Station Road, Batley.

13

The

Warehouses

A warehouse was originally any place — not necessarily a separate building — where wares were kept for storage or sale, both wholesale and retail. As late as the early nineteenth century Sparrow's Tea Warehouse and Harvey's Family Linen Warehouse on Ludgate Hill in London were essentially retail shops, although they may have had a wholesale department, as was often the case in those days.

In the course of the nineteenth century a more or less hard and fast division emerged: shops for the retail trade, warehouses for goods in transit, and warehouses for the storage and sale of goods wholesale. The third class had two divisions, depending on whether the warehouses were for goods sold in bulk, and usually by sample, such as corn, cotton, wool and coal, or for goods such as textiles, sold in smaller quantities as a result of inspection by the buyer or his agent. It is the last division with which this chapter is mainly concerned. The other types were essentially utilitarian, and their architecture, however impressive it might be because of the scale and logic of the design (Pl. 314), seldom went in for display or elaboration. Warehouses which were visited by buyers were a different matter.

Such warehouses existed in considerable numbers by the late eighteenth century, but had little identity as a building type. They could be the outlet of an individual mill and manufacturer, or the property of a merchant or warehouseman who was acting as middleman between manufacturer and buyer. They were almost invariably connected to the house in which the merchant or manufacturer lived; in the case of the latter there were quite often two partners, one living by the mill and the other by the warehouse. The two were separated because mills were dispersed over a considerable area, following the watercourses, whereas warehouses became concentrated in particular towns, for the convenience of buyers. By the early nineteenth century, for instance, Manchester, in addition to having its own mills, had become the sales centre for mills spread all over Lancashire.

STATION ROAD

314. A utilitarian warehouse of *c.* 1860 in Liverpool.
315. The original of the *palazzo* warehouse. Lamb's Warehouse, John Dalton Street, Manchester (W.H. Brakspear, 1846).
316. (top right) An essay in the *palazzo* style, by John Walters, Princess Street, Manchester.
317. (bottom right) Warehouse for Milligan, Forbes & Co., Bradford (Andrews and Delaunay, 1851-2).

Goods for sale were stored in part of the house, or in a building attached or close to it; if any attempt was made to impress the buyer with the prosperity or reliability of the business, it was likely to be in the house, where he was received and entertained.

The next stage came when merchant or partner moved out, and the premises were given over to warehousing, except, perhaps, for accommodation for employees of the firm on the top floor. This process was connected with the growth of trade and the development of suburbs. It is not always easy to establish whether individuals moved because they were attracted by suburban life, or because they wanted to take advantage of rising prices in central areas, and of the better return gained from premises given over to commercial use.

The process seems to have got under way at much the same time in London and the new cities of the north. William Hunt, for instance, father of William Holman Hunt, the Pre-Raphaelite painter, kept a warehouse for cotton and velvet thread in Wood Street, off Cheapside. In 1830 he stopped living on the premises and moved to the suburbs. A few years later he moved his business to a late-seventeenth-century house near the Guildhall. Here Holman Hunt remembered how: 'on the first floor the packing and ticketing of small parcels went on, and on two higher floors the stranger came upon the cause of a constant droning heard lower down. It was the rattling of a multitude of hand machines winding Brooks' cotton and thread into balls and on reels. When I was ascending to the upper floors my difficulty was to run through these apartments from the spring door stealthily and swiftly enough to escape the toll of kissing which the young women winders always exacted when I was caught.'[1]

In 1839 Love and Barton's *Manchester As It Is* described how merchants were moving to the suburbs from Mosley Street, previously the most fashionable street in the town, and how its houses were being converted into warehouses. One example in the neighbourhood was an eighteenth-century house in Cannon Street, which became the warehouse of the brothers Grant, the models for Dickens's Cheeryble brothers, who had a calico-printing works at Ramsbotham.[2]

Almost inevitably, as trade prospered (and it prospered greatly both in London and the northern cities), premises were rebuilt, or new warehouses appeared on virgin sites in convenient neighbourhoods. As Love and Barton put it: 'on land purchased at so high a rate new buildings have generally been erected; and, to make the most of it, a more than usual number of warehouses are raised on a limited space, the towering height of which make up for their contracted width'. And as buyers were now received at the warehouse rather than the residence (and the idea of architecture as advertisement was anyway on the increase), warehouses began to acquire pretensions. By 1839 Love and Barton were able to comment that many of the new buildings were 'imposing, and in some instances beautiful'. But it was not until the late 1840s that what was to become the standard type of Manchester warehouse, and be imitated all over England, emerged in full splendour.

Its inspiration was the Italian *palazzo*, as already adapted by Charles Barry for the clubhouses and private houses of London, and, more relevantly, for the Athenaeum in Manchester. This was built in 1837-9, as an educational centre for lectures, readings and meetings. In Barry's office at the time was a young man called W.H. Brakspear. Brakspear seems to have settled in Manchester, and in 1846 designed a new warehouse there for the firm of Lamb, in John Dalton Street. In it the *palazzo* was adapted for warehouse purposes: the ceiling heights were lowered, the ratio of window to wall increased, but the splendour remained (Pl. 315).[4]

Brakspear's career fizzled out, but his example was followed by other architects in Manchester, especially Edward Walters and J.E. Gregan. Walters's warehouse designed for James Brown, Son and Co. in 1851-2 was as imposing as Brakspear's, but more practical. It had an extra floor, an even higher ratio of window to wall, and was built of brick with stone dressings, whereas the brick in Brakspear's warehouse had been stuccoed to resemble stone. The principal floor of the Brown warehouse was raised up on a high basement to make it the right height for unloading goods from horse-pulled drays.[5]

Walters went on to design many more warehouses (Pl. 316). His designs were much imitated, not only in Manchester. In 1851-2 a warehouse at least as splendid as Brown's and closely modelled on it was built in Bradford to the design of Andrews and Delaunay, for Milligan Forbes and Co. (Pl. 317). Bradford, rather than Leeds, had become the main marketing centre for the Yorkshire woollen textile industry; it was the Yorkshire counterpart of Manchester, although it never quite acquired the overwhelming local supremacy of the latter city. Robert Milligan was a self-made Scotsman who from humping clothes on his back for sale in the Yorkshire villages had risen to become one of the richest merchants in Bradford and its first mayor.[6] James Brown was active in local government. The great warehouses were built by the ruling aristocracy of their towns.

Over the ensuing decades both Manchester and Bradford acquired large numbers of new warehouses, some of great splendour. For warehouses selling finished goods to the home or foreign trade (as opposed to those selling wool, cotton or yarn in bulk to local manufacturers), closeness to the main-line stations was essential, and architectural parade desirable. In Manchester a high proportion were still the outlets of individual mills, and under the same ownership; quite often, however, they also stocked goods from other mills. The Bradford warehouses more often belonged to independent merchants. At Manchester this type of warehouse was concentrated around Portland Street, between the London Road and Central Stations; in Bradford they were within easy walking distance of Exchange

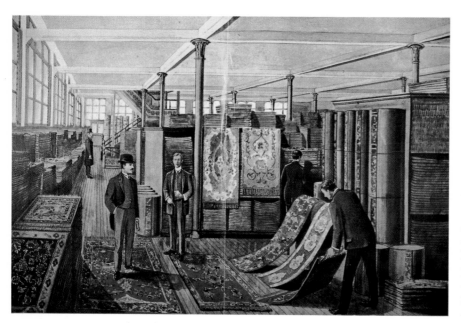

318. Inside a Manchester warehouse. Illustration from a brochure of *c.* 1880.

319. (top right)   Glazed backs of warehouses near Victoria Station, Manchester.

320, 321. (centre, bottom right).   Warehouse gates in Little Germany, Bradford.

Station. Both towns acquired Station Hotels as grand as the warehouses, for the entertainment of those who came to buy. More than half the Bradford warehouses were obliterated in the 1950s and 1960s, but some still survive in the district known as Little Germany; the name is due to the fact that much of Bradford's export trade was to Germany, and many (though by no means all) of the firms in the area were run by German families who had come to Bradford as a result.[8] There has been less destruction, on the whole, of Manchester warehouses, although many have gone, and the future of those that survive is often in doubt.

The warehouses had to strike a balance between display and convenience. Their organization was carefully worked out to achieve the maximum efficiency. They were mostly very high, by the standards of the time, six or seven storeys including the basement. Descriptions of warehouses in Bradford show how, as in contemporary breweries, the input was sent up to the top, and worked its way down. Goods arrived from mills, dye shops, goods stations or canal basins on drays, and were carried through arched entrances to loading and unloading bays; the fact that unloading took place away from the street is sometimes said to have been to prevent rival firms from seeing and copying the patterns, but seems as likely to have been for the convenience of being under cover or out of the traffic.

On arrival cloth was either sent out again to the finishers to be dyed, or taken by steam-powered lift up to the top floor. Here it was sorted, checked, measured, rolled out mechanically round boards, and labelled. The next few floors were given over to classified storage and displays (Pl. 318). This was by no means confined to different kinds of cloth, especially when Manchester and Bradford diversified into what was known as the 'fancy trade', from the 1850s onward, and stocked hats, ribbons, trimmings, shawls, umbrellas and so on. One room was usually set aside as a sample room, for goods which were sold by sample, or from pattern books.

On the ground floor or upper basement was the packing room, where goods were finally packed in hydraulic or steam-powered presses for dispatch. Here too were the selling rooms, where business was discussed and finalized with clients, the partners' or managers' offices and dining-room, and the counting house, from which invoices were sent out — round the world, in the case of an exporting house. In the basement were the steam-engine, store rooms and the employees' dining room.[9]

The father of the painter William Rothenstein had settled in Bradford and owned a warehouse in Little Germany. The family lived on Manningham Lane — the right place to live, in Bradford of that time. In his reminiscences, Rothenstein describes how, in the 1870s, the warehouse was: 'a place, to us children, of endless interest. There was an engine room, in which was a great steam-engine, and a man who looked after it. There were rooms full of machines for cutting and measuring cloth, and other rooms piled up to the ceiling with bales; and one room where beautiful labels, richly ornamented with gold, were attached to patterns. There were trucks, on which we could ride, and a lift — it was called a hoist — on which bales of cloth were lowered to the packing room; while outside, in the yard, lorries drawn by great horses with harness and heavy collars ornamented with brass, stood waiting to take the packing-cases to the railway. The warehousemen were patient and good-natured; we adored them all: the clerks, engineman, liftman and packers, and we grieved if anyone left the firm. Every Christmas a deputation from the warehouse came to the house to wish us a Merry Christmas.... My father had a passionate admiration for England, for the English character, and for the spirit of liberty for which, in his eyes, England stood. A staunch Liberal and free-trader, he admired the principles of Gladstone, Cobden and Bright; and he had read much of Carlyle, Ruskin, Darwin and Huxley.'[10]

The Bradford warehouses are built of local limestone, which is beautiful in colour and easy to carve. Manchester was not in a stone district, and the warehouses were almost all of brick, usually with stone dressings on the main façade, and sometimes with a little marble around the entrance. Structurally, the warehouses of both towns imitated local mills; the internal structure of those in Manchester was one of iron columns and iron or wood beams, that of those in Bradford all of wood, until the very end of the nineteenth century. Daylight was important, to facilitate work and enable examination of goods, and warehouses were often pierced with small light wells, painted white. At Manchester cast-iron construction could enable the back walls to be almost entirely glazed: the result is sometimes as impressive, in its own way, as the masonry fronts (Pl. 319).

For these the *palazzo* tradition remained the dominant one for several decades. Yorkshire and Lancashire merchants enjoyed comparisons with the merchant princes of the Italian Renaissance, and the style gave them what they wanted: an image of dignified prosperity, and a grand entrance for clients. But architects showed ingenuity in devising variations, which often took the buildings further and further away from their *palazzo* originals. The windows of each floor could be given different treatment. Sometimes they were linked vertically as well as horizontally. Windows with arched rather than flat tops were favoured as giving variety, but were less practical; arched windows let in less light. One solution to this was

241

to put flat-headed windows into an arched surround, and carry the arch above the ceiling level; another was to use shallow segmental-arched heads. Almost all warehouses had a bold surmounting cornice, a grand entrance for clients and a less grand entrance for goods: but even the latter were often given some magnificence by the great gates of ornamental ironwork which closed them (Pls. 320, 321).

Sometimes an unusual site suggested a special feature. In Vicar Lane in Little Germany the great warehouse designed by Lockwood and Mawson for Law, Russel and Co. in 1874 was on an acute-angled corner. The architects put the entrance on the corner, at the bottom of a frontispiece of piled-up Corinthian columns. Opposite is an equally ambitious warehouse designed by Lockwood and Mawson in 1871, also with a grand entry on the corner. The combination of these two mighty buildings, each six storeys high, facing each other at the entrance to narrow streets surrounded by other warehouses almost equally grand, is a dramatic one (Pl. 323). It was commented at the time that 'a stranger wonders to find such magnificent buildings in what appears to be more in the nature of a back street than anything else', but the narrowness of the streets is part of the drama (Pl. 322).[11]

Over the decades stylistic variations began to appear. There were a few Gothic warehouses, especially in Manchester; but their architects had to face the problem of what to do with the Gothic arch, which was inimical to daylight. The gigantic warehouses in Portland Street, Manchester, built in 1856 for S. and J. Watts, the monarchs of the fancy-goods trade, to the designs of Travis and Mangnall, used roof-top pavilions lit by rose windows to break up the length of the façade. In late-nineteenth-century Manchester glazed terracotta began to come in as an alternative to brick, and the introduction of passenger lifts made warehouses still higher. There is a fine constellation of these later warehouses along Whitworth Street, a new street carved out through slum property in the 1880s.

Manchester and Bradford always had the largest number of warehouses. Their warehouse districts were the first entirely business districts, with only a minimal residential element, to develop in England; the office business district was a later arrival. But in towns all over England there were constellations, small and large, of Victorian warehouses built to catch the eye. Their designers faced, and seldom solved, the same problems as in Manchester and Bradford. The desired image of prosperity and solidity had to be reconciled with the need to let in as much daylight as possible. In the great majority of cases the result was a compromise. Street

322. Looking down Vicar Lane, in Little Germany, Bradford.
323. Warehouses of the 1870s, designed by Lockwood and Mawson, at the opening of Vicar Lane, Bradford.
324, 325. (top and bottom right) Warehouses in Clerkenwell, London.

frontages entirely filled with metal and glass, although the most efficient in terms of daylighting, were a rarity; the use of window mullions in the form of slender iron columns was much more common.

London, especially the City, inevitably had large numbers of warehouses, although they were seldom as grand as the northern ones. Up till the end of the nineteenth century the financial district of the City covered a comparatively small area around the Bank of England and the Stock Exchange; the rest was a teeming mixture of buildings occupied by warehousemen, merchants, commission agents, shipping officers and dealers of all kinds, with towering utilitarian warehouses for heavy goods along the river. Comparatively little has survived bombing and redevelopment. The textile warehouses around St. Paul's Churchyard and Paternoster Lane have been almost entirely obliterated; it was in a coffee-house in Paternoster Lane, incidentally, that Charlotte Brontë always stayed when in London, preferring the City to the West End, as did Lucy Snowe in *Villette*, because it seemed 'so much more in earnest; its business, its rush, its roar are such serious things, sights, sounds.... At the West End you may be amused; but in the City you are deeply excited.'[12]

A few hop warehouses survive in Southwark, around the former Hop Exchange, but as hops were bought by sample at the Exchange, they do not go in for architectural display. In Eastcheap the vinegar warehouse designed by R.L. Roumieu in 1868 is a brilliant example of Gothic pyrotechnics. But the least altered Victorian commercial district in London is in Clerkenwell and Smithfields. In the second half of the nineteenth century it became an area of mixed printing works, small workshops and warehouses, and it still retains much of its architectural character (Pls. 324, 325).

In the late nineteenth century a number of London warehouses, in Smithfields and elsewhere, worked out a formula for an eye-catching front that also admitted plenty of daylight; the greater part of the front was given over to a single great arch, filled with more or less continuous glazing. Bradbury and Greatorex's warehouse in Aldermanbury (Pl. 326), built in about 1850, had devised an alternative formula, which for some reason failed to catch on, although it was well adapted to the language of classical architecture. The frontage was divided up by pilasters and entablatures, on a post-and-beam system, and the intervening spaces entirely filled with glass.[13]

Gothic was the ruling style for the warehouses of Bristol, of which all too many have been demolished. They dealt in a greater variety of goods than the Manchester and Bradford ones, and were less concentrated, tending to be mixed up with earlier and smaller buildings. Among them (in addition to some good buildings by E.W. Godwin) were two major masterpieces, Foster and Wood's Wills Tobacco warehouse (Pl. 329) in Redcliffe Street (1868), which has been demolished, and Ponton and Gough's granary for Wait and Jameson on the Welsh Back (1869), which survives (Pl. 328).[14] The

326. The Bradbury and Greatorex warehouse, Aldermanbury, London (*c.* 1850. Demolished).
327. Moorish detail on the Barran warehouse, St. Paul's Square, Leeds (Thomas Ambler, 1878).
328. (right) The former Wait and James Granary, Welsh Back, Bristol (Ponton and Gough, 1869).

former translated the Bradbury and Greatorex formula into Gothic: essentially it was a grid of masonry beams, piers and columns filled with glass and surmounted by a cornice of heroic scale. In the latter lighting was of little importance, and so, one might have thought, was architectural display. What was needed was a ventilated sieve, to prevent the corn from mildewing. A sieve was what Ponton and Gough produced, but it was made up of arches and pierced screens, all of polychromatic brick. The result was one of the most sensational achievements of Victorian architecture.

The warehouses in Leeds were never as numerous or, on the average, as grand as those in Bradford, but there are a few fine surviving examples and one eccentric *tour de force*, the huge warehouse designed in 1878 by Thomas Ambler in St. Paul's Square. This was built for John Barran, who pioneered the mass production of clothing in England, and established Leeds as the centre of the clothing industry. Barran, for reasons which remain obscure, commissioned a building with a strong admixture of Moorish or Islamic details, all executed in Doulton's terracotta, and culminating in tall bedizened pinnacles, like miniature minarets (Pl. 327).

Nottingham still has its Lace District, a compressed area of lace warehouses built in brick around narrow streets, and largely intact. Many were designed by the Nottingham architect, Thomas Hine, whose family had interests in the industry; as a central feature of his buildings, he favoured, and seems to have invented, a particular kind of square-headed window filled with stone tracery.

But the warehouses on Station Road, Batley, are at least as fine and much less well known. Batley, and its neighbour Dewsbury, were an exception to the great majority of smaller Yorkshire textile towns, which either sold direct from the mills or sent their cloth to be marketed in Bradford or Leeds. The reason may have been the nature of the speciality. They were the centres of the shoddy and mungo trades. Shoddy and its slightly younger brother mungo were a type of cloth woven from a wool fibre made by grinding up rags or old cloth, and combining it with a certain proportion of new thread. The industry was not, at first, considered respectable and was bitterly attacked because of its supposed infection with germs from the slums of England and Europe, and because the 'devil's dust' produced by the grinders infected the lungs unless proper precautions were taken.[15]

By the last decades of the century it had become accepted as a sensible method of recycling. But it was perhaps its early disrepute (from whence the adjective 'shoddy' derives) that made Leeds and Bradford unwilling to deal in it. Anyway, from the beginning shoddy and mungo were sold direct from Batley and Dewsbury, at first by auction and then from warehouses, which were almost always subsidiaries of individual mills.

From about 1840 until 1880 (when foreign competition took away what had been a virtual monopoly) the trade was exceedingly

prosperous. It turned Batley and Dewsbury from villages into towns, and produced warehouses the splendour of which was perhaps partly due to a desire to live down an ambivalent reputation. The best surviving group of warehouses in the two towns is on Station Road, Batley, which climbs up a steepish hill from the edge of the town to the station at which buyers arrived (and where there was formerly a grand Station Hotel, demolished in the 1960s).

The warehouses almost all date from between about 1860 and 1880. Ground values were lower than in Bradford or Manchester, and the warehouses are of three or four, rather than five or six, storeys. All are built of superb local stone, golden yellow, easy to carve, and still in vintage condition (Pls. 313, 330). The earlier warehouses are classical, some handsome but restrained, others enriched with the opulently wild detailing which sometimes flowered out of the profits of the Yorkshire textile trade. The Gothic style and even greater richness arrived in about 1870, introduced by a Batley firm of architects, Hanstock and Sheard. They favoured arches of Moorish flavour, voussoirs in alternating colours, and an abundance of carving, especially foliage capitals and a distinctive line in carved birds, winged dragons, and other animals. Behind the street front everything is utilitarian but solid, so that seen from the back the mass of unadorned stone looks like a line of fortifications climbing the hill. The line has gaps in it; some of the warehouses have been demolished, others are underused, or empty, or gutted by fire. But it is still a street of palaces, even if the palaces have fallen on hard days.

329. The Wills Tobacco Warehouse, Redcliffe Street, Bristol (Foster and Wood, 1868. Demolished).
330. A warehouse at the top of Station Road, Batley (probably by Hanstock and Sheard, *c*. 1875).
331. (right) One of the chimneys of the Tower Works, Leeds, built on the model of Giotto's campanile in Florence in 1899.

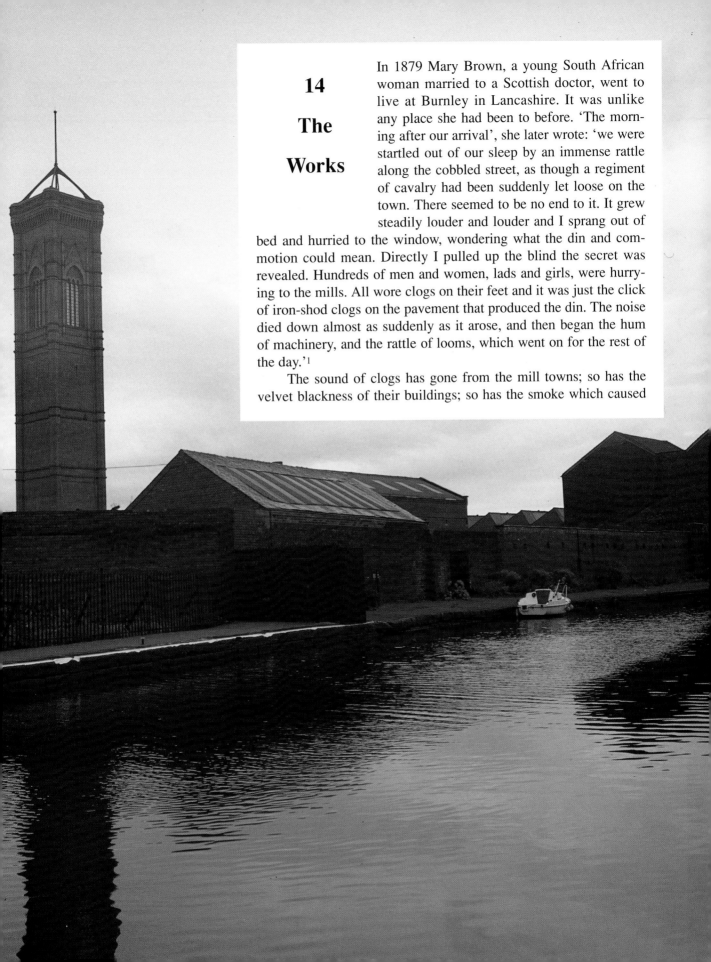

14

The

Works

In 1879 Mary Brown, a young South African woman married to a Scottish doctor, went to live at Burnley in Lancashire. It was unlike any place she had been to before. 'The morning after our arrival', she later wrote: 'we were startled out of our sleep by an immense rattle along the cobbled street, as though a regiment of cavalry had been suddenly let loose on the town. There seemed to be no end to it. It grew steadily louder and louder and I sprang out of bed and hurried to the window, wondering what the din and commotion could mean. Directly I pulled up the blind the secret was revealed. Hundreds of men and women, lads and girls, were hurrying to the mills. All wore clogs on their feet and it was just the click of iron-shod clogs on the pavement that produced the din. The noise died down almost as suddenly as it arose, and then began the hum of machinery, and the rattle of looms, which went on for the rest of the day.'[1]

The sound of clogs has gone from the mill towns; so has the velvet blackness of their buildings; so has the smoke which caused

With Compliments from the Smoke.

WIDNES WITH THE LID OFF, MAKES THE SUN HIDE HIS FACE.

332. 'With compliments from the smoke'. A Widnes postcard of the early 1900s.

333. Bolton mills after dark, from a photograph taken in about 1948.

334. (top right) Yorkshire mill town: looking down on Staithwaite.

335. (bottom right) The railway viaduct collides with a mill at Stockport.

it; so have the needle forests of factory chimneys which produced the smoke and loomed through it. The mills with their hundreds of windows stand, too often, empty or derelict, or vacant patches of land mark where they once were. The huge chapels where gargantuan organs loomed over equally gargantuan pulpits are empty, demolished or converted to other uses. A way of life has irrevocably vanished. It involved several million people for over a hundred years and produced most of the wealth on which the power and reputation of Britain was based.

It would be stupid to deny that there was much in this way of life that is better away. But when one looks back from the amorphousness of life today, it stands out, sharp and clear, as all of a piece. It had its own look, its own sounds, its own smells. Visually, it could be dramatic, and at times sublime — in the eighteenth-century sense of the word. The experience of coming as a stranger to see what remains of it is still a powerful one. The mills, the viaducts, the rows and rows of little houses, spilt over the hills and along the valleys, the hills themselves so wild and shapely, giving, by their contours, a shape to the towns, the stone everywhere, stone mills, stone viaducts, stone houses as solid as they are small, stone pavements, stone town halls, are all of a piece. Down in the plains,

248

especially in the undulating valley-seamed plain around Manchester, the drama subsides but does not disappear. It derived originally less from the landscape than from the forest of chimneys and proliferation of mills, most of which have gone; what is left is a sprawl of building going on and on, but still with dramatic episodes, like the mill poking through the great viaduct at Stockport (Pl. 335), the old town centre tumbling down the sides of the valley, and the huge mills that survive along the waterside above the town.

In general, what one sees is only a fragment, with the smoke, the blackness, the isolation, half the buildings and most of the poverty gone — as remote from the towns as they were in the nineteenth century as Cotswold towns and villages, with their boutiques, tourists, tended gardens, pony girls, trim verges and neat hedgerows are from the rough textile villages of the sixteenth and seventeenth centuries, even though, in both cases, many of the buildings are the same.

The impact remains strong enough, however, and the buildings can still excite and amaze, in spite of the fact that far larger ones are being put up today. When they first appeared among populations which had no experience of buildings of such size, or of the way of life which they produced, their impact must have been extraordinary.[2]

The first cotton and wool mills appeared in the 1760s, and were for spinning and carding. By the 1790s, they existed in considerable numbers, and some were very large. They were not confined to Lancashire and West Yorkshire; they appeared in Derbyshire and Cheshire, and in the south-west in Wiltshire and Gloucestershire as well. They were water-powered, and therefore strung out along rivers and streams with a sufficient fall to turn the water-wheels. For this reason they followed a pattern of settlement largely based on one which had begun to appear in the sixteenth or seventeenth centuries, if not before, when textile industries in these districts first began to develop, and fulling mills — tiny by comparison with the mills that were to come — had spread along the waterways, along with scattered groups of weavers' cottages and clothiers' houses. The developments of the Industrial Revolution before the spread of steam power made the existing pattern denser rather than changing it.

A mill on its own (unless it was enormous, like the steam-powered mill at Saltaire) was not sufficient to produce a town, but a group of two or three could double the size of a small town, or

make a little town out of a village. A site on the edge of an existing settlement was always desirable, because it could take advantage of existing facilities. The extra population attracted shops, banks, chapels and churches, and generated more population in doing so. Sites near canals were also in demand, for reasons of transport and because they could provide water for industrial purposes rather than power.

So one gets what became the typical pattern: thicker settlement along river valleys, especially those which also contained a canal, intensifying now and then into a town, often where a stream or smaller river came down to join the larger one; and further settlement up these tributary waterways, until they became too small to generate power and — very often — the moors closed in. The long-established textile village of Keighley, for instance, grew into a prosperous mill town with the coming of the Leeds and Liverpool canal and became the shopping and market centre for a string of mills leading up the valley to the growing mill villages of Haworth and Oxenthorpe.[3]

In the constellations of textile towns and villages which the waterway system produced, a few towns established themselves as bigger and more important than the rest. A frequent reason was that, in addition to having their own mills, they had become the marketing centres for their districts. This was especially the case in West Yorkshire, where Leeds, Halifax, Bradford, Huddersfield and Wakefield had all had outdoor cloth markets since at least the sixteenth century (usually promoted by the Lord of the Manor) and had consolidated their position by building cloth halls in the eighteenth. In Wiltshire and Gloucestershire, where cloth was all sent direct to London for

336. Mills on the canal at Huddersfield.
337. The former Crossley carpet mills at Halifax.
338. (top right) A masonry-and-timber mill of 1791 at Malmesbury.
339. (bottom right) Iron-and-concrete-framed mills on the canal at Manchester.

sale in the great marketing complex known as Blackwell Hall, this situation did not arise; and unlike the Yorkshire towns, none of those in the south-west developed to any great size.

Steam power, in the form of steam-powered mills and steam-served railways, made less difference to patterns of settlement than might have been expected. To a considerable extent, as with water power, it merely intensified the existing pattern. The natural tendency of railway promoters was to link existing centres. Although the steam-engine freed mills from dependence on fast-running water, water was still important for use in industrial processes and to supply the steam-engines. For this reason, many steam mills were built along canals (Pl. 336); a situation between a canal and a river became especially convenient, because mills could draw clean or relatively clean water from the canals on one side, and deposit their waste in the river on the other. Steam also enabled mills to be placed closer together, and produced the continuous wall of building along rivers or canals which amazed visitors to towns like Manchester, Halifax and Huddersfield (Pl. 337), and gained Trowbridge the appellation of the 'Southern Manchester'. Another dramatic combination which featured in many textile districts was a side-effect of steam power: a many-arched viaduct striding across a valley, above — or, as at Stockport, on top of — a many-windowed mill.

Water remained especially important in wool districts. It played a greater part in their manufacturing processes: basically wool had to be washed, and cotton did not. Once mills in cotton towns acquired a piped water supply and did not have to draw water for their engines from springs, running water or canals, they could move away from the latter more freely than in wool districts. Many cotton towns accordingly developed to considerably greater size and density than wool ones, even if they had no marketing element.

Steam all but killed certain textile districts, because they were too far from sources of coal supply. The most obvious casualties were the ancient textile centres of Devon and East Anglia. Wiltshire and Gloucestershire survived on coal from Somerset and the Welsh border, but the fact that the supplies were smaller and farther away than in the north put them at a disadvantage; they never enjoyed that sensational growth which was a feature of the northern districts in the nineteenth century.

Mill buildings were affected by two technological developments, gaslight and metal- or concrete-frame construction. The early mills, although often long and high, were invariably narrow, because they relied on daylight. Gas enabled them to be deeper — and also, in some cases, to run shifts through twenty-four hours at periods of peak business. Iron-frame construction was developed in the late eighteenth century in an endeavour to reduce the destruction of mills by fire, which was one of the great hazards of the industry at this date — not least because of the introduction of gas. It was developed for cotton mills, especially in Lancashire, rather than in

340. The Manningham Mill, Bradford (Andrews and Pepper, 1871-3).

the wool districts because the cotton dust produced by the manufacturing process was inflammable. Mill owners in wool districts were less eager to face up to the extra expense involved, and continued to use timber posts and floors. In terms of appearance the resulting difference was less than might have been expected (Pls. 338-40). Early iron-frame buildings never extended the frame to their external walls, which remained of masonry construction, as in the mills that relied on timber. In both cases the internal structure was largely self-supporting, so the mills could have bigger windows than the narrow early mills, when the external walls supported the floor. But they could not be too big, because the external walls still supported their own weight, and a small proportion of the floor.[4]

Iron-frame became popular in the decades between about 1790 and 1820, but grew markedly less so as it became clear that it was by no means fireproof. If the inflammable contents of a mill caught fire, the resultant heat cracked the exposed iron, and the building came down. This was not the case with concrete-frame construction, which was widely used in Lancashire mills from the mid-1890s. The concrete frame supported the external walls, and the brick was merely a cladding. As a result enormous early-twentieth-century mills, with a far higher proportion of window to wall, became a distinctive feature of Edwardian Lancashire, and in many cases replaced earlier less fireproof buildings.

Mills seldom went in for architectural display. A richly ornamented warehouse might help to sell the goods stored in it, but elaborate architecture was unlikely to have much effect on the sale of goods manufactured in a mill, because this normally took place elsewhere. On the whole, mills are impressive (if they are impressive) because of their size or number, and the contrast between them and the towns in their shadow or the wild country around them, not because of their architecture. None the less, a few ambitious or eccentric mill owners, or ones with money to spend, went in for architectural display (Pl. 340); and since it was against the temper of the nineteenth century to banish ornament entirely even in the most utilitarian building, many mills had a decorative element, however modest.

This usually derived from the architectural language of the time, and often from a pattern inaugurated in more ambitious types of building. Around 1800, for instance, mills sometimes had a central pediment, one or more Venetian windows, or a clock tower. An occasional feature of the mid-century were recessed arches running the height of the façade. Northern mills often made a feature of the staircase, which was put in a separate projection and carried up in the form of a tower containing a water tank. Sometimes the tower also contained the dust-extraction plants which factory laws made a required feature of cotton mills. Between about 1790 and 1840, Wiltshire and Gloucestershire mills were usually lit by small windows of dressed stone, set into the rougher stone of the walling; each window had an arched head and a central stone mullion carried up into the middle of each arch (Pl. 338). The arches perform no structural function, and the windows appear to be treated as they are largely for aesthetic reasons.[5]

Multi-storey mills were usually one element in a complex of buildings. This could include weaving sheds, in which a high level of daylight was desirable, so that they were usually single-storey buildings with long rows of clerestories for top lighting. There was often a separate small office block, sometimes more pretentious than the other buildings. And in steam mills there were, of course, the chimneys.

Most factory chimneys were as utilitarian as the mills. Their embellishment consisted, at most, of a projecting moulding at the summit and sometimes a ring of moulding beneath it. It was the cumulative effect of chimney after chimney, all belching smoke, which was their most memorable characteristic. The nearest equivalent were the slender and largely ornamental towers which were attached to the houses of medieval nobles in Italian hill towns — and which rose out of their skyline by the dozen, and in the biggest towns by the hundred. Their day has gone as much, and even more than, the day of factory chimneys; in both cases the stump is often all that survives. Most mill owners ran up their chimneys as a matter of practical necessity, but a few of the richer or more powerful competed, exactly as did Italian nobles, as to who could build the highest, more for prestige than use. In terms of height, Lancashire won. The highest recorded Italian tower rose 250 feet. The Blinkhorn chimney outside Bolton was 366 feet high, enabling a bird's-eye panorama of Bolton as seen from its summit to be published in 1842.[6] It has been demolished; among survivors the chimney of India Mill, at Darwen, rises 303 feet, and the Wainhouse tower, just outside Halifax, 235 feet.

The effect of the India Mill tower (Pl. 341) is still sensational — perhaps even more so than when it was first built, since only a handful of the town's other factory chimneys survive. It soars out of the stone-built town, but itself, apart from its base, is built of dark purple engineering bricks. Like most of the more ambitious factory chimneys it is modelled on Italian towers — not the domestic towers, however, which were mostly very plain, but church

341. The chimney of the India Mill at Darwen, 1867.

campaniles, such as that of St. Mark's, Venice. The Darwen tower was built in 1867 by Eccles Shurrock, Brother and Co., the biggest mill owners in Darwen (until they failed in 1882). Its foundations rest on a stone said to be the largest block to have been quarried apart from that used for Cleopatra's Needle. Thirty-five horses were needed to draw it from the quarry to its destination.[7]

The octagonal Wainhouse chimney (Pl. 343) is an even more elaborate tower of campanile type. Like the Darwen tower, it has a staircase running up it. It was built by J.E. Wainhouse as the chimney for a dye works. Almost inevitably, it became known as 'Wainhouse's Folly'. In fact it was never used, for Wainhouse sold his works before the chimney was completed, and gave the latter to the town as an outlook tower.[8]

Those coming by train to Leeds have the curious experience of seeing two Italian campaniles rising out of the industrial landscape, just before they draw into the station. Both are in fact chimneys built for the textile mill known as the Tower Works. The smaller and earlier one dates from 1864 and is modelled on a tower in Verona. The second one followed in 1899; uninformed passers-by were likely to take a minute or two to pierce through the disguise of black soot which encrusted it (until it was cleaned in 1989), and to realize that it was a reasonably close copy of Giotto's campanile next to the Duomo in Florence (Pl. 331).[9]

Mill towns were the commonest form of nineteenth-century industrial town but not, of course, the only one. There were steel and iron towns like Sheffield and Middlesbrough (and often foundries on the outskirts of textile towns, built to make machinery for the mills). There was the strange landscape of the Potteries (Pl. 342), developing with not unattractive randomness around the bottle-shaped kilns which followed the clay outcrops; today the kilns have mostly gone, and only the randomness remains. Swindon, Crewe and Wolverton were virtually new towns that grew up around railway workshops. The similar works at Doncaster developed on property belonging to the corporation, and brought it such wealth that the townspeople paid no rates until the later nineteenth century. There were the maltings and breweries that until recently dominated Burton-on-Trent, a town which owed its nineteenth-century growth and prosperity to the belief that the waters of the Trent had special qualities.[10]

But what tends to be forgotten is the extent to which Victorian industry penetrated to areas normally thought of as agricultural. Agriculture itself was in part industrialized, in that it made use of steam-driven tractors and threshing machines, and was almost entirely dependent on mass-produced tools and plant. Most areas had their own factories making these. Lincoln acquired new prosperity

342. A kiln at Burslem.
343. The Wainhouse chimney at Halifax.
344. (right) Brewery buildings of 1904 at Weymouth (originally John Groves and Sons Ltd.).

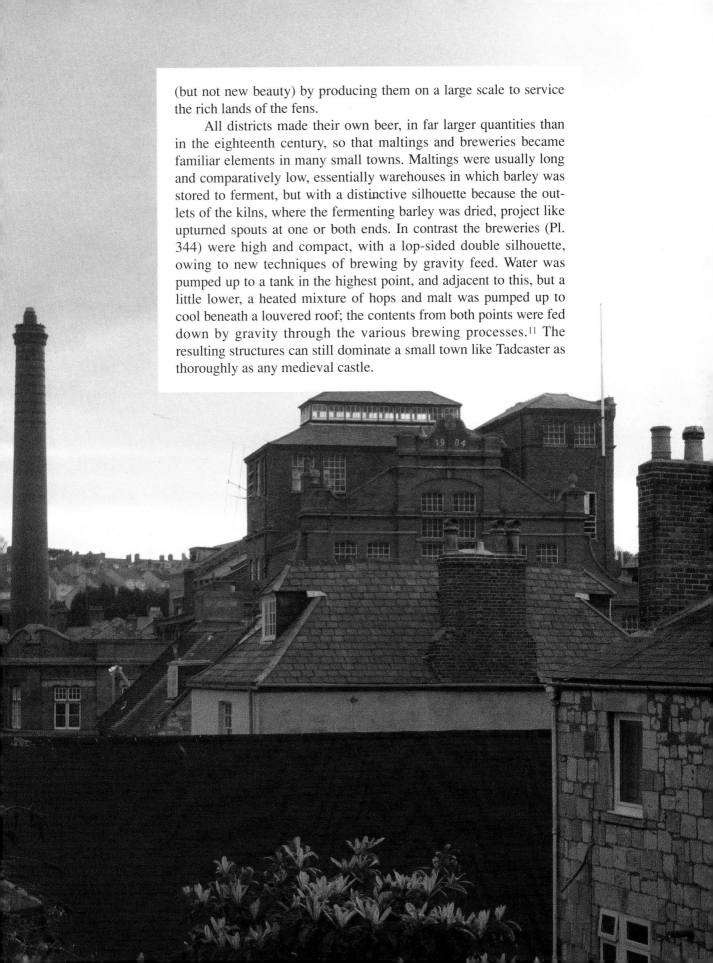

(but not new beauty) by producing them on a large scale to service the rich lands of the fens.

All districts made their own beer, in far larger quantities than in the eighteenth century, so that maltings and breweries became familiar elements in many small towns. Maltings were usually long and comparatively low, essentially warehouses in which barley was stored to ferment, but with a distinctive silhouette because the outlets of the kilns, where the fermenting barley was dried, project like upturned spouts at one or both ends. In contrast the breweries (Pl. 344) were high and compact, with a lop-sided double silhouette, owing to new techniques of brewing by gravity feed. Water was pumped up to a tank in the highest point, and adjacent to this, but a little lower, a heated mixture of hops and malt was pumped up to cool beneath a louvered roof; the contents from both points were fed down by gravity through the various brewing processes.[11] The resulting structures can still dominate a small town like Tadcaster as thoroughly as any medieval castle.

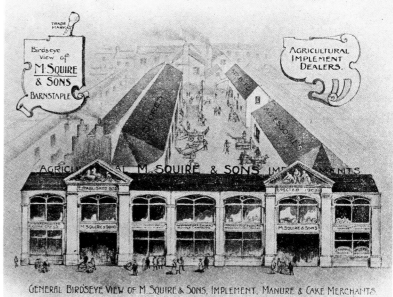

GENERAL BIRDSEYE VIEW OF M. SQUIRE & SONS, IMPLEMENT, MANURE & CAKE MERCHANTS.

345. (top left) Detail of M. Squire and Sons' Agricultural Works, Barnstaple (Alexander Lauder, 1903).
346. (top right) A bird's-eye view of Squire's from the firm's brochure.
347. (above) The Devon Art Pottery, Barnstaple.
348. (right) A hillside terrace in Preston.

Steam-powered machinery was widely used to cut timber, turn joinery, and make tiles or bricks. Barnstaple is an example of the kind of small industrial centre which could, as a result, appear in country districts. It was a market town, a reasonably flourishing small port, and had a resort and retirement element, represented by rows of stuccoed terraces stretching along the river Taw. By the 1880s it had acquired a number of flourishing industries, employing in all perhaps a thousand people. There were lace factories, a glove factory, an iron foundry, sawmills and the Raleigh Cabinet Works, which had a big factory facing the town across the river. In addition there were two successful potteries, the Royal Barum Ware Pottery and the Devon Art Pottery (Pl. 347). The latter had been founded in 1876 by W.O. Smith and his brother-in-law Alexander Lauder, an architect. It made a distinctive brick, and 'art' objects such as tiles, flowerpots, fountains and umbrella-stands. It had works outside the town and a showroom in it, in the form of a half-timbered building with infilling of its own tiles, designed by Lauder. Lauder, who was mayor in 1885 and 1886, was involved in the founding of the Barnstaple School of Science and Art; Smith was also a partner in the firm of Michael Squire, who made or merchandized agricultural implements, manure and cake. Lauder designed their premises in Tuly Street (Pl. 346), completed in 1903; the terracotta panels of agricultural implements which decorate the building (Pl. 345) were presumably made in the Devon Art Pottery.[12]

Long terraces for the workers in the various factories, and the works themselves, joined the other buildings in Barnstaple, but by no means overwhelmed them; the great covered Pannier Market behind the Guildhall (Pl. 277) provided a busy centre; the result was a thriving and pleasant little town.

15

The

Back

Streets

Shops, mills, banks, churches, monuments, and town halls, the high street and the main square, were the upper parts of the iceberg in Victorian towns, the bits that visitors saw, either because they were so large that they could not be ignored, or because they were in the quarters of the town which were visited. Most visitors also saw the rows of substantial villas which lined the approach roads, the homes of doctors, lawyers, bank managers, contractors and the richer shop owners, or passed the lodge gates leading to the opulent mansions of the mill owners. But they seldom penetrated under the water-line to the row after row of houses in which most of the inhabitants lived: shop assistants, bank clerks, factory workers, building labourers, canal workers, or dockers.

After the 1914-18 war many of these were to move into council estates. Huge areas of council housing, with their distinctive pattern of circuses, crescents, and avenues, joined the grids of speculative housing as the most easily recognizable areas on plans of all towns of more than modest size. But although the first council housing went up in a small way in Liverpool in the 1880s, council estates were not built on a large scale until the 1920s. A number of tenement blocks were put up in the bigger towns from the mid-nineteenth century onwards, mostly by trusts or foundations of a charitable nature, or at least charitable intent; but they catered only for a small percentage of the urban population, and were never popular.

349. Castle Lane, Bridgwater. A back street of the early eighteenth century.
350. Lumby's Terrace, Stamford, c. 1840. A matching row of houses on the other side of the yard has been demolished.

The majority lived in speculative housing of one kind or another; and the major part of this speculative housing was what is known as by-law housing, that is, housing built under the constraints of building regulations passed either locally or nationally, from the mid-nineteenth century onwards. It is ironic that vast swaths of this by-law housing were to be demolished in the post-war period, under the banner of slum clearance. Partly this was because standards had risen; but partly it was because houses which could not reasonably be described as slums, or were capable of improvement, conflicted with current fashions among planners and architects. So the little houses went, and tower blocks and tenements rose up, and all too often became slums far more rapidly and incontrovertibly than the housing which they replaced.

Before the mid-nineteenth century, building laws and regulations scarcely existed outside London, and even there were concerned with housing standards only in so far as they impinged on the public realm, rather than as they affected the health or living standards of their inhabitants. The London Building Acts of 1707, 1709 and 1774 were essentially about prevention of fire, and the convenience and drainage of the spaces between houses; the local acts passed for towns outside London were almost entirely concerned with the regulation, or creation, of public spaces.

Closer control of the quality of actual houses was left to ground landlords, or major leaseholders. Their concern was with maintaining the value of their property, and with the health and happiness of their tenants only in so far as they contributed to this. Leases of houses built for upper- or middle-class occupation were likely to contain stringent conditions as to maintenance of the property, and prohibitions of subletting, infilling, or use for industrial purposes. But in working-class areas the landlords' concern was more likely to be with maximizing their income by cramming in as many houses as possible. They would only do this, however, if they were confident of finding tenants. At Frome, between about 1680 and 1725, several fields on the edge of the town were developed with housing to cope with the town's textile boom.[1] A little less than half of this survives, but is still the most remarkable example of artisan housing of this date left in England. Another interesting survival is the row of artisan houses built by the Duke of Chandos behind his grand terraces in Castle Street, Bridgwater (Pl. 349). The houses at Frome contain two to six rooms, with the great majority somewhere in between the two extremes; they are very unpretentious, but all of them had sizeable gardens or yards, and many were built on plots a hundred feet or more in length. The houses were mainly occupied by self-employed weavers, carders, dyers and so on, working at home and making good money; such people were clearly not going to find housing of greater density acceptable.

The situation changed with the arrival of mass employment at mills or docks, as a result of which large numbers of people had to walk to and from work every day. The towns where this occurred — especially London, Manchester, Birmingham, Liverpool, Plymouth and Portsmouth — were those which were growing fastest in the eighteenth century, and in which lower-class housing was built in considerable quantities. Much of it took the form of courts, built on the gardens and backyards of existing houses, and usually approached by an archway piercing the parent house. Too much of what was built on new ground merely formalized and enlarged this pattern.

Courts were especially likely to appear where there was a shortage of building land. Around 1800 Nottingham, for instance, had a growing stocking and lace industry but was encircled by common land on which the freemen had grazing rights; they managed to block almost all building on this land until 1845, and the proliferation of courts and resulting overcrowding in Nottingham became notorious. A similar situation occurred, on a smaller scale and in less acute form, in the much smaller town of Stamford (Pl. 350). This was surrounded by a narrow band of manorial waste land, mainly used for grazing; beyond this was either an open-field system or the park of Burghley House. Encroachment on the waste started about 1800, but building on open fields was blocked until 1875, mainly by Lord Exeter, who owned Burghley, and was Lord of the Manor in Stamford. Between 1800 and 1875 most of what working-class housing was built took the form of courts, or closely packed housing on the waste land.[2]

The immediate results of development of this kind were over-high densities, minimum daylight and, usually, minimum sanitation; courts were often unpaved, and services usually consisted of a communal tap and a block of earth closets in each court. The ultimate result was cholera; the notorious epidemics of 1831, 1848-9 and 1866 killed nearly 40,000 people in London alone. It was cholera, and the fear of its recurrence, which made possible legislation which radically affected housing in Victorian towns all over England.

Legislation took two forms, the national Public Health Acts, of 1848, 1858 and 1866, and innumerable local Acts.[3] Up till 1866 the national Acts were discretionary, that is to say, it was left to the discretion of local authorities whether or not they adopted them. Many did so; but many other towns preferred to pass one or more local Acts, tailored to their needs and situations. It was rare for the local government of a town of any size to fail to take action of one kind or the other. Common principles behind new housing produced a basic similarity all over the country, but within this local traditions combined with variations in local Acts to introduce variety.

The pursuit of health was the common factor; it is significant that the local governments set up by the various national Acts to run towns which were not incorporated were called local boards of health. Current theories about health resulted in especial stress being laid on ventilation and sewage. The pursuit of good ventilation led to

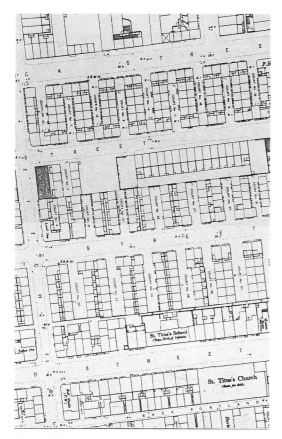

351. Different housing types, corner pubs, church and school in Sheffield.
352. (top right) Front doors and back-access arches grouped together in Bolton.
353. (bottom right) A back yard in Burnley.

wider spacing between terraces, both front and back, the disappearance of courts, and the outlawing of back-to-back housing in favour of houses with through ventilation. The pursuit of improved sanitation led to the installation of public sewage systems and the provision of adequate numbers of water-closets and water outlets: water outlets in each house, and water-closets in the houses or their backyards, or placed in communal groups, easily accessible from the houses. Outside water-closets were accepted and even encouraged, because by their nature they did not affect ventilation. The provision of gardens did not feature in legislation at all and, outside the tiny proportion of housing produced by the garden city movement, the idea that they were desirable only began to affect towns noticeably when the new London County Council was captured by garden city doctrine, and began to build what were called village estates in the early 1900s.

The commonest form of housing produced as a result of Acts both local and national was as follows.[4] Large areas were covered by row after row of identical terraces (Pl. 351). Slight changes in alignment and design marked where a field being developed by one builder gave way to a field being developed by another. Streets were long, lined with solidly-built two-storey houses, and wide — sometimes very wide — in proportion to the height of the houses. There were no trees and no front gardens, or, at best, a strip a few feet wide to one side of the front door, separated from the pavement by a two-foot wall.

The long streets were often punctuated by cross-streets. Off the cross-streets ran what still remain the most distinctive feature of by-law back streets: long back alleys, usually only a few feet wide, running between the high walls of little yards, the latter each stretching about 10 to 15 feet back from their respective houses and containing, originally, a shed for ashes and an outside water- or earth-closet (Pl. 353).

The back alleys were intended for the removal of waste, ashes, and rubbish, and of sewage in those streets which had outside earth-closets. The system was the same in miniature as the mews system, as developed in London and copied or adapted in provincial towns. Even the yards reflected London practice, in so far as London houses with mews access seldom had a garden — or for that matter, trees on the streets. But London houses had parks and squares within easy reach, or looked onto them. The square was a luxury which by-law housing did without. Admittedly, in smaller towns open country, often of great beauty, was usually in sight or in easy reach; but in big towns the street after street of little houses, unrelieved by trees or open spaces, could be very daunting.

There were many local variations. The prescribed minimum street width varied over the century, and from town to town; usually, it was increased by successive by-laws. In Manchester, for instance, it was fixed at 30 feet as early as 1830, and went up to 36 feet in

1868 and 42 feet in 1908. Middlesbrough fixed a minimum width of 20 feet in the 1850s, and increased this to 36 feet in 1876. Newcastle stipulated 40 feet in 1866. The combination of wide streets in front and little yards and narrow alleys behind seems odd today; the streets were far wider than was necessary for practical purposes (although today they come in convenient for car-parking) and could easily have been reduced to give the houses front gardens, or more space at the rear. The philosophy at work was perhaps one of distrust; space belonging to the houses was liable to neglect or misuse, wide streets could be controlled by the authorities and would remain uncluttered.

Arrangements at the back varied too. Quite often access was by means of arches cut through the terraces, rather than off cross-streets; these repeating archways could become a distinctive feature of the façades (Pl. 352). In some towns the back alleys were much wider than in others; in Manchester they were normally only 4 feet wide, in Burnley 12 feet, in Newcastle, Bolton and Barrow 20 feet.[5] In some the back lanes were used for normal everyday access, and they became sociable places; the front door was only used on special occasions. A few houses did not have backyards, at any rate until the end of the century; instead they had a wide communal yard, broken by blocks of privys and sheds. These were essentially a development of yards and, like them, enforced a high degree of communal life on the inhabitants.

In a few towns something even closer to the yard system survived under the by-laws, with improvements. By-law yards had to be open to the street, and the houses on them had to have back access, instead of being built back-to-back. Access both front and back was for pedestrians only. Usually the houses had little front gardens, often stipulated in the by-laws. This type of improved yard could be by no means unpleasant. They were especially popular in

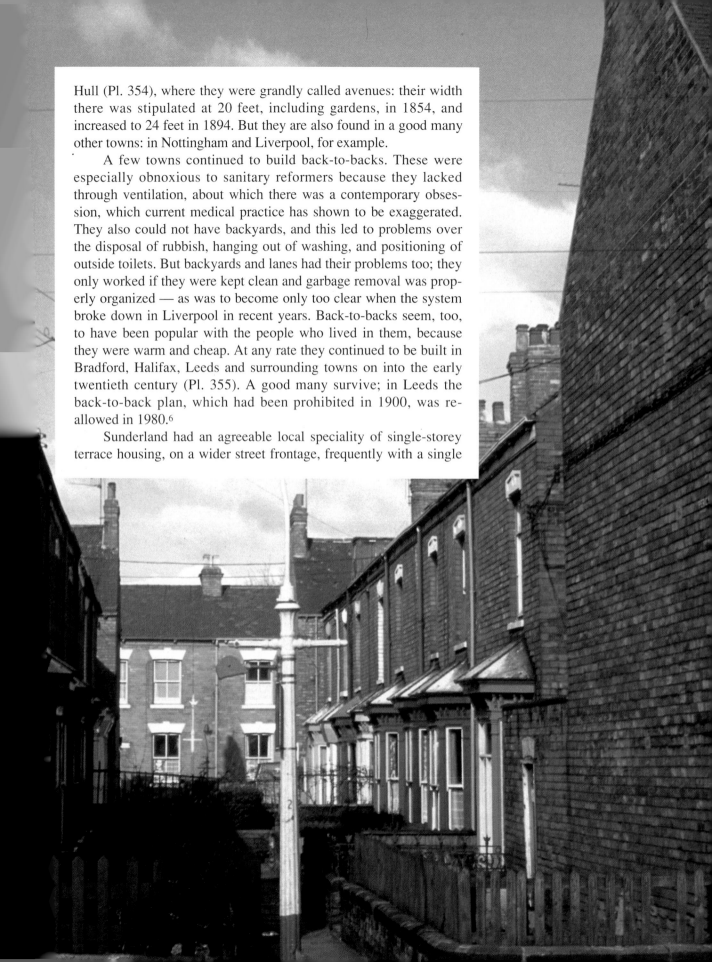

Hull (Pl. 354), where they were grandly called avenues: their width there was stipulated at 20 feet, including gardens, in 1854, and increased to 24 feet in 1894. But they are also found in a good many other towns: in Nottingham and Liverpool, for example.

A few towns continued to build back-to-backs. These were especially obnoxious to sanitary reformers because they lacked through ventilation, about which there was a contemporary obsession, which current medical practice has shown to be exaggerated. They also could not have backyards, and this led to problems over the disposal of rubbish, hanging out of washing, and positioning of outside toilets. But backyards and lanes had their problems too; they only worked if they were kept clean and garbage removal was properly organized — as was to become only too clear when the system broke down in Liverpool in recent years. Back-to-backs seem, too, to have been popular with the people who lived in them, because they were warm and cheap. At any rate they continued to be built in Bradford, Halifax, Leeds and surrounding towns on into the early twentieth century (Pl. 355). A good many survive; in Leeds the back-to-back plan, which had been prohibited in 1900, was re-allowed in 1980.[6]

Sunderland had an agreeable local speciality of single-storey terrace housing, on a wider street frontage, frequently with a single bedroom in the roof. Newcastle and Gateshead went in for what became known as Tyneside flats. Ex-ternally, these look almost exactly like conventional two-storey houses, except that the doors are grouped in pairs, and sometimes even in fours: every other door opens onto a staircase leading up to the first-floor flat, which also has another staircase down to its own yard. Variations of the two-storey flat are occasionally found in other towns (Pl. 356), including London, where they became known as cottage flats.[7]

Oddities and variations could appear when towns were built on steep hillsides. Apart from anything else, such a terrain almost inevitably broke up the monotony of endless parallel streets. In numerous York-shire towns one finds the at first sight eccentric but in fact logical and not displeasing practice of building houses with their eaves parallel to the slope (Pl. 357), instead of being stepped parallel to door and window lintels. In Hebden Bridge the slopes are so precipitous that what appears to be a two-storey terrace on one side sometimes turns out to have a second two-storey terrace fitted underneath it on the other. The resulting buildings are known locally as 'up-and-down houses' (Pls. 358, 359).

The vast majority of by-law housing is only two storeys high, without a basement. The plan is usually a variant on two-up, two-down, with a narrower back extension which tended to get longer and longer, especially in London. But the variety in façades can be considerable, especially in brick-built houses. Many of the stone terraces of northern mill towns are exceedingly simple, the only element in them approaching ornament being the contrast of the dressed stone of door and window surrounds with the darker, rougher, stone of the walling. Slightly more ambitious houses can have a classical door case, or variety is introduced by the contrast between doorways and arched entrances to the back alleys. Brick gave more scope for obtaining

354. (left) An avenue in Hull.
355. Back-to-backs and former corner shops at Queensbury near Halifax.
356. Two-storey flats in Plymouth.
357.   Sloping eaves at Darwen.

variety with little increase in expense, by the combination of bricks of different colours, the setting back or projection of courses, or the use of mass-produced terracotta ornament. Brick houses often had timber porches, of more or less elaboration.

Variety could also come from the treatment of windows. In some towns such as Nottingham, it was common to have no windows above the door — with bleak effect in the narrow three-storey houses which are relatively common in Nottingham back streets (Pl. 360). But the commonest variation was the bay window. Bay windows seem first to have appeared in by-law housing in about 1870. They were a status symbol, and two-storey bays carried more prestige than single-storey ones. In a common combination rows of terraced houses without bay windows open on a street of houses with them, often on a bigger street or one with a view, marking the move from the houses of the lower to those of the lower-middle classes (Pl. 361).

Nowhere did the bay window flourish more than in the housing built in the London suburbs between about 1870 and 1900. These were nearly all railway suburbs, most of the inhabitants of which commuted to work in the centre. They were lived in, to begin with, by the lower-middle classes. Working-class railway suburbs appeared with subsidized working men's trains later in the 1880s, and imitated the middle-class ones. The resulting houses were suburban, in the sense of being on the edge of the city, but built in terraces for those who could not afford detached or semi-detached villas. They all had back gardens, often very sizeable ones, and they almost invariably had two-storey bay windows. Porches and windows frequently sported stucco or terracotta capitals and other decoration; there could be stained

358, 359. 'Up and down' houses at Hebden Bridge. One terrace is built one on top of the other, with access at high and low level to either side.

360. (bottom right)   A back street in Nottingham.

glass in door lights and the upper lights of windows; owing to the length of the back extension the houses often have far more room than could be guessed from the street. They are by no means without their qualities, but it can be a relief to move from their monotonously bedizened façades to the sturdy simplicity of the stone terraces in northern mill towns.[8]

Back-street housing is almost invariably interspersed with other buildings, apart from the mills, the brewery, the power-station, or the gas works, in the shadow of which they often stand, and the existence of which produced them in the first place. Many areas generated their own shopping streets. In addition they were almost invariably punctuated by single corner shops (Pls. 355, 362). Other corners were occupied by pubs, unless there was a temperance developer or ground landlord. Every now and then there was almost invariably a Nonconformist chapel or a Church of England church, often built on a plot given by the ground landlord. Churches and chapels were usually accompanied by schools, or alternatively the street pattern was broken by a board school. The latter could tower above the houses, and so, often, could the churches, for building a big church in a poor district was a common form of piety for rich Victorians; sometimes, but by no means always, the donor was the owner of the local mill or works. The grandest example of contrast in scale was the noble and gigantic, even though unfinished, church of St. Bartholomew in Brighton, until the little houses around it were demolished by Brighton corporation in the 1970s.[9] In the district known as Jericho in Oxford, down by the railway and the reedy waters of the canal, the campanile of St. Barnabas still raises its head above terraces built for the workers in the Clarendon Press;

361. (left) Bay windows in Tiverton.
362. (right) A back street and corner shops in Darwen in about 1940 (demolished).

265

it was Thomas Combe, patron of Pre-Raphaelites and Printer to the University, who paid for it.

But the houses in Jericho are now lived in by undergraduates, or young academics and professionals. In London two-storey artisan houses are sold for several hundred thousand pounds. Up in the north, on the other hand, there are many areas of by-law housing which are still working-class. The pubs are still there, and so are the corner shops. The children are still playing in the streets — although now they are as often Indian or Pakistani boys playing cricket as English or Irish boys kicking a football. Sometimes a street or two has been demolished and replaced by playgrounds or a small park, bringing relief to the close grid of houses. There is less scouring of doorsteps and polishing of brass than there used to be, but many of the houses still suggest pride of ownership; fronts are gaily painted, new doors of doubtful design replace the old ones, lace curtains are raised in the middle or fanlights lit up, to display a piece of china or brass. It would be stupid to make too great claims for by-law housing, but it had, and has, its qualities.

363, 364. Back-street children in Liverpool (left) in the 1980s and (below) in about 1900, by the Steble fountain in William Brown Street.
365. (right) The bandstand in People's Park, Halifax.

16

The

Parks

Castle Meadow is a big field belonging to the town on the edge of Stamford, sandwiched between two branches of the river Welland, with a view of the town, the bridge, and the steeples of the town's many churches. There are self-sown trees along the banks, and an asphalt path running across it, but no other embellishment. It is just a field. On a hot summer day it is a very crowded field. Bicyclists zoom to and fro, groups knock, kick or throw balls, dogs are exercised, kites are flown, sunbathers sunbathe, couples lie in a clinch together under the trees.

There is nothing unusual about this. Its only interest is that similar activities have been going on on town fields for at least five hundred years. It is an example of a type of space which existed in many towns before the Victorian urge to improve, educate and edify turned the concept of the public field into that of the public park.[1]

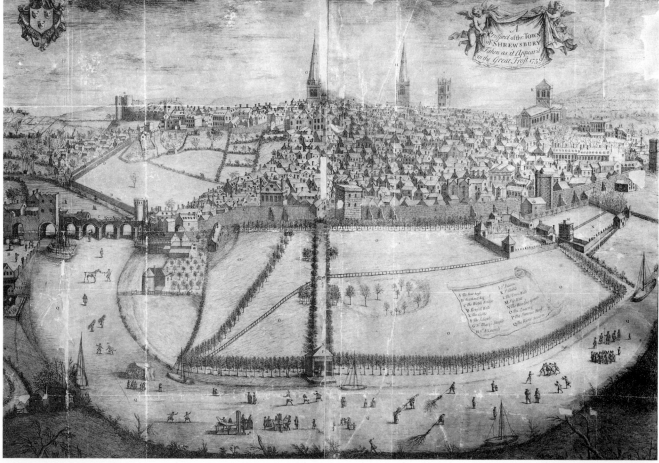

Most medieval towns had an area of open space belonging to the manor or to the corporation, on which the townspeople had rights of grazing and collecting fuel, and which they used for exercise and recreation, for football, archery, washing clothes and laying them out to dry, skating, if the fields were flooded and frozen in winter, or just strolling around on. Oxford had Port Meadow, Newcastle had the Town Moor, Norwich had Chapel Fields, Salisbury had the Quarry, London had Moorfields. All survive as public open spaces except Moorfields, which disappeared under Finsbury Circus and other building projects of the late eighteenth and early nineteenth centuries.

As related in chapter 8, some of these common fields were used in the seventeenth or eighteenth centuries for the new practice of social walking 'to see and be seen'. A surfaced path or paths were often laid down and rows of trees planted to either side. In Exeter the open space known as Northernhey, to the north of the city walls, was laid out with walks in 1612, and is still a public garden. Moorfields was levelled, raised, railed in, and planted with walks of trees, mostly at the expense of the corporation, between about 1605 and 1620.[2] The Quarry was planted with walks of trees in 1719 (Pls. 366, 367), and Chapel Fields in 1749. At the Quarry a boat-house was built on the Severn at the end of the central walk before 1739, and a bowling-green and tea garden established at one corner. Today, embellished with a bandstand and a war memorial, and with its walks replanted, it has become the principal park of the town.

Formal public walks also appeared in the royal parks in London. These were originally parks for hunting and other royal recreations, but were opened to the public in the sixteenth and seventeenth centuries. The Mall in St. James's Park was laid out and planted in 1660, and the Ring, for carriages, in Hyde Park at about the same time. The Broad Walk in Kensington Gardens was planted in 1726; it and the Gardens in general were occasionally opened to well-dressed members of the public under George II, and regularly in the spring and summer from about 1760. All these became places for social promenading.

The pleasure gardens of the eighteenth century were another type of recreational area. They were commercial concerns, offering music, refreshment, and an agreeable setting in return for an entry fee. The music was often played from a covered bandstand, the refreshments served to individual parties in alcoves or supper boxes opening onto the gardens. Most gardens had one principal walk, for promenading. At Vauxhall Gardens (Pl. 368) this led off into narrower, discreeter, darker walks in groves of trees to either side.

Vauxhall and Ranelagh were the two most famous pleasure gardens, but there were literally dozens of others in London, and most of the bigger provincial towns had at least one. Norwich had its own Vauxhall and Ranelagh, Newcastle the peculiarity of corporation-owned pleasure gardens at the Forth Walk, Bath its

366. (top left) The Quarry, Shrewsbury, before walks were laid out in 1719. From the picture attributed to John Bowen.

367. (bottom left) The Quarry in the Great Frost of 1759.

368. The main walk at Vauxhall Gardens, London. Detail from an engraving after a picture by Samuel Wale, *c.* 1750.

Spring, Grosvenor and Sydney Gardens.[3] The walks and gardens of the Cheltenham spas were essentially pleasure gardens.

The Sydney Gardens at Bath were perhaps the first to be laid out, at least in part, in the naturalistic landscape manner. They were designed by the Bath architect and landscape gardener Charles Harcourt Masters and opened in 1795, along with the Sydney Hotel. The hotel had a bandstand on the garden side, between crescents of open supper boxes. A broad central promenade led through the gardens from hotel and bandstand, and more intimate winding walks led off it. The gardens as described in 1801 anticipate several features of public parks: 'Sydney Gardens ... contains about 16 acres, interspersed with a great number of small, delightful groves, pleasant vistas, and charming lawns, intersected by serpentine walks, which at every turn meet with sweet, shady bowers, furnished with handsome seats, some composed by nature, others by art. It is decorated with waterfalls, stone and thatched pavilions, alcoves; the Kennet and Avon Canal running through, with two elegant cast-iron bridges thrown over it, after the manner of the Chinese; a sham castle planted with several pieces of cannon, bowling greens, swings, a labyrinth formed by enclosed pathways, the principal one of which, after many intricate windings, leads to a fine Merlin swing, and a grotto of antique appearance. On this way four thatched umbrellas are placed at equal distances from each other, which are intended to serve as a shelter from sudden rain and storms.'[4]

Sydney Gardens (which survived, much altered, as Sydney Park) were to have been surrounded with residential terraces. This was unusual for pleasure gardens. The garden view was clearly meant to make the terraces desirable. Owing to the building slump of the 1790s, only the southern ones were built. But this combination of pleasure gardens and terraces anticipated the residential parks of the early nineteenth century. Here the landscaped park and pleasure grounds which had originated as a country house amenity were attached to a group of town houses. This had already been achieved in miniature by the landscaping of town squares, as in Grosvenor Square in the 1770s, but residential parks carried the idea further.

They first appeared in John White's abortive proposals for a new park, made in 1809, and in Nash's plans for Regent's Park on the same site, as they developed from 1811. Both White's and Nash's schemes had what became typical elements of the fully developed residential park, inspired by similar features in country houses: lodge gates and lodge-keepers ensuring control of who came into the development; a carriage road accessible through the lodge gates, giving access to the houses and providing an agreeable drive through or round the park; and the park itself, embellished with winding walks, decorative planting and, if possible, a lake. Regent's Park also had a formal promenade, running along the east side. The parks were intended as an amenity for the residents, not for the general public; Regent's Park was not opened to the public until about 1840.

Both White's and Nash's plans bred numerous imitations, incorporating all or some of these features. They included what became Queen's Park, Brighton (1825), the intended villas surrounding which never materialized; Decimus Burton's Calverley Park, Tunbridge Wells (1829); Dawkes's The Park at Cheltenham (1833); Joseph Paxton's Upton Park at Slough (1842-3) and his Prince's Park at Liverpool (1842).[5] The latter was unusual in that the park was open to the public. All these had their lodge gates, carriage drive, and lake. Developments such as Amos Wild's Park Crescents in Worthing and Brighton (both *c*. 1829), or the communal gardens between the terraces off Ladbroke Grove (described in chapter 9) were cut-down versions of the same idea.

Meanwhile another type of urban park had developed, in the form of the zoological garden, the botanical garden, and the arboretum. These expressed an aspiration not previously connected with public open spaces in towns, and typical of the time: the desire to educate. This was sensibly combined with the desire to entertain and in addition many of the gardens incorporated a promenade.

The first ones were privately funded, usually by joint-stock companies. They recouped their expenditure by charging an entrance fee, but several had a philanthropic element, and were open free on certain days, for the benefit and improvement of the working classes. The earliest, but abortive, example was Henry Philips's project for an Oriental Gardens, conservatory and museum at Brighton. It was opened (without the conservatory) in 1825, but failed in 1827. It was followed by the Botanical Gardens in Birmingham, laid out in 1831, those in Sheffield (Pl. 369), laid out in 1834, the Zoological Society's and Royal Botanical Society's Gardens in Regent's Park, laid out in 1827 and 1839, and the Arboretum in Derby, laid out by Joseph Strutt in 1839-40, on land given by him to the town. The Botanical Gardens at Sheffield and in Regent's Park both incorporated handsome conservatories, with promenades in front of them.[6]

It was out of this varied background — public fields, public walks, pleasure gardens, residential parks, botanical or zoological gardens and arboretums — that the fully fledged public park emerged. One of the catalysts was the Parliamentary Select Committee on Public Walks, which presented its report in 1833. It had been appointed 'to consider the best means of securing open spaces in the vicinity of populous towns, as public walks and places of exercise calculated to promote the health and comfort of the inhabitants'. It resulted from concern that the big new towns, and the East End of London, had no such facilities. This was a new phenomenon; previously towns had been small enough for open country to be in easy reach, and most had their piece or pieces of common land as well. But not only were London and the northern towns growing at an alarming speed; in the process a good deal of common land was being enclosed and built over.

369. The conservatories in the Botanical Gardens, Sheffield.

The middle and upper classes were more concerned about the health and morals of the lower classes than their enjoyment. Walking in the fresh air was good for their health, and promenading for their morals. Promenading was seen as a means of civilizing the lower classes, just as a century earlier Beau Nash had seen it as a means of civilizing the upper and middle classes. As Robert Slaney put it in his evidence to the Select Committee: 'A man walking out with his family among his neighbours of different ranks will naturally be desirous to be properly clothed, and that his wife and children should be so also; but this desire, duly directed and controlled, is found by experience to be of the most powerful effect in promoting civilization and exciting industry.'[7] Walking was also thought to keep people out of the public houses. The emphasis of the report was on the provision of walks, not necessarily incorporated into parks. The need to provide open areas for sport featured little in it. The idea that games improved the character, which was to become so important later on in the century, was in its infancy; indeed working-class sports were still regarded with suspicion by many middle-class reformers.

The report suggested that the private sector should be responsible for providing the necessary walks, but that the government should assist where necessary. A meagre public fund of £10,000 was accordingly set up. In 1835 a private Act to enable the establishment of a public garden in any town where the majority of the rate-payers wanted it failed to get through Parliament. In 1838 the House of Commons recommended that in all future enclosures, open space should be left 'sufficient for purposes of exercise and recreation for the neighbouring population'. It was not until 1859 that the Recreation Grounds Act empowered local authorities to

370. A view in the Undercliffe cemetery, Bradford.
371. The view from the main walk in the park at Bolton, from the painting by Samuel Towers, *c*. 1895.

levy a rate for the laying out of parks, without the need to pass a local Act.[8]

Against this background of individual enthusiasm and tepid government support, the public-park movement got under way. Victoria Park, in the East End of London, opened (in a very unfinished state) in 1845. Queen's and Philips Parks, Manchester, and Peel Park, Salford, all opened in August 1846. Birkenhead Park opened in 1847. The five parks had different backgrounds. Like Regent's Park, Victoria Park (which was much the largest) was laid out by the Commissioners of Woods and Forests, partly out of the proceeds of selling what is now Lancaster House to the Duke of Sutherland. The Manchester and Salford parks were paid for by public subscription (topped up by £3000 from the government) but run by their respective corporations. Birkenhead Park was laid out by the commissioners who ran the new town of Birkenhead, under an Act of 1833. The provision of parks was often accompanied by the provision of public cemeteries, either by limited liability companies, or the corporations. Besides being necessary to relieve existing churchyards, they also were a means to healthy promenading in open space, with the bonus of the moral and social uplift which came from examining the tombs (Pl. 370).

372. The plan of Queen's Park, Bolton, in about 1920.

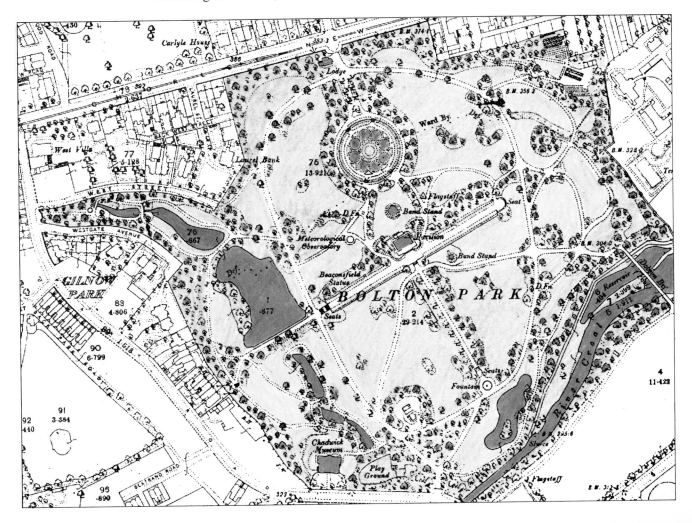

From the mid-century onwards, public parks appeared in increasing numbers. The great majority in England date from between 1850 and 1900. Sometimes a local notability presented the land and laid out the park on it, and the corporation or other local authority took it over. But often the corporation paid for everything out of the rates, particularly after the Recreation Ground Act of 1859. Quite a few parks were based on the purchase or gift of an existing private house or park, on the edge (or, more rarely, in the middle) of the town.

And so there emerged the familiar public park of today. In spite of later changes, it usually retains the lines of its Victorian design, and reflects the various influences out of which this grew. As in residential and country-house parks, it is entered by way of entrance gates of elaborate ironwork and a fanciful lodge. Inside the gates are a carriage drive, winding walks, a lake, shrubberies and bedded-out flowers, but also broad open spaces for games, kite-flying, exercising dogs and all the casual activity that had taken place on public fields. Prominent in some part of the park there is likely to be a promenade, often embellished with balustrades and statues, and sometimes with a bandstand adjoining, to enable the middle and lower classes to mix together in their Sunday clothes and parade to the sound of music, as their socially more elevated predecessors had done in the eighteenth century. Sometimes the promenade has a view beyond the park. The park at Bolton looked down on a sensational prospect of towers, mills and smoking chimneys; the view is still remarkable enough today, when most of the mills and chimneys have gone (Pl. 371).

The concerts put on in the bandstand, the refreshments on sale in refreshment kiosk, pavilion or tea gardens, the boats for hire on the lake, the occasional balloon ascent or fireworks display, and features such as a Chinese pagoda, a grotto, rustic seats or bridges and ornamental shelters were derived from pleasure gardens; in addition to which the educational tradition of the botanical gardens and their fellows was likely to produce a conservatory, a menagerie, or an aviary, an area for rare shrubs carefully labelled, and sometimes a museum or art gallery.

Anything to do with drink or gambling was taboo; this was the big difference between English parks and the French parks, which in other respects imitated them. The English objective was to get the working class out of the pubs and betting shops, not to supplement them. No municipal park had a racecourse (Alexandra Park, beneath Alexandra Palace in North London, which did, was laid out by a private company). Alcohol was never for sale (except occasionally, for a limited period and a special event). But drinking fountains were important weapons in the war against disease and drunkenness, and are much in evidence (Pl. 373). Many, especially in London, were erected under the aegis of the Metropolitan Drinking Fountain and Cattle Trough Association. This was founded in 1859

373. A drinking fountain in the park at Darwen.
374. On the promenade in People's Park, Halifax.
375. (right) A fountain of about 1890 in the Morrab Gardens, Penzance.

by Gurneys, Buxtons, and members of other philanthropic families, many of them Quakers. The Association supplied the cups and fountains, but the architectural or sculptural embellishment was often paid for by individual donors, as a suitable inscription seldom fails to record. Some were of great size and elaboration; others had a more modest charm, often grown poignant today when water has long ceased to flow out of their taps.[9]

Victorian park buildings offer many agreeable surprises. The promenade was sometimes made the setting for an especially elaborate display. That in the People's Park, Halifax, is flanked on one side by a pavilion and long screen walls embellished with fountains, on the other by balustrades, steps and rows of marble statues (Pl. 374). Effectively, it is a chunk of the gardens at Chatsworth brought to the people of Halifax by the Duke of Devonshire's protégé Joseph Paxton, who laid it out, and paid for by Francis Crossley, of Crossley's Carpets, whose mansion overlooked the park, and whose bust surveys the graffiti inside the pavilion.[10] Pavilion and fountains are embellished with inscriptions. One of these, from the Book of Proverbs, sums up the attitude behind all park promenades: 'The rich and poor meet together, the Lord's the maker of them all.'

Stanley Park, Liverpool, was laid out by the corporation to the designs of Edward Kemp, and opened in 1870 (Pls. 376, 377). A fine Gothic bridge, now derelict, a pretty Gothic shelter and a long Gothic arcade wrapped round three sides of the promenade were designed in the 1870s by E.R. Robson, architect to the corporation and later to the London School Board. The cloister looks across a bowling-green to an especially elaborate and handsome example of a cast-iron urinal, made in Glasgow at the Elmbank Foundry. There is usually plenty of good ironwork in Victorian parks, from cast-iron railings incorporating the crest of the corporation to elaborate conservatories, as at Sefton Park, Liverpool, through ornamental as opposed to drinking fountains (Pl. 375). But the most distinctive cast-iron buildings in parks are often the bandstands (Pl. 365). These derive from music pavilions in pleasure gardens, culminating in the delicate and inventive one that was installed in Cremorne Gardens in London in 1847, and soared in the gaslight above its dancing platform.[11]

Not all parks adhered to a similar pattern. Nottingham has a peculiar and distinctive system. As related in chapter 15, opposition from its freemen prevented the enclosure and building over of the common lands which

376, 377. On the lake and promenade in Stanley Park, Liverpool. The cloisters were designed by E.R.Robson in the 1860s.

276

encircled much of the town until 1850. In that year they were shared out by Enclosure Commissioners appointed by special Act of Parliament. These commissioners complied with the resolution passed by the House of Commons in 1838, and handed a percentage over to the corporation for laying out as public open space. Instead of this being concentrated in one mass, as in other towns, it was split up into different sections: a 19-acre arboretum, a 77-acre recreation ground (on the site of a former racecourse) which was mainly used for sport, two cemeteries and over a mile of pedestrian walks, running under avenues of trees between new villas, in the manner of the New Walk in Leicester. The result was a continuous green

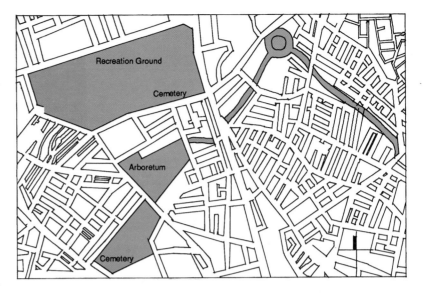

band, now wide, now narrow, threaded through the new part of the town and marked by massive stone piers of distinctive design, embellished with the city monogram (Pls. 378, 379).[12]

Many nineteenth-century spas and resorts followed the Tunbridge Wells and Bath tradition, and grew around inlets of greenery. As a result they were broken up by open spaces, instead of being built up solid like other towns, except for one or two blocks of parkland, usually out of the centre. The series of open spaces and gardens which leads to the sea front at Brighton has already been described. Another early example was at Dawlish (Pl. 380). In 1803 a local businessman, John Edye Manning, channelled a stream running down to the sea, and landscaped its water-meadows to provide an amenity for the terraces he built on either side. After flood damage in 1810, the area was re-laid out with the stream stepped to make little waterfalls, and rustic wooden bridges built over it. The whole space was later taken over by the corporation, and Dawlish spread around it.[13]

Harrogate grew up next to the great gondola-shaped common known as the Stray, or sometimes the Two Hundred Acre. The original settlement developed in the early nineteenth century, in two sections round the two prows of the gondola; in the course of the century they coalesced and the town leap-frogged over the main Stray to the south and expanded to the west around another common, Harlow Moor, which was laid out as the Valley Gardens.[14]

In the 1840s Scarborough expanded across a deep valley running down to the sea, to link up with the spa and its mineral springs below the cliffs to the south of the town. Expansion was encouraged by the building of the pedestrian Cliff Bridge across the valley in 1827, followed by a bridge for traffic in 1865. The bridges were built by joint-stock companies, the earlier of which leased the spa from the corporation. The valley was kept free of buildings,

378, 379. Nottingham's green belt, and one of the corporation gate piers along it.

except for the circular Rotunda Museum built by the Scarborough Philosophical Society in 1828-9, like a temple in a gentleman's park; greenery flows under the two bridges, and then laps along the cliffs, between terraces and sea, in the form of steeply sloping gardens, laid out by the Cliff Bridge Company and the corporation.[15]

Perhaps the most remarkable example of this type of development is at Bournemouth.[16] Up to 1811 this was open heath. Along the southern edge of the heath a series of deep valleys, known locally as chines, cut down through cliffs to the sea. The biggest contained a stream known as the Bourne. In 1806 an Enclosure Act divided the heath amongst local landowners; the largest portion went to Sir George Tapps and four patches were reserved as common land. In 1811 a Dorset landowner, John Tregonwell, bought a plot of land from Tapps, built a big house and some cottages to let to friends on it, and planted it with Scots pines. Other purchasers followed his example; the heath become a pine forest, and from 1835 a seaside resort of detached villas began to develop under and among pines, around the larger houses.

In 1841 Dr A.B. Granville visited Bournemouth, and was so impressed by its sheltered sites, sea breezes, and the 'balsamic effluvia' and health-giving properties of its pines that he gave it a puff in his influential *The Spas of England*, as potentially 'the very first invalid sea-watering place and winter residence for the most delicate constitutions in England'. He suggested that the mouth of the Bourne, below the bridge where the main road crossed the stream, should be laid out as a 'promenade-garden'.[17] His suggestion was taken up in 1848-9 when the Tapps (by now Tapps-Gervis) estate employed Decimus Burton to lay out part of the site. In 1869-73 the Bournemouth Improvement Commission, which had been set up in 1856, leased the valley below and above the bridge and created the Pleasure Gardens, running in a thin strip over a mile and a half inland (Pl. 381).

The chines were kept free of development and became pine-crammed gorges; the common lands were laid out as parks; more public gardens were formed and everywhere pines were preserved and new ones planted by the thousand. The villas spread. The bridge over the Bourne was enlarged into the Square, and became the hub of the town. As a local guide-book later put it: 'Belted by sea, woodland and common; crossed from end to end by a park of rare beauty, along the winding length of which a clear brook ripples; dotted here and there by wooded, flower-haunted nooks; rejoicing in roads that almost resemble forest glades in the luxuriance of their bordering trees; and with houses innumerable standing in grounds which are patches of the ancient forest, Bournemouth is, indeed, a town of gardens, greensward and trees.'[18]

380. The Lawn at Dawlish.
381. Looking across the Bourne and Pleasure Gardens to the Town Hall, Bournemouth.
382. (right) Looking out to sea from a villa in Lincombe Drive, Torquay.

17

The

Suburbs

Up till the mid-eigh-teenth century it was taken for granted that a man would live close to his work. Shopkeepers lived over their shops, bankers and lawyers over their offices, merchants and manufacturers next to their ware houses and workshops. Courtiers, peers and MPs either had lodgings in royal or government buildings or lived in walking distance of them. The rich were in the centre; what were then called the suburbs were mainly for the poor, who clustered in tenements outside the city gates, because it was cheap to do so.

At the same time, anyone who could afford it acquired somewhere in the country, or at least on the edge of the town, to retreat to. This might only be a summer-house in a garden, but such places had a way of developing into full-scale houses. At Bristol, for instance, the slopes up to the hill-tops around the city gradually filled up with the summer retreats of Bristol merchants. As early as 1590, or thereabouts, Sir John Young built the Red Lodge on the slopes of Kingsdown, at the end of the long garden which ran up from his house on the quay-side, ten minutes' walk away. In 1737 Giles Greville, apothecary, bought three fields on

Kingsdown, and built a tavern and four summer-houses on them, which soon became houses. At much the same time Bristol merchants began to build on Clifton Hill, a little further out from the centre. Paul Fisher's Palladian villa, designed by Isaac Ware, went up in 1746-50, and Thomas Goldney built Goldney House, with its wonderful grotto, in the 1720s and 1730s. But both Fisher and Goldney also had houses in the middle of Bristol.[1]

Summer residences appeared in the neighbourhood of all the bigger eighteenth-century towns, usually on high ground or by water, to catch the breeze. In London Hampstead and Highgate north of the river, Clapham and Streatham south of it, and the banks of the Thames upstream to Richmond and Twickenham had become popular places of retreat by the early eighteenth century, as had the villages on the edge of Epping Forest. At Liverpool Everton and Islington, above the town, were being colonized by the 1770s; the Hull merchants began to acquire retreats in or around the villages along the Humber in the same decade, so that to Anna Seward, passing through them in 1793, 'it seemed a drive of several miles through a gay garden, the pleasure grounds of each elegant and thick-sown villa extending from one to another.'[2]

Town-dwellers who could afford it often sent their wives and families out of town in the summer, and rode out to join them, sometimes daily, sometimes for the weekend or occasional nights. The less well-off hired lodgings for the purpose, the richer acquired a permanent house. Very often merchants and shopkeepers, or their widows, retired permanently to these summer resorts. As early as 1727 Defoe commented on the resulting 'prodigious increase' of the villages round London, 'being chiefly for the habitations of the richest citizens, such as either are able to keep two houses, one in the country and one in the city; or for such citizens as being rich, and having left off trade, live altogether in these neighbouring villages, for the pleasure and health of the latter part of their days'.[3] Some of these houses were detached, in their own grounds or gardens, but many were built in terraces on the town model.

The ideal of retreat from the cares of an active life or the heat of summer in the town to the 'serene enjoyment of the country' went back at least to Roman times, and was reinforced at the Renaissance. All educated people in the eighteenth century were brought up on Horace's celebration of the pleasures of his life in touch with nature in the country, and on Palladio's description of the villa as a place 'where the mind, fatigued by the agitations of the city, will be greatly restored and comforted, and be able quietly to attend the studies of letters, and contemplation.'[4]

In Roman and Renaissance times a villa was a farm with a gentleman's or nobleman's house on it. It was the country complement to his town house and served a double purpose; its farm supplied the town household, and its owners could retire to it from the town, especially in the summer. The word arrived in England in the seventeenth century, but it tended to lose its farming connotations and come to mean, as Dean Aldrich expressed it in the early eighteenth century, merely 'a house built for rural retirement'. As such the term could be, and was, applied both to a small house on the edge of, or close to, a town, with little land attached to it, and to a full-scale country house, on a large agricultural estate. If the emphasis was on the latter's status as the residence of a county family of standing, and a centre of authority and power, it was a 'seat'; if it was seen primarily as providing country enjoyments to a family in retreat from the town, it was a 'villa'.[5]

In the late eighteenth century the cottage began to offer an alternative to the villa as a genteel retreat. This followed a new attitude to working-class cottages, and the cottagers who lived in them. Gainsborough had been painting landscapes incorporating rustic figures and cottages since the 1750s, but it was not until the 1780s that his large-scale pictures of cottagers, portrayed individually or in groups in front of their cottages, became popular and commanded high prices as a result. The sentiment behind the paintings had much to do with Rousseau. Cottagers were simple, innocent, and to be envied, because they were free of the pretensions, worries and temptations of upper-class life, especially as lived in cities.

In 1798 James Malton published his *Essay on British Cottage Architecture*. This was partly concerned with advocating the cottage as a picturesque building type, partly with praising it as providing a way of life. 'The greatly affluent', he wrote, 'involuntarily sigh as they behold the modest care-excluding mansions of the lowly contented.' Thanks to Malton, they need sigh no longer, for he was the first architect to suggest that the upper and middle classes could lead the simple life in cottages, at least for part of the year. His *Essay* included fourteen designs, nine of which were appropriate as 'retreats for the gentleman'.[6]

Over the next thirty years numerous designs for genteel cottages were published and even more were built. 'Cottage' became a fashionable word. Many of the resulting buildings were only small villas under another name. The thatched roofs, porches and casement windows of others, Malton's included, had more resemblance to working-class cottages but incorporated extraneous features, which came to be seen as a radical part of the cottage image: verandas, which derived from the Indian bungalow, trellises which derived from French gardens, and flower gardens, and the flowering plants that climbed up trellises, porch and veranda. At one stage, Malton burst into verse:

> At the door of my straw-covered cot
> The rose and the jessamine blend ...[7]

But there seems to have been little or no tradition of flower gardens around country cottages in the eighteenth century; town artificers

383. A veranda at Sidmouth.

cultivated flowers, not country labourers or even country craftsmen.

The vogue for cottages coincided with a new attitude to the country. Life in the country villa had been seen as complementary to life in the town house, rather than inimical to it. Towns, whatever their drawbacks, were centres of civilization. Now the contrast began to be seen as one of innocence against corruption. Malton expressed this sentiment in a second book, published in 1802. Those 'who prefer the pure and tranquil retirement of the country to the fetid joys of the tumultuous city are they who take the most likely means to enjoy that blessing of life, happiness.' J.C. Loudon, in his *Treatise on Forming, Improving and Managing Country Residences* (1806), panned commerce and urban society as 'unnatural'. The only reason for engaging in commerce was to be able to 'retire to the country' and enjoy 'the *ease, liberty* and *independence* of a country residence'.[8]

To most of those who lived in or built them, however, cottages were just enjoyable places to be in, or perhaps a new form of toy. Many were built in and around seaside resorts. One of the best collections was at Sidmouth. Already by 1805 the number of 'simple houses scattered around' Sidmouth was remarked on, but it was only between 1805 and 1815 that distinctive thatched cottages-ornées appeared (Pls. 384-9), amongst them Knole Cottage, built for Lord le Despencer, Woodland Cottage, built for Lord Gwydir, and Sidcliff Cottage, built for Edward Boehm, a City banker with a house in St. James's Square. The latter's widow married John Bacon, the sculptor, and was celebrated in a poem, the gaily tripping couplets of which epitomize the apparently artless artificiality of these pretty buildings:

384-389. Six Sidmouth cottages of the early nineteenth century: (top) Clifton Cottage, (centre) Knowle Cottage, (bottom) Powys Cottage, (top right) Woodbine Cottage (centre) Camden Cottage, (bottom) Belmont Cottage.

Mrs Boehm
Wrote a poem
On the Sidmouth air.
Mr Boehm
Read the poem
And built a cottage there.
Mr Bacon
All forsaken
Wandered to the spot.
Mrs Bacon
He has taken
Partner of his lot.
As they longer
Live, the stronger
Their affection grows.
Every season
They with reason
Bless the spot they chose.[9]

Others were built in considerable numbers around London, and the larger provincial towns, and feature among the designs in the many books on cottage and villa architecture which were published from 1800 onwards. By then a major change was already beginning to take place in the suburbs. In the last decades of the eighteenth century merchants and professional men had begun to make their suburban villas or cottages their main place of residence, and to commute from them into the town. The change, which was to be momentous for towns and cities all over the world, is hard to document precisely. In 1790, William Roscoe, the Liverpool banker, reformer and philanthropist, moved from his house in central Liverpool to a suburban one in Islington, which became his only home. A little earlier the Thornton family of City of London merchants began to live for most of the year around Clapham Common, and provided the nucleus of what later became known as the Clapham Sect.[10]

No doubt there were occasional earlier examples; and by 1800 they were fairly common. The practice of having both a town and a suburban house lingered on for some decades; Constable, for instance, had

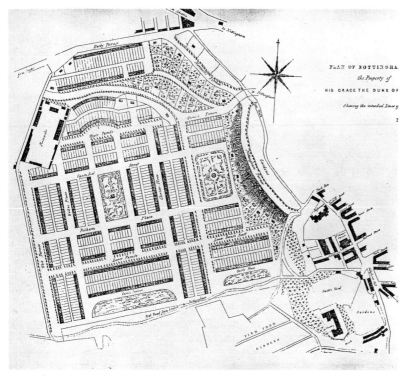

390, 391. Two schemes for developing the Park at Nottingham. By (top) P.F. Robinson (1828), and (bottom) T. Picken (c. 1840).

a house in Charlotte Street and a house in Hampstead from about 1827 until his death in 1837; there are examples in Hull up till the 1850s.[11] But by the mid-century it had become unusual; families opted for a house in the town, or a house in the suburbs, but not for both.

What caused this move — which ultimately became a rush — to the suburbs? With the growth of commerce and industry property in town centres was becoming more expensive, and property in the centre with a garden not only more expensive still, but very hard to find. Fog and dirt were increasingly a problem; the factory and household smoke, that was to blacken all large cities or industrial towns, was already beginning to belch. The cumulative effect of bad or non-existent drainage and tainted water was making central areas more unhealthy. In 1818, for instance, Louis Michael Simon, an insurance broker, three of whose six children had died in infancy when he was living in the Minories, by the Tower of London, moved out to Blackheath — not to a villa, however, but to the Paragon, a half-and-half compromise between a row of villas and a terrace, on which otherwise free-standing semi-detached houses are joined to adjoining pairs at ground-floor level. His son was the future Sir John Simon, one of the greatest of Victorian sanitary reformers.[12]

Such factors had begun to produce a move out of the centre from the 1770s onward: but it was primarily a move into new terraces. Merchants and professional men had begun to abandon their old houses, let or sell them to become warehouses and offices, and move out — to the terraces of Bloomsbury and Islington in London, to Rodney Street and its neighbours in Liverpool, to St. John Street and its neighbours in Manchester. The next wave of expansion produced more villas than terraces. The change is vividly demonstrated by two schemes for building over the park of Nottingham Castle (Pls. 390, 391). In the first (abortive) scheme, of 1828, most of the proposed housing consisted of terraces; the 1840 scheme provided for almost nothing but villas, and was what was finally built, in a slightly different form.[13]

One attraction of a villa was undoubtedly its garden. The late-eighteenth-century terraces normally had small gardens; their possession of them was one of the reasons for moving into them. The new villas, being further out and on cheaper building land, could have much bigger ones. The desire for such a garden was clearly growing among people who lived in towns. Behind it was a general feeling that life in the country was preferable to life in the town, so that if one had to live in the town one should make one's home as close to a house in the country as possible. A suburban villa provided something approaching the garden, the privacy, and even the carriage drive of a country house. It was also more suited to domestic life: it provided the ideal setting in which the merchant, after a hard day's work in the unattractive but necessary ambience of the busy commercial world, could be welcomed with 'happy greetings by wife and children whenever he returned from his struggle with the contending currents of the world's seething sea without'.[14]

And so in 1818 one finds John James Ruskin moving with his wife into a five-storey terrace house with a small garden in Hunter Street, off Brunswick Square, two miles from his wine business in the City; hiring summer lodgings in Hampstead or Dulwich; and then, in 1823, moving with their four-year-old son John to a semi-detached house of much the same size, but with a front garden, a carriage sweep, and a back garden 70 yards long by 20, on Herne Hill, four miles from his office. Here, as John Ruskin later put it, the view was 'over softly wreathing distances of domestic wood' his mother found 'her chief personal pleasure in her flowers', and 'the little domain answered every purpose of Paradise to me' — except that, unlike the Garden of Eden, '*all* the fruit was forbidden'.[15]

When the Herne Hill villa was built, in around 1805, its first occupant was John Jones, who had a draper's shop in Cheapside. It was one of two pairs, presumably built by one developer. The inevitable result of the fashion for villas and cottages was that they began to be built as speculative developments, instead of for individual clients. Two ambitious schemes for estates of semi-detached cottages or villas were designed for the Eyre estate in St. John's Wood, North London, in 1794 and 1803.[16] Neither came to anything, but between about 1807 and 1820 a more haphazard layout of villas and cottages covered much of the estate, and made it the first villa suburb in England. In 1823 John Nash designed Park Village West and East, a planned layout of pretty villas on either side of a canal to the north-east of Regent's Park. Decimus Burton's Calverley Park villas at Tunbridge Wells were started in 1828. More planned estates followed in the 1830s and 1840s, and by the 1850s they were being built, or at least projected, everywhere. The development of these early estates was facilitated by the introduction of

392. A villa in Lincombe Drive, Torquay.

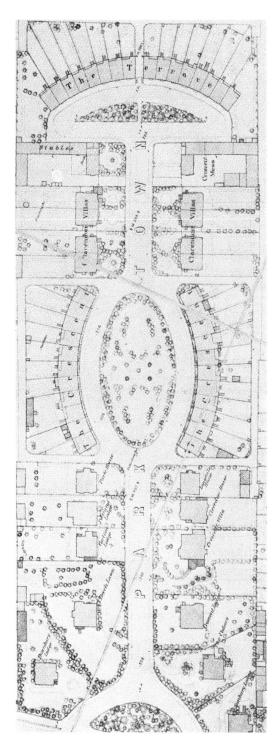

393. Park Town, Oxford, as laid out by S.L. Seckham and William Baxter in 1853-5.

394. (top right) Design by George Godwin for a villa estate at Ashford, c. 1860.

395. (bottom right) Unexecuted design by Henry Kendall for laying out land at Harlesden, north of London, c. 1850.

horse-drawn omnibus services, their later explosion by the arrival of suburban railways, which dramatically increased the commuting range.

By the second half of the nineteenth century the change was complete. Outside London and a few seaside or inland resorts, the middle and upper-middle classes were living in villas, not terraces. Even the upper classes, who lived in terrace houses when they came to London for the season, were likely to spend the winter or summer in villas or cottages in Sidmouth, Torquay (Pls. 382, 392) or Scarborough, and, later, at Westgate-on-Sea or Cromer. Most big towns acquired one particular villa estate or area, where most of the best families lived. In Birmingham they lived in Edgbaston; in Liverpool around Sefton Park; in Nottingham in the Park; in Leicester in Stoneygate; in Bradford along or off Manningham Lane. Even a much smaller place like Abingdon had its prestigious area of villas around Albert Park, and every town had at least one row of solid successful villas along one of the roads leading out of the town.

Common patterns can be seen in villa estates all over the country (Pls. 393-5). There are three main types of layout: a geometric one, based on squares, circuses and crescents; a picturesque one, of winding roads; and a grid, or series of parallel streets. The earlier estates quite often combine terraces and villas. The neatest example of this is perhaps Park Town in Oxford (Pl. 393). This was laid out between 1853 and 1855, with S.L. Seckham as architect, and William Baxter, former curator of the Oxford Botanic Gardens, to design 'ornamental gardens and pleasure grounds well stocked with trees and flowering shrubs'.[17] Later layouts usually had no terraces (except, if appropriate, a terrace of shops) and often no communal gardens. The social element had given way to the idea of individual privacy. But 'Park' continued to feature in the name of many estates even where there was no park.

A church was considered desirable, as a guarantee of respectability, if no more. Sometimes it was made a focal feature, in the centre of a central square, or closing the main vista. The roads were often planted with trees and many estates were separated from the outside world by gates and, not infrequently, a lodge. The architecture of individual villas inevitably changed over the decades. The earlier villas were often stuccoed and delicate in their architecture; the high Victorian villas were far solider, often to the verge of grimness. They were invariably of stone or brick, and often in two or more colours, especially if they were of brick. Towards the end of the century a degree of delicacy returned, in the form of turned woodwork around the porch or veranda and white-painted sash-windows, with small panes at least in the top half of the sashes.

At least as much care went into the planning and design of Victorian villa estates as into the residential areas of Georgian towns. In their own way, they are as successful. By their nature they can never

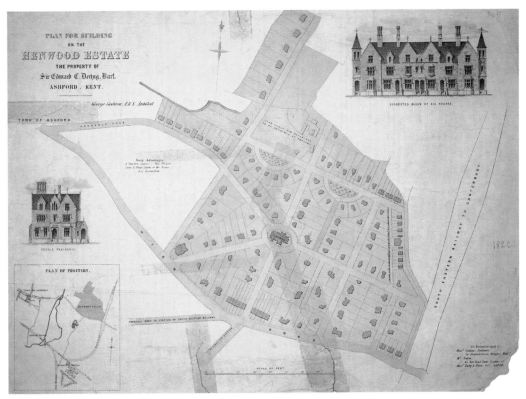

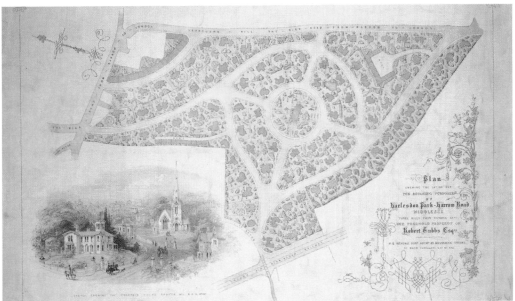

have the integrated architectural effect of a Georgian terrace: it is the trees which cement them together rather than the buildings. But, at their best, they abundantly succeeded in creating what those who came to live in them wanted: an atmosphere of security and seclusion amidst greenery.

Within this security a nation-wide way of life grew up. It had various focal points, of almost ritual sanctity. Around nine o'clock,

in a railway suburb, the front gate of every house disgorged a man in top hat and frock coat, who walked down to the station — itself often designed to harmonize with the surrounding villas. There were no women in the resulting procession, for none of the wives worked. Katherine Chorley described the Manchester suburb of Alderley Edge: 'After the 9.18 train had pulled out of the station, the Edge became exclusively female. You never saw a man on the hill roads, unless it were the doctor or the plumber, and you never saw a man in anyone's house except the gardener or the coachman. The quiet day was given over to correspondence, overseeing the servants and gardeners, and paying morning calls, until the evening train came in and the male procession took place again in reverse.'[18]

The unpublished diaries of C.S. Lucy[19] throw a vivid light on suburban life in North Oxford in the 1880s (Pl. 397). Bliss was it then to be alive — at least for the pretty daughter of a prosperous tradesman with as yet only a handful of girl-undergraduates to offer competition. The university provided young men, balls, concerts, extension lectures, Union debates, boat-races, or football and cricket matches in the Parks. Which young man did or did not bow to one was carefully noted in the diary. In winter there was skating on Port Meadow, in the summer tennis at home or the Tennis Club, geology excursions, picnics, boating, swimming and parties.

The Lucys did not own a carriage, but almost everything was within reach of a walk — or, for the more daring, of a bicycle. 'In the evening Mr Dixon brought up his flute and played and sang; he came on his bicycle, and Edith and I tried it.' Lessons at the School of Art produced more young men, and there were further lessons in shorthand and dancing. The Ragged School and the Zenana Mission gave an opening for good works, but fun came first: 'It was the Zenana Mission meeting but Katie and I thought the Parks a better pasture land.' A similar way of life is epitomized, a decade later, in Charles Gere's picture of the Gere family and their friends, in the garden of their home, Sandhurst Villa, at Leamington Spa (Pl. 396).

396.   Charles Gere, *The Tennis Party* (1900). Painted outside the artist's own villa in Leamington.
397.   A view in North Oxford.
398. (right)   Looking up to the Winter Gardens, Blackpool.

18

The

Bright

Lights

In 1900 Blackpool was one of the wonder towns of England. Within fifty years it had grown from a dim little village to a city of pleasure which stretched five miles along the coast, and had a resident population of 47,000, and a holiday population, at peak periods, of at least 100,000 more. Those who could squeeze out from the jam-packed crowds on the beach (Pl. 399) could see a range of buildings dedicated to enjoyment which was unequalled anywhere else in the world. To the left the compact mass of the Alhambra rose in a cliff of brickwork to a skyline of pyramidal towers. To the right was the long line of the Winter Gardens — the egg-shaped glass dome of its entrance hall, the hunched profile of the Empress Ballroom, the lofty skeletal web of the Ferris wheel. In the centre was the Tower itself (Pl. 402), Blackpool's tribute to Paris, finished five years after the Eiffel Tower, and although only just over half as high as its model, offering a much greater variety of entertainment in the building which was wrapped round its base — to the detriment, perhaps, of its architectural lines. The whole panorama was also visible across the domed kiosks and fretted Indian Pavilion on the North Pier; to the right two more piers, each with its own kiosks and pavilions, stretched out from the Promenade; to the left the auditoria of the Grand Theatre and the Hippodrome rose above shops and lodging-houses. Along the Promenade trundled, day and night, the first electric trams to be introduced to England, just as the Promenade itself was the first in the world to be lit by electric light; and at night the great beacon light at the top of the Tower circulated over the town, the sea and the plain of the Lancashire Fylde.

Each of the three main complexes provided its own world. The Winter Gardens incorporated two theatres, the Opera House (which put on much more than opera) and the Pavilion; round the latter the horseshoe-shaped promenade of the actual Winter Gardens provided a glass-covered avenue or bower of tropical vegetation; off the promenade the Indian Lounge led to the huge Empress Ballroom, a cathedral of dancing 189 feet long and 110 feet wide. The Alhambra combined a circus, a theatre and a ballroom, the last not quite so large as the Empress Ballroom, but even more extravagant in the lushness of its rococo decoration. Inside the Tower an entry fee of sixpence gave access to numerous restaurants and dining rooms, one of enormous size; an aquarium, disguised as a grotto; a menagerie and monkey house; an Olde Englishe Village (all under glass) in which visitors could buy presents and souvenirs; a conservatory, and an open-air promenade above it; and above all, a circus (for another sixpence) and a ballroom. The circus (Pl. 401) was (and is) on ground level, between the four legs of the Tower, but legs and everything else are clothed with glittering decoration in the Indian style; a great central pendant hangs above the circus ring, which could, and can, be flooded for water ballets and carnivals. At 90 by 150 feet the ballroom was smaller than the Empress, but it remains

the most richly decorated large space in England. Half ballroom, half theatre, rising up through two tiers of balconies to a vast coved ceiling on which gods and goddesses disport amidst gilded plaster work and crystal chandeliers, culminating in a huge stage which was later to be supplied with one of the world's biggest Wurlitzer organs, it enabled the mill hands of Lancashire to dance together in a setting as superficially glittering as anything provided for the court of Versailles, and a great deal larger (Pl. 400).[1]

The clientele of Blackpool was by no means entirely working-class. The hotels, terraces and crescents on the northern end of the Promenade catered for middle-class visitors, who occupied the more expensive seats in the theatres and patronized the 'first-class' restaurant in the Tower. Blackpool had in fact been planned as a resort for the better-off, on the model of other resorts all round the coast. It was for such a clientele that the North Pier was built in 1863, and the first buildings of the Winter Gardens opened in 1878.

399. (left) On the beach at Blackpool, from an old photograph.
400. Old-time dancing in the ballroom of the Tower, Blackpool (Frank Matcham, 1899).

291

But during the 1880s and 1890s the wages of the mill workers were rising in real terms, a week's summer holiday by the sea became an accepted and essential part of their lives, and in increasing numbers they took the train to Blackpool — at first by no means to the delight of the resort industry in the town. A symbolic incident occurred in August 1879. Mrs Ellen Lamb, reciting decorously in the Winter Gardens Pavilion, was interrupted by a voice from the audience shouting 'Give us a comic song'. In 1887 Sarah Bernhardt received such a bad reception in the Pavilion that she walked out in a fury; the audience could not hear what she said, and when they did hear, were indignant to discover that it was in French.[2]

By then the Gardens were on the verge of bankruptcy. They were rescued by the importation of a manager from London, William (always known as Bill) Holland. Holland saw that there was money in large working-class audiences, and set out to attract them. His motto was 'Give 'em what they want'. He built on a new Opera House, and inaugurated it with a season of Gilbert and Sullivan. In the Pavilion spectacular dance shows, at which John Tiller's Tiller Girls kicked up their shapely legs in amazing unison, went down much better than Sarah Bernhardt. Some of the shareholders protested; as one of them put it, 'the new manager is entirely mistaking the

401. The circus between the legs of the Blackpool Tower, redecorated in the Indian style in 1899.
402. (right) Looking towards Blackpool Tower from under the North Pier.

character of the establishment he is taking over'. They ceased to complain when the Gardens paid an 8 per cent dividend.[3]

Holland's success encouraged others. The opening of the Tower in 1894 introduced a war among entrepreneurs. The Tower cost £300,000, put up by the 3,000 shareholders of a limited-liability company. The dominant force behind it was John Bickerstaff, the chairman of the company. He was as enterprising as Bill Holland, but a native. He came from a Blackpool fishing family, and crewed for its lifeboat as a young man, besides running the successful pub which his father had built on the front. He then moved into local politics, and served as mayor in 1889-91. There were few aspects of Blackpool in which he was not involved. He was chairman of the Clifton Hotel Company and the Blackpool Passenger Steamboat Company, and a director of the Blackpool Electric Tramways. He was knighted in 1926. For years he was the best-known figure in the town. He was easily recognizable by the yachting cap which seems never to have left his head, and featured in flowers among the wreaths at his funeral.[4]

From the start the Tower was a financial success. Holland fought back at the Winter Gardens by adding the Empress Ballroom and the Ferris wheel, but died in 1895, the year before they were completed. Bickerstaff retaliated in his turn, by turning his circus into an Indian extravaganza, and converting the former Assembly Hall or Grand Pavilion into the amazing ballroom. Both were inaugurated in 1899.

Meanwhile a second rival had appeared, in the shape of the Alhambra, which opened in the same year. By now the phenomenal success of Blackpool seemed like a law of life, and the shares of the companies which were started up to build piers, entertainment buildings, tramways, hotels and housing estates sold like hot cakes on the Manchester Stock Exchange. £382,000 was rapidly subscribed for the Alhambra, of which no less than £234,000 — an amazing sum for the period — went on buying the site. The almost immediate failure of the venture marked the collapse of the great 1890s boom. Blackpool recovered, however, and so did the Alhambra — but only after it had been bought by the Tower Company (for only £131,000), and re-opened as the Palace in 1904.[5]

A third character can be pulled out of the galaxy of Blackpool personalities of this period: the Revd J.S. Balmer, minister of the United Methodist Free Church, active in temperance and Sunday Observance societies, against all drinking and dancing in the town, and critical of the corporation for encouraging it. In 1899 he wrote to the newspapers in a state of shock. He had tried out a penny-in-the-slot machine on the promenade, advertising 'Parisian Scenes'. 'I thought perhaps the pictures meant some beautiful representations of Paris, and dropped a penny in one of those abominable slots. It was like looking through the gateway to perdition.' But Balmer lived in the same street as Bill Holland and paid tribute to their relationship,

403. Burning the effigy of the Pope on Guy Fawkes' night, Lewes, from a painting of 1892.

after Holland's sudden death, in December 1895: 'He does not belong to my church, nor to my school of thought, but that is not a reason why I should not be neighbourly with a man living near me.' Holland, like Bickerstaff, belonged to the Church of England, but was not, perhaps, a religious man; certainly the Freemasons played a much more prominent role than the clergyman at his funeral, which was one of the biggest ever held in Blackpool.[6]

By examining Balmer's point of view, and pursuing Holland's career back to his London origins, one can get some idea of the opposing forces which lay behind Blackpool in the 1890s, and the flowering of the leisure industry all over England. One may also understand the reasons for the lack of hostility between the two men.

One of the main subjects about which Victorians disagreed was the use of leisure. Was it a safety valve, enabling people to let off the steam which had been built up by the repressions of their working life? Or a time for rest? Or a time to meet like-minded people in enjoyable conditions? Or an opportunity for self-improvement? Not least, should Sunday be a day of leisure, or a day devoted to the service of God?[7]

Attitudes varied widely between two poles, the Nonconformist and Evangelical view at one end, and the traditional attitude of the working-classes at the other. Balmer represented the former. He belonged to a tradition which derived from the rise of the Wesleyans and the Evangelical movement in the Church of England in the late eighteenth century. Sunday was God's day, on which any non-religious activity, however harmless or meritorious in itself, was to be avoided. On other days leisure should be used for self-improvement — moral and intellectual improvement, and physical improvement only in so far as it contributed to them. Pleasure was a distraction from godliness. The theatre, the music-hall, the racecourse, the public-house and the ballroom were all taboo.

The majority of the working classes felt differently. After having worked excessively hard for six days a week, they saw Sunday either as an opportunity for sleep, or a time to let themselves go, in terms of drink, food, sex, gambling, noise and violence. What it was not, except for a minority, was a day on which to go to church.

There were numerous stages in between. Pleasure was, perhaps, acceptable in moderation; young men should be allowed to sow their wild oats; a religious Sunday morning could be followed by a secular afternoon; letting off steam on certain occasions, such as Derby Day, was not only allowable, but could be a way of bringing the classes together.

In the first three-quarters of the nineteenth century the Non-conformist and Evangelical lobby grew in power. Its members not only ordered their own lives, but tried to remould the lives of others by converting them, or by banning or limiting activities they found undesirable, by legislative or other means. They had their greatest success with traditional working-class enjoyments, especially those confined to the working classes, or in which the general move towards godliness and respectability had reduced upper- and middle-class participation to unimportance. The wild Guy Fawkes celebrations at Lewes survived (and still take place) perhaps because their anti-Catholic bias won support from the Protestant middle classes (Pl. 403). But pleasure gardens, fairs, boxing matches, cock fights, bull-baiting and bull-running were banned or ceased to take place all over the country. St. Bartholomew's Fair, the acrobats, fire-eaters, roundabouts, animal shows and gambling dens of which had enabled Londoners of all classes to run wild since the sixteenth century, became more and more disreputable, and was closed in 1855.

The approach had a positive side. Dedicated efforts were made to provide the working classes with an alternative, in the form of

404. Bull-running in Stamford, *c.* 1800. From an anonymous painting in Stamford Town Hall.

what became known as 'rational recreation' — with parks, museums, libraries, evening lectures and classes, concerts, Sunday School outings, coffee public houses, and opportunities for 'healthy' sport. The movement was only partially successful. It never appealed to more than a small segment of the working classes, if an important one. Its effectiveness was limited by the fact that many of those who supported it were also extreme advocates of Sunday observance, and managed to prevent, for instance, museums being opened, or even music being played in the parks, on Sunday; on the other hand it was to give the working classes a chance of recreation outside Sundays that the Saturday half-holiday was introduced by law in 1850.

The working classes resented and resisted any curtailment of their traditional amusements; in the late 1830s, for instance, the army had to be called in to help the police in suppressing the annual bull-running (Pl. 404) which for centuries had taken place through the streets of Stamford.[8] They received a certain amount of sympathy, and some activities, like big race-meetings, had too much support even to come near suppression. In addition, they managed to develop new amusements, of which the music-hall was the most important, or to remould activities devised for them by their superiors into forms which they found more attractive — bringing alcohol into working men's clubs, for instance, or taking public-school spirit out of football.

But the middle classes were not monolithic. Today, when 'Victorian middle-class morality' is talked about, what is meant is the morality of the strait-laced, puritanical, Nonconformist middle class, as though that was the only type there was. In fact one can distinguish two main strands. These can be described as godly and ungodly, as long as one recognizes that the ungodly were not necessarily anti-godly, or even irreligious. Both strands can be traced at every social level, but the stronghold of godliness was among the middle classes.

The godly middle classes were serious-minded, strict-living, and hard-working; many, though not all, were self-made. They supported, and not infrequently endowed, public libraries and baths, Athenaeums, Mechanics' Institutes, and temperance halls. They voted Liberal, preached free trade, attended chapel, and were critical of the upper classes. They can be watched in action all over England, but especially in London and the industrial towns. In Bolton, for instance, they joined with the Evangelicals, and fought, ultimately without success, for the suppression of the Star Music Hall, which in the 1840s and 1850s was perhaps the most popular music-hall in the north of England.[9] In Nottingham, when the Theatre Royal was rebuilt in 1865, the Revd H. Hervey leapt into print: 'It is thought by the right-hearted that to expend £15,000 upon a play-house, in a town where efforts are daily put forth to improve the morale and religion of the young, is the height of folly and sin.'

A similar note was struck in the same town about twenty years later by Samuel Johnson, the town clerk. When opening a coffee public house in the town, he referred to the Talbot Inn and Music Hall as 'the flaunting Talbot, a source of immorality and degradation' (Pl. 406). Both buildings were opened in 1876 by Edward Barker Cox, a steel-bar manufacturer. The Talbot was one of the biggest and busiest public houses in the Midlands. Cox was a keen fox-hunter, and treasurer of the South Nottinghamshire Hunt; his obituary described him as an intimate of Lord Harrington, the Hunt's MFH.[10]

Virtually every Victorian town had its Coxes — and, more generally, a section of its middle class which voted Conservative, attended the Church of England, admired the upper classes, imitated them to the best of their ability, and aimed to join them if they made enough money to do so. They included professional people, manufacturers, merchants, bankers, brewers, builders, publicans and tradesmen. Often they were conscious of having superior origins to those of self-made Nonconformists; some shopkeepers affiliated with the upper classes, because upper-class custom was important to them.[11]

405. Acrobats in the Alhambra, London.

These 'ungodly' middle classes could be as hard-working or good at making money as their godly counterparts. But as a group they were less rigid in their attitude to amusements, both their own and other people's. In particular, they followed the upper classes in a tenderness towards traditional working-class amusements. In Shrewsbury, for instance, the annual Shrewsbury Show, at which, since the Middle Ages, the town guilds had marched in procession to feast and enjoy themselves on Kingsland common, was coming under attack from the Nonconformist and Evangelical lobby in the 1840s, as an encouragement of drunkenness and immorality; but in the 1850s and 1860s another strand of opinion in the town joined with local landowners to defend it, on the grounds that 'all work and no play makes Jack a dull boy', that it would help 'revive the harmony of feudal days' or, as the mayor put it, make 'the lower, middle and the higher classes unite together for mutual enjoyment'.[12] In Bolton, the *Bolton Chronicle* expressed a similar point of view when it came to the support of the Star Music Hall in 1852: 'the Singing Saloons or Singing Halls are the best guarantee for recreation and approach nearer to the inclinations and customs of the working classes than any other institution of the present age.'[13] Among the middle classes of this persuasion, there was always a

406. The bar of the Talbot, Nottingham, in the late nineteenth century.

sizeable proportion which hunted, raced, danced, drank, fornicated and gambled with as much dedication as any wild young marquess.

One model for such people was the 'swell', a type who was to be found right down the social scale, though at some stage he was likely to merge into the 'masher'. A swell was the antithesis of Nonconformist ideals. He lived and dressed with style, splendidly careless of money and morality. As an example of an aristocratic swell one can take the first Earl of Londesborough. This superb shot and whip, owner of a string of houses and an income of £100,000 a year, moved from country house to country house, from Ascot to Cowes, and Cowes to Cricket Week at Scarborough, scattering his great fortune in a collage of actresses, racehorses, powdered footmen, yachts, and coaches as gleaming as the horses which drew them.[14]

But sporting brewers, rich tradesmen's sons, theatrical managers, journalists, bookies, publicans, clerks and shop attendants all aimed as best they could for the same swagger and style. Here Bill Holland returns to the picture. For it was when he was lessee and manager of the Canterbury Music Hall in London, between 1867 and 1870, that George Leybourne sang the song and created the character of 'Champagne Charlie', to such effect that a 'Champagne Charlie' became a synonym for any middle- or lower-class swell. The character was as much a creation of Holland's as Leybourne's. He established it with the same gift for publicity that he was later to show at Blackpool. He bought Leybourne a coach and four, equipped it with elaborate harness for the horses and postilions in cherry-and-black uniforms, and sent him driving from music-hall to music-hall, to racecourses and Hyde Park, wearing a fur-collared coat, smoking a big cigar, and calling in at bars to distribute bottles of champagne.[15]

Music-halls had developed out of the singing rooms built onto pubs in the 1830s and 1840s. By the 1860s they had proliferated, especially in London and the northern towns. The solo acts were being supplemented by elaborate acrobatics, ballets, and floor shows (Pl. 405). Their architecture, especially in the bigger halls, was becoming more elaborate. They still relied on a basis of working-class support, but their clientele was spreading. In London, in particular, there was a hierarchy of music-halls: little halls in back streets, with a working-class audience; big halls in the suburbs, with a sizeable mixture of shop-keepers and tradesmen, with their wives, in the audience; halls like the Oxford in Oxford Street, and the Canterbury in Lambeth, frequented by swells in evening dress; and the halls around Leicester Square, especially the Alhambra and, later, the Empire, where one might find peers, Rothschilds and maharajahs, attracted, perhaps, less by the show than by the high-class prostitutes on the promenade in the Empire, and the chorus-girls who came from dancing the cancan to mix with the audience in the Alhambra buffet.[16]

The middle-class swell was scornfully described in 1888, in a pamphlet entitled *Tempted London*: 'The full-dressed men to be found in such a place comprise the loafers of the West End, the sons of the big shopkeepers, the smaller members of the Stock Exchange, the livery-stable keepers, the West-End wine-bar proprietors, and all those men who, daily brought into contact with gentlemen, fancy they have only to arrange their feathers to become counterparts of the bird.'[17] Such people were also

407. Henry Isaac Butterfield, worsted manufacturer, in his drawing-rooms at Cliffe Castle, Keighley, *c.* 1880. He had a second house in Paris.

likely to be found on and around the great dancing platform in Cremorne, or in other London pleasure gardens. The life they lived, the values they represented, were the antithesis of those of the godly middle classes. But they had their own style — as one can see if one takes yet another look at Bill Holland.

From his emergence from his family drapery business to put his capital into Weston's Music Hall in 1866, until his death at Blackpool at the age of fifty-eight in 1895, Holland — 'the People's Caterer', as he liked to call himself – was constantly in the public eye, constantly thinking up new forms of entertainment, and constantly alternating between affluence and bankruptcy. When he died the *Blackpool Gazette* commented: 'William Holland's worst friend was undoubtedly William Holland. He was prodigal with his money, and played ducks and drakes with what must originally have been a strong constitution. If there was any "fun" going, William Holland must be in at the very thick of it.' At different times, he owned or leased five London music-halls. He put on bullfights at the Agricultural Hall in Islington, and lost all his money. He put on gorgeous pantomimes at Covent Garden. For many years he ran the North Woolwich Gardens, and popularized them by holding postman's races, barmaid shows, baby shows, cat shows, and a beard and moustache show — which he won himself. He was a genial fellow, full of good stories: about how he had escaped from North

Woolwich Gardens by balloon to avoid a bailiff, or how he had attended the opening race-meeting at Alexandra Palace with 'Champagne Charlie' Leybourne, in his gorgeous equipage, and been ushered by the police through cheering crowds, in mistake for the Prince of Wales. As the *Daily Telegraph* commented, at the time of his death: 'Mr Holland's burly figure and long waxed moustaches were as well known as are the personal characteristics of our leading statesmen.' His portrait makes clear that his model in this respect was Napoleon III, not the Prince of Wales, and introduces another element to the story.[18]

For the godly the Paris of the Second Empire and the Third Republic stood for immorality and wickedness; for the ungodly it was the place where life was lived as it ought to be. Its influence pervaded their own life-style; it was not just a matter of imperials and waxed moustaches, or reading French novels. Second Empire opulence, heavy hangings, inlaid furniture, painted ceilings and proliferating bronze, marble and china bric-à-brac is frequently met in later Victorian England. At differing levels of lavishness and discrimination one can find it in Rothschild houses, in the houses of successful northern manufacturers (Pl. 407),[19] and in the saloon bars of the more lavish public houses (Pl. 406). Above all, French influence is apparent in the theatres, music-halls, and circuses which, like the public houses, were built or altered in increasing numbers in and around the 1890s. The numbers were, in fact, so great that, in London and the bigger towns, there were almost no theatres or pubs of any consequence which were not largely or entirely remodelled.

There were two main reasons for this: more working-class money, and an increasing middle-class appetite for diversion. To this can be added an increasing skill among those who provided the diversions in raising capital and selling their wares. The working-class prosperity which had caused the growth of Blackpool was having a similar influence in towns all over the country. Lancashire mill hands were a little earlier in taking seaside holidays than working people in other parts of the country, but their example was soon followed. Resorts all round the coast began to swell in size and produce new buildings to entertain their new clientele (Pl. 408). When at home the same people had more money to spend in the bars, and on a night out once a month or even once a week.[20]

The number of middle-class people who wanted to be entertained was growing too, partly for straightforward reasons of population growth, partly because there were more of them, and partly because an increasing proportion were diverging from the straight and narrow path of godliness. By the end of the nineteenth century the Industrial Revolution had been under way for a century. Second- or third-generation families, whose parents or grandparents had made their money by hard work, long hours, and a refusal to be diverted, were able to relax, and to react against their parents' way of life. As Richard Le Gallienne put it at the time: 'a New Spirit of

408. (right) The pier at Plymouth, from the painting by Charles Ginner, 1923.

409.   The Grand Theatre, Leeds (George Corson, 1878).

Pleasure is abroad amongst us, and one that blows from no mere coteries of hedonistic philosophers, but comes on the four winds.'[21]

New theatres and music-halls all over England were one result. But the new spirit of pleasure was helped along by concessions on both sides. Pubs aimed to attract respectable members of both sexes with the blazing fires, thick carpets, comfortable chairs and potted palms in their new saloon bars. Both the theatre and the music-hall promoted their image as places which had purged themselves of anything that could shock. Those who ran them had always protested that they were not as bad as they were painted. In 1854 the manager of the Star in Bolton had spoken up for his music-hall as a place which combined 'social enjoyment with wholesome instruction'. In 1865, when the Revd Hervey was castigating the new Theatre Royal, Nottingham, as 'the height of folly and sin', its promoters declared that 'we call upon our fellows to assist us in our endeavours to make the theatre a place of innocent recreation and of moral and intellectual culture'.[22] But in the 1880s and 1890s such efforts became more effective, or at any rate were more widely believed in.

Music-hall managers imposed their own censorship and laid down provisos such as that 'any artiste giving expression to anything obscene or vulgar in song, saying or gesture, or of political, religious or local matters, will subject themselves to instant dismissal'. 'Music Hall' with its connotation of vulgarity was increasingly replaced by 'Theatre of Varieties'. Bill Holland played a part in this development. The *Blackpool Gazette* commended him as 'among the first of the managers in London to develop the lighter and brighter side of the music hall programme — to eradicate the vulgar and the loud ...'.[23] This probably explains the Revd Bulmer's relatively kindly feelings towards him.

On the opening night of the Grand Theatre in Leeds (Pl. 409) in November 1878, the manager, Wilson Barrett, made a speech. He described how only a few years ago in Leeds 'it was difficult to get respectable people into the theatre. But such ideas were being rapidly swept away' (applause). He himself promised to produce only 'plays that would not bring a blush to the youngest girl who might enter the theatre'. The new building was the most lavish theatre out of London; its promoters included some of the richest and best-established people in Leeds, Liberals and Nonconformists among them; their primary object was 'the elevation of the drama in Leeds'. Even so, the *Leeds Mercury*, whose proprietor, Edward Baines, was a rigid Nonconformist, is said to have continued to refuse to accept theatrical advertisements or publish reviews of theatrical performances.[24]

The next two decades were to make clear that Barrett was right, and that Baines was rowing against the tide. When Shaftesbury Avenue and Charing Cross Road were formed in the late 1880s, they included no less than seven theatres and eight public houses; that the Avenue should have been named in honour of the Earl of Shaftesbury, a strict Evangelical who was no friend either to the drink interest or the theatre, and that a memorial to him, in the form of a figure of Love, should have presided over the prostitutes of Piccadilly Circus was one of the more curious vagaries of the period.[25]

Music-halls and variety theatres became not only acceptable, but even chic. Young middle-class people attended them as a way of showing their escape from their parents' values. Painters and writers began to frequent them, in emulation of their equivalents across the Channel. As early as 1876 Whistler painted Conny Gilchrist, the child skipper who was to skip from the music-hall stage to a viscountess's coronet. Sickert began painting music-hall scenes in the late 1880s; in the 1890s the halls were being frequented by Beerbohm and Rudyard Kipling, along with Ernest Dowson, Arthur Symons and all the Decadents. Albert Chevalier took time off from them to sing his coster songs in West End drawing-rooms. By 1905 a biography of Charles Morton, pioneer manager of music-halls, commented with unction: 'the once despised and often properly despised music halls of the Metropolis have become splendid variety theatres, worthy of (and often receiving) the patronage of the Highest in the Land'. Between 1880 and 1910 variety theatres were being built in large numbers all over the country. Although many straightforward theatres were built in the same period, they were far outnumbered and (outside London) exceeded in lavishness and size by variety theatres.[26]

Their success was aided by improved financing. Both theatres and music-halls had previously offered a dubious investment. Individual entrepreneurs such as Bill Holland had moved from property to property, and oscillated between success and failure, intensely vulnerable through lack of capital. Few theatres were as

410. The London Coliseum (Frank Matcham, 1904), from a contemporary illustration in *The Sphere*.

successful as the Britannia, Hoxton, where fifty-eight years of well-managed popular melodrama created a fortune of £126,000 for the Lane family, and lifted Samuel Lane into the Royal Thames Yacht Club.[27]

Limited joint-stock companies owning single theatres or music-halls appeared in some numbers in the 1880s. They often paid wildly fluctuating dividends, and seem mainly to have been supported by their local clientele. A company owning a chain could iron out individual successes and failures. Big companies of this type were made possible by improved techniques of flotation. The most impressive expression of this was the formation of Moss Empires Ltd., in 1899. It was a merger of the separate variety chains already formed by H.E. Moss, Oswald Stoll and Richard Thornton, coming from the backgrounds of an Edinburgh fairground, a Liverpool music-hall, and a Newcastle pub respectively. Moss Empires had capital of £1,400,000, and owned or built large 'Empire' variety theatres all over Scotland, Wales, London (Pl. 410), and the north of England.[28]

Other chains included one of southern music-halls, built up by Walter de Frece (of a Liverpool music-hall-owning family, and married to Vesta Tilley), and the Hippodrome group, built up by Tom Barrasford, the son of a Newcastle publican. By 1903, in which year he went public, Barrasford had acquired a chain of fifteen variety theatres. Over the next few years, according to his grandson, he conducted a vendetta against Oswald Stoll, who had banned him from his theatres on the grounds that Barrasford was poaching his performers. 'The direct result of this was that my grandfather resolved to build a bigger and better music hall in every town and city, in direct opposition to the existing Moss and Stoll Empires.'[29] True or not, in the next few years Barrasford Hippodromes were built in close proximity to Empires in at least five cities.

Something of the same empire-building can be seen in the London pub world of the 1880s and '90s. It started with publican speculators building up groups of pubs, doing them up or rebuilding them, and buying and selling them at a great rate. Then the breweries moved in to secure their outlets, raised capital by going public, and bought pubs in large numbers. The liveliest, though not the largest, buyer was the Cannon Brewery, remarkable for the lavishness of the pubs which it built, and for the ebullient fox-hunting Toryism of its partners.[30]

The demand and the finance were available: it remained to evolve the architecture. Theatres and pubs needed to attract attention, get the public inside and put them in the right mood. They needed to suggest gaiety, and fun, to make people feel that they were escaping from everyday life, having a good time, and living like lords — or pashas. Both achieved this by a lavish use of ornament, of brightly coloured, glittering, reflecting or faceted surfaces, and curves as abandoned as Lottie Collins dancing (Pl. 413). Both played tricks with scale and proportion, exaggerated, used any style which suited their fancy, and mixed styles and periods together with the ebullience of a fancy-dress ball.

Having similar aims and a common ancestry, they inevitably had elements in common, but they also each drew on a different set of images. Theatres dipped into a rich past of theatres, especially baroque and rococo — but more, one suspects, as revived and developed in nineteenth-century Paris than in their original form. Although elements from different periods and other styles were mixed together without compunction, on the whole their interiors moved chronologically from the opulence of Louis XIV through the gaiety of Louis XV to the elegance of Louis XVI — arriving at the last stage in the early 1900s. An occasional alternative was the Indian style, perhaps used merely because it was exotic, perhaps because it suggested dancing girls and voluptuous rites, perhaps because of the British Empire. But the immediate inspiration came from Paris, from the Indian-style Eden Theatre of Variety, the huge elephants' heads adorning which featured in a number of English variety theatres of the 1890s (Pl. 415).[31]

The pub had different connotations. It was a mixture of a house, in which the landlord entertained his guests, and a shop, in which drink was sold across the counter. The art of the late Victorian pub was to take both aspects and exaggerate them. The many-shelved overmantels loaded with pretty objects that were fashionable in 'artistic' drawing-rooms were transformed into towering shrines of bottles and glasses behind the bar (Pl. 411). The curving glass and elaborate timber framework of contemporary shop-fronts were adapted to flash and sparkle with embossed and engraved decoration (Pl. 412). Their stylistic inspiration was mostly English, the same mixture of Jacobean and Georgian elements that was to be found in contemporary houses under the confusing denomination of 'Queen Anne'. But French influence was apparent too, in domes and mansard roofs on the exterior, in bronze statues and ornaments

411. (top left)   The main bars at the Philharmonic, Liverpool (Walter Thomas, 1895-1900).
412. (bottom left)   The Prince Alfred, Maida Vale, London (*c.* 1898).
413.   Lottie Collins dancing Ta-ra-ra-BOOM-de-ay, from a caricature of 1895.
414.   Detail from a late-nineteenth-century fairground organ.

and plush curtains inside, and in the rococo motifs that whirled and sparkled over the windows and mirrors, using the technique known as French embossing.[32]

Lavish decoration in both theatres and pubs was made especially easy because of new techniques of producing, or mass-producing, ornament. In pubs tiles, machine-cut joinery, decorated glass, embossed lincrusta on walls and ceilings, and cast-iron columns and trimmings for exterior and interior were all readily and relatively inexpensively available. Similar elements were found in theatres. But the particular material which eased the creation of the latter was fibrous plaster, modelled, coloured or gilded to produce cherubs, swags, and scrolls on balcony fronts, domes and caryatids over and between the boxes, and a riot of sculpture and ornament around the proscenium arch.

It was appropriate that Felix de Jong, the leading supplier of fibrous plaster, should be the close friend, and ultimately the executor, of Frank Matcham, the most successful and ebullient theatre architect of the period. It was Matcham who designed the Tower ballroom at Blackpool, along with the Grand Theatre and Winter Gardens Opera House. In all, between 1879 and 1912 he designed over 150 theatres (Pls. 410, 415). He worked for clients all over Britain, but his most important patrons were H.E. Moss and Oswald Stoll. In a similar fashion the practice of Matcham's main rival, Bertie Crewe, was based on designing Barrasford's Hippodromes.[33]

Contemporary architects and critics tended to be patronizing about the architecture of pubs and theatres — especially variety theatres. In 1890 Edwin Sachs commented on the lavish decoration of the London Alhambra, as it was rebuilt after a fire in 1883. It resulted, he wrote, 'not ... from any interest taken by its owners in architecture, but merely in the way of gorgeous advertisement, not dissimilar from the motives which occasion the elaborate fittings of a public house.'[34] But, after all, 'gorgeous advertisement' is a reasonable enough aim for a certain kind of architecture. It is true that few of the pubs or theatres of the time can stand up to criticism in terms of the logic or coherence of their design, still less of the scholarship of their detail. They are slapdash; their architects were prepared to paper over any awkward junctions or difficult corners by a row of mirrors, or an application of gilt or fibrous plaster. But in terms of achieving what they set out to achieve, of suggesting mystery and romance when the lights were turned down in the theatre, or glamour and gaiety when the pubs blazed out in the streets at night, few types of architecture have been more successful.

415. Inside the Olympia, Liverpool (Frank Matcham, 1905).
416. (right) A tasteful arrangement of concrete and flowers.

Epilogue

Contemplating the vast literature of town planning that crams shelf after shelf in the library of the Royal Institute of British Architects with official publications and books by experts or enthusiasts, anyone who has been travelling round the towns of England can be excused for asking himself 'what on earth went wrong?'

MULBERRY HOUSE
FACTORIES TO LET
CityEstates
051-227 3911 Ex.123
Kingsway House, Hatton Garden, Liverpool L69 2DJ
LIVERPOOL CITY COUNCIL

English towns started on a dangerous course two hundred years ago. Rural romanticism and the influence of the Enlightenment achieved wonderful results in late Georgian towns, but the points of view behind them were ultimately to have a disastrous effect. Project Thomas Harrison and the heroic polygons and semi-circles of his design for Chester Castle, and one ends up with a borough engineer massacring his town by means of the ruthless geometry of an inner ring road. Project the lovely interpenetration of town and greenery at Bath, and one ends up with that same borough engineer jumping into his car at the end of the day and driving off from the town which he is destroying to his house in a nearby village.

Disciples of the Enlightenment preached the clean sweep, the fresh start and the grand geometric plan. Tradition had to give way before rational analysis. New cities were better than old ones, because old ones were untidy, illogical, and full of problems. Ideal cities were best of all, because their designers did not have to make compromises in the course of building them.

Rural romanticism implied that the country was a better place than the town, because it was closer to nature. Towns were only bearable insofar as they resembled the country. A small country town was the best kind of town, because the country lay all round it and soaked all through it. Thomas Hardy epitomized the type, when he described Dorchester, thinly disguised as Casterbridge, as 'the complement of the rural life around; not its urban opposite. Bees and butterflies in the cornfields at the top of the town, who desired to get to the meads at the bottom, took no circuitous course, but flew straight down High Street without any apparent consciousness that they were traversing strange latitudes.' Bigger towns, where such a relationship was not possible, had to do the best they could. Threading them with parks and open spaces was one way of making them supportable; building detached or semi-detached houses in their own gardens on tree-lined roads another. Living outside the town altogether, and commuting in, was the best solution of all.

One might expect rural romantics and the children of the Enlightenment to pursue opposing courses. A poor-law workhouse, rotating its wards like the spoke of a wheel as the supreme rational solution to the problem of poverty, seems a long way removed from the modest vernacular of a traditional country town or village. But in fact the two groups had a way of joining forces. The earlier ideal towns of the nineteenth century, like James Silk-Buckingham's Victoria or Pemberton's Queen Victoria Town, combined Enlightenment plans with Enlightenment architecture, or something not so far removed from it. In the course of the nineteenth century, as the ideal of the Garden City evolved, the urban terraces of the earlier plans gave way to rows of cottages — or villas trying to look like cottages.

Ebenezer Howard's ideal Garden City of 1898 (the first to be so called) and the projected or realized garden cities or garden suburbs, planned industrial settlements and London County Council estates that followed (or, in one or two cases, anticipated Howard by a few years) developed what was to become a stereotype: Enlightenment plans, vernacular architecture. A framework of grand avenues, crescents and circuses was made up of terraces or semi-detached houses based on village or small-town models and built of brick, roughcast, half-timbering or tile hanging, with low-swept roofs, gables, leaded casements, prominent chimney-stacks, small front gardens and sizeable back ones. Even the multi-storey flats that were built out of necessity rather than choice to replace slums in central areas were often tricked out with the same vernacular detailing.

The result covered, and still covers, many square miles around the larger English cities, and features conspicuously on the outskirts of any English town of any size. Very often it was combined with a bypass, product of the burgeoning motor age. A familiar townscape resulted: stretches of tree-lined dual carriageway linking the roundabouts, houses set back behind feeder roads to either side, the occasional parade of shops, and otherwise acre after acre of little houses, semi-detached or in short rows, stretching back from the bypass on a spacious geometry of circuses, crescents and avenues that is immediately recognizable on any town plan. All this reflected garden-city ideals. Many of the new estates were in fact planned by architects or planners, such as Barry Parker or Raymond Unwin, who were closely associated with the garden city movement.

Town planning developed out of the garden city. The Town and Country Planning Association, which first took that name in 1932, had been founded in 1902 as the Garden City Association. The ideals of town planners reflected their pedigree. A few individuals, of whom Patrick Geddes is the best known, envisaged the possibility of an organic development and reordering of existing towns, but most thought in terms of new towns, or large new areas attached to existing towns and radically different from them. Their interest in central areas was confined to demolishing slums and replacing them with new housing equally unrelated to the existing town fabric.

But what was a slum, and did it have to be cleared? In 1939 Dr. Aubrey T. Westlake wrote an article attacking the destruction of working-class terraces in Wapping, and their replacement by flats. He pointed out that the inhabitants had no desire to be moved, and that the back gardens and yards of their houses, however, small, were intensively used and formed an essential part of working-class life. A mile or two away the Nichol in Spitalfields had been a notorious slum, which featured as the Jago in Arthur Morrison's best-selling novel *A Child of the Jago* (1896). It was demolished at the end of the century, to make way for one of the first LCC estates.

Old photographs show brick terraces of two-storey cottages, with big weavers' windows on the first floor. They would probably sell for a couple of hundred thousand pounds each in Spitalfields today. But the possibility of renovating and improving, rather than demolishing, never had serious consideration. The phrase 'slum clearance' carried all before it.

Outside the areas of slum clearance, comparatively little changed in town centres between the Wars. Cinemas appeared, as a supplement to, or replacement of, theatres; cars increasingly replaced horse traffic in the streets and evoked garages and motor showrooms; some shops and banks were rebuilt, some shop-fronts replaced, the big chains began to make their first appearance, and a sprinkling of towns acquired a new county or town hall, and a piece of *Beaux-Arts* planning to set it off. But on the whole, a Victorian returning to walk down and around the high street of his home town forty years after the death of Queen Victoria would still have felt at home.

One major change, however, there had been and it is still in progress. The middle classes were deserting the towns. The fabric remained, but the middle classes were living in it less and less. Rural romanticism was pulling them to the country, or at least the outer suburbs, and first railways and then cars helped them on their way. In her *Manchester Made Them* Katherine Chorley remarked on the effect this was already having on Manchester before the 1914-18 War. In the nineteenth century the people whom Manchester made and who made Manchester took it for granted that they would also run Manchester. If they moved to suburbs, these were still within easy reach of the centre. As they moved further out they also moved out of local government. The golf-club replaced the town hall as the focus of their lives.

In Liverpool the opening of the Mersey Tunnel in the 1920s transformed the city. Its prosperous middle classes began to take to their cars in the evening, and drive to their snug villas in the pseudo-countryside of the Wirral, across the water from Liverpool. The grand terraces around the newly-emerging cathedral were gradually abandoned to prostitutes and down-and-outs. A similar phenomenon could be observed in all large cities, except London. But it was also beginning to take place in smaller towns all over the country, even if to a lesser extent.

The importance of this change can scarcely be exaggerated. It is the middle classes, on the whole, who write the history books and the social studies, and they have tended to find it more romantic or interesting to write about classes other than their own. There are endless studies of working-class life in towns, and a series of prestigious and impressive books has analyzed the activities of the great families which own or owned large portions of them. Studies of the middle-class contribution are few and far between. But it was the middle classes who created the towns, whether acting communally in the polite society of the eighteenth century, or by means of the aggressive town corporations of the nineteenth, or in the form of individuals such as Thomas Bunn in Frome or Benjamin Hammet in Taunton. Even in towns owned by great families, it is often the middle-class servants of the great, rather than their employers, who have set the pace. William Kitson in Torquay, and G.A. Wallis in Eastbourne, exerted at least as much influence on their home towns as the Palks and the Devonshires, whose estates they administered. A town without a prosperous, powerful resident middle class is a town in trouble, and so is a town in which the middle class think that the country is better.

The various forces which had been at work in towns came to the boil in post-war England. Filled with high hopes and ideals, the committed set about building a new Britain. Planning was to be an essential means towards this. Planners found themselves endowed with increasing status and power. A new and important strain was added to the existing tradition, however. It derived from continental theories of town-planning, especially as developed by Le Corbusier. These reflected Enlightenment values unadulterated by any romanticism about the country. Tower blocks rising out of open greensward and the stripped lines of the Modern Movement replaced the village and the vernacular as the desirable model.

One might have expected garden-city men to fight with modern-movement men. Some of them did, admittedly, but on the whole the two disciplines merged, or discovered ways of living together. Roughly speaking they divided the field. Tower blocks inspired by the Modern Movement were built in or around existing towns, along with an admixture of terrace housing, and on the basis of a greatly extended policy of slum clearance. The garden city tradition was adapted for the New Towns, which formed one of the spearheads of post-war planning; even in New Towns, however, an occasional tower block showed that their planners were keeping up with new ideas.

Meanwhile, old towns suffered. For Le Corbusier the traditional street, on which they were based, was hopelessly out of date. Cities should consist of discrete buildings, the bigger the better, with space flowing around and, if possible, underneath them. Streets were tolerated in garden cities, but so opened up as to lose all the characteristics of the traditional town street. Both Corbusian and garden city planners had little if any sympathy with the concept of a town as a slow growth, which should be delicately dealt with. 'Comprehensive redevelopment' was the accepted phrase. The listing of buildings of historic and architectural interest, as a means of protecting them, had been introduced in 1944. But many, and perhaps most, planners envisaged that towns were going to be largely rebuilt over the ensuing decades, around a few isolated historic buildings; only in a limited number of historic towns would the occasional entire street be preserved. In the interval, any demolition that brought light and space into towns, and opened them up, was to be welcomed.

But, as is very evident in contemporary periodicals, the energies and interests of planners and planning committees were absorbed in creating, discussing and arguing about new towns and new housing. 'Slum clearance' went on apace to make the latter possible. Otherwise, town centres were left to traffic engineers, and to developers eager to provide new shopping precincts. Both new roads and shopping precincts were the result of a great and growing increase in car ownership and road traffic, and the pressure that this put on conventional towns. One result was that shoppers, especially village shoppers, had an increasing choice. They could drive to the town which they preferred, and which offered the best facilities. Town councils began to worry that their own town would lose out, unless it kept itself up-to-date with a nice new precinct.

The concept of the outer and inner ring road, with feeders from them going in and out of the town, like the spokes of a wheel, dated from before the 1939-45 War. After it, it became an accepted and recommended Ministry of Transport formula. It was adopted for most new towns: an outer ring road serving a circuit of low-density housing, based on neighbourhood centres providing small shops and local services, and an inner ring road giving access to the car-parks of the main shopping centre — in which no one lived. Exactly the same system was applied to old towns all over the country. An inner ring road was built, or existing roads adapted and widened to make one. Multi-storey car-parks were strung out along it, giving access to the centre, and to the new shopping precinct, if there was one. Fewer and fewer people lived in the centre: the upper storeys above shops became empty or were used for storage, big old houses became offices, and their gardens became car-parks. The simple geometry of the ring road became the equivalent of the simple geometry of the late-eighteenth-century prison. It was applied to existing towns with the ruthlessness of a guillotine. Cruel but necessary surgery was going to lead to a new world.

One can argue, in the case of many towns, whether or not inner ring roads were necessary, but they were certainly not needed as close to the centre as they were often built, strangling the heart of the town in a noose of roaring traffic. The destruction of historic or interesting buildings, the ripping apart of towns, in order to provide precincts, ring roads and car-parks, the unnecessary demolition of entire neighbourhoods in the name of slum clearance or comprehensive redevelopment, adds up to one of the most melancholy chapters in the history of English towns. But most people in Burnley or Bury, for instance, when their Victorian centres were torn apart in order to introduce new shopping centres, were probably unaware that they were losing anything of value. Their old buildings were soot-encrusted and out of fashion; few people as yet took Victorian buildings seriously, even if they represented the most prosperous and active period of the town in which they lived. The new deal, when it came, was seldom a good one, however, for the replacements were almost always banal, second-rate and shoddily constructed.

By 1960 the destruction that had already taken place was very great, and was still going on. But the tide was about to turn, as the general public became aware of what it was losing. A new climate of opinion began to develop. Local and national amenity societies, which had been protesting without much effect, found their number and effectiveness increasing. Government, both local and national, began to swing in the direction of conservation.

The dry list of Acts of Parliament and government directives covers a momentous change. Anyone travelling round English towns will soon become aware that the fact that their qualities have survived at all, however damaged and scarred, is almost entirely due to the system of listed buildings, conservation areas and grants, and the support which this has received from the central government and local people.

In this changed climate, Enlightenment values, as expressed by comprehensive redevelopment, master plans, gigantism, tower blocks and the architecture of the Modern Movement, have taken a beating. Perhaps too much so; faced with a really large hole in a town or city, few planners or architects have any idea how to fill it. But rural romanticism is as lively as ever. It can be spotted in the emphasis on the country town as the best kind of English town; in the often-stated view that London is a collection of villages; in the belief that the problems of an inner city can be solved by planting a million trees; in the fallacious but wide-spread theory that Georgian towns were lovingly created by country-house owners; in the National Trust's huge portfolio of country properties compared to its tiny portfolio of town ones; and in the increasing migration of townspeople to villages and country cottages, whether in order to commute from them, or to try and make them the bases for a new life in the country.

It is possible to realise the value and strength of English feelings about the country, and yet to deplore the effect these have had on the towns. Anyone who defends compact, traditional towns, however, must be inflicted on occasion by doubt. So many people *do* want to live in a detached house with a garden, and *do* want to shop once a month by car. Computer technology makes dispersal of work much easier. All old towns contain large number of houses which are too big for single-family use, and of other buildings — churches, chapels, warehouses, factories, railway stations and so on — which have lost their original function. Is the traditional town simply becoming irrelevant to contemporary needs?

A drive from New York to Boston, through the interminable belt of East Coast suburbia, can act as an antidote to feelings of this kind. The problem of how to keep traditional towns alive, without destroying what makes life worth living in them, remains. There is no easy answer, no grand, sweeping solution. But to love one's own town, and to learn everything one can about its history and what gives it its individuality, is at least a step in the right direction.

NOTES

The place of publication is London, unless stated otherwise.
DNB Dictionary of National Biography
VCH Victoria County Histories
RCHM Royal Commission on Historical Monuments (England)

NOTES TO CHAPTER 1

1. *Purefoy Letters 1735-53*, ed. G. Eland (1931), I, p. xxiii.
2. *The Agrarian History of England and Wales*, ed. J. Thirsk (Cambridge, 1967), IV, pp. 467-78 and Fig. 9.
3. ibid., p. 469. Some authorities consider it to have been a churchyard cross, rather than a market one.
4. For Elizabethan markets see *Hugh Alley's Caveat —The Markets of London in 1598*, ed. V. and C. Barron (1989).
5. Mass Observation, *Brown's and Chester: Portrait of a Shop 1780-1946* (1947), pp. 57-8.
6. Based on the description in Defoe, *A Tour through the Whole Island of Great Britain*, ed. G.D.H. Cole (1927), II, pp. 611-13.
7. See *City of Salisbury* (RCHM, 1980), I, pp. xi-xii and plan on p. 60; also reproduced in M. Girouard, *Cities and People* (London and New Haven, 1985), p. 18.
8. C.B. Rowntree, *Saffron Walden Then and Now* (Chelmsford, 1952); D. Monteith, *Saffron Walden and its Environs* (M.A. thesis, 1958, deposited in Saffron Walden Public Library).
9. For a discussion of 'encroachment' in Broad Street, Ludlow, see D. Lloyd, *Broad Street: its Houses and Residents through Eight Centuries* (Ludlow Research Paper 3, Birmingham, 1979), pp. 14-15.
10. There is a useful list of corn exchanges, with dates and cost, in C. Cunningham, *Victorian and Edwardian Town Halls* (1981), pp. 245-99.
11. Local information.
12. Fairs are treated at some length in Thirsk, *Agrarian History* (n. 2), pp. 532-43.
13. Information Wilhelmine Harrod.
14. For a graphic medieval representation of the market cross as centre of the town, see the earliest plan reproduced in W. George, *Some Account of the Oldest Plan of Bristol* (Bristol, 1881).
15. Leominster Town Hall was bought and moved in 1853 by John Arkwright, to save it from demolition, and has appropriately reverted to public use as the offices of Leominster Borough Council.
16. For the administration and legal background of markets see Thirsk, *Agrarian History* (n.2), pp. 467, 480-8, and accompanying references.
17. For Louth see R.S. Bayley, *Notitiae Ludae* (1834), pp. 56 ff.; for the Palmers' Guild, Ludlow, see *Shropshire* (VCH, 1973), II, pp. 134-40. Its property records, and the subsequent corporation records, are in the County Record Office, Shrewsbury, and form a basis for any detailed study of Ludlow.
18. R.H. Mottram, *John Crome of Norwich* (1931), pp. 46-7, 128-9.
19. Pishey Thompson, *History and Antiquities of Boston* (1856), p.305. For venison feasts see, e.g., J. Bodman, *A Concise History of Trowbridge* (Bristol, 1814), p. 24.
20. Letter, Bath Corporation to W. Pulteney, *c.* 1770, quot. R.S. Neale, *Bath 1680-1850: a Social History* (1981), p. 233.
21. For Warwick see P. Styles, 'The Corporation of Warwick, 1660-1835', *Transactions and Proceedings of the Birmingham Archaeological Society for 1935*, I.ix (1938), pp. 9-122.
22. M. Chubb, 'A Forebear and his Hobby', *The Countryman* , Winter 1963, p. 282. Mark Girouard, 'Country Town Portfolio', *Country Life*, 7 Dec.,

1989.
23. Plan and quotation of contemporary description in W. Ison, *The Georgian Buildings of Bath* (1948), pp. 86-7.
24. Newcastle, 1691 (demolished); York, 1725; London, 1739. At Bristol an existing house in Queen Square was bought for Mansion House, 1783. The Mansion House in Doncaster was never residential.
25. Mass Observation, *Brown's and Chester* (n. 5), p.56.
26. S. and B. Webb, *English Local Government*, 9 vols. (1906-29; reissued 1963), III, pp. 536 (Norwich), 418 (Leeds). Eneas Mackenzie, *Account of Newcastle-upon-Tyne* (Newcastle, 1827), pp. 641-2 (Newcastle).
27. J. Toulmin, *History of the Town of Taunton* (Taunton, 1791), p. 283; J. Bensusan-Butt, *A Friend to his Country, or the Recovery of the Charter* (typescript, Colchester Public Library, 1972).
28. J. Picton, *Memorials of Liverpool* (2nd edn., 1875), I, p. 233.
29. Thompson, *Boston* (n. 19), pp. 227, 252-3.
30. C. Brown, *History of Newark-on-Trent* (1904), II, p. 296. For plans, and description of original arrangement of the town hall, see G. Richardson, *New Vitruvius Britannicus* (1802-10), II, Pls. 11-14 and text.
31. Styles, 'Corporation of Warwick' (n. 21), p. 105.

NOTES TO CHAPTER 2

1. *The Journeys of Celia Fiennes*, ed. C. Morris (1947), p. 210.
2. See list of 'ships useing the Coale Trade at Newcastle', J. Brand, *History of Newcastle* (1788), II, p. 677, reprinted in E. Hughes, *North Country Life in the Eighteenth Century* (Oxford, 1952), I, p. 201.
3. R. Weatherill, *The Ancient Port of Whitby* (Whitby, 1908), pp. 18-19.
4. Fiennes, *Journeys* (n. 1), p. 92.
5. W.G. Hoskins, *Industry, Trade and People in Exeter,* 2nd edn. (Exeter, 1968).
6. For the Billingsgate coal trade see Hughes, *North Country Life* (n. 2), esp. I, pp. 100-7.
7. The classic studies of English waterways before the canal age remain T.S. Willan, *The English Coasting Trade 1600-1750* (Manchester, 1938) and *River Navigation in England 1600-1750* (Oxford, 1936).
8. See Willan, *River Navigation*, especially the maps on pp. vi, 32, 68. Small boats could get beyond York to Ferrybridge.
9. ibid., pp. 38, 53, 59-60, 117, 148.
10. ibid., pp. 42-4.
11. The connection has been convincingly argued by Dr Eric Till, in an unpublished history of Stamford, of which he kindly let me see the typescript.
12. Defoe, *Tour* (Ch. 1, n. 6), II, p. 447.
13. Bayley, *Notitiae Ludae* (Ch. 1, n. 17), p. 110.
14. *Correspondence of Alexander Pope*, ed. G. Sherburn (1956), IV, pp. 201-5.
15. Letter from S. Leigh, *History of Boston Series,* No. 3 (Boston, 1971), pp. 16-17.
16. For the origins of the quayside area at Newcastle see Northumberland Archaeological Society, *The Quayside Area of Newcastle upon Tyne in the Middle Ages* (Newcastle, 1989). The foreshore was partly made-up land, created by rubbish deposits from the town.
17. N. Ritchie-Noakes, *Liverpool's Historic Waterfront: the World's First Mercantile Dock System,* (1984), pp. 19-22 etc.
18. C.J. Palmer, *Perlustration of Great Yarmouth* , (1872), I, pp. 132-6.
19. G. Jackson, *Hull in the Eighteenth Century* (Oxford, 1972). p. 235.
20. Defoe, *Tour*, II, p. 437; J.H. Bettey, *Bristol Observed: Visitors'*

Impressions of the City from Domesday to the Blitz (Bristol, 1986), pp. 46, 52, 54, 68.

21. *City of York* (RCHM, 1981), V, pp. 151-2.

22. See A.A. Garner, *The Fydells of Boston* (Boston, 1987).

23. See D. James, *Lancaster*, 2nd edn. (Clapham, N. Yorks., 1980), pp. 32-46 and bibliography.

24. The history of London's docks is usefully summarized in *London: the Port of the Empire* (Port of London Authority, 1914). See also the more detailed account of the down-river docks in Weale, *Pictorial Handbook of London* (1854), pp. 339-44.

25. *Yorkshire: East Riding* (VCH, 1969), I, p. 185. See G. Jackson, *Hull in the Eighteenth Century* (Oxford, 1972). Ownership plan of 1772-3 and river elevations redrawn from photographs of *c.* 1864 in Hall, *Georgian Hull* pp. 22-6.

26. Fiennes, *Journeys*, pp. 245-9.

NOTES TO CHAPTER 3

1. The fullest account of country administration before the County Councils remains that of S. and B. Webb, *English Local Government*, I, pp. 279-607. See also B. Keith-Lucas, *The Unreformed Local Government System* (1980), pp. 40-74.

2. British Library Add. MS 37732, ff. 284-301.

3. Reported in the *Derby Mercury,* 15-22 March 1787, pp. 15-22.

4. R. Furneaux, *William Wilberforce* (1974), p. 29.

5. For accounts of assize procedures see *The Office of the Clerk of Assize* (1682), esp. pp. 24f.; J.S. Cockburn, *A History of English Assizes 1558-1714* (1972), pp. 297-302; J.J. Sheahan, *History and Description of Hull* (1864), p. 110. For assizes in their social aspect see *Derby Mercury,* July 1733; R.W. Ketton-Cremer, 'Assize Week in Norwich, 1688', *Norfolk Archaeology* , XXIV (1932), pp. 15f.; *Diary of Sylas Neville*, ed. B. Cozens-Hardy (Oxford, 1950), pp. 174-5. *Passages from the Diaries of Mrs Philip Lybbe Powys*, ed. E.J. Climenson (1899), p. 208.

6. A.M. Leighton to her mother: letter in Shropshire Record Office, quoted J. Cornforth, 'Shrewsbury III', *Country Life,* 3 November 1977, p. 1306.

7. For illustrations of Westminster Hall when used in this way, *History of the King's Works,* V, ed. H.M. Colvin (1964), Fig. 10 (engraving after H. Gravelot, *c.* 1745).

8. J. Noake, *Notes and Queries for Worcestershire* (1856), p. 279.

9. For County Hall, Derby, see H.M. Colvin, 'Eaton, George', in *Biographical Dictionary of British Architects 1600-1840* (1979). S. Glover and T. Noble, *History and Gazetteer of the County of Derby* (1829), I, pp. 472-3, with plan showing new courts added in 1829. The stairs for prisoners' access survive at the Crown Court end of the original hall. For Shire Hall, York (demolished *c.* 1770), see *City of York* (RCHM, 1972), II, p. 64; E. Croft-Murray and P. Hulton, *Catalogue of British Drawings* (British Museum, London, 1960), Pl. 249.

10. G. Jackson-Stops, 'The Sessions House, Northampton', *Country Life,* 21 August 1986, pp. 588-90.

11. V. Green, *History and Antiquities of Worcester* (1796), II, pp. 6-11, with list of subscribers.

12. For plans and elevations of Nottingham and York, see J. Gandon and J. Woolfe, *Vitruvius Britannicus* (1771), V, Pls. 72-7; Richardson, *New Vitruvius Britannicus* (1808), II, Pls. 1-4.

13. Richardson, *New Vitruvius* (Clerkenwell), I, Pls. XXXIV-XXXV; (Stafford), II, Pls. 7-10.

14. E.A.L. Moir, 'Sir George Onesiphoros Paul', *Gloucestershire Studies*, ed. H.P.R. Finberg (Leicester, 1957), p. 220.

15. Designs and documentation for Chester Castle are in the quarter sessions papers in Cheshire County Record Office; further drawings at Grosvenor Museum, Chester, and Weaver Hall Museum, Northwich.

16. For Ipswich see L.J. Redstone, *Ipswich through the Ages* (Ipswich, 1948), pp. 102-3; for Abingdon, J. Townsend, *A History of Abingdon* (1910), p. 153.

17. Address to Queen and Speech at Opening of Leeds Town Hall, 1850, quoted A. Briggs, *Victorian Cities* (1963), pp. 174, 179.

NOTES TO CHAPTER 4

1. F. Little, *A Monument of Christian Magnificence* (2nd edn., Oxford, 1873), p. 93.

2. For Guild and Hospital see *Berkshire* (VCH), II, p. 92; A.E. Preston, *Christ's Hospital, Abingdon* (Oxford, 1930); J. Carter and J. Smith, *Give and Take: Scenes from the History of Christ's Hospital, Abingdon, 1553-1900* (Oxford, 1981).

3. For the Tomkins family see Townsend, *Abingdon* (Ch. 3, n. 16), p. 146; L.G.R. Naylor, *The Malthouse of Joseph Tomkins* (pamphlet, Abingdon Public Library, *c.* 1965); E.A. Payne, *The Baptists of Berkshire* (1951).

4. *City of York* (RCHM), V, pp. 82-91; M. Sellers, *The York Mercers and Merchant Adventurers* (Surtees Society, CXXIX, 1917).

5. For this and subsequently mentioned almshouses see especially W.H. Godfrey, *The English Almshouse* (1955), with numerous plans.

6. For parish government and organization see Webb, *English Local Government*, I, pp. 3-276; Keith-Lucas, *Unreformed Local Government* (Ch. 3, n. 1), pp. 75-107. For Poor Relief in the parishes see *English Local Government*, VII, *passim*.

7. For an account of parish government in one vestry see M. Girouard, 'Local Government in Spitalfields in the Eighteenth Century', in Girouard et al, *The Saving of Spitalfields* (1989), pp. 35-48.

8. The court met in the south aisle, in which there are memorials to several proctors. *City of York* (RCHM), V, pp. 39-40.

9. For the part played by clergy in county government in Cheshire see *Cheshire* (VCH, 1979), II, pp. 61-2.

10. See Webb, *English Local Government*, I, pp. 134-43, for the importance of parish meetings in St. Nicholas, Liverpool.

11. For the Georgian ordering of churches see G.W.O. Addleshaw and F. Etchells, *The Architectural Setting of Anglican Worship* (1948), pp. 148-202.

NOTES TO CHAPTER 5

1. The classic account of the legal and historical background of burgage tenure is J. Tait, *The Medieval English Borough* (1936; 2nd edn. 1969). For the results in terms of town plans see W. Beresford, *New Towns of the Middle Ages*, 2nd edn., (Gloucester, 1988), pp. 154-5, 254-7; C. Platt, *The English Medieval Town* (1976), pp. 51-5; D.W. Lloyd, *The Making of English Towns* (1984), especially pp. 38-41.

2. M.E. Speight and D. Lloyd, *Ludlow Houses and their Residents* (Ludlow Research Paper I, 1978), pp. 2-3.

3. J. Boswell, *The Life of Samuel Johnson* (Everyman edition, 1906), I, p. 455; II, p. 288.

4. *A Survey of Whitby and the Surrounding Area*, ed. G.H.J. Day (Eton, 1958), p. 63 and Pl. 7.

5. R.Thoroton, *Survey of Nottinghamshire*, ed. J. Throsby (1790-7), II, p. 81; C. Campbell, *Vitruvius Britannicus* (1725) III, Pl. 55; T.C. Hine, *Nottingham, its Castle etc.* (Nottingham, 1876), p. 47.

6. Display in local history section, Brighton Museum and Art Gallery.

7. The field pattern before development is shown in the town plan included in T. Troughton, *History of Liverpool* (1810).

8. Pope, *Dunciad*, II, l. 272.

NOTES TO INTERLUDE I

1. See L.E. Klein, *The Rise of Politeness in England, 1660-1715* (doctoral dissertation, Johns Hopkins University, Baltimore, 1983). I am most grateful to Dr Klein for sending me the abstract and ch. 5 ('The City and the Town') of this unpublished thesis. I have also drawn ideas from J.G.A. Pocock's essay in R. Ajello *et al.*, eds., *L'Età dei Lumi: studi storici sul settecento europeo in onore di Franco Venturi* (Naples, 1985), I, pp. 525-62.
2. Shaftesbury, *Characteristics*, ed. J.M. Robertson (1900), I, p. 46; 'Essay upon Conversation', in *Miscellanies by Henry Fielding, Esq.*, ed. H.K. Miller (Oxford, 1972), p. 123.
3. John Toland, *Description of Epsom* (2nd edn., 1727), II, pp. 105-6.
4. Marjorie Williams, *Lady Luxborough goes to Bath* (Oxford, 1946), p. 5.
5. *Hary-O*, ed. Sir G. Leveson-Gower (1940), p. 74.
6. O. Goldsmith, *Life of Richard Nash of Bath* (1762), p.24.
7. J. Wood, *Essay towards a Description of Bath* (2nd edn., 1762), pp. 437f. (Bath schedule); Prévost, *Le Pour et Le Contre*, No. 38 (1734), pp. 173-4; quoted A. Barbeau, *Life and Letters at Bath in the Eighteenth Century* (1904), p. 81; Williams, *Lady Luxborough* (n. 4), p. 5; Goldsmith, *Life of Nash* (n. 6), p.5;Pierce Egan, *Walks through Bath* (1819).
8. Quoted without date, L. Melville, *Bath under Beau Nash* (1907), pp. 217-8, giving as source, 'Topographical Tracts'.
9. Abbé Le Blanc, *Lettres d'un Français* (1745) II; trans. *Letters on the English and French Nations* (1747), p.378
10. British Library Add. MS 30867, ff. 62-5, quoted C. Chenevix Trench, *Portrait of a Patriot* (Edinburgh, 1962), p. 12.
11. For Bath architecture see Ison, *Bath* (Ch. 1, n. 23); J. Lees-Milne and D. Ford, *Images of Bath* (Richmond-upon-Thames, 1982).
12. O. Warner, *A Portrait of Lord Nelson* (1958), pp. 17, 21; *The Diary of a Country Parson*, ed. J. Beresford (Oxford, 1924-9), especially entries for 7 October 1792, 13 June 1797.
13. Pocock, *Età dei Lumi* (n. 1), pp. 539-42.
14. Description in Anon., *A Journey from London to Scarborough* (1733).
15. Diary of W. Knatchbull and his cousin, quoted in *Country Life*, 8 February 1973, p. 334.
16. F. Drake, *Eboracum: the History and Antiquities of York* (York, 1736), p. 241.
17. A. Rosen, 'Winchester in Transition, 1580-1700', in *Country Towns in Pre-industrial England*, ed. P. Clark (Leicester, 1981), pp. 179-80.
18. 'Quo (dilatante negotio) gloria pristina novo Eboraci splendore obumbretur'. The full inscription is given in the Assembly Rooms Minute Book, York City Record Office.
19. See J. Ingamells, 'Art in Eighteenth Century York', *Country Life*, 10 June 1971, pp. 1412-14; 17 June 1971, pp. 1530-2.
20. E. Burke, 'Letters on a Regicide Peace, 1796', in *Works* (1826 edn.), VIII, pp. 172-3.
21. *Nottingham Journal*, 6 January 1781, quoted Cornelius Brown, *Newark* (Ch. 1, n. 30) II, p. 291.
22. Powys, *Diaries* (Ch. 3, n. 5), p. 152.
23. Woolcombe Diaries, West Devon Record Office, Plymouth.
24. Shaftesbury, *Characteristics* (1723), II, p. 175. See also, for example, Pope, *Essay on Man*, IV, 396: 'True self love and social are the same'.
25. Mary Gwladys Jones, *The Charity School Movement: A Study of Eighteenth-Century Puritanism in Action* (Cambridge, 1938).
26. For improvement trusts and commissions see Webb, *English Local Government*, IV, pp.152-349; Keith-Lucas, *Unreformed Local Government* (Ch. 3, n. 1), pp. 108-31. There is no single list of relevant Acts, but they can be extracted with reasonable ease from the chronological *Table of the Statutes, Part I 1235-1950* (HMSO, 1988).
27. J. Gwynn, *London and Westminster Improved, to which is Prefixed a Discourse on Public Magnificence* (1766), p. 20.
28. For charity schools see Jones, *Charity School Movement* (n. 25).
29. G. Hadley, *A New and Complete History ... of Kingston-upon-Hull* (1788), p. 380.
30. For eighteenth-century hospitals see J. Woodward, *To Do the Sick No Harm* (1974), with list (not complete) of hospital foundations, pp. 147-8.
31. Woodward, op. cit. (n. 25); Jones, *Charity School Movement*; *Salisbury* (RCHM, 1980), I, pp. 52-3, with plans.
32. *An Account of the Establishment of the County Hospital at Winchester* (1737), Benefit 15.
33. Robin Evans, *The Fabrication of Virtue: English Prison Architecture 1750-1840* (Cambridge, 1982), is an admirably comprehensive, richly illustrated and stimulating monograph on the subject.
34. For Blackburn's prisons, see Colvin, *British Architects.*(Ch. 3, n. 9).
35. The designs and accounts for Abingdon are in Berkshire County Record Office, Reading: Q/AG/2/1 and I/AG/2/5.
36. Moir, *Paul* (Ch. 3, n. 14).
37. For Bayly, see *D.N.B.* and M. De Lacy, *Prison Reform in Lancashire* (Stanford, Calif., 1986), especially pp. 10-82, 93-8. He is listed among Bill of Rights Society members in British Library Add. MS 30883, ff. 86-7.
38. A. Gibb, *The Story of Telford* (1935), pp. 11-19; *The House of Commons 1754-90*, ed. L. Namier and J. Brook (1964), III, pp. 341-3; Ison, *Georgian Buildings of Bath* (Ch. 1, n. 23), pp. 164-7, 200-1.
39. For Foster and Young, see *DNB*; for Alexander, see Colvin, *British Architects* (Ch. 3, n. 9).
40. See R.E. Schofield, *The Lunar Society of Birmingham* (Oxford, 1963). A full-scale study of literary, philosophical and related societies remains to be written; but see T. Fawcett, 'Self-Improvement Societies: the early "Lit. and Phils." ', in *Life in the Georgian Town* (Georgian Group symposium, 1985, published 1986), pp. 15-25. Examples include Manchester (1781), Derby (1783), Newcastle-upon-Tyne (1793), Liverpool (1814), Whitby (1823), Halifax (1830), Chichester (1831), Ludlow (1833), Leicester (1835) and Bradford (1839).
41. Both inscriptions quoted in R. Welford, *Men of Mark "twixt Tyne and Tweed* (1895), III, pp. 108-9.
42. Introductory memoir in J. Murray, *Travels of the Imagination* (1828), p. iv.

NOTES TO CHAPTER 6

1. C. Hussey, in one of four articles on Ludlow, published *Country Life*, December 1945 and February 1946.
2. See Lloyd, *Broad Street* (Ch. 1, n. 9). I am most grateful to Mr Lloyd for further information and suggestions concerning Broad Street residents.
3. The recollections of a slightly later rector's daughter, Mary Sneade, in Herts. Record Office, are quoted in C. Oman, *Ayot Rectory* (1965).
4. Lloyd, *Broad Street*, p. 36.
5. Namier and Brook, *House of Commons* (Interlude I, n. 38), II, p. 303.
6. Powys, *Diaries* (Ch. 3, n. 5), p. 135.
7. Defoe, *Tour* (Ch. 1, n. 6), pp. 446-7.
8. J. Macky, *A Journey through England* (3rd edn., 1732), II, pp. 152-3.
9. *The Torrington Diaries*, ed. C.B. Andrews (1934), I, pp. 130-1.
10. D. Lloyd, *Dinham House and its Grounds* (pamphlet, Ludlow, 1982). Knight bought Croft Castle in the 1750s, but the remodelling of the house dates from the time of his son-in-law, Thomas Johnes, in 1765.
11. R. Francis and P. Klein, *The Organ and Organists of Ludlow Parish Church* (Ludlow, 1982), pp. 12-15; D. Lloyd and P. Klein, *Ludlow: a Historic Town in Words and Pictures* (Chichester, 1984), pp. 71-2.
12. Lloyd and Klein, *Ludlow*, p. 86, with further quotation.

13. See Colvin, *British Architects* (Ch.3, n. 9); Lloyd, *Broad Street* (Ch. 1, n. 9), p. 56.

14. See Colvin, *British Architects*, and J. Harris, 'Pritchard Redividus', in *Historians of Great Britain* (1968), II, pp. 17-24.

15. A. Clifton-Taylor, *Six English Towns* (1978), p. 162.

16. Styles, 'Corporation of Warwick' (Ch. 1, n. 21).

17. R.I. and S. Wilberforce, *William Wilberforce* (1880-2), I, p. 292; Walker, *Wakefield* (Ch. 3, n. 17), p. 405.

18. P. de la R. du Prey, *John Soane: the Making of an Architect* (Chicago, 1982), pp. 112-14, 123-4, 139-42, 233; B. Cozens-Hardy and E.A. Kent, *The Mayors of Norwich 1403 - 1835* (Norwich, 1938), pp. 130, 140.

19. Cozens-Hardy and Kent, *Mayors of Norwich*, pp. 117, 143; T. Fawcett, 'The Thorpe Water-Frolic', *Norfolk Archaeology,* CXXXV.

20. For Stanford, see S.D. Chapman, 'Enterprise and Innovation in the British Hosiery Industry', in *Textile History,* V (1974), pp. 14-37. For Whitby see G. Young, *Picture of Whitby and its environs* (1840), one of the best of eighteenth and early nineteenth-century local histories, and articles by M. Girouard, *Country Life,* 5 and 12 May 1988, pp. 182-4, 138-41.

21. See R. Robson, *The Attorney in Eighteenth Century England* (Cambridge, 1959).

22. J.D. Nichol, 'Social and Political Stability in Eighteenth Century Provincial Life: a Study of the Career of John Ashby of Shrewsbury', *Shropshire Archaeological Studies,* LIX, pp. 53-62.

23. See the chapter on Walter in H. Erskine-Hill, *The Social Milieu of Alexander Pope* (New Haven and London, 1975), pp. 103-31.

24. Colvin, *British Architects* (Ch. 3, n. 9), under Harrison; quarter sessions records, Cheshire County Record Office, Chester.

25. Stebbing Shaw, *Staffordshire* (1798), I, pp. 66-7; M. Craven, *The Derby Townhouse* (Derby, 1987), pp. 90-5.

26. Gaskell, *Cranford* (1853), ch. 1.

27. Now in Shropshire Record Office, Shrewsbury.

28. Swift, *Journal to Stella,* 25 December 1711.

29. Boswell, *Life of Johnson,* I, pp. 627-36.

30. All three houses now belong to their respective local authorities. The Commandery and Christchurch Mansion are open to the public, St. Edmund's College has become the Council House.

31. Campbell, *Vitruvius Britannicus* (1717), II, Pl. 87; it was demolished *c.* 1760.

32. J. Hervey, 1st Earl of Bristol, *Diary,* ed. S.H.A. Hervey (Wells, 1894), entries for 13 May 1708 and 31 August 1710; *Letter-Books,* ed. S.H.A. Hervey (Wells, 1894), II, pp. 145-390; III, pp. 151-3. The house was sold by the Hervey family well before 1782, according to *A Description of ... Bury St. Edmunds,* 3rd edn., revised G. Ashby (1782), p. 73.

33. See *The House of Commons 1715-54,* ed. R. Sedgwick (1970), I, p. 362.

34. For W. Landor see *D.N.B.,* under 'Walter Savage Landor'; for Wood, G. Tyack, 'Thomas Ward and the Warwickshire Country House', *Architectural History,* 27 (1984), pp. 534-42. Macky, quoted in *Journey* (n. 8), II, p. 183.

35. There are many country gentry, for instance, in a voting list of Whig householders, 1754, from the Attingham papers (transcript in Shropshire Record Office, Shrewsbury), although ownership of a house does not necessarily imply occupation. Rules of the Hunt (1769), with signatures of the original members, are also in the Shropshire Record Office.

36. Assembly Room subscription lists, York City Archives M.23/1, p. 4, M.23/19.

37. Typescript by Mrs. M.T. Halford, in County Record Office, Shrewsbury.

38. For example, designs possibly for Little Salisbury House, London (1600), A.P. Baggs, 'Two Designs by Simon Basil', *Architectural History,* 27 (1984), pp. 104-10.

39. For example, 9 Grosvenor Square had a first-floor dining-room in 1757, but it had become a drawing-room by 1785. *Survey of London,* XL (1980), p. 124.

40. K. Downes, 'The Kings Weston Book of Drawings', *Architectural History,* 10 (1967), p. 28 and Fig. 77.

41. British Library Add. MS 22226, f. 11.

42. Pückler-Muskau, *Tour in England, Ireland and France in the year 1828 and 1829* (1832), III, pp. 341-2.

43. For the rebuilding of Warwick after the 1694 fire (under an Act modelled on the London ones), see P. Borsay, *The English Urban Renaissance* (Oxford, 1989), pp. 90-5.

44. These and other pattern books are comprehensively listed in J. Archer, *The Literature of British Domestic Architecture 1715-1842* (Cambridge, Mass., 1985).

45. Quoted in Colvin, *British Architects* (Ch. 3, n. 9), under Brettingham.

46. See n. 14, above.

47. J. Bensusan-Butt, *Unsung Architects of Eighteenth-Century Colchester* (typescript, Colchester Public Library, 1966).

NOTES TO CHAPTER 7

1. Austen, *Northanger Abbey* (1818), ch. 2.

2. 'Rules for the Assembly Room' by William Dawson, Master of Ceremonies, 1777, quoted in R. Cruttwell (publisher), *New Bath Guide* (1780 edition).

3. La Rochefoucauld, *A Frenchman in England, 1784* (Cambridge, 1933), pp. 57-9.

4. Sheridan, *The Rivals* (1775), Act II, Scene I.

5. id., *The Ridotto of Bath* (1771), reprinted in *Plays and Poems of Richard Brinsley Sheridan,* ed. R.C. Rhodes (Oxford, 1928), III, pp. 120-1.

6. W. Tyte, *Bath in the Eighteenth Century* (1903), p. 29.

7. J. Penrose, *Letters from Bath, 1766-67* (Gloucester, 1983), p. 174.

8. O. Warner, *Lord Nelson* (Interlude I, n. 12), pp. 45-6; cf. P. Thicknesse, *New Prose Bath Guide* (1778): 'The wit of man could not contrive a more certain method to defeat the efficacy of all medicine, or endanger the life of those who come to Bath for their health, than attending a Dress Ball in full season'.

9. There is no monograph on assembly rooms. This chapter develops out of my three articles in *Country Life,* 21 August, 11 September, 2 October 1986, pp. 540-55, 766-8, 1057-9.

10. York Assembly Minute Book, York City Record Office, M23/1, 7 August 1732, 12 July 1736, 1 July 1746; R. Davies, *Walks through the City of York* (1854), quoted in C.B. Knight, *History of the City of York* (1944), p. 595.

11. W. Watson, *Historical Account of the Ancient Port and Town of Wisbech* (Wisbech, 1827), p. 363.

12. For a good description of a Norwich card assembly, see letter from W. Herring to W. Patteson, 15 October 1778 (Patteson MSS, Norfolk Record Office, Norwich).

13. Defoe, *Tour* (Ch. 1, n. 6), I, pp. 51-2, 186, 217.

14. Macky, *Journey* (Ch. 6, n. 8), p. II p. 40.

15. *Letters and Works of Lady Mary Wortley Montagu,* ed. W. Moy Thomas (1893), II, p. 298.

16. ibid., I, p. 207.

17. Bristol Letter-Books (Ch. 6, n. 8), II, pp. 91-2; Jackson, *Hull in the Eighteenth Century* (Ch. 2, n. 25), p. 269; Macky, *Journey* , II, p. 235; *Austen Papers 1704-1856,* ed. R.A. Austen-Leigh, p. 166; Austen, *Pride and Prejudice* (1813), ch. 3.

18. Cholmondeley MSS, Cambridge University Library, CH/P58/11 (communicated by Dr. E. Till); York Assembly Minute Book (n. 10), 10 April 1755; M. Elwin, *The Noels and the Milbankes* (1967), pp. 166-8.

19. Papers, advertisements, etc. relating to the dispute collected in *The Bath Contest* (1769; copy in Bath City Library). See also Cruttwell, *New Bath Guide* (n. 2).

20. Macky, *Journey*, II, p. 235; *Letters from Lady Jane Coke*, ed. Mrs A. Rathbone (1899), p. 8; Byng, *Diaries* (Ch. 6, n. 9), II, p. 175, and see an even more extreme account by Mrs Gaskell, quoted in W. Gérin, *Elizabeth Gaskell* (Oxford, 1976), p. 21.

21. There is no apparent social discrimination in the rules of Buxton Assembly Room (1788), reprinted R.G. Heape, *Buxton under the Dukes of Devonshire* (1948), p. 32.

22. Assembly Room papers, York City Record Office M23/4, collated with lists of York freemen.

23. M. Boddy and J. West, *Weymouth* (Wimborne, 1983), pp. 62-3; Heape, *Buxton*, and W. Bott, *A Description of Buxton* (1796).

24. Description of Newark Town Hall, Richardson, *New Vitruvius* (1808), II; Edward Miller, *History and Antiquities of Doncaster* (Doncaster, 1804), p. 140.

25. S. Derrick, *Letters* (1767), II, p. 83; W. White, *Hampshire* (1859), p. 65; *The Winchester Guide* (1780 edn.), pp. 79-80.

26. York: printed and MS subscription lists, York City Archives M23/1, p. 4, M23/19. Bristol (tontine): W. Ison, *Georgian Buildings of Bristol* (1952), p. 109. Norwich: lease, Norfolk Record Office, Norwich, MC 97/76. Derby: lists, S. Glover, *History of the County of Derby* (1829), II, p. 456. Bath (tontine): lists, Bath City Record Office. Newcastle: list, *A Short History of the Old Assembly Rooms* (pamphlet 634, Tyne and Wear Archives, Newcastle), p. 2. Bury St. Edmunds: list, E. Gillingwater, *Historic and Descriptive Account of St. Edmundsbury* (1804), p. 265. Plymouth: tontine advertisement, 1810 (West Devon Record Office, Plymouth).

27. Drake, *Eboracum* (Interlude I, n. 16), p. 338; lease, Norfolk Record Office (see n. 26), and B. Cozens-Hardy, *Norfolk Archaeology*, XXVII, p. 380 f.; Management Committee Proceedings, Bath City Record Office (its first meeting took place in Colborne's house, and he was also chairman of the building committee); J. Brand, *History and Antiquities of Newcastle-upon-Tyne* (1789), I, p. 595, and Welford, *Men of Mark* (Interlude I, n. 41), pp. 108-10.

28. York Assembly Minute Book (n. 10), 16 and 18 April 1731 (Irwin house); many references to King's Manor in Robinson correspondence, Vyner Collection, Sheepson Library, Leeds (information Jennifer Kauer); *A Norfolk Tour* (1829), II, p. 1082, quoted in *Crossgrove's News*, 1722 and 1727; Jackson, *Hull* (Ch. 2, n. 25), p. 268; Phillips, *History and Antiquities of Shrewsbury* (2nd edn., enlarged), p. 13; Thompson, *Boston* (Ch. 1, n. 19), p. 235, for date of sash-windows which seem contemporary with other fittings.

29. Ison, *Bath* (Ch. 1, n. 23), p. 50.

30. Letter, 4 May 1730, transcribed in Minute Book (n. 10).

31. Minute Book, 31 March, 5 May, 4 August 1732, 1 July 1751, 20 November 1752, 20 February, 31 December 1754.

32. W. Field, *Historical and Descriptive Account of Warwick and Leamington* (1815), pp. 79-81.

33. It is possible, however, that such raised daises were occupied by the Queen or Governess of the Assembly. A canopied throne seems to be shown in a view of the County Assembly Rooms, Lincoln, *Illustrated London News*, 10 February 1850.

34. The lion over the assembly-room apse was carved by J. Nelson, who worked regularly for Pritchard; R. Gunnis, *Dictionary of British Sculptors 1660-1851* (1953), under Nelson; Harris, 'Pritchard Redivivus' (Ch. 6, n. 14), pp. 17, 19.

35. attr. F.G. Fisher, *Brighton New Guide* (1800), p. 13.

36. Austen, *Persuasion* (1818), ch. 19.

37. Pückler-Muskau, *Tour* (Ch. 6, n. 42).

38. Egan, *Walks through Bath* (Interlude I, n. 7), p. 133; *Jackson's Oxford Journal*, quoted in *News of a Country Town*, ed. J. Townsend (Oxford, 1914), sub. 1833. Separate 'Subscription Trades Assemblies' were held at Stamford as early as 1787 (*Stamford Mercury*, 16 and 23 November).

39. But Manchester Assembly Rooms flourished into the 1920s. See K. Chorley, *Manchester Made Them* (1950), pp. 145, 223, 263-4.

40. Poster in Stamford Museum.

NOTES TO CHAPTER 8

1. *A Foreign View of England in the Reign of George I and George II* , ed. M. van Muyden (1902), pp. 47-8.

2. R. Phillips, *A Morning Walk from London to Kew* (1817), quoted in J. Timbs, *Curiosities of London* (1867 edn.), p. 653.

3. See Interlude I (n. 8).

4. Fiennes, *Journeys* (Ch. 2, n. 1), p. 227; H. Owen and J.B. Blakeway, *History of Shrewsbury* (1825), I, p. 506; H. Jones, *Shrewsbury Quarry, a Poem* (Shrewsbury, 1769), pp. 8-9.

5. J. Toland, *Description of Epsom* (1749 edition), pp. 225, 343.

6. John Wood, *Description of Bath* (1749 edn.), pp. 25, 343.

7. ibid., p.346, and plan reproduced Ison, *Bath* (Ch. 1, n. 23), p. 128.

8. ibid., p. 350, and plan reproduced Ison, p. 146.

9. Knight, *History of York*, p. 538; R. Davies, *Walks through York* (Ch. 7, n. 10) (1880), p. 89; R. Taprell, *Barnstaple, a Poem* (1806); J.B. Gribble, *Memorials of Barnstaple* (Barnstaple, 1830), pp. 593-4.

10. Cozens-Hardy and Kent, *Mayors of Norwich* (Ch. 6, n. 18), p. 129; W. Honeycombe (pseud.), *The History of Pudica* (1754), pp. 21-2; Picton, *Memorials of Liverpool* (Ch. 1, n. 28), II, pp. 262-3; J. Simmons, *Leicester Past and Present* (1974), I, p. 127; G. Potts, 'New Walk in the Nineteenth Century', *Trans. Leicester Archaeological Society* , 44 (1968-9), pp. 72-3.

11. Erskine-Hill, *Social Milieu of Pope* (Ch. 6, n. 23), pp. 29-31; P. Morant, *History and Antiquities of Colchester* (1748), II, p. 4; *The Cambrian Balnea or Guide to the Watering Places of Wales* (1825), pp. 29-31; W. White, *History of Norfolk* (1845), pp. 506-7; A. Pope, 'The Walks and Avenues of Dorchester', *Proc. Dorset Natural History and Antiquarian Society, XXXVIII* (1918), pp. 23-33.

12. Fiennes, *Journeys* (Ch. 2, n. 1), p. 92; Boddy and West, *Weymouth* (Ch. 7, n. 23), pp. 62-3, 70; Delamotte, *The Weymouth Guide* (1789 edn.); *Sherborne Mercury*, 15 June 1789. There is no mention of the esplanade in Delamotte's 1785 guide.

13. E. Butcher, *An Excursion from Sidmouth to Chester* (1805), pp. 449-50; id., *A New Guide Descriptive of the Beauties of Sidmouth* (1810), pp. 51-2.

14. An engraving of the interior of Hall's especially handsome library at Margate (1789) is illustrated in J.H. Plumb, *Georgian Delights* (1980), p. 70.

15. The Earl of Egremont was a shareholder in the Chain Pier, which was painted for him by Turner accordingly (information Lord Egremont). For Cromer, see A.C. Savin, *Cromer* (1936), p. 30, quoting from a guide of *c.* 1840.

16. Byng, *Torrington Diaries* (Ch. 6, n. 9), III, p. 233.

17. Taprell, *Barnstaple* (n. 9).

18. H. Davies, *Stranger's Guide to Cheltenham* (1843), p. 191.

19. F.E. Witts, *Diary of a Cotswold Parson*, ed. D. Verey (Gloucester, 1978), pp. 86, 102-6.

NOTES TO CHAPTER 9

1. *City of York* (RCHM, 1981), V, pp. 143-6. For the late-medieval terrace in Spon Street, Coventry, see C. Platt, *The English Medieval Town* (1976), p. 68.

2. For Covent Garden and its prototypes see *Survey of London*, XXXVI (1970), pp. 64-76; Girouard, *Cities and People* (Ch. 1, n. 7), pp. 128, 174.

3. J. Coad, *Historic Architecture of the Royal Navy* (1983), pp. 20-1, 95-6.

4. Ison, *Bristol*, (Ch. 7, n.26) pp. 149-52.

5. Colvin, *British Architects* (Ch. 3, n. 9), under Aldrich.

6. J. Ralph, *Critical View of the Publick Buildings of London* (1734), pp. 34, 101.

7. For all aspects of Grosvenor Square see *Survey of London*, XXXIX(1977) and XL (1980).

8. For Wood's idiosyncratic approach to Bath (as much neo-Celtic as neo-Roman), see T. Mowl and B. Earnshaw, *John Wood, Architect of Obsession* (Bath, 1988).

9. [Burney], *Diaries and Letters of Madame d'Arblay*, ed. C. Barrett (1904-5), I, p. 327.

10. Wood, *Essay* (Interlude I, n. 7), p. 346.

11. See vignette of Buckingham House in John Sheffield, Duke of Buckingham, 'A Letter to the D[uke] of Sh[rewsbury]', *Works* (1729), II, pp. 253 f.

12. Ralph, *Critical View* (n. 6), p. 33.

13. W. Lowndes, *The Royal Crescent in Bath* (Bristol, 1981), p. 54; Burney, *Diaries* (n. 9), I, p. 329; Austen, *Northanger Abbey* (1818), ch. 5; Egan, *Walks* (Interlude I, n. 7), p. 162.

14. S. Derrick, *Letters* (Dublin, 1767), pp. 50-2.

15. *Survey of London*, XL (1980), p. 115 and Pl. 28B.

16. Sir T. Robinson to Lord Carlisle, 23 December 1734, *Carlisle* (HMC), p. 143.

17. *Critical Observations* (2nd edn., 1771), p. 13. This used to be wrongly attributed to James Stuart.

18. J. Gwynn, *London and Westminster Improved* (1766), p. 14.

19. Watson, *Wisbech*, (Ch. 7. n. 11), pp. 131-4.

20. *The Town of Stamford* (RCHM, 1977), pp. 115-16.

21. For the Ladbroke estate development, see *Survey of London*, XXXVII (1972), pp. 194-257.

NOTES TO CHAPTER 10

1. For Frome and T. Bunn see T. Bunn, *Answers to Inquiries respecting Frome Selwood* (1851); M. McGarvie, *The Book of Frome* (Buckingham, 1980), esp. pp. 105, 113-14. The Minute Book of the Trustees set up by the 1757 Act, including lists of trustees, is in Somerset County Record Office, Taunton, SRO DD/LW 27.

2. For Warwick, see Borsay, *Urban Renaissance* (Ch. 6, n. 43), p. 92; for Blandford, *County of Dorset* (RCHM, 1970), III, part I, pp. 16-18.

3. The relevant Acts for the provincial towns are 33.George.II.c.52 (Bristol); 6.George.III.c.77 (Shrewsbury); 9.George. III.c.84 (Worcester).

4. T.R. Nash, *Collections for the History of Worcestershire* (1781-2), II, cxv-vi.

5. See G.H. Kite and H.P. Palmer, *Taunton: its History and Market Trust* (Taunton, 1926); J. Toulmin, *The History of the Town of Taunton* (Taunton, 1791), p. 179; reprinted Toulmin and Savage, *Taunton* (1822), p. 581 etc. The enabling market Act is 9.Geo.III.44 (1768).

6. Toulmin, *Taunton*, p. 179.

7. ibid., p. 183.

8. For Hammet, see Namier and Brooke, *Commons*, (Interlude I, n. 38) p. 575; Kite and Palmer, *Taunton* (n. 5), pp. 29, 93; E.J. Chapman, 'Taunton Turnpike Trusts', in *Notes on County History* (Adult Education Department, Bristol University, 1950), pp. 21-30.

9. Toulmin and Savage, *Taunton*, p. 184.

10. See Brand, *Newcastle*, (Ch. 2, n. 2) I, p. 524 f.; Common Council Minutes, Tyne and Wear Archives, Newcastle; W. Collard and M. Ross, *Views of Newcastle-upon-Tyne* (1842), pp. 36, 73 (Collingwood Street and markets).

11. *City of Liverpool Municipal Archives and Records*, ed. J.A. Picton (Liverpool, 1886), II, pp. 258 f., 264-72.

12. Picton, *Liverpool Municipal Archives*, pp. 365-6; *Report ... of a Court of Inquiry into the existing state of the Corporation of Liverpool ... before his Majesty's Commissioner*s (Liverpool, 1833).

13. S. McIntyre, 'Bath: the Rise of a Resort Town, 1660-1800', *Country Towns in Pre-industrial England*, ed. P. Clark (Leicester, 1981), pp. 222-36; Bath Improvement Act, 29.Geo.III.c.89; Commissioners' papers, Bath Improvement Act (Bath City Archives).

14. Neale, *Bath* (Ch. 1, n. 20), pp. 256, 261.

15. Ison, *Bath* (Ch. I, n. 23), pp. 57-65, 168-9. The façade of the remodelled Cross Bath was in fact designed by J. Palmer after Baldwin's dismissal.

16. Evans, *Fabrication of Virtue* (Interlude I, n. 33), pp. 121, 125, Pl. 53; E. Inglis-Jones, *Peacocks in Paradise* (1950); *The House of Commons 1790-1820*, ed. R.G. Thorne (1986), IV, p. 636.

17. J. Preston, *Picture of Yarmouth* (Yarmouth, 1819), p. 225; enabling Act, 50.Geo.III.c.23.

18. *Dictionary of London*, ed. C. Hibbert and B. Weinreb (1983), under King William Street, London Bridge, Moorgate.

19. D. Wholmsley, 'Market Forces and Urban Growth: the Influence of the Ramsden Family on the Growth of Huddersfield, 1716-1853', *Journal of Regional and Local Studies*, IV, no. 2 (Autumn, 1984), pp. 27-57. The Ramsden estate papers (Huddersfield Public Library) have very little relative to this period. A site in King Street was being leased in 1802 (DD/R/dd/VII No. 55), and the whole layout is shown on George Crosland's plan, 1826. For Kaye, see E.A. Hilary Haigh, 'Joseph Kaye, a Builder of Huddersfield', *Old West Riding*, IV, no. 1 (Spring, 1984).

20. J. Summerson, *The Life and Work of John Nash Architect* (1980), pp. 60-2 (Fordyce), and *passim*.

21. The standard sources for this period in Brighton are A. Dale, *Fashionable Brighton* (1947) and id., *Brighton Town and Brighton People* (Chichester, 1976).

22. J. Wallis, *Brighton Townsman and Visitor's Directory* (1828 edn.), p. 13.

23. ibid.

24. J.A. Erredge, *History of Brighthelmstone* (Brighton, 1862), p. 311.

25. A.B. Granville, *The Spas of England* (1841), II, p. 568.

26. Collard and Ross, *Views of Newcastle* (n. 10), p. 78.

27. For Grainger's Newcastle see L. Wilkes and G. Dodds, *Tyneside Classical: the Newcastle of Grainger, Dobson and Clayton* (1964); article by Jones and Honeyman, *Archaeological Aeliana* (4th series), XXIX, pp. 239 f.

28. For Torquay, for example, see J.T. White, *History of Torquay* (Torquay, 1878); for Eastbourne, D. Cannadine, *Lords and Landlords: the Aristocracy and the Towns 1774-1967* (Leicester, 1980), pp. 243-4, 273, 291, 296-7.

NOTES TO INTERLUDE II

1. A. Clarke, *Effects of the Factory System* (1899), pp. 36-7.

2. G. Gilbert Scott, *Personal and Professional Recollections* (1879), p. 88.

3. Thorne, *Commons* (Ch.10, n. 16), II, pp. 257-8. *Town of Stamford* (RCHM, 1977), pp. 134-6.

4. Rogers, *Making of Stamford*, pp. 96; *Stamford* (RCHM), pp. 134, 158-9; *Stamford Mercury*, 1840s, *passim*; sale catalogue of Newcomb estate in Stamford (Stamford Museum, 1919).

5. *Leeds Mercury*, 1, 8, 15 December 1849.

6. Wholmsley, 'Market Forces' (Ch. 10, n. 19); plans, Ramsden papers (Huddersfield Public Library).

7. See Interlude I, p. 99 and n. 40.

8. For example, new Assembly Rooms erected in Ludlow, 1840, also containing library, billiard room and associated museum. D. Lloyd, *The History of Ludlow Museum 1833-1983* (Ludlow, 1983).

9. There is no general work on Mechanics Institutes, but see M. Tylecote, *Mechanics' Institutes of Lancashire and Yorkshire before 1851* (1957).

10. A. Conan Doyle, 'The Naval Treaty', *The Complete Sherlock Holmes Short Stories* (1928 edn.), p. 515.

11. G. Kitson Clark, *The Making of Victorian England* (1962), p. 169.
12. The idea of the gentleman, and the increasing tolerance of late Victorian England, are treated at some length in my *Return to Camelot: Chivalry and the English Gentleman* (London and New Haven, 1981), and *Sweetness and Light: The Queen Anne Movement 1860-1900* (Oxford, 1977).

NOTES TO CHAPTER 11

1. A useful study is J. Redlich, *Local Government in England* (1903).
2. E.M. Sigsworth, 'Bradford and its Worsted Industry under Victoria', *Bradford Textile Society* (1952-3), pp. 63-70; J. Fieldhouse, *Bradford* (1981 edn.), p. 178; E. Midwinter, *Old Liverpool* (Newton Abbot, 1952), p. 104; Picton, *Memorials of Liverpool* (Ch. 1, n. 28), I, p. 569; E.A. McBride, *Elan* (Welsh Water Estates, 1987), p. 29; R.P. and E. Taylor, *Rochdale Retrospect* (1956), pp. 140-1.
3. Briggs, *Victorian Cities* (Ch. 3, n. 17) pp. 230-1.
4. *Survey of London*, XXXI, pp. 68-71.
5. The only monograph on the subject is C. Cunningham, *Victorian and Edwardian Town Halls* (1981). This includes a useful chronological list of town halls and associated buildings, with dates, architects and dimensions.
6. Ison, *Bristol* (Ch. 7, n. 26), p. 109.
7. J. Foulston, *Public Buildings erected in the West of England* (1838), p. 55. *John's Plymouth Directory* (1823), and later guidebooks and directories. For Taunton, see Ch. 10, p. 175.
8. J.A. Langford, *A Century of Birmingham Life* (1868); J.T. Bunce, *History of the Corporation of Birmingham* (1878), p. 92; Gill and Briggs, *History of Birmingham* (1952), I, pp.197-9.
9. ibid., pp. 399-400; Cunningham, *Town Halls* (n. 5), pp. 43-4, 222-3.
10. ibid., pp. 36-8.
11. ibid., pp. 38-44; Briggs, *Victorian Cities*, pp. 174, 179; plan in *Building News,* IV (1858), p. 794.
12. Quoted in Briggs, *Victorian Cities*, p. 161; Cunningham, *Town Halls*, pp. 39, 43.
13. For the Fieldens' buildings in Todmorden see D. Linstrum, *West Yorkshire: Architects and Architecture* (1978), pp. 84, 226, 354-5.
14. For the Gibsons and Saffron Walden see D. Hopkinson, 'Quaker Influence in an Essex Town', *Country Life*, 16 November 1968, pp. 1672-4.
15. See the excellent monograph by R. de Z. Hall, *Halifax Town Hall* (Halifax, 1963).
16. Quoted ibid., pp. 42-3.
17. Visit described and illustrated in *Illustrated London News*, 15 August 1863.
18. Hall, *Halifax Town Hall*, pp. 72-4.
19. Cunningham, *Town Halls*, pp. 195-8; Taylor, *Rochdale Retrospect* (n. 2), pp.115-8; *Rochdale Observer, passim.*
20. *Rochdale Observer*, 1878.
21. Perhaps the earliest Gothic town hall to be built was the undistinguished one in Bishop's Auckland, adapted by J. Johnstone from a winning competitition design by J.P. Jones (1860), and built in 1860-2 (Cunningham, *Town Halls*, pp. 150-1).
22. J.S. Courtney, *Half a Century of Penzance* (1878), p. 135; corporation minutes and designs, DC Penwith 819/26, in Cornwall County Record Office, Truro. In 1836 designs by H.J. Whitling, made for the unreformed corporation, were shelved by the reformed one as being too expensive, and replaced by similar and only slightly less expensive designs by W. Harris.
23. J. Clegg, *Annals of Bolton* (Bolton, 1888), pp. 111, 130-3.
24. W.F. Gardiner, *Barnstaple 1837-97* (Barnstaple, 1897); L. Lamplugh, *Barnstaple: Town on the Taw* (Chichester, 1983), pp. 124-6.
25. Clegg, *Bolton* (n. 23), pp. 98-102.
26. ibid., Section II, pp. 84-6.

27. Inscription on North Bridge; obituary, *Halifax Courier* (1887). The statue was 'erected by his fellow townsmen'.
28. J. James, *Continuations and Additions to the History of Bradford* (1866), II, p. 118.
29. R.A. Church, *Economic and Social Change in a Midland Town* (1966), pp. 340-1.
30. Picton, *Memorials of Liverpool*, II, pp. 220-3, 446.
31. W.A. Munford, *Penny Rate: Aspects of British Public Library History 1850-1950* (1951); W.A. Munford, *William Ewart M.P.* (1960).

NOTES TO CHAPTER 12

1. Mass Observation, *Brown's and Chester* (Ch. 1, n. 5), pp. 17-18.
2. Some of Papworth's shop designs survive in the RIBA Drawings Collection. But according to the *Somerset House Gazette and Literary Museum,* XLIX (11 September 1824) , p. 399, J. Linnell Bond's shop for Marsh and Tatham in Mount Street, Mayfair, was the 'first shop front acknowledged to have been worthy the name of architecture, and ... the origin of all the expense and splendour that has succeeded'. No record of this design, which dated from *c.* 1807-8, is known to survive (*Survey of London*, XL, p. 317).
3. *Reminiscences of an Old Draper*, ed. W.H. Ablett (1876), pp. 142-3.
4. ibid., p. 89.
5. Colvin, *British Architects (*Ch. 3, n. 9), under Taylor; illustration in J. Tallis, *London Street Views* (supp. 14 of the 1847 edition; facsimile, 1969, p. 274).
6. A. Briggs, *Friends of the People: a Century History of Lewis's* (1956).
7. G. Gilbert Scott, *Remarks on Secular and Domestic Architecture* (1857), p. 174.
8. The standard work on arcades is J. F. Geist's formidable *Arcades: the History of a Building Type* (trans. Cambridge, Mass., 1983). This covers arcades round the world, and includes an invaluable (though not comprehensive) gazetteer, with full entries for the more important arcades.
9. For useful general accounts of the development of banking in the late eighteenth and nineteenth centuries, see J.F. Ashby, *Story of the Bank* (1934), and W.F. Crick, *A Hundred Years of Joint-Stock Banking* (1936).
10. See *D.N.B.* for Beaumont's life.
11. J. Weale, *Pictorial Handbook of London* (Ch. 2, n. 24), p. 110. For nineteenth-century insurance buildings generally, see C. Walford, *The Insurance Cyclopaedia* (1871-86).
12. Crick, *Joint-Stock Banking* (n. 9), pp. 249-50.
13. *City of York* (RCHM, 1981), V, p. 167.
14. M. Ross and W. Collard, *Newcastle*(Ch. 10, n. 10), p. 78.
15. For Cockerell's banks, see D. Watkin, *The Life and Works of C.R. Cockerell* (1974), pp. 214-31.
16. The West of England and South Wales Bank failed in December 1878; J.F. Nicholls and J. Taylor, *Bristol Past and Present* (Bristol, 1881-2), III, p. 354.
17. For a list of Gibson's banks see his obituary, *Builder*, 21 June, 1890, p. 449. Photographs of the best of them are in a book of late Victorian photographs of his work, in the RIBA Library.

NOTES TO CHAPTER 13

1. W. Holman Hunt, *Pre-Raphaelitism and the Pre-Raphaelite Brotherhood* (1905), I, p. 7.
2. Love and Barton, *Manchester as It Is* (Manchester, 1839; facsimile 1971), pp. 200-1; T. Swindells, *Manchester Streets and Manchester Men* (3rd

series, Manchester, 1907), pp. 133-4, with photographs.

3. Love and Barton, *Manchester as It Is*, p. 201.

4. *British Architect,* I (1874); *Builder*, 21 June 1890, p. 449; 30 April 1898, p. 423.

5. Brown warehouse illustrated, *Illustrated London News*, 14 May 1853.

6. J.S. Roberts, *Little Germany* (City Trail 3, Bradford Art Galleries and Museums, 1977; available Bradford Public Library), pp. 3-4.

7. I have had much help and information from Alison Cooper, who is preparing a Ph.D. thesis on Manchester warehouses for the University of Manchester. There is also useful material in W. A. Shaw, *Manchester Old and New* (Manchester, 1894), II, pp. 1-72, and in Swindells, *Manchester Streets and Manchester Men* (n. 2),*passim*.

8. Roberts, *Little Germany* (n. 6), especially 'The Bradford Warehouse', pp. 7-20. For a more detailed study, see J.S. Roberts, *The Bradford Textile Warehouse 1770-1914* (M.Sc. thesis, University of Bradford, 1976). See also 'Bradford and its Manufacturers', *The Warehouseman and Draper*, special supplement, 1899.

9. Based on the description in 'The Henrys of Manchester and Bradford', *Fortunes Made in Business* (1887), III, pp. 201-51.

10. W. Rothenstein, *Men and Memories* (1931-2), I, p. 7.

11. 'Bradford and its Manufacturers' (n. 8).

12. C. Bronte, *Villette*, ch. 6.

13. Study of photographs and the Post Office Directories suggest that the original façade was built on the site of 5-6 Aldermanbury in about 1855, and subsequently extended over 7-9 in the same style. The building was demolished in the 1960s.

14. For the Wills building see 'Work in Bristol', *Bristol Times and Mirror* (Bristol, 1883). For the granary and the grain trade, see Nicholls and Taylor, *Bristol Past and Present* (Ch. 12, n. 16), III, pp. 242-4.

15. S. Jubb, *History of the Shoddy Trade* (1860); J. Willans, *Batley Past and Present: Rise and Progress Since the Introduction of Shoddy* (1880); N. Moir and Associates, *Batley at Work: the Rise and Fall of a Textile Town* (1974).

NOTES TO CHAPTER 14

1. *Mrs John Brown, 1847-1935*, ed. A. James and N. Hills (1937), pp. 29-30.

2. The section on mills in this chapter owes much to the following sources: K. Rogers, *Wiltshire and Somerset Woollen Mills* (Edington, 1976); *Satanic Mills: Industrial Architecture in the Pennines* (SAVE Britain's Heritage, *c.* 1979); O. Ashmore, *The Industrial Archaeology of Stockport* (Manchester, 1975); C. Aspin, *The Cotton Industry* (Aylesbury, 1981); J.H. Longworth, *The Cotton Mills of Bolton 1780-1985: a Historical Directory* (Bolton Museum and Art Gallery, 1987); M. Stratton and B. Trinder, *Stanley Mill: an Evaluation* (Research Paper 12, Institute of Industrial Archaeology, Birmingham, 1987).

3. For the origin and spread of mills in and near Keighley, see J. Hodgson, *Textile Manufacture and other Industries in Keighley* (Keighley, 1879).

4. Stratton and Trinder, *Stanley Mill* (n. 2), has a thorough analysis of an individual iron-framed mill, and account of its technological context; see also the relevant articles in A. Rees, *Cyclopaedia* (1802-20), and N.B. Harte's article on it in *Textile History, 5* (1974), pp. 119-27.

5. Rogers, *Wiltshire and Somerset Woollen Mills* (n. 2), pp. 46-9; Stratton and Trinder, *Stanley Mill*, pp. 28-32; J.M. Richards, *The Functional Tradition in Early Industrial Buildings* (1958), pp. 75-105.

6. Longworth, *Cotton Mills of Bolton* (n. 2), plate and note, p. 121.

7. J.G. Shaw, *Darwen and its People* (Blackburn, 1889), p. 150; *Darwen Guide* (1907 edn.).

8. T.W. Hanson, *The Story of Old Halifax* (1920), p. 267; see also C.T. Rhodes, *History of Old Skircoat Moor and Savile Park* (1908).

9. D. Linstrum, *Historic Architecture of Leeds* (Newcastle upon Tyne, 1969), p. 53.

10. M. Binney, 'The Home of John Barleycorn', *Country Life*, 15 June 1978, pp. 1764-5.

11. A. Barnard, *Noted Breweries of Great Britain and Ireland* (1889-91); F. Sheppard, *Brakspear's Brewery, Henley on Thames, 1779-1979* (Henley, 1979), for a thorough history of one country brewery; Hook Norton Brewery Co. Ltd., *Hook Norton: a Heritage Brewery* (Hook Norton, *c.* 1980), for a useful diagram and photographs of the brewing process.

12. H.W. Strong, *Industries of North Devon, 1889*, reprinted and ed. B.D. Hughes (Newton Abbot, 1971); Lamplugh, *Barnstaple* (Ch. 11, n. 24), pp. 112-3, 164.

NOTES TO CHAPTER 15

1. *Early Industrial Housing: the Trinity Area of Frome* (RCHM, 1981).

2. *Town of Stamford* (RCHM, 1977), pp. xliv-v, 161-2. For early courts see C.W. Chalklin, *The Provincial Towns of Georgian England. A Study of the Building Process 1740-1820* (1974), pp. 196-217; and for courts in one town, I.C. Taylor, 'The Court and Cellar Dwelling: Eighteenth-Century Origins of the Liverpool Slum', *Trans. Historical Societies of Lancashire and Cheshire*, 122 (1970), pp. 67-91.

3. An interesting approach to Victorian sanitary legislation is by way of E. Chadwick and Sir J. Simon: *English Sanitary Institutions* (1897); R.A. Lewis, *Edwin Chadwick and the Public Health Movement 1832-54* (1952); S.E. Finer, *Life and Times of Sir Edwin Chadwick* (1952); R. Lambert, *Sir John Simon 1816-19 and English Social Administration* (1963).

4. For by-law housing, and terrace housing generally, I have drawn heavily on S. Muthesius's invaluable *The English Terraced House* (New Haven and London, 1982). See also J. Burnett, *A Social History of Housing* (Newton Abbot, 1978); J.N. Tarn, *5% Philanthropy. An Account of Houses in Urban Areas 1840-1914* (Cambridge, 1975).

5. Wide back alleys may be related to houses with earth closets only, where the alleys had to accommodate a horse and cart, as described in A. Williams, *36 Stewart Street, Bolton: an Exercise in Nostalgia* (Victoria, B.C., 1978), p. 28.

6. Muthesius, *English Terraced House* (n. 4), p. 123.

7. ibid., pp. 130-7.

8. For London suburban terraces see D. Olsen, *The Growth of Victorian London* (1976), pp. 187-293, and for a sympathetic view of their advantages, N. Taylor, *The Village in the City* (1973).

9. It would be interesting to establish to what extent its founder the Rev. A.D. Wagner's heroic church-building in Brighton was subsidized by his undoubted activities as a speculative house-builder. It is hard to see how it could have been financed entirely out of his inherited fortune. See A. Dale and A.R. Wagner, *The Wagners of Brighton* (1983), especially pp. 118, 128.

NOTES TO CHAPTER 16

1. See J. Drakard, *History of Stamford* (1822).

2. R. Izacke, *Antiquities of the City of Exeter* (1724 edn.), p. 145; F. Lambert, 'Some Recent Excavations in London III: Moorfields', *Archaeologia, LXXI* (1921), pp. 75-94.

3. T. Fawcett, 'The Norwich Pleasure Gardens', *Norfolk Archaeology*, XXXV (1972), pp. 382-99; T. Oliver, *A New Picture of Newcastle upon Tyne* (1831, facsimile 1970), pp. 58-60; Ison, *Bath* (Ch. 1, n. 23), pp. 92-8.

4. Ison, p. 98, quoting *New Bath Guide* (1801).

5. Dale, *Fashionable Brighton* (Ch. 10, n. 21), p. 164, Pl. 79; C. Hussey,

'Calverley Park, Tunbridge Wells', *Country Life*, 1 and 8 May 1969, pp. 1080-3, 1166-9; printed plan, *c.* 1825, among Busby drawings, RIBA Drawing Collection; J. Pigott Smith, plan of Brighton (1826); Girouard, *Cities and People*, Pl. 236; G.F. Chadwick, *The Work of Sir Joseph Paxton* (1961), pp. 44-71.

6. Dale, *Fashionable Brighton*, pp. 171-7; M. Hadfield, 'Garden Design Ahead of its Time', *Country Life*, 7 May 1970, pp. 1070-1 (Birmingham); M.L. Simo, *London and the Landscape* (New Haven and London, 1988), pp. 178-85, 191-205 (Birmingham and Derby); K. Lemon, 'Botany by Citizens' Request', *Country Life*, 14 April 1983, pp. 920-22 (Sheffield).

7. *Evidence before the Select Committee on Public Walks* (1833), p. 9.

8. For public parks and park legislation in general in the nineteenth century see G.F. Chadwick, *The Park and the Town* (1966).

9. M. Girouard, 'A Hundred Years of Free Water', *Country Life*, 2 April 1959, pp. 149-50.

10. Chadwick, *Paxton* (n. 5), pp. 65-6, 195-6. For the Crossleys in Halifax, see M. Girouard, *The Victorian Country House* (New Haven and London, 1979), pp. 205-12.

11. Picton, *Memorials of Liverpool* (Ch. 1, n. 28), II, pp. 412-13; W.W. Wroth, *Cremorne and the Later London Gardens* (1907).

12. R. Mellors, *The Gardens, Parks and Walks of Nottingham and District* (Nottingham, 1926).

13. W.G. Hoskins, *Devon* (1954), p. 387; G. Griffiths, *The Book of Dawlish* (Buckingham, 1984), p. 39.

14. W. Grainge, *History and Topography of Harrogate* (1871), pp. 178-80.

15. Prospectus, Scarborough Cliff Bridge Company (British Library, 1826).

16. C.H. Mate and C. Riddle, *Bournemouth 1810-1910* (Bournemouth, 1910); R. Roberts, 'The Corporation as Impresario'; *Leisure in Britain 1780-1939*, ed. J.K. Walton and W. Walvin (Manchester, 1983), pp. 136-57.

17. A.B. Granville, *The Spas of England* (1841), II, pp. 514-17.

18. *Guide to Bournemouth, Poole and District* (18th edn., *c.* 1935), p. 49.

NOTES TO CHAPTER 17

1. J. Latimer, *Annals of Bristol in the Eighteenth Century* (1893), p. 205; K.M. Armistead, 'The Red Lodge', *Country Life*, CXXVIII (1960), pp. 238-41; J. Latimer, 'Clifton in 1746', *Bristol and Gloucester Archaeological Society*, XXIII (1900-1), p. 312.

2. K.J. Allison, *Hull Gent seeks Country Residence 1750-1850* (East Yorkshire Local History Society, Beverley, 1981), p. 6.

3. Defoe, *Tour* (Ch. 1, n. 6), I, p. 6.

4. Palladio, *Architecture*, trans. I. Ware (1738), pp. 46-7.

5. See the discussion of English use of the word 'villa' in J. Archer, *The Literature of British Domestic Architecture 1715-1842* (Cambridge, Mass., 1985), pp. 59-67.

6. J. Malton, *Essay on British Cottage Architecture* (1798), p. 6.

7. J. Malton, *Collection of Designs for Rural Retreats* (1802), p. v.

8. J.C. Loudon, *A Treatise on Forming, Improving and Managing Country Residences* (1806), I, pp. 4-5.

9. The cottages were illustrated and described in a series of publications issued by two Sidmouth booksellers, J. Wallis and J. Marsh. See *Sidmouth: a History* (Sidmouth Museum, 1987), pp. 48-70.

10. E.M. Forster, *Marianne Thornton* (1956), p. 16; J. Picton, *Memorials of Liverpool* (1875), II, pp. 360-1.

11. C.R. Leslie, *Memoirs of the Life of John Constable* (Oxford, 1951), pp. 162f.; Allison, *Hull Gent* (n. 2), p. 8.

12. R. Lambert, *Sir John Simon, 1816-1904* (1963), pp. 16-17.

13. K. Brand, *The Park Estate, Nottingham* (Nottingham Civic Society, *c.* 1985).

14. *Building Societies' Gazette*, 22 May 1889, p. 44.

15. *Praeterita*, I, sect. 38-9, in Ruskin, *Works*, ed. Cook and Wedderburn (1908), XXXV, pp. 35-6.

16. Reproduced Girouard, *Cities and People* (Ch. 1, n. 7), Pl. 231.

17. A monograph by Tanis Hinchcliffe on North Oxford is approaching publication.

18. K. Chorley, *Manchester Made Them* (1950), pp. 147-69.

19. These diaries belong to Christina Colvin, and are on loan to Oxford Public Library.

NOTES TO CHAPTER 18

1. For the history of Blackpool, see A. Clarke, *The Story of Blackpool* (1923); J.K. Walton, *The Social Development of Blackpool 1788-1914* (Ph.D. thesis, Lancaster University, 1974); B. Turner and S. Palmer, *The Blackpool Story* (1976); B. Curtis, *Blackpool Tower* (Lavenham, 1988).

2. Turner and Palmer, *Blackpool Story*, pp. 40-4.

3. ibid., pp. 44-5; Clarke, *Story of Blackpool*, p. 218; *Blackpool Gazette*, 20 August 1912.

4. Clarke, *Story of Blackpool*, pp. 17, 24-5, 47; Turner and Palmer, *Blackpool Story*, pp. 173, 226-7, 293; Curtis, *Blackpool Tower*, p. 20; obituary, *Blackpool Gazette*, 9 August 1930.

5. Turner and Palmer, *Blackpool Story.*

6. ibid., p. 57; Balmer obituary, *Blackpool Gazette*, 1 November 1910; Balmer on Holland, *Blackpool Gazette*, 3 January 1896; Holland funeral, ibid. The influence of Freemasonry on the entertainment industry, and on urban development generally from the eighteenth century onwards deserves more study than it has received.

7. For Victorian attitudes to leisure, see Peter Bailey, *Leisure and Class in Victorian England* (1978).

8. R.W. Malcolmson, *Popular Recreation in English Society* (Cambridge, 1973), pp. 126-33.

9. R. Poole, *Popular Leisure and the Music Hall in Nineteenth Century Bolton* (University of Leicester Occasional Paper 22, 1982), pp. 45-9; Bailey, *Leisure and Class* (n. 7), pp. 19, 31, 33.

10. R.S. Tresidder, *Nottingham Pubs* (Nottingham Civic Society, 1980), p. 20.

11. For the two groups in Lancashire see J.K. Walton, *Lancashire: A Social History 1558-1939* (Manchester, 1987), pp. 125-40, 221-38.

12. P. Price, 'The Decline and Fall of the Old Shrewsbury Show', in *Victorian Shrewsbury: Studies in the History of a County Town*, ed. B. Trinder (Shrewsbury, 1984), pp. 145-55.

13. Bailey, *Leisure and Class*, p. 33.

14. For Londesborough see O. Sitwell, *Left Hand, Right Hand* (1945), pp. 124-47, 252-60.

15. *Blackpool Gazette*, 3 January 1896, p. 2; A. Waters and R. Hunter, *The Illustrated Victorian Song Book* (London, *c.* 1979), pp. 92-4. The champagne firm of Moët et Chandon sponsored Leybourne in the role, an early example of promotional advertising.

16. D.F. Cheshire, *Music Hall in Britain* (Newton Abbot, 1974), pp. 36-42. Article on music halls by F. Anstey, *Harper's*, XXI (1891) Europe; [LXXXII, America], pp. 190-202.

17. Quoted ibid., p. 86.

18. Obituaries, *Daily Telegraph*, 30 December 1895; *Blackpool Gazette*, 3 January 1896, p. 6; F. Boase, *Modern English Biography* (1912), V, supplement II, pp. 686-7.

19. For example, the francophile H.I. Butterfield of Cliffe Castle, Keighley; *Cliffe Castle: a Restoration Project* (Bradford Art Galleries and Museums, 1989), pp. 1-3.

20. J.K. Walton, *The English Seaside Resort: A Social History 1750-1914* (Leicester, 1985), pp. 5-44.

21. Quoted in H. Jackson, *The Eighteen-Nineties* (1922). I have not found the original location.
22. Quoted in E. Bryson, *'Owd Yer Tight* (Nottingham, 1967), p. 35.
23. *Blackpool Gazette*, 3 January 1896.
24. *The Grand Theatre and Opera House, Leeds. First Hundred Years, 1878-1978* (Leeds, 1978); *Leeds Mercury*, 19 November 1878; G.R. Sims, *My Life* (1917), p. 111. It seems likely that Sims was exaggerating.
25. *Survey of London* , XXXI, pp. 68-84.
26. R. Emmons, *Walter Richard Sickert* (1942), p. 47; Cheshire, *Music Hall* (n. 16), pp. 88-91; W.H. Morton and H.C. Newton, *60 Years Stage Service* (1905), p. 208; Penwell illustrated Anstey's article in *Harper's* (n. 16).
27. A.L. Cranford, *Sam and Sallie* (1933).

28. G.J. Mellor, *The Northern Music Hall* (Newcastle, 1970), p. 136.
29. ibid., p. 159.
30. M. Girouard, *Victorian Pubs* (1975), pp. 78-80, 117-18.
31. The Eden Theatre is illustrated and described in Vol. II of E.O. Sachs, *Modern Opera Houses and Theatres* (1896-8).
32. Girouard, *Victorian Pubs*, pp. 95-102, 141.
33. *Frank Matcham, Theatre Architect*, ed. B. Mercer Walker (Belfast, 1980). This is the only monograph on an English theatre architect, but has a chapter by V. Glasstone on Matcham's contemporaries, including Crewe (pp. 82-94). See also Glasstone, *Victorian and Edwardian Theatres* (1975).
34. Sachs, *Modern Opera Houses* (n. 31), p. 42.

PHOTOGRAPHIC CREDITS

Louth Town Council, Louth (photograph National Art Collections Fund): front and back endpapers; Peter Burton and Harland Walshaw: p. i, 1, 4, 14, 18, 19, 20, 22, 26, 28, 37, 38, 45, 48, 49, 50, 51, 52, 55, 56, 58, 60, 64, 73, 74, 75, 84, 88, 94, 96, 112, 113, 117, 127, 128, 131, 137, 139, 156, 164, 167, 177, 178, 198, 212, 213, 214, 215, 219, 222, 224, 230, 231, 233, 238, 239, 240, 251, 259, 269, 270, 271, 272, 276, 282, 283, 293, 301, 302, 305, 327, 331, 355, 361, 369, 377, 380, 382, 383, 392, 397, 400, 401, 411, 412, 414; Lefevre Gallery: pp. ii-iii; Michael Andrews: p. v; Mark Girouard: 2, 10, 21, 23, 24, 25, 30, 31, 46, 47, 54, 67, 69, 70, 71, 80, 81, 83, 86, 90, 95, 109, 122, 130, 132, 133, 134, 135, 136, 138, 148, 149, 153, 154, 157, 158, 159, 169, 182, 194, 196, 200, 201, 206, 207, 209, 216, 217, 227, 232, 237, 241, 242, 243, 244, 246, 247, 248, 253, 258, 261, 263, 273, 275, 279, 280, 281, 284, 285, 294, 295, 303, 307, 309, 311, 312, 314, 316, 317, 319, 320, 321, 324, 325, 330, 335, 342, 344, 348, 349, 350, 352, 356, 360, 363, 370, 373, 374, 375, 376, 379, 381, 398, 402; City of Peterborough Museum Services: 3; Nottingham County Library Service (photograph W.E. Middleton and Son, Ltd.): 5, 6, 390, 406; Grosvenor Museum, Chester: 8, 59; Neil Wright: 9; Norfolk Museums Service (Norwich Castle Museum): 11, 129; Martin Gledhill, artwork: 12, 35, 42, 62, 121, 155, 174, 225, 226, 228, 229, 234, 378; Nottingham City Museums: 13, 391; British Museum, London: 16, 203, 287; Edward Piper: 17, 77, 85, 151, 195, 210, 218, 220, 249, 250, 251, 255, 260, 266, 277, 322, 328, 334, 336, 337, 339, 340, 341, 343, 345, 347, 357, 358, 359, 365; Worcester City Council: 27; Oxfordshire County Council, Central Library (photograph John Peacock): 29; by courtesy of the Revd N. Chubb, and Admiral Blake Museum, Bridgwater: 32, 57, 144, 145, 146, 147; Sutcliffe Gallery, Whitby: 33; Lincolnshire County Council Recreational Services (Usher Gallery, Lincoln): 34, 168; Wisbech and Fenland Museum: 36; Tate Gallery, London: 39, 170; City of Bristol Museum and Art Gallery: 40, 44, 92, 152, 180, 199; Yale Center for British Art (Paul Mellon Collection): 41, 189, 192, 366; National Museums and Galleries on Merseyside: 43, 118, 364; Sir Reresby Sitwell, Bart: 53; Bodleian Library, Oxford: 61, 367; National Gallery of Ireland: 63; British Broadcasting Corporation, London (photograph by Geoff Howard): 65; Royal Commission on Historical Monuments, England (Crown copyright reserved): 66, 79, 89, 91, 306; IPC Magazines/Country Life: 72, 143; Christ's Hospital, Abingdon: 76; National Monuments Record, London: 78, 154, 252, 326, 329, 338; University of East Anglia (Sainsbury Centre): 82; North Yorkshire County Council (County Archives): 87; The Olde House, Shrewsbury: 93; University of Cambridge Committee for Aerial Photography: 97; Christie, Manson and Woods, London: 100; Victoria Art Gallery, Bath (photograph Flotek): 101, 161; British Library, London: 103, 104, 105, 106, 141, 142, 197; York City Art Gallery: 107, 186; Newark Museum: 108; Thomas Coram Foundation for Children, London: 110, 111; Cheshire County Council: 114; Tyne and Wear Museums Services: 115; Guildhall Library, London: 116, 120; the Trustees of Sir John Soane's Museum, London: 119; Midland Bank, London (photographs Geremy Butler): 123, 124, 125, 126; Lady Serena James: 140; Bath Reference Library: 160, 171, 173, 204, 205; National Trust (England): 162; Bruce Allsopp and Ursula Clark: 163; Derby Museums and Art Gallery: 166; A.F. Kersting AllP, FRPS: 175; Buxton Library: 176; Dorset County Council (Weymouth Libraries Local Studies Collection): 181; Frick Collection, New York: 183; Board of Trustees, Victoria and Albert Museum, London: 184; Courtauld Institute, London: 185; Scarborough Borough Council: 187; Presteigne Parish Church (photograph Christopher Dalton): 188; Royal Pavilion, Art Gallery and Museum, Brighton: 190, 191, 193; Ashmolean Museum, Oxford: 202; Royal Institute of British Architects, London (photographs Geremy Butler): 211, 291, 394, 395; Somerset County Council (Local History Library): 223; Bungay Museum: 245; Eastbourne Central Library: 254; School of Architecture, University of Manchester: 256; Leeds City Council (Central Library): 262; H.C. Stacey (photograph Phase Three Services): 264, 265; Town Hall, Rochdale: 268; Christopher Ketchell Collection, Hull: 274; Bolton Metropolitan Borough (Department of Planning and Development): 278; Birmingham Public Libraries (Reference Library): 286; Bolton History Museum (photograph John Parkinson-Jones FIIP): 288, 289; Bath City Archives: 290; Judy Thomas: 296; R. Coxeter: 297; Wiltshire County Council (County Record Office): 298, 299; M.K. Benson, Company Archive Consultant, Lewis's Ltd., Liverpool: 300; West Devon Area Central Library, Plymouth: 304; Leeds City Art Gallery (photograph Richard Green): 310; Asadour Guzelian: 313, 323; Alison Cooper: 346; Bolton Museum and Art Gallery: 332, 333; Messrs. Gliddon and Squire, Barnstaple: 346; Stefan Muthesius: 351, 353, 354; John Garland: 362; The Museum, Sidmouth: 384, 385, 386, 387, 388, 389; Cheltenham Art Gallery and Museums (photograph Bridgeman Art Library): 396; Lewes Museum (photograph Edward Reeves): 403; Lincolnshire County Council (Stamford Museum): 404; Mander and Mitchenson Theatre Collection, London: 405; Bradford Art Galleries and Museums (Cliffe Castle): 407; Plymouth Museums and Art Gallery: 408; Victor Glasshouse Collection: 409, 410, 415.

INDEX